Research Guide to Central America and the Caribbean

Research Guide to Central America and the Caribbean

Kenneth J. Grieb
EDITOR-IN-CHIEF

ASSOCIATE EDITORS

Ralph Lee Woodward, Jr.
Central America

Graeme S. Mount
The English Caribbean

Thomas Mathews
The Spanish, Dutch, and French Caribbean

The University of Wisconsin Press

Published 1985

The University of Wisconsin Press
114 North Murray Street
Madison, Wisconsin 53715

The University of Wisconsin Press, Ltd.
1 Gower Street
London WC1E 6HA, England

Copyright © 1985
The Board of Regents of the University of Wisconsin System
All rights reserved

First printing

Printed in the United States of America

For LC CIP information see the colophon

ISBN 0-299-10050-2

Contents

v

Descriptions of Archives and Resource Depositories

      The Caribbean
      Topical Essays

Contents   ix

Descriptions of Archives and Resource Depositories

        Joan E. Mount

80   The Maritime Provinces of Canada 382
        Harold H. Robertson

81   Central Canada 385
        David R. Murray

82   Great Britain 387
        Brinsley Samaroo

**83   Archives and Libraries in the United States Containing
        Materials Dealing with Bermuda, Jamaica, and the
        Bahamas** 392
        Edward W. Chester

        Contributors 399

        Index 405

Preface

This volume is a collaborative effort, involving scholars from the United States, Central America, the Caribbean, Canada, and Europe, to identify the archival resources regarding the Central American and Caribbean region available to historians, and to indicate future directions for research about the region. The project was initiated during the 1970s by the Caribé–Centro America Committee of the Conference on Latin American History, the major national organization of historians in the United States specializing in this region. While existing scholarship about the region is extensive, much still awaits the researcher. With study of the region increasing, it is certainly an appropriate time to provide a guide to archival resources, which were often known only to those with research experience in the area. To be sure, the undertaking was ambitious, and the time required for completion far exceeded the original expectations.

Collectively the authors encompass a broad range of institutions and a wide geographical distribution. Most are historians, since this project focuses on archival resources and was designed principally for historians. Representatives of other disciplines in the social sciences and the humanities, including archivists and librarians, are included where appropriate. The resulting volume should be of interest to students and researchers in a wide range of fields.

Each contributor has personal experience in the archives he is describing, as well as familiarity with existing scholarship regarding the region. The editorial team includes scholars specializing in each of the subregions involved. The large number of North American contributors reflects the extensive publication about this region in the United States. In some cases political turmoil or restrictions in the area affected the mix of participants. This was particularly true in the case of Cuba, where local scholars declined to contribute despite a visit to that nation by the associate editor for the Spanish Caribbean.

Inevitably space considerations played an important role, given the broad scope of the volume. Both the number of chapters and the size of each were affected, limiting the coverage of topics as well as the types of information provided. The intent was to point to future directions and identify major resource depositories, rather than to provide specific topics or indicate all possible sources available. Admittedly this involved some painful judgments by the editorial team and the contributors. All would have welcomed more space to amplify coverage, but the size of the volume clearly indicates the necessity of compromise between comprehensiveness and affordability. In this effort the overall allocation of space was the responsibility of the editor-in-chief, while the regional associate editors determined the chapter topics and selected the contributors.

The *Guide* contains two types of articles: descriptions of major archival depositories or research centers, and topical essays suggesting future directions for research. The approach of each author to these themes varies, and the overall perspective is part of the value of such a collaborative effort. While efforts were made to assure that all the articles in each section were parallel in scope, uniformity of data was not mandated. Instead each author was allowed to select what he or she considered important within space limitations and overall guidelines indicating focus.

The archival descriptions are designed to provide basic information about available materials. They indicate the scope of the holdings, unique aspects or restrictions, availability, hours of operation, and prevailing conditions. Due to space limitations, no effort was made to catalogue the holdings of each institution. Instead, the focus is on the type and scope of sources contained in each depository. The existence of indices or guides is indicated where appropriate. Particular procedures and requisite types of information and documentation important in gaining access to the materials are also noted when applicable. Many of the articles contain comments about the limits of the materials available, reflecting past practices or natural disasters. The depositories described are principally those of the governments involved, and therefore identify the location of the extant official records. The major libraries and newspaper depositories are also included, though these necessarily are treated more generally. These articles should enable the researcher, whether a novice or a veteran, to rapidly identify the specific holdings of interest to him and the principal locations of his major sources.

The topical essays serve to indicate future directions, topics yet to be studied, and gaps in existing research. They suggest a wide array of potential subjects to those searching for ideas, and highlight the questions scholars working in the area are presently asking. The approaches of the various authors are diverse. Some discuss existing literature and scholarship to indicate the present situation, while others focus directly on areas that require more investigation. Many refer to specific unexploited resources that await examination by scholars.

There are, of course, some differences in approach and coverage both among the authors and the various sections. For example, a depository covered in the Central American section is not necessarily discussed in the Caribbean section if the sources it contains regarding each area are the same. Similarly, the Central American topical essays focus more specifically on individual countries and particular centuries, while the Caribbean section contains more general essays covering the entire region topically. Hence essays may have applications beyond their specific focus, just as archival descriptions may provide information of interest to researchers concerned with other subregions within the area. The contributors also reflect a broad range of conceptual, theoretical, research, and ideological approaches. This diversity means that suggestions in a particular essay may have applications beyond the topic, region, or country being addressed. In the process the volume encompasses the various scholarly trends throughout the region and among those studying it.

The essays contained herein should facilitate the already-rising interest in and study of this important region and broaden the possibilities for multiarchival research by scholars, whatever their topical interest or country focus. Thanks are due the many contributors who provided these original essays for sharing their experiences and offering their time to this endeavor, and particularly the associate editors for their tireless efforts throughout the process.

Kenneth J. Grieb

Research Guide to Central America and the Caribbean

1 Materials Regarding Central America and the Caribbean in the National Archives of the United States
Kenneth J. Grieb

Researchers seeking information on Central America and the Caribbean will find the National Archives and Records Service of the United States a veritable gold mine. Because of the United States' extensive involvement in Central American and Caribbean affairs, these records provide insights, not just into United States relations with these nations, but also regarding interaction among the states of the region and their internal affairs.

It is scarcely surprising that the records of the Department of State constitute the largest and most valuable portion of the resources dealing with Central America and the Caribbean in the National Archives. State Department documents, contained in Record Group 59, are located in the Legislative, Judicial, and Diplomatic Branch of the archives. Until 1906, the records were divided into four categories: instructions to United States diplomatic and consular representatives; dispatches received from these envoys; notes to foreign legations and embassies in the United States; and missives received from these agencies. Using materials from this period is rather cumbersome, since each separate series must be consulted. From 1906 to 1910, a system of subject files was employed. This format is also somewhat cumbersome, as the establishment of files depended upon the foresight of the clerk, resulting in wide variations of length. Since the file numbers were assigned in sequence of creation, they offer no clues to their contents without use of the department's indices and guides.

In 1910 a new system was adopted, establishing consolidated decimal files organized by nation, with internal subject headings. The two most useful major series are 800 for Internal Affairs and 700 for International Relations. The remaining digits identify the countries involved, with the decimals signifying the subgroupings. This system renders all items readily identifiable. Thus the 711.14 file encompasses relations between the United States (11) and Guatemala (14), while the 712.14 file contains records regarding relations between Guatemala (14) and Mexico (12). The 816.00 file contains general political records relating to the internal affairs of El Salvador. Guides for identifying the country numbers and the various subsections are readily available. Individual documents are identified by slash numbers, with each item having an individual digit until 1944.

Thereafter the documents, instead of being numbered sequentially in order of receipt, were numbered by date. For example, a dispatch sent November 11, 1944, will bear the slash number 11–1144. While this enables grouping in sequence, it also means that several documents bear the same number, thus introducing another form of confusion in citations. The decimal files contain all correspondence relating to a specific country, regardless of source. The 800 group contains the reports of American diplomatic representatives regarding internal events, and the directives, exchanges, and analyses from the department regarding these matters, as well as related information from other posts. These reports encompass a broad range of topics, though coverage varies with the country, the time, and the size of the United States diplomatic establishment there. In general, United States diplomatic posts in Central America and the Caribbean were rather small, but since this was an area of prime American interest during the nineteenth and early twentieth centuries, they were among the earliest established and have been continually manned.

The basic State Department files can be supplemented by the Post Records, in Record Group 84, which contain the archives of virtually every diplomatic establishment abroad. This includes the consulates, legations, and embassies. These files contain the raw data upon which communications to the department were based, such as memoranda of conversations, as well as communications between posts not necessarily transmitted to Washington. As such, they offer a valuable supplement that is often overlooked by scholars. The materials in this group are more variable than the general series, and their usefulness is often dependent upon how systematic and thorough a particular mission head was in his record keeping.

Consular records also constitute a valuable source within the State Department records, particularly during the nineteenth century, when the consulates outnumbered the few small diplomatic missions in this region.

While the aforementioned groups encompass the bulk of the State Department records relevant to the region, there are many other useful categories. Although far too numerous to list, they include such divisions as the Records of Boundary and Claims Commissions and Arbitrations, in Record Group 76, which contain in case files all negotiations regarding United States claims against other countries and all arbitrations in which the United States was involved, either as a party or as adjudicator. Frequent U.S. arbitration activities in this region make this a large and important group of documents. The Records of International Conferences, Commissions, and Expositions, in Record Group 43, contain material relating to and assembled for each of the various Pan-American and Inter-American conferences, with sections regarding each of the participants. Of particular interest to Central Americanists are the collections relating to the Washington conferences and the electoral missions in Nicaragua, which are also encompassed within this group.

The records of other agencies of the United States government also contain extensive information, though in more modest quantities than those of the State Department.

The second most important group of materials for the study of Central America and the Caribbean can be found in the Military Branch. This, of course, reflects the numerous interventions of the late nineteenth and early twentieth centuries, as well as the cooperation of World War II and the continued presence of some bases in the region. The scholar wishing to tap these resources may need some staff assistance, as the records are gathered in large consolidated files by office, rendering it necessary to know what office was in charge of each operation and also to cope with overlapping or changing jurisdictions. A competent staff and extensive finding aids provide ample assistance in dealing with this problem. Records are scattered over a wide variety of offices, with each important only for certain countries or events. In the Army Section, the Records of the Office of the Secretary of War, Record Group 107, contain some correspondence relative to operations in Cuba. The files of the Adjutant General's Office, broken into two chronological divisions—1780–1917, Record Group 94, and post-1917, Record Group 407—while containing considerable material relating to Mexico, offer relatively little to the Caribbeanist or the Central Americanist, save for some data relating to the Spanish-American War. Far more valuable to scholars interested in this region are the Records of the War Department General and Special Staffs, Record Group 165, which include files regarding political and police matters in Cuba and Panama, several more specialized studies of some interest, and, most significant, the dispatches of the Military Intelligence Division, which contain the reports of United States military attachés. These are most valuable in the post–World War I era, when the United States began stationing attachés abroad in significant numbers. Special studies relating to many topics, particularly regarding Cuba and Puerto Rico, can also be found in this section. The files of the Office of the Chief of Engineers, Record Group 77, include several canal studies and pertinent harbor surveys. The Records of United States Army Overseas Operations and Commands (1898–1942), Record Group 395, house information relative to units stationed in Cuba, Puerto Rico, and Panama, as well as various aspects of the Spanish-American War. Other groups of interest in the Army Section include the Records of the Military Government of Cuba, Record Group 140; Records of the Provisional Government of Cuba, Record Group 199; and the Records of the Dominican Customs Receivership, Record Group 139.

Records of the Navy Department, contained within the Military Branch, are also highly significant for students of the Caribbean and Central American region, because a considerable number of the United States military interventions in this area were conducted by marines, and hence were under the jurisdiction of the navy. Data relating to many of these can be found in the General Records of the Department of the Navy, Record Group 80. Reports and files in this group concern Honduras (1910–11), Haiti (1917), the Dominican Republic (1917), and Nicaragua (1927–32), the latter relating to the election supervision. The general collections of correspondence from officers, arranged by rank and date rather than by country, also contain some pertinent material. The Records of the Office of Naval Intelligence (1888–1914) consist primarily of reports from squadron commanders in the Caribbean and along the coasts of Central America, and include considerable information regarding these areas, although they are somewhat spotty, depending on the disposition of units at any given moment. More valuable are a series of subject files for the years 1909–30, which contain records relating to Costa Rica, Cuba, the Dominican Republic, Haiti, Honduras, and Nicaragua. Each of these is classified separately, facilitating consultation. The Records of the Office of the Chief of Naval Operations, Record Group 38, contain the Records of the Military Government of Santo Domingo as well as the Correspondence with the American High Commissioner in that country. The Records of the United States Marine Corps, Record Group 127, include a section regarding detachments abroad that encompass data on Cuba, Haiti, and Nicaragua, constituting the correspondence relative to the interventions in those nations. In addition to the major items listed above, there are also several smaller, scattered items relating to this region, to which the staff can provide guidance.

The National Archives also have custody of other categories of records which contain some material of interest to scholars of this region, though the relevant portions are less extensive and spotty, hence their importance varies with particular topics. For example, the records of independent executive agencies include the files of the various canal commissions under a grouping of Records of the Panama Canal, Record Group 185, as well as the Records of the Spanish Governors of Puerto Rico, Record Group 186. Depending on the topic, additional information can be found in the legislative records, which contain materials relative to and records of congressional investigations and committees, from both the House and the Senate. Customs and port records can be found in the Treasury Department papers, while the Interior Department Section contains the files of such agencies as the Bureau of Insular Affairs and the Office of Territories. Such departments as Agriculture and Commerce offer scattered reports regarding trade, agriculture, and economic aspects, as well as correspondence from commercial and agricultural attachés, during the years when such agents were stationed in any particular country. Numerous special agencies, particularly during the period of World War II, are also filed separately and will contain in their Latin American sections some records of interest to scholars of these eras.

In addition, scholars should also be aware of the various presidential libraries scattered around the country, which are under the jurisdiction of the National Archives and Records Service and which house the correspondence and office files of the nation's chief executives. The amount of material relevant to any particular topic is often quite small, for in modern times the responsibilities of the presidency are so broad that only urgent matters make their way to the White House, much less to the Oval Office. Nonetheless, such files are useful in determining the importance attached to a particular matter and do provide useful insights into questions regarded as major issues at the time. Scholars would be well advised, however, to utilize the resources of the National Archives before consulting private papers or the presidential libraries, for they will find that the bulk of the information relating to any particular incident or question is contained in the department-level files, where most questions are handled.

At the present time, there are few restrictions on materials for the pre–World War II era. With some exceptions involving classified materials, most records through 1950 in all branches are open and readily accessible. Even the materials that are still classified can often be obtained through requests or via freedom-of-information channels. The greatest problems will be encountered in the military records, intelligence-gathering agencies, or in presidential papers, which can be restricted. In general, however, most executive departments now have automatic procedures to declassify materials after a set period, usually twenty or twenty-five years, which automatically and constantly makes additional material available. For example, State Department Papers become available to researchers upon publication of the relevant volume of the series Papers Relating to the Foreign Relations of the United States. This has greatly simplified consultation, and constitutes a significant improvement over earlier procedures, which involved restricted periods.

Substantial portions of the available documents have been microfilmed for the convenience of researchers. The State Department Decimal Files for most of the countries of the region through 1929, a substantial portion of the Consular Records and some of the Presidential Papers are available in this form. Despite the convenience of this program, investigators should realize that only the Decimal Files and Consular Records are microfilmed. While they include much of the relevant documentation, other pertinent and highly important papers, such as the files of the internal State Department offices, the Post Records, and records of other agencies, are not available on microfilm. Hence, while the use of the microfilms enables a substantial amount of research closer to home, it does not substitute for a trip to the National Archives, which remains necessary to consult other files and cross references. Since filming of the 1910–29 file groups is still in progress, materials beyond this date are not as yet available in this form.

Central America

2 Hapsburg Central America
Historical Sources and Research Possibilities
Murdo J. MacLeod

The long stretch of about two hundred years in Central America between Christopher Columbus' first glimpse of land in the Gulf of Honduras and the death of the last, unhappy Spanish Hapsburg has had a most intermittent and uneven historiography.

During the colonial period itself, four great chroniclers—Francisco Antonio de Fuentes y Guzmán, Antonio de Remesal, Francisco Vázquez, and Francisco Ximénez—quite literally put the area on the map for the Western world. After 1750 historians such as Domingo Juarros, José Milla y Vidaurre, Hubert H. Bancroft, Francisco de Paula García Peláez, León Fernández, and Tomás Ayón continued the tradition of the long, detailed narrative account until the twentieth century.[1]

The first half of the twentieth century did not produce the flourishing historiography of other Latin American areas for the years before 1700. Dedicated Central American pioneers such as León Fernández and the indefatigable archivist José Joaquín Pardo compiled invaluable documentary series; local scholars such as Jorge Lardé y Larín, Ernesto Chinchilla Aguilar, and Carlos Monge Alfaro enriched the long narrative tradition of their *antepasados;* and Spanish scholars such as Carmelo Sáenz de Santa María and Pablo Alvarez Rubiano showed that the former colonial offspring were still of interest in the mother country. Many of these writers continue to produce works of significance. But with a few notable exceptions—some of the writings of Robert Chamberlain come to mind—Central America before the 1960s did not draw modern scholars with modern concerns, especially in the U.S. and Europe.[2]

All this has changed since the 1960s. Specialists such as Manuel Rubio Sánchez on economic history and export crops, Severo Martínez Peláez on the emergence of class and class conflict, André Saint-Lu on Church and intellectual history, and William Sherman on Indian labor have turned to early colonial Central America in a modern manner and with today's

---

1. The best and most current guide to the bibliography of colonial Central America is Sidney David Markman, *Colonial Central America: A Bibliography* (Tempe, Arizona, 1977). See also Murdo J. MacLeod, "Colonial Latin America: Central America," in *Latin America: A Guide to the Historical Literature*, 228–36 (Austin, 1971).

2. The works of these authors may be found in the two bibliographies cited in note 1.

debates in their minds.[3] A new generation of Ph.D. students in the U.S., for example, Christopher Lutz, Robert Wasserstrom and David Radell, have investigated in previously barren fields—urban society and demography, ethnic relations, and historical geography.[4] This miniboom should not discourage others who think of Hapsburg Central America as a possible area of interest. The surface has hardly been scratched. Many areas of historical inquiry, which have produced numerous volumes and essays in neighboring Mexico, have yet to draw a single student for the Audiencia de Guatemala.

The scholar who wishes to do research on a topic which covers all of the geographical area once called the Audiencia de Guatemala (i.e., Chiapas through Costa Rica) must be prepared to travel. Archival sources are abundant, but often poorly ordered and horribly scattered around the globe. Printed documentary sources should not be ignored as a first step. In addition to those mentioned above and others which limit themselves to the Audiencia de Guatemala, the student must search in the great Spanish and Mexican multivolume collections. Foreign travelers' accounts of the period are also useful and entertaining.[5]

Prospective topics for study are almost limitless, but some topics present themselves more clearly because (1) certain groundwork has been done, (2) the topical gaps are particularly glaring, or (3) certain geographical areas have been neglected. One should begin, perhaps, by establishing the geographical context and by putting the people into it. Historical geography and historical demography in Hapsburg Central America are fields where some excellent but hesitant starts have been made, and where enormous quantities of documents can yield much more definitive results. Historical geography has much more to tell about soils and changes in soils, about changes in ground cover over the first two centuries of Spanish rule, about the impact of new animals and agricultural methods on

3. E.g., Manuel Rubio Sánchez, *Historia del añil o xiquilite en Centro América*, 2 vols. (San Salvador, 1976–78); Severo Martínez Peláez, *La patria del criollo: Ensayo de interpretación de la realidad colonial guatemalteca* (Guatemala, 1971); André Saint-Lu, *Condition coloniale et conscience créole: Guatemala, 1524–1821* (Paris, 1971); William L. Sherman, *Forced Native Labor in Sixteenth-Century Central America* (Lincoln, 1979).

4. Christopher H. Lutz, "Santiago de Guatemala, 1541–1773: The Sociodemographic History of a Spanish American Colonial City," Ph.D. dissertation (University of Wisconsin–Madison, 1976); David R. Radell, "An Historical Geography of Western Nicaragua: The Spheres of Influence of León, Granada and Managua, 1519–1965," Ph.D. dissertation (University of California, Berkeley, 1969); Robert F. Wasserstrom, "White Fathers and Red Souls: Indian-Ladino Relations in Highland Chiapas, 1528–1973," Ph.D. dissertation (Harvard University, 1976).

5. See, for example, the various Colecciones de documentos inéditos . . . and the collections compiled in Mexico by Francisco del Paso y Troncoso. The travel accounts by such as John Cockburn and Thomas Gage are rich in detail and pleasant to read.

soils and vegetation, about the interaction between climate and altitude and the new society which emerged after the conquest. Using the pioneering works of Denevan, Veblen, and Johannessen as springboards, the historical geographer can be the first to pursue such topics in many parts of Hapsburg Central America.[6]

Central American colonial demography has made considerable advances in the last decade. But so far it resembles nothing more than the scattered pieces of a puzzle. All agree on a drastic decline in the indigenous population after the Spanish conquest, but few agree on the size of the disaster. It is also obvious that the impact varied according to region, climate, altitude, and Spanish economic activity.

During the seventeenth century the apparently simple population pattern began to disintegrate. The decline continued in some areas, leading here to a complete extinction of the identifiably Indian population, there to delayed or partial revivals in the eighteenth century. The core area of Nicaragua would seem to be an example of extinction, while Chiapas gives evidence of delayed but significant demographic recovery.[7] In areas where Indian populations remained the large majority, demographic recovery often began in the early or mid-seventeenth century, but the patterns are intricate and varied. Even neighboring parishes recovered at different rates, for a whole variety of possible reasons.

Obviously related to Indian demography is the relative size, rates of growth, and reasons for growth among the three other population groups in Hapsburg Central America. Whites, *castas*, and blacks grew in number throughout the colonial period, with a few interesting but temporary reverses, but not all regions and groups grew at the same rates. Such questions bring the scholar very quickly to other large topics of interest such as miscegenation (or *mestizaje*), the slave trade and slave numbers, interregional migration, movement between rural areas and cities, and differences in morbidity and mortality between highlands and lowlands, town and country, intensive workplaces and extensive livestock raising, and much else.[8] Tribute records, parish records of births, confirmations, marriages, and deaths, and secular and ecclesiastical *visita* records are

6. William M. Denevan, *The Upland Pine Forests of Nicaragua: A Study in Cultural Plant Geography* (Berkeley and Los Angeles, 1961); Thomas T. Veblen, "The Ecological, Cultural, and Historical Bases of Forest Preservation in Totonicapán, Guatemala," Ph.D. dissertation (University of California, Berkeley, 1975); Carl L. Johannessen, *Savannas of Interior Honduras* (Berkeley and Los Angeles, 1963).

7. The annual meeting of the American Society for Ethnohistory held in Albany, New York, in October 1979 was devoted to Guatemalan demography. Several papers were devoted to the colonial period and will be published shortly.

8. For a discussion of one of these problems, see Magnus Morner, "La Política de Segregación y el Mestizaje en la Audiencia de Guatemala," *Revista de Indias*, 24, 95–96 (1964): 137–51. Work on the other topics mentioned is just beginning.

quite abundant in the archives of both Central America and Spain and await the student interested in these and other matters.

The history of food supply and diet is a bridge between some of the above questions and cultural history. What were the connections between such factors as famines, dearths, crop failures, new European crop introductions such as wheat or pigs, local plagues, locusts, economic dislocation, and the gradual changes in diet, especially Indian diet, after the conquest?[9] And how much was diet a function of deterministic necessities, how much a question of cultural preferences and dictates? Many Central American historians know of anecdotes and brief documentary references to such matters as the prestige of wheat compared to lowly maize—one, the staple of the European conquerors; the other, the staple of the conquered.

Population, mortality, food supply, and diet lead next to the source of most food. How was the land used, abused, divided, and held? Studies of land use would quickly lead scholars to a consideration of the impact of Central America's great commercial crops such as cacao and indigo. While the general histories of these two boom crops are known, the internal and social histories of the merchants, growers, middlemen, and laborers involved in them are not.[10] Land tenure is another vast unknown during the first two centuries of Spanish rule. Hacienda studies, so much in vogue in Mexico and Peru, have attracted few students in Central America, and most of the work done so far has been at the macro level.[11]

The influences of men and women upon one another, either singly or in groups and classes, also offer numerous prospects. The conquest itself has been fairly well covered. There are adequate biographies of several of the leading conquerors, and well-researched, thorough histories of the conquests of Honduras and Chiapas.[12] But the impact of the Spanish arrival and settlement upon individuals and groups, in its fine grain, is hardly

9. For comparative purposes, see the article by Sherburne F. Cook and Woodrow Borah, "Indian Food Production and Consumption in Central Mexico Before and After the Conquest (1500–1650)," in their *Essays in Population History,* Vol. 3, 129–76 (Berkeley and Los Angeles, 1979).

10. For indigo, see the work by Rubio Sánchez, *El añil.* For cacao, see J. F. Bergman, "The Distribution of Cacao Cultivation in Pre-Columbian America," *Annals of the Association of American Geographers,* 59 (1969): 85–96, and his more specific "Cacao and its Production in Central America," *Tijdschrift voor economische en sociale Geografie,* 48 (1957): 43–49.

11. Costa Rica is somewhat of an exception. See the numerous essays by Carlos Meléndez Ch. on land and land tenure.

12. E.g., Pablo Alvarez Rubiano, *Pedrarias Dávila* (Madrid, 1954); Robert S. Chamberlain, *The Conquest and Colonization of Honduras, 1502–1550* (Washington, D.C., 1953).

known. What, for example, became of Chorti society? Here was a particular group, tribe, or nation with its own distinguishable language and culture. In much modified form this group remains unique today. Feldman
has assembled a catalogue of documents on the Chorti, and such a case
study would be of immense value.[13] Similar studies of Indian groups are
possible in areas where Indians survived in numbers.

In the same vein little is known of the impact of the New World of
Central America on Spanish society. Lutz, Markman, and others have
pointed the way, but so far the whole world of the city, the hacienda, the
convent, and the monastery in Hapsburg Central America awaits curious
scholars.[14]

From the above it should be obvious that research opportunities in
Hapsburg Central America are so varied as to defy cataloguing. Nevertheless, it is worth adding a few more words of advice, which may aid the
student further in his selection of topics, times, and places. In general,
Guatemala (which included El Salvador) and Costa Rica, especially in the
last decade, have drawn most of those interested in Central America. Nicaragua, Chiapas, and Soconusco have been studied by very few scholars
with modern concerns. Honduras is almost terra incognita, apart from a
few suggestive works by researchers such as West.[15]

Notable also is the concentration of research in certain epochs. The
beginning and end of the colonial period draw the attention of scholars,
the middle does not. This seventeenth-century gap is not limited to Central
America, of course. In general, there is a considerable corpus of modern
writing up to about 1620. But the "real" or classic seventeenth century,
running from that date to the late 1680s, is known only in roughest outlines. Even more neglected has been the crucial and complicated period
between 1690 and 1730—a period of war, disasters, revolts, shortages, at
the same time it saw Central America emerging from its commercial isolation, renewing old ties with Mexico and Peru, and establishing new ones
with Jamaica, Cuba, and the northern European world beyond. The para-
doxical nature of these years, with their different impacts on Indian, casta,
and Spanish societies, requires a sophisticated explanation.

And one last word of caution and exhortation. Central America is not
the most "prestigious" area of Latin America in which to study. It does
not have the importance of core areas such as Mexico and Peru, and its

13. Lawrence H. Feldman, *A Survey of Chorti Manuscript Resources in Central America* (Columbia, Missouri, 1978).

14. On Spanish colonial architecture and the society which created it, see Sidney David
Markman, *Colonial Architecture of Antigua Guatemala* (Philadelphia, 1966).

15. Robert C. West, "The Mining Economy of Honduras during the Colonial Period,"
Actas del XXXIII Congreso Internacional de Americanistas, 2 (1959): 767–77.

disintegration into five nations, a Mexican state, and a British colony after independence may have further decreased its relative significance or attractiveness to modern eyes. As a result scholars who work on Central American colonial history may not attract the attention which they no doubt feel they deserve. (Of course it could also be argued that this is a sort of benign neglect. Neither do such scholars attract the sharp criticism that many deserve.) Because of this situation Central American colonial history runs the danger of sinking into cliquish parochialism. There are several ways of avoiding this. Scholars working in colonial Central America should keep in mind the possibilities of the case study. This would make them more interesting to scholars working on other areas and force them out of their parochialism. In a similar vein Central Americanists have made little use of the comparative method. A comparison with other secondary areas such as Cuba, Venezuela, or Chile would give students of the colonial period a better idea of what was unique or similar about colonial Central America, and would open the Central Americanist's eyes to broader Latin American horizons. Finally, the scholar interested in Hapsburg Central America should search diligently for models, theories, or ideas which have "worked" in other areas, not with a view to forcing them willy nilly on the Central American reality, but to test them there with a view to giving Central American history a wider framework and a place in the exciting world of historical theory. What is rare and exciting about Hapsburg Central America is that one has the opportunity to be a pioneer *and* a contributor to the large discussions which intrigue the scholarly world.

3   Research Topics for Bourbon Central America, 1700–1821
Mario Rodríguez

The recent literature on the Bourbons underscores the commitment of the dynasty to the process of modernization in the Spanish-speaking world. The vaunted Bourbon Reforms, for example, prepared the ground for the type of liberalism that emerged in southern Spain from 1810 to 1814 in the "Cádiz Experiment." Charles III and his talented ministers envisioned a modern Spanish nation as they pursued a program of "enlightened despotism," one in which efficient governmental institutions promised to guarantee subjects of the king equal and fair treatment before the law.

Despite some concessions to local rule, a central (unitary) authority was responsible for guiding the entire process. Its primary objective was to foment a national economy on the peninsula which, by capitalizing upon the bountiful resources of the empire, would assure Spain's economic independence; perhaps, in the long run, it might even secure her hegemony in international matters. Guided by the best thinkers of the Enlightenment, Bourbon statesmen aspired to reform Spanish society in keeping with their ambitious political and economic aims.

To what extent did the Bourbons succeed in creating the proper atmosphere for modernization overseas? What were the consequences of their efforts? Those are vital questions that interest students of the colonial as well as the early national periods of Central American history. A serious obstacle, however, is the amount of pertinent documentation. Private archives are difficult to come by. Materials controlled by the Church are not always readily available to scholars. Yet, there are still large quantities of documents in the archives of Guatemala, Spain, and Costa Rica that have not been quarried adequately. Recent books on colonial Hispanic America have demonstrated in convincing form the usefulness of notarial documentation for meaningful insights into society, demography, and economy. These materials include the *protocolos, padrones, tierras, testamentos, bautismos, tributos, registros de parroquia,* and sundry pieces that exist in the archives.

This new documentation should provide greater depth to what already is known about the political, economic, and social history of Bourbon Central America. The extant publications, moreover, can serve as guides to the general developments of that period. They point out lacunae and suggest questions that remain to be answered. Anyone proposing to do research on the political developments of that area, for example, should first consult the works of Héctor Humberto Samayoa Guevara on the intendancies, Ernesto Chinchilla Aguilar on the municipal history of Guatemala City, and Severo Martínez Peláez on the creoles' political and social structures.[1] Economic studies include the well-documented studies of Troy S. Floyd, Manuel Rubio Sánchez, Robert S. Smith, Francisco de Solano Pérez-Lila, Valentín Solórzano Fernández, Ralph Woodward, Jr., and Miles Wortman.[2] Murdo MacLeod's historical treatment of Central

1. Héctor Humberto Samayoa Guevara, *La intendencia en el Reyno de Guatemala* (Guatemala, 1969); Ernesto Chinchilla Aguilar, *El ayuntamiento colonial de la ciudad de Guatemala* (Guatemala, 1961); and Severo Martínez Peláez, *La patria del criollo: Ensayo de interpretación de la realidad colonial guatemalteca* (Guatemala, 1971). These studies cite the older standard works as well.

2. Troy S. Floyd, "Bourbon Palliatives and the Central American Mining Industry, 1765–1800," *The Americas,* 18 (1961): 103–25, and "The Guatemalan Merchants, the Gov-

America's economy, moreover, extends to 1720.[3] In the socioeconomic field, there are works on the guild system of Guatemala City by Samayoa and on the Mayas of the eighteenth century by Solano, in addition to the above-mentioned book by Martínez.[4] John Tate Lanning and Virgilio Rodríguez Beteta have dealt with intellectual affairs and Carlos Martínez Durán is still a standard reference for the medical history of the period.[5] A three-volume manuscript on the *protomedicato* by the late John Tate Lanning is being prepared for press by Professor John TePaske. This author's *The Cádiz Experiment in Central America, 1808 to 1826* (Berkeley, 1978) stresses the indebtedness of Spanish and Central American liberalism to the Bourbon Reforms. All these studies, and many more that cannot be listed here, set forth the major lines of Bourbon developments and suggest where greater depth of research is needed.

In view of the constant warfare of the eighteenth century, the Bourbons had little alternative but to rationalize government in Central America if they hoped to prevail over the British. This rivalry with Great Britain, which Professor Floyd has treated, was an expensive proposition.[6] This military drain greatly affected the fate of the reform program in Central America, simply by distracting available revenues. It is also important to recognize the nature of the military establishment in the area from 1764 forward, along the lines set down by Professor Lyle McAlister's monograph on Mexico.[7] How successful were the Bourbons in establishing mil-

---

ernment, and the *Provincianos, 1750–1800*," *Hispanic American Historical Review,* 41 (1961): 90–110; Manuel Rubio Sánchez, "El añil o xiquilite," *Anales de la Sociedad de Geografía e Historia* (Guatemala), 26 (1952): 313–49; Robert S. Smith, "Indigo Production and Trade in Colonial Guatemala," *Hispanic American Historical Review,* 39 (1959): 181–211, and "Origins of the Consulado of Guatemala," ibid., 26 (1946): 150–€1; Francisco de Solano y Pérez Lila, *Estudio historico y socioeconómico de Guatemala durante el siglo XVIII* (Madrid, 1970); Valentín Solórzano Fernández, *Historia de la evolución económica de Guatemala* (México, 1947); Ralph Lee Woodward, Jr., *Class Privilege and Economic Development* (Chapel Hill, 1966); and Miles Wortman, "Bourbon Reforms in Central America: 1750–1786," *The Americas,* 32 (1975): 222–38.

3. Murdo J. MacLeod, *Spanish Central America: A Socioeconomic History, 1520–1720* (Berkeley, 1973).

4. Héctor Humberto Samayoa Guevara, *Los gremios de artesanos en la ciudad de Guatemala, 1524–1821* (Guatemala, 1962); Francisco de Solano Pérez-Lila, *Los mayas del siglo XVIII: Pervivencia y transformación indígena guatemalteca durante la administración borbónica* (Madrid, 1974); Severo Martínez Peláez, *La patria.*

5. John Tate Lanning, *The Eighteenth-Century Enlightenment in the University of San Carlos de Guatemala* (Ithaca, New York, 1956); Virgilio Rodríguez Beteta, *Evolución de las ideas* (Paris, 1929); Carlos Martínez Durán, *Las ciencias médicas en Guatemala: Origen y evolución* (3d ed., Guatemala, 1964).

6. Troy S. Floyd, *The Anglo-Spanish Struggle for Mosquitia* (Albuquerque, 1967).

7. Lyle McAlister, *The Fuero Militar in New Spain* (Gainesville, 1957).

itias, the "citizen-soldiers" of Central America? How did future leaders of the area react to service in the militias and on the battlefield? Did it convince José Francisco Barrundia that it was a worthwhile reform? He had served in the Dragones, a cavalry unit, along with Antonio Juarros, a man who strongly conditioned his career in politics. Finally, a good biography of Captain General Matías de Gálvez, who had a brilliant career in Central America before he left for Mexico City to serve as viceroy of New Spain, is needed.

A comprehensive work on administrative reforms in Central America is still lacking, especially one dealing with the practical realities in the various intendancies and the *gobierno* of Costa Rica. The latter, for all practical purposes, was virtually autonomous. These various regional governments constituted the future states and countries of Central America. It is therefore crucial to study in detail their experiences under the Bourbons, the growth of their home-rule aspirations, and the relentless drive toward independence. A model study for Costa Rica, which stresses the popularity of Governor Tomás Acosta, already exists.[8] The fact that Acosta was Cuban raises a key issue that has been preoccupying scholars of the Bourbon era in other parts of Spanish America. How many *criollos,* from Central America and elsewhere in the New World, served in the expanded bureaucracy of the Bourbon world? Where did they serve? What ranks and what positions did they enjoy? What impact did they have upon local creoles? Were they important in propagating a love for the region in which they served, thus nurturing an incipient sense of nationalism? To what extent did they encourage a continental nationalism or "Americanism"— an increasing consciousness and identification of the criollos with the concept of "America"? Also, it is important to determine what influence Central Americans had upon peninsular-born officials in their midst, thanks to marital or social ties. Was this influence as pronounced in Central America as some writers have shown for Chile, Peru, and Mexico?

The presence of other Americans in Central America during the Bourbon era is intriguing. The Cuban Acosta was not alone. Professor Lanning has written about the famous Narciso Esparragosa, a Venezuelan medical expert, who was a leader at the University of San Carlos de Guatemala.[9] Professor Chandler has evaluated the role played by Jacobo de Villaurrutia as an *oidor* of the Audiencia de Guatemala from 1794 to 1804.[10] Domin-

8. Ligia Estrada Molina, *La Costa Rica de don Tomás de Acosta* (San José, Costa Rica, 1965).

9. John Tate Lanning, *Dr. Narciso Esparragosa y Gallardo* (Caracas, 1953), Colección Historia, II.

10. Dewitt S. Chandler, "Jacobo de Villaurrutia and the Audiencia of Guatemala, 1794–1804," *The Americas,* 32 (1976): 402–16.

ican-born, Villaurrutia was the principal founder of the Economic Society in Guatemala City and a recognized champion of "Americanism." Chandler also mentioned the judge, Manuel del Campo y Ricas, who apparently was Costa Rican by birth. The Colombian Antonio García Redondo was the dean of the Cathedral Chapter in Guatemala and an articulate defender of the Indians. There undoubtedly were many more. Did Bourbon policy encourage such mobility, deliberately or unintentionally?

By emphasizing and popularizing economic developmentalism, Bourbon leaders consciously strove to foment a strong sense of respect, love, and pride for things Spanish. In other words, they were encouraging a modern feeling of nationalism within the Spanish-speaking world, and their success in this regard was remarkable. It permeated the atmosphere at Cádiz and was evident throughout the wars for independence in many parts of Spanish America. This strong sentiment in favor of Spain had a varied potential. It helps to explain the loyalist feelings in some areas of the New World. It might have led to an integrated Spanish nation in which ex-colonials were destined to play a leading role—the objective of Americans at Cádiz. It might also have served as the basis for the creation of a commonwealth of nations in the Spanish world. This was the goal envisioned in the various plans to establish feudal monarchies overseas, all of them closely connected to the Crown in Madrid. These alternatives, of course, did not materialize for many reasons.

There was an interesting residue that resulted from the Bourbons' program of nationalism. Their nationalistic objectives depended heavily upon a concurrent buildup of regional sentiment and pride—a loyalty to a region that presumably would dovetail with the greater nationalism and which would tend to reinforce it. It can be contended that this is what happened when Bourbon leaders encouraged the establishment of regional intendancies, of new regional *consulados,* and of new regional economic societies by the end of the eighteenth century. In doing so, Bourbon leaders were following through on a well-known assumption among practitioners of the Enlightenment: namely, that the people of a given region were more capable of regulating and guiding their own destinies than distant bureaucrats who knew very little about local conditions. After all, this was a key recommendation in the celebrated Informe de Ley Agraria of 1795.[11] The regional emphasis prevailed at Cádiz and in the home-rule projects and aspirations reflected by the future leaders of Central America. It might be argued, in short, that the Bourbons fostered a series of loyal-

11. Gaspar de Jovellanos, "Informe de la Sociedad Económica de Madrid al Real y Supremo Consejo de Castilla en el expediente de Ley Agraria," in *Obras de Jovellanos,* ed. Venceslao de Linares y Pacheco, Vol. 7, 29–185 (3 vols., Barcelona, 1839–40).

ties that had a key impact upon the Americas at various levels. For example, a Costa Rican found it easy to develop a fierce pride about his local area and its economic potential. He was able, moreover, to project this feeling on to a larger regional area that comprised all of Central America; from there, to all of Spanish America; and, finally, to all of the New World, including the non-Spanish-speaking areas of the Americas. Of course, there were other factors that fed this range of American loyalties: the Enlightenment's obsession with nature was a case in point. There was the widely held belief that the individual could best regenerate himself and his society in the New World, where the natural and historical conditions were more propitious. Furthermore, the former English colonies of North America had launched a successful movement of anticolonialism as well as a program of modernization in keeping with the spirit of the age. All these elements, including the Bourbon contribution, aided the propagation of "Americanism" in the Spanish world—a hypothesis which students of Bourbon Central America should be prepared to test.

Bourbonists should likewise consider the increasingly important role played by Americans in the Spanish bureaucracy from 1808 forward. There were various reasons for this: first, Spain desperately needed American support in the war against France; second, Spanish Americans thereby gained more bargaining power in their relations with authorities in Spain; third, the "Cádiz Experiment" encouraged more American appointments, given the premise of equality between Spaniards and Americans; and, finally, the minister of the Indies after the restoration of Ferdinand VII continued the policy of more appointments for Americans. The role of these appointees during the wars of independence deserves to be studied seriously. A few examples should prove the point. José de Aycinena, the son of the first marquis of that name in Central America, was asked to serve on the prestigious Consejo de Estado, one of six Americans who worked in that corporation during the first constitutional period. Later, Ferdinand VII assigned him to the Consejo de Indias, where his presence helped to reverse the baneful actions of Captain General José de Bustamante in Central America. Aycinena also helped the Nicaraguan Miguel de Larreinaga to win a position on the Audiencia de Guatemala. This learned jurist, moreover, was a key figure in the adoption of educational reforms in the Spanish world before returning to Guatemala City. The "Cádiz Experiment," also, was the training ground for Central Americans like José Francisco Barrundia. There were many others who gained valuable political experience during those years; they are awaiting their biographers. Vicente Aycinena, José's brother and the second marquis to hold the title, was elected Jefe Político Superior of Guatemala in 1814—a post which he was unable to fill because of death and the end of the first constitutional period. The neglect of Antonio Juarros in Central American historiography has been lamentable. His uncle is remembered because of his publications; but the nephew, because he died before independence, has been practically forgotten. Yet, he was equal in stature to the Honduran savant José del Valle. Another figure whose biography is long overdue is Juan Fermín Aycinena, the first marquis of that name and one of the most dynamic entrepreneurs of the eighteenth century.

Municipal institutions throughout Central America, including the Ayuntamiento de Guatemala, require thoughtful monographs. The ideas of the count of Campomanes on the advantages of elected officials had a sounding board among councilmen in Guatemala City; and it is interesting to note that Spaniards on that corporation were stronger champions of that particular reform than Americans, at least initially. The origin of the practice of sharing municipal posts between creoles and peninsulars needs to be explained. In addition, the municipal structures and practices of the "Cádiz Experiment" throughout Central America need further investigation, especially where the documentation is available (Costa Rica and Quezaltenango). The municipal experience in Chiapas, which was part of the Kingdom of Guatemala, should be compared with the Central American counterparts. In fact, the municipal structures and administrative practices of the national period throughout Central America and Chiapas should be studied and compared to the Cádiz predecessor, especially since the latter already outlined in considerable detail the jefe político system. The states-rights pretensions of the Guatemalan highlands (Los Altos) is another theme worth considering. Finally, the Indians' reaction to the program of modernization in the "Cádiz Experiment" is a subject that should throw much light on the pre–Rafael Carrera period in Guatemalan history, eliminating perhaps much of the romanticism that has characterized some writing on that theme.

The general lines of economic developmentalism in Bourbon Central America are clear enough, but the specifics need further elaboration and research. For example, the Bourbons fostered laissez-faire economics: greater competition in an open society that found the authorities in Madrid protecting the outlying provinces, the so-called *provincianos;* the support of a more adequate and extensive infrastructure (roads, bridges, harbors, etc.) that would further undermine the merchant capitalists in Guatemala City and their stranglehold over the provinces; the incentives for establishing an indigo association that might stabilize prices and provide necessary funding, again relieving the provincianos from a dependency upon Guatemala City interests; the classification of new lands from the royal domain that would be available to small farmers, thus protecting the Indians, for example, from the intrusions of larger corporations or from the mestizos in their midst; the opening up of the guilds to new elements, thereby avoiding the restrictive practices of the past; the promotion of the textile industry in Central America through special demonstrations or by encouraging the measures taken by the Economic Society of Guatemala; the financial assistance in the transfer of the government and peoples from Antigua to the new capital of Guatemala City after the devastating earthquake of 1773; the official support of the authorities in Madrid and in Guatemala City for the consulado and the economic society founded in the 1790s; the encouragement of all manner of publications dealing with the problems of economic developmentalism in Central America; and many other manifestations of the Bourbon commitment to the modernization of the economy. All these themes can still be studied with profit, some to a greater extent than others, depending upon the available documentation. Samayoa, for example, admits that he did not fully exploit all the materials for the guild system in Guatemala City, and he urges the study of guilds in other parts of Central America. Smith has written about the forced-labor system adopted by the Bourbons, contrasting it with the long-standing policy of defending the Indians in Guatemala. Expediency prevailed over principle, it would appear. There is room for much more study of the condition of both rural and urban labor, according to Professor Smith. Although the indigo industry is well known, graphs on other economic endeavors of the period are needed.

Perhaps one of the most neglected economic themes in Bourbon Central America is contraband, a topic that historians seem to avoid like the plague. Yet, the Bourbons were obsessed with stamping out all illegal activities or open defiance of economic measures. Prospective researchers would do well to review the imaginative methodology employed by Professor William Sharp in his study of the Colombian Chocó during the colonial years.[12] Reasonable estimates of the illegal traffic and practices are sorely needed. The major problem is to determine the type of documentation that will yield the stingy facts, however fragmentary. Scholars should also concern themselves with the commercial contacts between Central America and the markets in Mexico, South America, and the Philippines for the years not covered by Professor MacLeod.

In furthering an open economy, the Bourbons supported the outlying provinces as opposed to "the establishment," the merchant capitalists in Guatemala City, who controlled the Kingdom of Guatemala economically

12. William Frederick Sharp, *Slavery on the Spanish Frontier: The Colombian Chocó, 1680–1810* (Norman, Oklahoma, 1976).

through their close contacts with a network of *alcaldes mayores*. The Crown's objective was to reestablish control over the fiscal and governmental machinery; in the process, however, it also fostered a regionalism that was hostile to the former capital and unfortunate for the future of Central American unionism.

Up to this point, the emphasis has been primarily upon the Bourbon contribution to an open economy. There is another side of the coin: the fiscal reforms introduced from 1768 to 1780. According to Professor Wortman, the Bourbons succeeded in increasing revenues by taking over the various *estancos,* or franchises, on tobacco, salt, playing cards, *aguardiente,* etc. These monopolies, and others like the *chicha* preceding independence, need to be studied carefully. Were they all taken over by the Crown? Or did the Crown later revert to farming out the estancos? Moreover, what kind of a reaction did the various estancos provoke among all classes of people? It was a major grievance at the time of independence and a current that runs throughout the national history of Guatemala. Judging from the complaints of Central Americans at Cádiz, the overhead administrative cost for the hated tobacco monopoly was 50 percent.[13] If this is true, then it is possible that the alleged revenue increases of the Bourbon Reforms are misleading. Although a monograph on the Costa Rican tobacco industry exists, others are needed for Guatemala and Chiapas.[14]

There are still many questions that remain unanswered concerning the condition of the Indian in Bourbon Central America. Careful land-retention studies, like those of Professor William Taylor for Oaxaca and other Mexicanists, can be utilized as models by Central Americanists. Were the *ejidos* of the Indians abused or respected by local officials, Spanish or otherwise? How did the tribute system work? This author is particularly interested in the *cajas de comunidad,* a fund drawn in part from the tribute revenue and intended to protect the Indians in times of adversity. Apparently these revenues were tapped frequently for *donativos* to the government, which was always in a financial pinch, or were spent for sundry items that had nothing to do with the Indians. After 1789 with the publication of the manuscript of José Campillo y Cosío, *New System of Economic Government for America,* the defense of the Indians once again became popular in the Spanish-speaking world. To what extent was this defense a humanitarian concern or the result of a need for labor in the

13. *Diario de las Cortes* (Cádiz), March 14, 1812, referring to a letter sent to him by the Ayuntamiento de Guatemala, August 13, 1811.
14. Marco Antonio Fallas, *La factoria de tabacos de Costa Rica* (San José, Costa Rica, 1972).

programs for economic development? Perhaps it was both; at any rate, there is no doubt that it contributed heavily to the strong current of *indigenismo* at the Cortes of Cádiz.

In a report written by the Guatemalan consulado, instructing the Guatemalan deputy to Parliament on the developmental measures that it favored, a dynamic group of merchants from northern Spain—Asturianos and Vascos, for the most part—came to the defense of the Indians. They especially desired an aggressive program of agrarian reform that would benefit the natives. Strongly pro-*indígena,* these northerners were also antilatifundistas and in favor of small farmers. The diversification of agriculture and the development of the area's industrial potential were additional measures they sought. This was the Spanish faction that followed José del Valle in the constitutional elections of 1820; it was also responsible for the minority report of the Ayuntamiento of Guatemala City to Father Antonio Larrazábal, the area's representative at Cádiz. A socioeconomic study of this enterprising group of Spanish merchants would clarify the policies of the preindependence period.

The notarial documentation should prove to be particularly useful in revealing the nature of society in Bourbon Central America, rural and urban. What was the extent of the dislocation that attended the earthquake of 1773, as well as the decline of indigo prices? There was a general economic depression, which apparently caused the unemployed to flock to the urban nuclei. Crime was rampant, and the potential for social revolution was great, judging from a report from the Ayuntamiento of Guatemala City, which likened conditions there to those in France before the Revolution. The Cádiz governments tried to meet the challenge, but revenues were in short supply. Here is a theme worthy of a talented observer.

The Church in Bourbon Central America likewise raises key questions that need to be answered. How did the regalist policies affect the hierarchy and structure of the Church, especially after the investigations of Bishop Pedro Cortés Larraz (1768–72)? There appears to have been an awareness that a tighter ecclesiastical administration might enhance the projected political reforms, leading to the consideration of new bishoprics, perhaps in the Intendancy of San Salvador. How did the clergy function in the rural areas, and what was the nature of the subsidies provided by the Indians? More study of the missionary effort throughout Central America and not just on the Anglo-Spanish frontier, which Professor Floyd has described, would be helpful. Did the clergy in urban zones help to educate the unemployed by establishing public schools, as in Mexico? What was the Church's financial role in the program of economic developmentalism? These are all legitimate questions, which have been posed for other areas of Spanish America, and Central Americanists should also focus on them.

It is this author's contention that perhaps the Bourbons' greatest success in the process of modernization took place in the Church, in the form of the education and upgrading of the ecclesiastical personnel throughout the Spanish-speaking world. Nowhere was it more evident than in the "Cádiz Experiment," where clergymen were leaders in the reform process. In Spain, Central America, and Mexico they were consistently preferred by the electorate for political office. Moreover, this was mainly because of their progressivism, not a result of any obscurantist views. Judging from the "Instructions" to Father Larrazábal, Guatemalans favored a regalist stand. The various religious orders were in step with the times. According to Father Goicoechea, the curriculum for the Franciscan order was exemplary in reflecting the new ideas of the Enlightenment. The social work and the popularity of the Bethlemite order, founded in Guatemala, should provide a rewarding project for some investigators. The education of the clergy in Bourbon Central America is a theme which should be given a high priority among scholars.

Finally, the role of the artisan groups throughout Central America requires a dispassionate study, if that is possible. Although apathetic in the initial stages of the "Cádiz Experiment," artisans, at least in Guatemala City, pursued their objectives dynamically under the leadership of José del Valle.

Hence Bourbon Central America is still open for investigators who are willing to utilize the new documentation or rework the older veins from the broader perspective of the modernization attempted by the Bourbon leaders in the area's political, economic, and life styles.

4   Guatemala
David McCreery

From the conquest, social, economic, and political forces have been at work in Guatemala, shaping a nation of unusual complexity. Problems important not only to Latin America but to the whole of the Third World manifest themselves in peculiarly acute forms in the fabric of the nation's changing situation: export monoculture, latifundia and minifundia, coerced labor, race and class conflict, political and social violence, authoritarianism, and the impacts of foreign domination are only the most obvious. But if this complexity creates exciting opportunities for investigation, it also places heavy demands on the researcher. The best work will require not only an interdisciplinary approach but well-formulated questions or hypotheses rooted in broad and applicable theory.

Political History

The central concern of political activity is power: its origins and site, how it is or is not made effective in a given situation, and to what ends it is used. While for most of the national period the Guatemalan state has been quite effective in controlling the countryside and repressing regionalism and local competition,[1] the structure of the regime prior to the 1940s remained little more than *caciquismo* writ large, or *caudillaje*.[2] Little is known about the process of central decision making or the means, other than the too common violence, utilized to mobilize support for, or at least acquiescence to, state policy. The Archivo General de Centro América (AGCA) contains an abundance of material, including presidential papers of Reyna Barrios and Estrada Cabrera and perhaps others, which might be used to address this question. What role has ideology versus personal or family connections? Which social groups or structural features of national society facilitated or obstructed, for example, the Carrera-Conservative alliance, Estrada Cabrera's "Dictatorship of Twenty Years," or Ubico's regime?[3]

Whereas present knowledge of the executive rarely rises above the level of polemic, even less is known about the other elements of the central government. What were the activities of the cabinet ministries and ministers and what importance had they? Did power bases exist in the governmental hierarchy independent of the *caudillo?* What was the role of the departmental governors, several of whom went on to more prominent positions in subsequent administrations?[4] By contrast, because it typically had scant real power, the National Assembly prior to 1944 would be a less interesting object of study, and techniques such as role-call analysis could

1. Good introductions to the problems of local control include R. Kerns. ed., *The Caciques* (Albuquerque, 1973); and R. Bartra, ed., *Caciquismo en el México rural* (México, 1975).

2. E. Wolf and E. Hansen, "Caudillo Politics: A Structural Analysis," *Comparative Studies in Society and History,* 9 (1967): 168–79.

3. In addition to the standard works on Barrios, which could stand to be updated, there is a recent monograph on Ubico by K. Grieb, *Guatemalan Caudillo* (Athens, Ohio, 1979); and R. L. Woodward has underway a book on Carrera.

4. In its uncatalogued holdings the AGCA has literally tons of the papers of the departmental governors. Information on the more successful of the jefes políticos can be found in O. Zea Carascosa, *Semblanza: Ministerio de la Defensa Nacional* (Guatemala, 1971); on Ubico's early career, see J. Pitti, "Jorge Ubico and Guatemalan Politics in the 1920's," Ph.D. dissertation (University of New Mexico, 1975).

be expected to reveal little about political decision making, though they might reveal something about interelite cleavages.

A number of books and articles about the democratic decade (1944–54) exist, but many seem today too obviously soaked in Cold War rhetoric.[5] Recently, on the other hand, studies have tended to focus on subjects, e.g., the 1954 U.S. intervention,[6] which can be investigated outside the AGCA. In part this reflects the continuing difficulty of working on 1944–54 in Guatemala, as well as the related problem that the materials contained in the national archives for the years after 1944 remain in almost total disarray. Exiles aside, participants in the 1944–54 governments are not generally good sources of information: many have been killed in the years since 1954, and those who survive tend, not illogically, to prefer a low profile and are usually reluctant to talk openly to researchers.[7] On the other hand, projects utilizing published materials, e.g., formal aspects of political life such as electoral campaigns, party ideology, or political education and the growth of public consciousness, can be effectively pursued in the unusually wide variety of newspapers and periodicals permitted to appear during these years. Most worthwhile questions about the political life of the short-lived republic remain to be asked, but when and under what circumstances they can be answered remain to be seen.

Probably no important political institution in modern Guatemala is less well understood than the military.[8] Though exceptions have been made, military materials in the AGCA are normally closed to investigators. Considerable information on at least the overt political activities of the officer class, however, could be gleaned from conventional sources. What have been the origins and composition of the officer corps? A study of recruitment and socialization in the Politécnica would be useful.[9] What political

5. Compare, for example, J. Rozzoto, *El carácter de la revolución guatemalteca* (México, 1958) with R. Schneider, *Communism in Guatemala* (New York, 1958); for one of the classics of this period, see S. Newbold [R. Adams], "Receptivity to Communist-Fomented Agitation in Rural Guatemala," *Economic Development and Cultural Change,* 5, 4(1957): 335–61.

6. J. Aybar, *Dependency and Intervention: The Case of Guatemala in 1954* (Boulder, 1979); S. Schlesinger and S. Kinzer, *Bitter Fruit: The Untold Story of the American Coup in Guatemala* (New York, 1982); R. Immerman, *The CIA in Guatemala* (Austin, 1982); and S. Jonas, *Guatemala: plan piloto para el continente* (San José, Costa Rica, 1981).

7. This, at least, has been the author's experience.

8. The chapter "The Development of the Military" in R. Adams, *Crucifixion by Power* (Austin, 1970) is a superb beginning.

9. For a description of the activities of the Politécnica, see F. Samayoa C., *La Escuela Politécnica atraves de su historia* (Guatemala, 1964). A good example of what can be done with seemingly ordinary and uncontroversial military materials is "Quantitative and Cartographical Exploitation of French Military Archives, 1819–1826," by E. Le Roy and P. Dumont in *Historical Studies Today,* ed. F. Gilbert and S. Graubaud (New York, 1972).

role did this group traditionally see for itself, and when and how did it seek to implement this role? What of its links to other groups in society? Was the military simply a servant of the landed elite, or had it goals of its own? What were the political implications of foreign training missions and, with World War II, foreign aid? The specifics of military involvement in historical events from the Reforma to the Banana War of 1930 to the Revolution of 1944–54 must still be clarified.

In the years since 1954 the national politics of Guatemala has become almost exclusively the product of the interaction of a newly "professionalized" military and an increasingly complex agro-industrial elite.[10] But if military officers have been at the heart of every important political decision since the betrayal of the Reform governments, their role as keepers of a repressive society makes them unlikely and unwilling candidates for investigation. The impacts of U.S. and Israeli political and military ideology on the thinking and plans of the officer corps, the campaigns during the 1960s in the Oriente and Sierra de las Minas, and the renewed fighting since 1976 need to be studied,[11] as does the guerrilla response.[12] Does Guatemala's army have a *línea dura* and a Sorbonne, or do the internal disputes which surface occasionally reflect only personalist rivalries and competition between *promociones?*

The stock of "elite lore" for Guatemala remains remarkably limited.[13] We know more about the despised Indian than we do about the dominant national or regional and local families. Evidence suggests they are a group with a relatively high rate of circulation, a significant correlation of economic and political power, and a growing internal diversity and, hence, tendency toward disunity. A fairly undifferentiated ruling faction of mer-

10. For the politics of the 1950s and 1960s, see M. Jamail, "Guatemala, 1944–1972: The Politics of Aborted Revolution," Ph.D. dissertation (University of Arizona, 1972); the best treatments of the recent involvement of the military in politics are George Black's articles in *NACLA: Report on the Americas,* 17, 1(January–February 1983) and 2(March–April 1983), being reissued in an expanded book version by Zed Press.

11. A good introduction is G. Aguillera Peralta, *La violencia en Guatemala como fenómeno político* (México, 1971), and "Efectos cuantitativos de la política de terror del estado guatemalteco en relación al movimiento popular," *Estudios sociales centroamericanos,* 9, 27(septiembre–diciembre 1980): 217–49.

12. On the EGP (Guerrilla Army of the Poor) see M. Payeras, *Los días de la selva* (La Habana, 1980) and documents reprinted in *Contemporary Marxism,* 3 (Summer 1981). The "New Resources" section of the *NACLA: Report on the Americas* frequently lists Left solidarity publications on Central America; excerpts from a number of these together with newspaper articles and original essays are brought together in J. Fried et al., eds., *Guatemala in Rebellion: Unfinished History* (New York, 1983).

13. For an interesting treatment in an unlikely source, see F. Goldman, "The Girls of Guatemala," *Esquire,* 95, 3(March 1981): 38–45; more scholarly is E. Quintana, *Historia de la generación de 1920* (Guatemala, 1971).

chants and landowners in the nineteenth century gave way to one crosscut by divisions based on new activities in industry, distribution, and agricultural and mineral raw-material exports. As well, and almost alone among the Central American states, Guatemala has a significant middle sector, the interests of which tend to be linked to the domestic market and appear at times to have been at odds with those of the more cosmopolitan haute bourgeoisie.[14] Class position, particularly when one speaks of regional and local elites, is crosscut also by race, especially that peculiarly Guatemalan category, the *ladino*. Collective biographies of political officeholders at various levels, if telling little about the institutional operation of government, might reveal much about elite composition and its changes over time. Most aspects of elite political activity (e.g., clubs and associations, pressure and interest groups, political parties when they functioned, and the class and family alliances of politics) need to be identified and followed over time.[15] Material is available to enable much more study of *los que mandan* in Guatemala.

The majority of Guatemala's population historically has participated in politics only at the local level if at all. Preliminary indications are that major changes have occurred in community political life since the late nineteenth century.[16] Increasing penetration of world capitalism in the form of land and labor demands for coffee production, together with the policies of an effective liberal central state, undermined what remained of local, and particularly Indian local, autonomy. In the apparent absence, except perhaps for the years 1944–54, of the necessary preconditions, have meaningful elections been possible and, if so, how and when? If not, how has the state manipulated the electoral process and "delivered" the vote?[17] By what institutional, or perhaps more important, extra-institutional means does the state enforce its mandate? What is the role of violence in Guatemala's local politics?[18] Useful to begin with would be a

14. The postcolonial class structure of Guatemala is examined from a *dependentista* perspective in C. Guzman-Böckler and J-L. Herbert, *Guatemala: una interpretación histórico-social* (México, 1970).

15. A study of interest-group politics of particular utility for its clear statement of concepts and problems is P. Smith, *The Politics of Wheat and Beef in Argentina* (New York, 1969).

16. For example, R. Adams, ed., *Community Culture and National Change* (New Orleans, 1972); and W. Smith, *The Fiesta System and Economic Change* (New York, 1976).

17. Ballots for the elections of the 1970s are on deposit in the AGCA. For a "ground-level" view of local politics during the 1970s, see J. Sexton, ed., *Son of Tecun Uman* (Tucson, 1981).

18. An examination of political violence at the local level, which effectively combines techniques of history and anthropology, can be found in A. Blok, *The Mafia in a Sicilian Village, 1860–1960* (New York, 1974).

series of microhistorical studies from which regional and interethnic comparisons could be drawn.[19]

Economic History

There is an obvious need for a general economic history of the national period.[20] A new synthesis could, by imaginatively exploiting available but widely scattered secondary material, update existing standard treatments to incorporate the results of recent empirical research and take up problems and theoretical questions, e.g., "dependency" versus modes of production, much debated in recent years.

Most areas of the history of the national-period economy await serious monographic treatment. For example, it is agriculture which has sustained—albeit unequally—most Guatemalans. Anthropologists provide some insight into changes in the countryside, but typically they only sketch these changes as a preliminary to basically synchronic analyses.[21] Studies by economists stress technical factors but give scant attention to political economy. From the colonial period Guatemala produced agricultural exports, but the shift to coffee after 1850 provoked unprecedented changes in most aspects of national life. A valuable exercise would be to bring together the available published material on this crop (much of the material is repetitive and could be "boiled down") and compare this with the experiences of other coffee-monoculture economies.[22] Other areas remain to be examined. The labor systems need to be studied.[23] The capital

---

19. For comparative history, including an extensive bibliography, see M. Morner, J. de Viñuela, and J. French, "Comparative Approaches in Latin American History," *Latin American Research Review*, 17, 3(1982): 55–89.

20. This is not to deny the value of V. Solorzano's *Evolución económica de Guatemala* (Guatemala, 1947) but simply to point out that it is now more than thirty years old.

21. Happily, an exception is R. Carmack, *Historia social de los Quichés* (Guatemala, 1979).

22. A preliminary effort for Central America can be found in C. Cardoso, "Historia económica del café en Centroamérica (siglo XIX): estudio comparativo," *Estudios sociales centroamericanos*, 4, 10(1975): 9–55. A model study of a coffee economy is M. Palacios, *Coffee in Colombia: An Economic, Social and Political History* (Cambridge, 1980). The chief problem for the study of coffee, or for that matter any of Guatemala's commercial crops, is the lack of accessible plantation records. The only generally available set of such papers is the Dieseldorff collection at Tulane University: G. Náñez Falcón, "Erwin Paul Dieseldorff, German Entrepreneur in the Alta Verapaz of Guatemala, 1889–1937," Ph.D. dissertation (Tulane University, 1970). Julio C. Cambranes has used these papers in the preparation of a projected three-volume study of coffee in Guatemala; see his essay: J. Cambranes, "Café sangriento," Vol. 3, 18–31 *Polémica* (San José, Costa Rica).

23. The author is at work on an examination of agricultural labor systems from the late colonial period to 1978. A portion of the results of this research has been published: D. McCreery, "Debt Servitude in Rural Guatemala, 1876–1936," *Hispanic American Historical Review*, 63, 4(1983): 735–59.

and commercial structure of coffee production and trade is largely unexplored, as is the operation of the large, usually foreign-controlled, wholesale and commission houses of the capital.[24] How profitable was coffee, and who made the profits? Too little is known about the banana industry or the more recent exports of cotton, cattle, and cardamon. What were the effects of the export revolution on agricultural production, particularly food, for the domestic market?

Increased agricultural exports led to new patterns of trade and commerce. The growth of monoculture tended to discourage creation of a diversified communication network which might have fostered internal integration or stimulated the domestic market.[25] There are few studies of Guatemala's international commerce.[26] What did the nation trade and with whom? Was Guatemala's trade with Latin America and Mexico as unimportant as is usually assumed? How did the inflow of wealth from agricultural exports affect the internal economy? The effects of monopoly control of areas of the national economy need to be studied.[27] There are descriptions and analyses of the Indians' "solar" market systems, but what of the rural ladinos, both in the countryside and the small towns, or the urban retail merchants? How have patterns of regional and interregional trade changed over time? Studies of currency, credit, and inflation in the twentieth century and of the country's international financial position are sorely needed. What were the costs, and who paid them, of Guatemala's ruinous inflation in the 1890s or the pegging of the *quetzal* to the dollar since the 1920s? Particularly serious is the lack of adequate price series for the years prior to the 1950s[28] or any serious attempt to study more recent

24. The Ph.D. dissertation of M. Domínguez, "The Development of the Technological and Scientific Coffee Industry in Guatemala, 1830–1930" (Tulane University, 1970), includes material on the capital structure of coffee production and trade; and G. Náñez Falcón, "German Contributions to the Economic Development of the Alta Verapaz of Guatemala, 1865–1900," M.A. thesis (Tulane University, 1961) in part treats the activities of German-owned coffee brokerage and import houses in Guatemala City.

25. C. Smith has worked extensively on patterns of internal trade and development in the Occidente, both in her Ph.D. dissertation—"The Domestic Marketing System in Western Guatemala: An Economic, Locational, and Cultural Analysis" (Stanford University, 1972)—and in more recent unpublished manuscripts such as "Local Response to Global Process: Social and Economic Transitions in Western Guatemala" (1982).

26. See T. Schoonover, "Central American Commerce and Maritime Activity," *Latin American Research Review*, 13, 2(1978): 157–69.

27. LaBarge suggests the developmental advantages of "imperfect competition": R. LaBarge, *Impact of the United Fruit Company on the Economic Development of Guatemala, 1946–1954* (New Orleans, 1960); an alternative view of the company is to be found in "United Fruit Is not Chiquita," in *Guatemala,* ed. S. Jonas and D. Tobis (Berkeley, 1974).

28. For the 1920s, for example, prices on a monthly basis by municipality are available in the papers of the departmental governors.

trends. Without these, investigation of real wages and living standards, profitability, or investment patterns is impossible.

For most Guatemalans agriculture has meant precarious subsistence or peasant production sometimes eked out with petty-commodity handicrafts or trade. Vignettes of this life are more numerous than are serious historical studies.[29] Evidence suggests that crops and techniques have not changed greatly from the late colonial period; this lack of change is the central problem of the small agriculturist's life. Land tenure has been the chief variant.[30] Based on the laws and the few available studies,[31] it is thought that Indian villages lost much of their communal lands in the years during and after the Reforma, but hard information is scarce: How was the land taken, by whom, and from whom, and to what uses was it put? Was land engrossed for production or simply to "shake out" cheap labor? These questions call for local studies making use of ethnohistorical and oral history techniques from which—keeping in mind the famous dictum that anything you can say about Guatemala is both right and wrong— generalizations might be possible. Municipal archives, while usually chaotic, at least promise manageable quantities of materials.[32] A tedious but useful exercise would be to trace land transactions for a sample of municipalities from the original titles in the AGCA through the subsequent resales, divisions, and consolidations recorded in the ledgers of the Registro de Propiedad Inmueble. Similar questions arise about the disposition of Church lands in the nineteenth century and the origins and fate of fruit company property in the twentieth. What of the *faja transversal* and the "zone of the generals" in the Alta Verapaz?

Prior to World War II Guatemala had no appreciable industrial capacity or production. Except for railroad construction, most of what passed for industry was in fact artisan work. In recent years there has been some growth in consumer light industries, but many of these are little more than

29. Anthropologists are beginning now to restudy communities originally investigated in the 1930s and 1940s. For example, see Hinshaw, *Panajachel: A Guatemalan Town in Thirty Years Perspective* (Pittsburg, 1975); and J. Watanabe, "Cambios económicos en Santiago Chimaltenango, Guatemala," *Mesoamérica* (Guatemala), 1, 2(junio 1981): 20–41.

30. A starting point for any study of this topic should be K. Duncan and I. Rutledge, eds., *Land and Labor in Latin America* (Cambridge, 1977); for comparison, see R. Palmer and N. Parsons, eds., *The Roots of Rural Poverty in Central and Southern Africa* (Berkeley, 1977).

31. The best of these is S. Davis, "Land of Our Ancestors: A Study of Land Tenure and Inheritance in the Highlands of Guatemala," Ph.D. dissertation (Harvard University, 1970); on the more current situation, see Instituto de Investigaciones Económicas y Sociales de Occidente (I.I.E.S.O.), *Guatemala: Estructura agraria del altiplano occidental* (Quetzaltenango, 1976).

32. A major contribution to historical research in Guatemala would be the inspection and inventory of surviving municipal archives.

the "last touch" operations of multinationals and are meant to supply the limited middle-class market gathered together by the Central American Common Market.[33] At the same time, however, the not insubstantial local entrepreneurial faction competes with and promotes interests not necessarily identical to those of the multinationals and their allies. When and under what circumstances do these groups in turn oppose or cooperate with the more traditional agro-export-based elites? What is the extent of and basis for overlap of membership and interests?[34] Information on organized labor and its peasant allies is scarce.[35] Because working-class organizations commonly are criticized for their supposed readiness to resort to violence, the systematic denial to them by the Guatemalan state, over the last thirty years, of their legal rights and of the opportunity for peaceful change must be clearly documented.

Both academic and activist dependentistas find Guatemala of particular interest.[36] Dependency as a concept, however, remains more graphic than analytic and thus easy prey to assaults from its flanks. If those who embrace this approach are to avoid the French vice of replying to criticism by simply restating their theory in more strident terms, they must systematize their insights and attend to gaps presently papered over with polemic. More attention must be given, for example, to the genesis of modern dependency in the nineteenth-century world of competing metropoli and incomplete hegemony. Dependency needs more adequate treatments of "race" and "class" and must clarify its relationship to Marxist analysis.

33. More extensive than most but otherwise unfortunately typical of the books available on the CACM is W. Cline and E. Delgado, *Economic Integration in Central America* (Washington, D.C., 1978).

34. To begin, see Carole Snee, "Guatemala's Bourgeoisie: The Top 20 Families," in *Guatemala,* ed. Jonas and Tobis.

35. A piece which is often overlooked is N. Pearson, "Guatemala: The Peasant Union Movement, 1944–1954" in *Latin American Peasant Movements*, ed. H. Landsberger (Ithaca, 1969). The most comprehensive, though now badly outdated, study of labor remains E. Bishop, "The Guatemalan Labor Movement, 1944–1959," Ph.D. dissertation (University of Wisconsin, 1959).

36. The standard introduction to "dependency" in Latin America is R. Chilcote and J. Edelstein, eds., *Latin America: The Struggle with Dependency and Beyond* (New York, 1974), which includes summaries of the positions of the major theorists and chapters on various countries including Guatemala; useful critiques—there are many—include R. Bath and D. James, "Dependency Analysis of Latin America: Some Criticisms, Some Suggestions," *Latin American Research Review,* 11, 3(1976): 3–54; D. Ray, "The Dependency Model of Latin American Underdevelopment: Three Basic Fallacies," *Journal of Interamerican Studies and World Affairs,* 15 (1973): 4–20; D. Platt, "Dependency in Nineteenth-Century Latin America," *Latin American Research Review*, 15, 1(1980): 113–30; and, from the Left, "Dependency and Marxism," a special issue of *Latin American Perspectives* (ed. Ronald H. Chilcote), 8, 3–4(Summer and Fall 1981).

In general, dependency has played an important role in breaking the stranglehold of "value free" positivism on North American social science and indicates potential for continued development.

Social History

The social history of Guatemala is extraordinarily rich in opportunities for the researcher. Groups which are defined and which identify themselves in ethnic, socioeconomic, and cultural terms overlap, intersect, and interact, resulting in combinations and situations perplexing to the observer and to the participants alike. Basic studies of the composition of social classes and class factions of and for themselves need to be undertaken. There has been much attention to Indian-ladino relations, but, again, without much attention to changes over the past two hundred years.[37] The mechanisms and rhythm of the spread of national culture to and within the western highlands and the Alta Verapaz remain unclear. Writers have ignored the social history of the ladino/mestizo Oriente as well as that of the Caribbean and Pacific coasts.[38] What of the thousands of West Indian blacks who turned Puerto Barrios into a roaring frontier town at the turn of the century? Little is known even today about rural life outside Indian areas and perhaps even less about the inhabitants of the small towns and provincial centers which withered from relatively substantial communities in the eighteenth and nineteenth centuries to dusty backwaters in the twentieth.

Yet to be traced is Guatemala City's emergence as a "primate city" typical of the Third World. This ought to be examined in spatial[39] and population terms as well as from the perspectives of housing, sewage and water, public transportation, and police and fire services. Treatment of these problems must, of course, embrace not simply technical considerations but the economic and class bases of urban development as well.[40] Crime, violence, and the activities of the "dangerous class"[41] might be studied for the nineteenth and early twentieth centuries, using the AGCA's copious police and court files and the papers of the department's governor. Much of the city's explosive growth has been very recent, resulting in

37. Among other exceptions to this generalization are K. Warren, *The Symbolism of Subordination: Indian Identity in a Guatemalan Town* (Austin, 1978); and B. Colby and P. van den Berghe, *Ixil Country* (Berkeley, 1969).

38. The chapter on Guatemala in R. Adams, *Cultural Surveys of Panama–Nicaragua–Guatemala–El Salvador* (Washington, D.C., 1957), focuses on the mestizo/ladino areas.

39. T. Caplow, *La ecología social de la ciudad de Guatemala* (Guatemala, 1966).

40. An excellent study is B. Roberts, *Organizing Strangers: Poor Families in Guatemala City* (Austin, 1973).

41. Useful models would be R. Cobb, *The Police and the People in Paris* (Oxford, 1970); or L. Chevalier, *Labouring Classes and Dangerous Classes* (New York, 1973).

records of a quality far surpassing those for the years prior to 1945. The problem is one of access.

Although several recent studies have greatly improved the situation, much work is still to be done on the historical demography of the country.[42] The quality of census statistics for the nineteenth and first half of the twentieth centuries probably does not lend itself to sophisticated manipulation, but it should be adequate to indicate general trends and magnitudes. What, for example, have been the effects of the export revolution on the health and mortality of the rural and urban classes? What has urbanization done to the population of the capital? Analyses of migration and population mobility need more historical depth. On the subject of immigration, there are studies of the nineteenth-century Verapaz schemes, but what of the country's most persistent immigrants, the Salvadoreños?

The role of ideas and ideology also merits attention. Needed are studies of all levels of the educational system. These should go beyond the familiar collections of documents to examine the social contexts of education and its relationship to economic and political life in specific historical circumstances.[43] Another institution in Guatemala involved historically with the dissemination and control of ideas has been the Catholic church; studies of most Church activities are lacking, at least in part because of inaccessibility of Church archives. One might, though, be able to combine newspapers with Church publications and interviews to study, for example, the rise and the state of social consciousness in the lower ranks of the clergy.[44] Even in the colonial period, however, the Church failed to gain an ideological monopoly, and, since independence[45] its role as arbiter of ideas has been further threatened by new religious and secular systems which offer alternative world views, e.g., Protestantism—of particular interest given the *evangélicos* recent involvement in politics—liberalism, positivism, social Darwinism, and Marxism.

It should be abundantly clear that much of the history of modern Gua-

42. J. Early, *The Demographic Structure and Evolution of a Peasant Society: The Guatemalan Population* (Boca Raton, 1982); and R. Carmack, J. Early, and C. Lutz, eds., *The Historical Demography of Guatemala* (Albany, New York, 1982); see also, R. L. Woodward, "Crecimiento de población en Centro América durante la primera mitad del siglo de la independencia nacional: investigación reciente y estimados hasta la fecha," *Mesoamérica*, 1, 1(1980): 219–31.

43. The fact that, for example, political factions and the state have felt it necessary to murder fifty to seventy primary and secondary school teachers a year in recent years, as well as scores of university faculty over the last decade, suggests the importance of exploring this topic.

44. Worth looking at in this context is P. Lernoux, *Cry of the People* (New York, 1980).

45. For a study of the struggle in recent years between traditional Indian Catholicism and Acción Católica, see R. Falla, *Quiché rebelde* (Guatemala, 1978).

temala has yet to be written. Indeed, a serious problem for the investigator can be precisely a lack of ancillary secondary material, which would allow examination of the broader implications of a given problem. More seriously, given the continuing sociopolitical tensions and violence in the country, many of the most interesting topics remain touchy or even potentially dangerous, if not always for the researcher, then frequently for those of the local population who cooperate with him. The historian, to repeat, to work successfully on Guatemala, should employ an adequate research design, set upon solid theoretical foundations and illuminated where applicable by comparisons. To those who proceed in this manner, Guatemalan history offers the chance to do genuinely original research of importance beyond narrow national boundaries.

5   Belize
Wayne M. Clegern

Belize developed in fair analogy to the islands of the Caribbean, but its primary products, logwood and mahogany, produced a unique social pattern. The development of Belize featured piracy in the seventeenth century, logwood in the first two-thirds of the eighteenth, mahogany in the late eighteenth and early nineteenth, extensive commerce with Spanish Central America by the early nineteenth, and long-wave depression in the late nineteenth century. Until the twentieth century agricultural production remained slight and resulted in a poor internal marketing system. Even after World War II the colony remained a net importer of foodstuffs. Irregular political ties to Great Britain before 1862, a labor base of African slavery until the 1830s, and a white population which remained miniscule, all reflected or perpetuated an economy tied to extractive production for the world market.

The historiography of British Honduras has reflected this condition. Not until the twentieth century would it have been possible to collect a significant bibliography for the history of that exotic "Coast." Most writing about Belize was buried in government memoranda and commission reports, although there were some outstanding eye-witness accounts such as Captain George Henderson, *An Account of the British Settlement at Honduras . . .* (London, 1809), and occasional local histories such as Archibald Gibbs, *British Honduras: An Historical and Descriptive Account of the Colony from Its Settlement, 1670* (London, 1883). The present dispute between Great Britain and Guatemala over British Honduras, which originated in the Anglo-Guatemalan treaty of 1859 and became a public issue in the twentieth century, produced the bulk of writings which can be categorized as historical. The climax of Guatemalan publications came in the documentary, *White Book, Controversy between Guatemala and Great Britain Relative to the Convention of 1859 on Territorial Matters* (Guatemala, 1938), and in the three-hundred-page summation by José Luis Mendoza, *Great Britain and her Treaties on Belize* (2d ed., Guatemala, 1959; 1st ed. in Spanish, 1942).

In a sense, works published in the 1960s completed the treaty phase of Belizean historiography and started a new one, which gave serious general consideration to Belizean society itself. R. A. Humphreys, *The Diplomatic History of British Honduras, 1638–1901* (Oxford, 1961) summarized the corpus of diplomatic literature in masterful fashion and rather completed British presentation of the matter. D. A. G. Waddell, *British Honduras: An Historical and Contemporary Survey* (Oxford, 1961) dealt with diplomatic questions but moved on to an analytical consideration of what kind of society existed in Belize and how it had developed. W. M. Clegern, *British Honduras: Colonial Dean End, 1859–1900* (Baton Rouge, 1967) dealt with origins of the diplomatic dispute, utilizing Belizean, British, and Guatemalan archives, and created a domestic narrative for the colony in the late nineteenth century by systematic use of Belize newspapers.

In the 1970s the role of Belize in the Third World became an issue. Narda Leon Dobson, who had done research in London and Belize earlier, made a serious attempt in *A History of Belize* (London, 1973) to treat social questions in Belizean history from a viewpoint calculated somewhere between London and Belize. Her approach appeared to be completely inadequate to a new generation represented by C. H. Grant (*The Making of Modern Belize* [Cambridge, 1976]) and O. Nigel Bolland (*Formation of a Colonial Society* [Baltimore, 1977]). These works, thoroughly researched, express an aggressive Third World philosophy which calls for the writing of "people's history." (N.B., see Grant's essay review of Dobson's work, in *Caribbean Studies*, 14 [1974]: 181–88). In its scholarly roots this new Belizean school grows both from research trends in Caribbean social science of the last quarter century (cf. Sidney Mintz, *Caribbean Transformations* [Chicago, 1974]) and from an openness to Third World Marxism. Both Grant and Bolland were trained in Jamaica and England, and both did extensive fieldwork in Belize.

Their work bears comparison with Jesse Lemisch's advocacy of a "people's history" for the United States (cf. "The American Revolution Bicentennial and the Papers of Great White Men," *AHA Newsletter*, 9, 5[November 1971]: 7–21). They argue that the real history of Belize has yet to be written, because, excepting some of the works listed above, most of the colony's historiography is vacuous, imperialist, or "racialist." Bolland (*Colonial Society*) sees the history of the colony as involving three classes: labor (basically racial castes), white settlers, and metropolitan groups (government and capitalists). He maintains that the settler group was eliminated from this equation by 1871, when the legislative assembly was eliminated, and that the common people have confronted metropolitan forces directly since then.

Clearly missing from the historiography of Belize is a single-volume, comprehensive narrative history exhibiting high literary merit. Such a volume would utilize fully the bibliography now extant and would incorporate the insight of a native Belizean. It should draw authentically on the folklore of British Honduras. Otherwise, although many local problems await clarification, Belize's needs for historical research are not urgent, because all scholars, foreign and domestic, can now avail themselves of reliable works covering the breadth of the country's history.[1] Overviews are available in Humphreys, Waddell, and Dobson. A chronology of Belizean society from beginning to present can be assembled from the works of Bolland, Clegern, and Grant. All six of these works provide significant bibliographies. Belize does offer unexpected opportunities for the historical researcher because of its marginal location—much as its settlers found a serendipitous existence in the logwood, mahogany, and Central American trades in the seventeenth and eighteenth centuries. From the vantage point of Belize, the historian can sometimes gain unique insights into Mexican, Guatemalan, and Caribbean affairs. Again, publications on Belize since World War II, both in history and the social sciences, have established Belize as a recognizable scholarly arena for any researcher.

While its historiography has improved steadily since 1945, much light remains to be thrown on matters of local interest which might take on broader significance. For example, across the Gulf of Mexico, at the mouth of the Mississippi River, stands a community and navigational point called The Balize. It has been on maps of Louisiana and the Gulf since French times and obviously carries the French name for beacon. This circumstance goes unmentioned in the debate on the name origin of the town of Belize (sometimes called The Belize) and the Belize River on the Bay of Honduras, a debate which features the name of an English seaman (Wallace), gives serious consideration to a Mayan word for wood,

1. Ralph Lee Woodward, Jr., comp., *Belize* (World Bibliographical Series, Vol. 21; Santa Barbara, 1980) is indispensable. Since the mid-1970s several serial publications sponsored by St. John's College in Belize have made major contributions to Belizean historiography (cf. Woodward).

and downplays the possibility of the Spanish word for beacon, *balisa*. Not even the authoritative J. A. Calderón Quijano, *Belice 1663(?)–1821: historia de los establecimientos británicos del Rio Valís hasta la independencia de hispanoamérica* (Sevilla, 1944), mentions the Louisiana coincidence. No direct evidence has been reported to support provenance of the name from the French or Spanish words for beacon, but French phraseology was widely used by the Caribbean buccaneers; and who has determined, factually, that the Spanish failed to establish a navigational reference point at the principal estuary between Guatemala and Yucatán? This is a minute example of the many questions of local interest which remain entirely open in the history of Belize.

Political independence for Belize, September 21, 1981, resolved the Hamlet-style dilemma posed by the still unsatisfied Guatemalan claim. The situation had grown more complex since 1945. Not only the desires of Belize, Guatemala, Mexico, the United States, and Great Britain had to be considered, but also the attitudes of Cuba, of the variously related ex-British islands in the Caribbean, and of the no-longer monolithic Spanish-American mainland countries. Security for Belize awaits a kind of international stability which the Caribbean has yet to experience, but aspects of Belize's history and society will continue to require the scholar's consideration.

Even before 1804 when a Spanish official bewailed oppression of Central America by Belizean commerce ("O Walis, almacén de nuestra desgracia y esponja de nuestras minas!"), and after 1975 when an eminent scholar asserted the universal significance of so frail a craft as Belize setting sail on the seas of independence (W. J. M. MacKenzie, in the forward to Grant's book), the English community on the Bay of Honduras drew and will draw attention to itself.

6   El Salvador
Derek N. Kerr

El Salvador, the smallest but most densely populated state of the American mainland, as an area of investigation offers the researcher certain practical advantages not found in most other areas of Latin America. In a country as small as El Salvador, it is possible to study in microcosm the familiar phenomena that present themselves in other countries of Latin America (i.e., monoculture, latifundia, oligarchic power, militarism) without the formidable task which studying nations as vast and diverse as Brazil,

Mexico, or Argentina would present. As in most Central American areas, the scholarship in Salvadoran history has been very thin. A few notable exceptions stand out because of their excellent methodology and scholarship. Rodolfo Barón Castro's demographic study of El Salvador is the most complete scientific investigation of the origin and development of Salvadoran society from pre-Hispanic times to the 1940s.[1] David Browning's *El Salvador, Landscape and Society* (Oxford, 1971) evaluates the relationship between man and land in El Salvador from precolonial times to the present. *El Salvador* (London, 1973) by Alastair White gives a concise historical overview of the total independence period but deals mainly with contemporary twentieth-century Salvadoran politics.

Only a glimpse of these scholarly works will unveil myriads of research opportunities left unexplored. Browning has intimated the need for a more thorough investigation of the relationship between Indians and *ladinos*. Relations between the Spanish and the Pipils remain unexplored. Evidence in the AGCA indicates numerous complaints of Indian and ladino abuse at the hands of the minute Spanish population. Why did the Indians of El Salvador become so much more "ladinoized" than their counterparts in neighboring Guatemala? The role of El Salvador as the economic powerhouse of the Audiencia de Guatemala has been slightly underplayed by historians. What were the effects of the changing economy on the landscape and the people with each adaptation of a new cash crop such as cacao, Peruvian balsam, indigo, coffee, sugar, and cotton? El Salvador lends itself well to a study similar to that of Stanley J. Stein's in Vassouras, Brazil.[2] The development of the coffee oligarchy in the late nineteenth century with all its political, social, and economic ramifications still requires further research.[3] Liberalism, positivism, and social Darwinism, which drifted into El Salvador from Justo Rufino Barrios' Guatemala, played roles in Salvadoran ideology. Monographic studies of the origins of the *finqueros* would reveal much of the roots of the present Salvadoran elite. An article by Robert T. Aubey provides a good beginning for the study of Salvadoran elites.[4] With the emergence of the liberal faction

1. David Browning, *La Población de El Salvador* (Madrid, 1942).

2. Stanley J. Stein, *Vassouras: A Brazilian Coffee County, 1850–1900* (Cambridge, Massachusetts, 1957).

3. Derek N. Kerr, "The Role of the Coffee Industry in the History of El Salvador, 1840–1906," M.A. thesis (University of Calgary, 1977) deals with the establishment of the coffee oligarchy in the late nineteenth century. Also useful is Warren Dean, "The Planter as Entrepreneur: The Case of São Paulo," *Hispanic American Historical Review,* 46 (May 1966): 138–52.

4. Robert T. Aubey, "Entrepreneurial Formation in El Salvador," *Explorations in Entrepreneurial History,* 6 (1969): 268–85.

under Field Marshal Santiago González in 1871, El Salvador experienced a surge of Westernization and became locked into an agro-export-oriented economy. New biographies of President Gerardo Barrios and his successors are needed to assist in the interpretation of today's civil insurrection in El Salvador. The entire period of Salvadoran history from the establishment of the intendancy onward is crucial to the understanding of the contemporary conflict in El Salvador.

Nineteenth-century Salvadoran historiography contains innumerable gaps waiting to be filled. It is hoped political stability will soon return to allow the researcher safe access to the archives, parish records, and private collections. The AGCA contains much of the documentation until the collapse of the Central American Federation in 1839. The U.S. consular dispatches from El Salvador in the U.S. National Archives, Washington, D.C., contain valuable information concerning agriculture, the economy, health, and social conditions, and U.S.–Salvadoran relations. Although Thomas P. Anderson's *Matanza*[5] is a well-documented account of the revolt of 1932, a study should be made of the entire social-political history of Izalco to explain the independent stance which has persisted among its inhabitants since colonial times. The separate department of Sonsonate also deserves special attention. Manuel Rubio Sánchez has documented much of the contraband activity through the port of Acajutla in colonial times.[6] Much of this documentation is waiting at the AGCA to be mined. Little investigation has been done of the various immigration schemes to attract Europeans to invest in Salvadoran coffee estates. The abolished *tierras comunales* of the Indians created the land pool needed for the coffee boom plus the large labor force to work the *fincas*. The social problems and dislocation contributed to much of Salvador's present-day social upheaval. A social history written from the "bottom up" would cast an entirely different perspective on nineteenth-century Salvadoran events.

As in Guatemala, the role of the military and *caudillismo* weighs heavily in Salvadoran politics. Only one major study in English has covered the Salvadoran military.[7] Further investigation should explore the influence of foreign military missions, the development of military academies, and the infiltration of the coffee elites into the military ranks. Many of the comments of David J. McCreery regarding the military and national police

5. Thomas P. Anderson, *Matanza, El Salvador's Communist Revolt of 1932* (Lincoln, 1971).

6. Manuel Rubio Sánchez, *Historia de El Realejo* (San José, Costa Rica, 1975).

7. Robert Varney Elam, "Appeals to Arms: The Army and Politics in El Salvador, 1931–1964," Ph.D. dissertation (University of New Mexico, 1970) contains an introductory section on the history of the Salvadoran military; see also Stephen L. Rozman, "The Socialization of Military Rule in El Salvador," Ph.D. dissertation (University of Nebraska, 1970).

of Guatemala equally apply in El Salvador, particularly concerning the use of violence against the labor unions in the 1960s and 1970s. Like Ubico's powerful machine in Guatemala, the presidency of General Maximiliano Hernández Martínez from 1932 to 1944 deserves a thorough study, similar to Kenneth J. Grieb's *Guatemalan Caudillo*.[8] Another period worthy of major investigation is the 1913–27 dynasty of the Meléndez-Quiñonez family. The intellectual and diplomat Alberto Masferrer, a neglected philosopher of this period, reflected an early humanitarian ideology in contraposition to the Marxist-Leninism which began to infiltrate the labor union organizations in urban San Salvador in the 1920s. The presidencies of Pío Romero Bosque (1927–31) and his successor, Arturo Araujo (1931), demonstrated the liberal swing which politics had taken in Central America in the late 1920s. Biographical articles would be useful on several Salvadoran notables: Agustín Farabundo Martí, Abel Cuenca, Miguel Marmól, Tomás Regalado, don Herbert de Sola, Felix Choussy, and don Jaime Hill.

Salvadoran history would facilitate a comparative approach. A French geographer, Jean Tricart, employed a comparison of El Salvador with the Ivory Coast coffee developments.[9] Similar sociological, political, economical, and historical problems exist in other Third World areas of Africa, Latin America, and Southeast Asia. Because of El Salvador's extremely explosive population situation, a thorough demographic history would continue the work begun by Barón Castro in 1942. The first population war of the twentieth century, the "Fútbol War of 100 Hours" in 1969, deserves thorough study. Migration of Salvadoreños throughout Central America is a persistent problem awaiting scholarly examination.

Stephen Webre's study of the beginnings of the Christian Democratic party in Salvadoran politics serves as an excellent prelude to further research of contemporary Salvador of the 1980s.[10] The present revolutionary guerrilla activity in El Salvador also invites examination of such factors as the origins, ideology, and leadership of these groups. What role has liberation theology played in Salvadoran politics? Studies of the effects of success of the Sandinistas in Nicaragua upon the revolutionaries of Salvador and a biography of Archbishop Arturo Romero as a revolu-

8. Kenneth J. Grieb, *Guatemalan Caudillo: The Regime of Jorge Ubico, Guatemala, 1931–1944* (Athens, Ohio, 1979); see also K. Grieb's "The United States and the Rise of General Maximiliano Hernández Martínez," *Journal of Latin American Studies*, 3 (November 1971): 151–72.

9. Jean Tricart, "Apropos du cas Salvador: le geographe et la développement économique et social," *Développement et civilisations*, 10 (avril–juin 1962): 80–91.

10. Stephen Webre, *José Napoléon Duarte and the Christian Democratic Party in Salvadoran Politics, 1960–1972* (Baton Rouge, 1979).

tionary figure of the 1970s would be helpful. Agrarian reform, though only just begun, has been a persistent demand of the underprivileged in El Salvador and should be examined as one of the basic themes of the nation's history. David Browning's historical geography speculates upon the future of the Salvadoran landscape.

Though the archival situation of El Salvador is poor for the nineteenth century because of the fire of 1899, which destroyed the archives, private collections, newspapers, *memorias,* parish, and municipal records do exist. The history of El Salvador, though studied by local academics, awaits foreign scholarship, just as a hidden Spanish galleon overflowing with pieces of eight beckons the treasure hunter.

7   Honduras
Kenneth V. Finney

Despite the general surge in Latin American studies, Honduran scholarship is nearly as underdeveloped today as it was thirty years ago, when William Stokes wrote in his widely disseminated monograph, *Honduras: An Area Study in Government* (Madison, 1950), that "it is impossible to find an accurate, recent study of Honduran government in either Spanish or English." Although Stokes wrote only of the country's political system, his observation holds for other dimensions of Honduran society in 1950, and still today. In fact, those interested in the history of this Central American republic eventually begin to suspect that even the social scientists who take up its study are infected with the contagion of Banana Republic underdevelopment. What else could account for the embarrassing lack of published monographic research on Honduras? Yet this very neglect might, under certain conditions, prove benign. Alexander Gershenkron's "advantages of backwardness" might spill over from the economic into the intellectual domain. By choosing topics carefully and working up research designs skillfully, scholars who henceforth pursue Honduran history since 1823 should be able to avoid the interpretative false starts and conceptual dead ends that have sidetracked their more proliferate fellow Latin Americanists. In short, it is possible that Honduran studies might begin to flourish in some fashion if Honduranists could implement, test, and modify the best of the available theoretical frameworks developed elsewhere by their colleagues.

Honduran economic history is relatively better served by current scholarship than other dimensions. Even in the historical accounts of its economy, however, much of what has been done needs to be redone in view of recent reinterpretations. The banana industry, for example, badly needs reexamination by someone sagacious enough to supersede the passé conceptual cliches of both anti-imperialist exposés and agribusiness apologies, diligent enough to seek out fresh sources of data, and insightful enough to deduce in what amounts to very nearly a vacuum what it all meant to the Honduran people and society.[1] The work of Thomas Karnes on the Standard Fruit Company points toward a renaissance of "ripe" Honduran banana studies.[2]

The perfidious saga of the Honduras Interoceanic Railroad and associated foreign debt, for almost a century a millstone that thwarted most developmental schemes, is now pretty much untangled.[3] The same is true for the late nineteenth-century mining boom.[4] Although mining continued to be economically significant after 1900, its course during the twentieth century is imperfectly understood. Moreover, there appear to have been ties between the Honduran mining industry and those of El Salvador and Nicaragua. What were these ties? Were they important? Finally, a thorough company history of the giant New York and Honduras Rosario Mining Company would be a valuable and viable study.

Other dimensions of Honduran economic history remain virtually blank. Almost nothing is known about the structure and evolution of the nontropical-fruit agrarian sectors, notwithstanding the fact that corn and

1. On the anti-imperialist side, there are the two well-known studies of Charles D. Kepner, Jr., *Social Aspects of the Banana Industry* (New York, 1936), and with Jay H. Soothill, *The Banana Empire* (New York, 1935), plus the more recent survey by V. Lainez and V. Meza, "El enclave bananero en la historia de Honduras," *Estudios sociales centroamericanos*, 2 (May–August 1973): 115–56. On the agribusiness side, there is Charles M. Wilson, *Empire in Green and Gold* (New York, 1947); Henry B. Arthur, et al., *Tropical Agribusiness Structures and Adjustments—Bananas* (Boston, 1968); and Stacy May and Galo Plaza, *The United Fruit Company in Latin America* (Washington, D.C., 1958).

2. Thomas L. Karnes, *Tropical Enterprise: The Standard Fruit and Steamship Company in Latin America (Baton Rouge, 1978)*.

3. The debt issue has been given its definitive treatment by Gene S. Yeager, "The Honduran Foreign Debt, 1825–1953," Ph.D. dissertation (Tulane University, 1975). On the railroad see also Yeager; Charles L. Stansifer, "E. George Squier and The Honduras Interoceanic Railroad Project," *Hispanic American Historical Review*, 46 (1966): 1–27; and Delmer G. Ross, *Visionaries and Swindlers* (Mobile, 1975).

4. Elements of the mining industry are available in John C. Pine, "The Honduras Mining Boom, 1880–1900," M.A. thesis (University of Chicago, 1947); Charles A. Brand, "The Background of Capitalistic Underdevelopment: Honduras to 1913," Ph.D. dissertation (University of Pittsburgh, 1972); and James F. Vivian, "Major E. A. Burke: The Honduran Exile, 1889–1928," *Louisiana History*, 15 (1974): 157–94. Every dimension of the industry during the late nineteenth and early twentieth centuries is covered in Kenneth V. Finney, "Precious Metal Mining and the Modernization of Honduras," Ph.D.dissertation (Tulane University, 1973).

bean milpas and cattle haciendas—not fruit plantations—provided the material basis for existence for the vast majority of Hondurans up to the present. Murdo MacLeod's finds for the colonial period offer a tentative baseline and William Durham's recent work on the human ecological background of the 1969 "Fútbol War" will provide a convenient terminus,[5] but until historians plow the admittedly infertile documentary sources for the intervening hiatus and eke out whatever insights possible about the subsistence or "traditional" agrarian sector of the country, scholars shall be doomed to rely on the time-worn, hardly distortion-free clichés gleaned from episodic travelogues. If scholars cannot discern at least the main features of the Honduras variation on the latifundia-minifundia theme, how are they to ascertain the scope and significance of the cattle ranching of the famous Olancho *hacendados,* understand the impact of the tobacco manufactories of Copán, reconstruct the record of mahogany and other tropical timbering enterprises, or even, for that matter, fully unravel the development of the dominant banana industry itself? Partial evidence on these matters is to be had in the land titles extant in the Honduran archives and microfilmed by the Honduran Instituto Nacional Agraria. This information, if woven together competently with other corroborative sources available, would amplify understanding several fold. Moreover, Johannessen's pioneering work on the Comayagua savannas suggests that the nondocumentary approaches of the ethnohistorian, anthropologist, and geographer might be fruitfully employed.[6]

Honduran commercial, transportation, and monetary histories also remain almost wholly to be written. Long-distance trade to and from Honduras has not only ebbed and flowed dramatically but has rapidly shifted its orientation: now and again dominated by the Fonseca Gulf outlet on the Pacific coast; later preferring the north coast shipping facilities. The underlying dynamics of the ebb and flow of trade in general and the Janus-like alternation of Atlantic and Pacific routes both beg investigation.[7] Partial statistics on this trade appear in the official newspapers and in government reports extant in the National Archives. The Honduran business elite deserves at least a summary treatment. The late nineteenth-century Hon-

5. Murdo J. MacLeod, *Spanish Central America* (Berkeley, 1973); William H. Durham, *Scarcity and Survival in Central America, Ecological Origins of the Soccer War* (Stanford, 1979).

6. Carl L. Johannessen, *Savannas of Interior Honduras* (Berkeley, 1963).

7. During the late nineteenth century, for example, consular dispatches reveal that the Caribbean ports were repeatedly closed by yellow fever quarantines. This exogenous influence needs to be integrated into the continuing struggle between Comayagua, Tegucigalpa, and San Pedro Sula for dominance and the successive export-product dependencies created by the process of serial diversification.

duran plutocrats—the Francisco Planas, Jerónimo Zelayas, Ramón Midences, Pedro Abadies, and the Rossners—are all but unknown to their countrymen today, and the country's twentieth-century economic titan, Santos Soto, is only vaguely remembered. Although sufficient data to construct a sophisticated quantitative collective biography of these elites probably do not exist, a careful descriptive analysis would throw much needed light on the underlying structure and operations of the Honduran economic system, political forms, and social structure. Although the main outlines of the transportation and communication infrastructure have been rather well done for the late nineteenth century,[8] the story needs to be traced at least up to the 1950s when rather complete official accounts begin, since virtually everyone blames the country's lack of progress on an inadequate transport infrastructure. In addition, the pioneering air transportation industry needs further research.[9]

Although decent compilations of labor laws exist, the labor history of Honduras remains almost altogether blank. The famous 1954 banana strike needs to be reassessed using oral history techniques before all the participants die off.[10] Labor organization patterns immediately prior to 1954 need to be studied to ascertain the roots and background of this labor explosion. Moreover, the 1954 strike must be studied apart from the intellectual cold war straightjackets. The union movement since 1954, while an acutely sensitive political issue, also needs scholarly examination as a study of the aftermath of the 1954 strike.[11]

The political history of Honduras still runs rather to polemics. The iron *caudillos* of the early and middle nineteenth century—Francisco Ferrera, Trinidad Cabañas, José Santos Guardiola, and even Francisco Morazán— need to be considered by nonpartisan biographers able to weave their stories around the times and circumstances in which they functioned. The data now being organized and catalogued in the national archive in Tegucigalpa should be utilized to the fullest in any such reevaluations. For the period after 1876, the possibility for presidential biographies becomes

8. Gene Yeager, "Honduran Transportation and Communication Development: The Rise of Tegucigalpa, 1876–1900," M.A. thesis (Tulane University, 1972).

9. See Frans Blom, *Airminded Honduras* (1935); and George S. Roper, "TACA Makes History Over Central America," *Inter-American Quarterly,* 3 (January 1941): 26–51. The Honduran's early transition to air transport belies their reputation for general backwardness.

10. See John D. Martz, *Central America: The Crisis and the Challenge* (Chapel Hill, 1959); Mario Posas Amador, "El movimiento obrero hondureño: la huelga de 1954 y sus consecuencias," *Estudios sociales centroamericanos,* 5, 15(1976): 93–127; see also Posas Amador's 1976 thesis from the University of Costa Rica, "El movimiento obrero hondureño: huelgas y lucha sindical en el enclave bananero (1916–1955)."

11. See for example, Robert L. MacCameron, "Organized Labor in Honduras: 1954–1963," Ph.D. dissertation (State University of New York at Buffalo, 1976).

much more sanguine. Ample material remains both in Honduras and in other depositories[12] for reexamination of the lives and times of Marco Aurelio Soto, Luis Bográn, and Policarpo Bonilla.[13] The fascinating career of Manuel Bonilla lies waiting, buried in the newspapers, diplomatic reports, and official records. The most serious need today, however, is for a competent biography of Tiburcio Carías Andino, who, as president from 1933 to 1949, shaped the contours of contemporary Honduras. Notwithstanding his towering influence, there is little in the way of a systematic account of the man or his regime.[14]

The abnormal degree of outside manipulation and intervention by foreigners in Honduran internal politics has been noted often, but most discussions fail to get beyond superficial observations: banana politics, boundary disputes, and various rounds of Central American unionism. More noteworthy than these episodic occurrences is the remarkable nomadism of Honduran political elites. Many important Honduran *políticos* had prominent careers in other Central American countries. For example Marco Aurelio Soto held high office in the Justo Rufino Barrios regime before inaugurating the Edad de Oro in Honduras, and José María Moncada served as Manuel Bonilla's secretary of government before he became president of Nicaragua.[15] The roles played by non–Central Americans—especially citizens of the United States[16] and Great Britain[17]—in

12. In particular, the British and American government reports are replete with information and by themselves tell rather complete stories. For instance, from diplomatic sources, Daniel J. J. Ross wrote a rather complete account of the 1924 "revolution," "The Honduras Revolution of 1924 and American Intervention," M.A. thesis (University of Florida, 1969).

13. For don Policarpo there is a massive but uncritical biography and a great many personal papers in various states of decay in the Honduran National Archives. Before they completely biodegrade, someone should reassess his life's work.

14. For Carías there is William Stokes' well-documented but surprisingly static study, *Honduras: An Area Study in Government* (Madison, 1950), and other less cautious bits and pieces: e.g., William Krehm, *Democracia y tiranias en el Caribé* (México, 1949); Daniel Hernández, *La justificación historico de la actual prolongación en el poder* (La Esperanza, Honduras, 1940); Gilberto Gonzáles y Contreras, *El último caudillo* (México, 1946); Russell H. Fritzgibbon, "'Continuismo' in Central America," *Inter-American Quarterly*, 2 (July 1940): 56–74.

15. For Soto see Rómulo E. Durón *Biografía del Doctor Marco Aurelio Soto* (Tegucigalpa, 1944). José María Moncada wrote three accounts that underscore his central role in Honduran political affairs in the early years of this century: *Cosas de Centro América* (Madrid, 1908), *La revolución de 1903 y el golpe de estado del 8 de febrero de 1904* (Tegucigalpa, 1904), and *Deuda del ferrocarril de Honduras* (Tegucigalpa, 1904).

16. Stansifer, "E. George Squier"; Hermann B. Deutsche, *The Incredible Yanqui: The Career of Lee Christmas* (London and New York, 1931); Dana G. Munro, *Intervention and Dollar Diplomacy in the Caribbean, 1900–1921* (Princeton, 1964); and George W. Baker,

Honduran affairs are some of the better-known chapters in Honduran history. Other important groups of foreigners, however, remain unstudied. More than one Cuban patriot sought asylum in Honduras after failing to gain the island's independence on the first try. These refugees introduced a certain degree of sophistication into Honduras during the last half of the nineteenth century.[18] Subsequently, Spanish intellectuals, recruited to man various academic and administrative positions, permeated the country with their influence in a myriad of ways. German import-export merchants held considerable mercantile sway from the early 1880s until dispossessed during the backlash against all things German during the world wars. The so-called (in Honduras) Turcos entered Honduran commerce in the early twentieth century and continue to fill an important economic role in the country that has not been examined for its political or its social implications. In each of these cases documents in Cuba, Germany, or the Middle East might supplement those extant in Honduras.

Stokes made a commendable effort to untangle the regional political tensions: between Comayagua and Tegucigalpa, a rivalry that traces its roots far back into the colonial era; and more recently between the internal highland center around Tegucigalpa and the north-coast complex radiating out from San Pedro Sula.[19] Several recent studies have scrutinized parts of these regional conflicts, but the theme needs to be considered systematically and explained in terms more convincing than mere *patria chica* rivalry.[20] Whatever the explanation, it should be able to make sense of the sign which stood along the road to Juticalpa all during the Carías regime; it read: You are now entering the free Republic of Olancho.[21]

The administrative-bureaucratic history of the country rests almost entirely on Stoke's discussion. This topic urgently requires reassessment given the "flood" of articles and monographs arguing that unmitigated *personalismo* marked Honduran politics until 1950, when outside political

---

"Ideals and Realities in the Wilson Administrations's Relations with Honduras," *The Americas,* 21 (1964): 3–19, for example.

17. Frederick Chatfield was perhaps the most notorious such British intervener in Honduras affairs. Mario Rodríguez, *A Palmerstonian Diplomat in Central America* (Tucson, 1964).

18. Tomás Estrada Palma, later to be president of Cuba, spent part of his exile in Honduras.

19. Stokes, *Honduras.*

20. Yeager, "Honduran Transportation"; William K. Crowley, "San Pedro Sula, Honduras: The Order and Disorder of the Pubescent Period in Central America's Most Rapidly Growing City," Ph.D. dissertation (University of Oregon, 1972).

21. That even non-Olanchanos repeat this particular anecdote with obvious relish suggests perhaps the texture of legitimacy obtained by the central government.

experts and economic technicians came to the rescue and imposed a sem-
blance of bureaucratic order on the country.[22] This thesis of abrupt discontinuity in 1950 is currently in vogue but is not altogether convincing—
especially since no one is in a position to offer concrete evidence either
way.[23] In particular, better information is needed on the National Congress, the military, and formal and informal interest groups that exercised
at least minimal political power. For example, someone with a flair for
psychohistory might attempt to explain the sudden rise of a generation of
important anti-American, anti-imperialist intellectuals—Angél Zúñiga
Huete, Froylan Turcios, and Matías Funes among others—in the second
and third decades of this century.

In what might be loosely labeled social history, almost everything needs
to be done. There is, however, little archival data available, and the social
historian who intends to pursue his research in Honduran history will per-
force be called to demonstrate extra ingenuity in squeezing what information is available for the last drop of significance and creating alternative
sources of data to supplement the written record. Given the rapid accom-
modation of the *hondureños* to "modernized" lifestyles, many priceless
opportunities to conduct oral history are evaporating. For instance, as recently as the early 1970s, itinerate circus troupes traveling by mule
through the hinterland on a yearly circuit brought excitement and enter-
tainment to the hill folk off the main roads.[24] These circuses date back at
least to the 1880s.[25] During the last ten years, however, the circuses for
one reason or the other have stopped making the rounds. The failure to
study this phenomenon in the only way possible—by interviewing those
who manned it—will sweep away forever an invaluable piece of Honduran popular culture.

More conventional social topics continue to be viable. Much has been

22. Robert A. White, *Mass Communications and the Popular Promotion Strategy of
Rural Development in Honduras* (Sanford, 1976); and James A. Morris and Steve C. Ropp,
"Corporatism and Dependent Development: A Honduran Case Study," *Latin American Re-
search Review,* 12 (1977): 27–68.

23. This discontinuity is less than meets the eye. Mostly it is a matter of a sharp transition in record keeping (in itself an important, but not paramount transformation). Reality is
surely underreported prior to the 1950s and probably overreported thereafter. The sharp
ascent in the figures collected suggests that great changes are taking place, whereas in
reality what is now being reported has been functioning all along but ignored. In short, the
Hondurans as of 1950 are in much the same position as the hick farm boy gone to college
who discovered that he spoke prose.

24. Interview with Kenneth V. Finney, Santa Cruz de Guayape, Olancho, Honduras
(December 1970).

25. See Cecil Charles, *Honduras: The Land of Great Depths* (Chicago and New York,
1890).

done on the residual Indian populations—the Jicaque, Payas, and Moskitos—but much of it has been done by ethnologists and anthropologists with concerns distinct from that of history.[26] This work needs to be translated into a historical framework. The role of blacks in Honduras is much more important than the almost total paucity of information would suggest. Two waves of Afro-Americans, the early colonial mining-slave imports and the twentieth-century voluntary migrations from the British Caribbean, have swept into Honduras. Race mixture (rather thorough if the outward visible signs are not misleading) and race relations need careful scrutiny, for they may well reveal particular nuances not common to other mixed Latin American societies.[27] In general, demographic history is for the time being almost wholly a matter of intuition and folk traditions. What was the impact of the frequent migration of young men from remote villages to the north coast? After spending approximately ten years working in the banana stands, these young men almost always returned to their home villages. Why did they return? How did their return affect their home villages? Is this nomadism a continuation of the late nineteenth-century similar migrations into El Salvador and Nicaragua during the periodic famines of surplus young men, all of whom returned at the first news of a good crop or employment prospects at home? What impact did the cut off of this alternative source of employment have on the small villages nestled in the hills and valleys of central Honduras?[28] Did this restriction relate at all to the 1969 "Fútbol War"?

The somewhat nebulous influence of the Catholic church has come down in bits and pieces. This institution needs its historian, especially since the clergy in Honduras, as elsewhere in Latin America, now seems to be splitting into radical and conservative factions.

In short, Honduran history remains to be written. Why this is so is explained in part by the size of the country: it is small and therefore in the eyes of some it need not require much serious attention. In part the neglect of Honduran history can also be explained by the fact that the Hondurans have failed in all those activities that count in the "real" world: they have failed to modernize; they have so far failed to pose either an ideological threat or opportunity for interbloc brinkmanship by one or the other of the superpowers; and they have not discovered oil or any other natural re-

26. Eduard Conzemius, "Ethnological Notes on the Black Carib," *American Anthropologist,* 30 (1928): 183–205, and "Los indios Payas de Honduras," *Journal de la Société des Américanistes de Paris,* 19 (1927): 245–302.

27. William S. Stokes, "The Racial Factor in Honduran Politics," *Modern Language Forum,* 29 (March 1944): 25–30, asserts that Afro-Hondurans have been presidents and congressmen in ratios all out of proportion to their numbers in the population.

28. Interview, Kenneth V. Finney (December 1970).

source Eldorado. "Also rans" almost never get broad press coverage or in-depth historical coverage.[29]

The current state of historical studies, however, suggests the need for a second look at Honduran studies (and its equivalent elsewhere). Mature historical analysis transcends the mere compilation of facts and interpretations. It asks genuine, important questions that concern the investigator and his times. For this reason history must be continuously rewritten and reappraised.[30] The problem arises in that important questions almost always tend to be complicated. Moreover the data bank holding the answers to these questions is, in most first-rate countries, forbiddingly mountainous. Faced by this double complication, the researcher has three courses of action open. He may opt to specialize: limit the questions to be posed to the data in some reductive fashion. In short, ask fewer, less complex, and partial questions and trust that parallel efforts by colleagues will mesh with his own work so as to provide answers to the important questions. Sometimes this in fact happens, but more often it merely results in hit-and-miss scholarship and dissipation of effort. A second approach, increasingly followed especially by quantitative historians, is to persist in asking the important questions, but to pursue the answers selectively. In such cases one samples the sources rather than examining them in their totality. This approach, of course, risks, to one degree or another, providing partial, perhaps even incorrect, answers.

The third option, available to the would-be historian of Honduras, is to persist in asking the "Big Questions" but to do so within the confines of a limited population (e.g., Honduras). Upon reaching fairly solid conclusions, one could then generalize them beyond the borders in larger and larger concentric circles.[31] Therefore, at least as long as the nation state retains its legitimacy as the natural geographic unit of analysis, the study of Honduras makes much good sense. Even if subsequently the "world system" becomes the primary unit of analysis, every investigator will still need to begin somewhere. Why not begin in a small country like Hondu-

29. As Simon Schama reminds us, "No scholar cares much to keep company with calamity for long." Simon Schama, *Patriots and Liberators: Revolution in The Netherlands, 1780–1813* (New York, 1977), as quoted in Charles Wilson, "Velvet Revolution?" *New York Review of Books*, 24 (June 9, 1977): 31. Of course calamity at least has the perverse appeal of all "bad news." Backwardness on the other hand seems just plain boring.

30. See Theodore Zeldin, "The Destruction of the Peasants," *New York Review of Books*, 24 (November 24, 1977): 45; and Christopher Hill, "Political Animal," *New York Review of Books*, 24 (June 9, 1977): 39, for recent justification of the need for revisionism (which of course presumes a vision to revise).

31. Undoubtedly the best example of this sort of analysis is Rodney C. Stares, "La economía campesina en la zona sur, 1950–1970: Su desarrollo y perspectivas para el futuro," unpublished paper (Choluteca, Honduras, 1972).

ras, which can be encompassed conceptually, rather than drift disorient-
edly amid a mass of data and awash in a welter of competing conceptual
designs of a Brazil or a Mexico or an Argentina?

8   Nicaragua
Charles L. Stansifer and Richard Millett

It is a sad fact that nineteenth-century Nicaraguan history is known only
in political outline. What little scholarly research has been done on this
hundred-year period focuses heavily on the rivalry between the Conservative and Liberal parties. Within this framework research has gone little
beyond the superficial struggle for power and the chronicling of specifically political events or military confrontations. Biographies, sadly, deal
only with a handful of major figures, and none of these is based on a
comprehensive collection of private papers.

The two most violent decades in Nicaragua's nineteenth-century history,
the 1820s and 1850s, have received, not surprisingly, the most attention.
It is the latter decade, because of the international importance given to
Nicaragua by the invasions of William Walker and his band of filibusters,
which has drawn the greatest number of scholarly investigators. The crucial years of the formation and consolidation of the state, from 1830 to
1850, and the period of Conservative party domination (1861–93), which
coincided with the rapid expansion of coffee production, have received the
least attention.

Apart from the partisan political rivalry, the principal thread in Nicaraguan historical narrative is the interoceanic transit route. Non-Nicaraguan
historians of Nicaragua have of course concentrated their research efforts
on the transit route and have shown little inclination to investigate or in-
terpret the Nicaraguan political system. These historians, with few exceptions, can be said scarcely to have identified, let alone analyzed, underlying social, economic, and cultural issues. At least the international
pressures on Nicaragua and its strategic importance as a transit route have
been carefully studied.[1] The effects of these pressures on the Nicaraguan
socioeconomic system are largely unknown.

Before identifying specific areas of research needs and opportunities, it

1. Examples of such studies are William O. Scroggs, *Filibusters and Financiers* (New
York, 1916); and David Folkman, *The Nicaragua Route* (Salt Lake City, 1972). See also
the various studies of Richard W. Van Alstyne.

is good to pinpoint other areas of strength in the historiography of nineteenth-century Nicaragua. Two Nicaraguan historians, José Dolores Gámez and Tomás Ayón, contemporaries of the last half of the nineteenth century, stand out as pioneers of their time. Both authored government-sponsored, comprehensive, interpretative histories of Nicaragua. Ayón's *Historia de Nicaragua,* which was intended to cover until 1852 but only reached 1821, was published in three volumes (1882–89).[2] A Conservative sponsored by a Conservative government, Ayón wrote favorably of Spain and the Catholic church. In contrast, Gámez, who had an active newspaper and political career as a Liberal, denigrated Nicaragua's Spanish colonial background and the Catholic church. Gámez, in 1889, published a good general history of Nicaragua to 1860.[3] Later, he wrote a detailed, documented narrative of the Nicaraguan Mosquito Coast.[4] His other historical writings include biographies and documentary collections.

Both Ayón and Gámez, especially Gámez, advocated historical research based on documentary evidence. They could do little to recover the historical records of Nicaragua lost to destructive civil strife and administrative neglect, but they pioneered in locating documents pertaining to Nicaragua in the archives of other countries. However, Gámez, who made a special effort in his publications to relate Nicaraguan history to events in other countries, ignored the colonial period because of his anti-Spanish bias. As a cabinet officer in the administration of Liberal dictator José Santos Zelaya (1893–1909), he concentrated on collecting, preserving, and publishing postindependence documents.

Except for a few superficial surveys of Nicaraguan history published in the twentieth century, no other comprehensive histories of Nicaragua besides those of Ayón and Gámez exist. Nevertheless, four twentieth-century writers on nineteenth-century Nicaraguan history merit discussion. They are José Coronel Urtecho, Andrés Vega Bolaños, Franco Cerutti, and Jorge Eduardo Arellano. The gaps they leave are essentially the research needs of Nicaraguan nineteenth-century history.

Of these only Coronel attempted a comprehensive history of Nicaragua. A poet, essayist, and historian, Coronel began a general, interpretative history entitled *Refleciones sobre la historia de Nicaragua.* The first volume, a brilliant apology for the Spanish period and lament of the move-

2. For a fuller discussion of Nicaragua's historiographical strengths, see Carlos Molina Arguello, "Bibliografía historiográfica de Nicaragua," *Revista interamericano de bibliografía,* 4 (January–June 1954): 9–22.

3. José Dolores Gámez, *Historia de Nicaragua desde los tiempos prehistóricos hasta 1860, en sus replaciones con España, México y Centro América* (Managua, 1889).

4. José Dolores Gámez, *Historia de la Costa de Mosquitos hasta 1894* (Managua, 1939).

ment for independence, was published in 1962. The second and third volumes, published in 1962 and 1967, respectively, became mired in the intricacies of the civil war of the 1820s and the conflicting interpretations of Chester Zelaya Goodman's admirable *Nicaragua en la independencia* (San José, Costa Rica, 1971). The great promise of a reflective, balanced interpretation of the nineteenth-century Nicaraguan political system remains unfulfilled.

The contribution of Vega Bolaños was to refocus attention on the need for documentation. As minister to Spain for more than a decade, Vega Bolaños enjoyed an unparalleled opportunity to mine the Archives of the Indies and other archives in Spain, resulting in the seventeen-volume set of colonial documents known as the *Colección Somoza*. Substantial as this effort was, Vega Bolaños may have done an even greater service to Nicaraguan historiography by collecting and publishing several volumes of documents pertaining to the nineteenth century.[5]

The Italian Franco Cerutti's indefatigable efforts to discover the complete works of writers of the late nineteenth century have led to a number of literary-historical studies and anthologies. Parenthetically, it may be noted that literary historians the world over have gathered material on the great Nicaraguan poet Rubén Darío and have published voluminously on his life and works. Until Cerutti began his work, few of these Darío enthusiasts gave any attention to the cultural milieu from which Darío sprang. Cerutti has painstakingly concentrated on the lesser Nicaraguan lights of the Darío period and in the process has revealed that Nicaragua enjoyed a far more vigorous intellectual life in the late nineteenth century than most observers suspected. His eruditely edited works of Enrique Guzmán and Pío Bolaños are especially noteworthy.[6]

Jorge Arellano, through his interest in diverse Nicaraguan institutions, provides a badly needed perspective on political events. His *Historia de la Universidad de León* (2 vols., León, Nicaragua, 1973–74) carefully written mainly on the basis of published materials, provides unexpected insights into political events and cultural life in nineteenth-century Nicaragua. A number of specialized studies, such as his biography of Tomás Ruiz, a Nicaraguan Indian priest at the time of independence, provide

5. For example, Andrés Vega Bolaños, *Gobernantes de Nicaragua: notas y documentos* (Managua, 1944); *Los atendados del Superintendente de Belice, 1840–1842* (Managua, 1971), and *Bombardeo y destrucción del Puerto de San Juan del Norte de Nicaragua* (Managua, 1970).

6. Franco Cerutti, *Enrique Guzmán: Editoriales de la prensa, 1878* (Managua, 1977); *Las pequeñeces cuiscomeñas de Antón Colorado* (Managua, 1974); *Las gacetillas, 1878–1894* (Managua, 1975); *Obras de don Pío Bolaños* (2 vols., Managua, 1976–77).

understanding of attitudes toward Indians and of religion.[7] Equally important are his studies of Nicaraguan literature and art.[8]

Despite the efforts of the above-mentioned Nicaraguan scholars, there
are enormous gaps in Nicaraguan historiography. With the exceptions of
William Walker and Rubén Darío, no major Nicaraguan figure of the nineteenth century has been thoroughly studied.[9] Unfortunately, in the absence
of private or public collections of correspondence, no thoroughly documented studies can be expected. If the rich and powerful have been neglected, the poor and powerless have been ignored altogether. No studies
of miners, *campesinos,* workers, or women exist. Few Nicaraguan histories give any attention to professional associations, interest groups, or the
middle classes of the nineteenth century. Poor census records and the
scarcity of documentation of ranches and corporate agricultural enterprises
limit the opportunities for such research, but the need is there.

Other specific aspects of social history are neglected in the existing
literature. The story of immigrants and internal migrations is untold, except for a recent study of Germans in Nicaragua.[10] Foreign scientists and
businessmen await discovery, although a few foreign diplomats have attracted scholars. Community studies are noticeably absent. Unlike the predominantly Indian countries of Latin America, Nicaragua attracted practically no anthropologists, ethnographers, or geographers in the nineteenth
century, leaving a gap in the history of small towns and Indian *barrios*
that will be difficult to fill. There is no adequate history of any Nicaraguan
city, and, despite repeated references to the importance of the rivalry between León and Granada in the nineteenth century, there is no study of
this rivalry.[11]

Regional histories are also scarce. Julián N. Guerrero and Lola Soriano
have done splendid work in their efforts to write monographs on each of
Nicaragua's sixteen departments, but the individual studies contain little

7. Jorge Eduardo Arellano, *El padre indio Tomás Ruiz, prócer de Centroamérica* (Managua, 1979).

8. Jorge Eduardo Arellano, *Panorama de la literatura nicaragüense: época anterior a
Darío, 1503–1881* (Managua, 1967), and *Pintura y escultura en Nicaragua* (Managua,
1978).

9. Molina Arguello, "Bibliografía historiográfica," 21–22, lists the fifteen or sixteen best
biographies of nineteenth-century Nicaraguans.

10. Goetz von Houwald, *Los alemanes en Nicaragua* (Managua, 1975).

11. The best historical study of Managua is that of Gratus Halftermeyer, *Historia de
Managua: data desde el siglo XVIII hasta hoy* (4th ed., Managua, 1965), but its casual,
anecdotal approach leaves much to be desired. Most of the few historical studies that have
been done on the other cities and towns of Nicaragua may be found reprinted in the pages
of the *Revista conservadora del pensamiento centroamericano.*

analysis or interpretation. Nicaragua's least populated department, Zelaya, has captured a disproportionate share of scholarly attention because of international controversies over Nicaraguan sovereignty on the Atlantic coast, but the few successful scholarly treatments illustrate what could be done if scholarly weapons were turned on the other departments.[12]

As for public health and medicine the pages of nineteenth-century Nicaraguan history are largely blank. With the possible exception of folk medicine, there is no aspect of medicine, disease, nursing, or pharmacy that is adequately treated in the literature on nineteenth-century Nicaragua. The history of women, households, child raising, and other aspects of family life in Nicaragua, especially as related to the nineteenth century, has as yet no practitioners.

Although no comprehensive economic study of the nineteenth century exists, several recent provocative theses, dissertations, and monographs point the way to opportunities for challenging research. José Salomón Delgado's attempt to trace agricultural landholding and work patterns in the period of the thirty years of Conservative rule should be followed up.[13] Ilva Fernández' and José Santos Quant's analyses of the economic history of the Zelaya period should be projected backward.[14] Trade, commerce, entrepreneurship, exports, and land tenure need to be examined on a regional as well as a national and international basis. National borrowing and expenditure patterns, if thoroughly studied, should clarify issues of class stratification as well as concentrations of wealth. Specific industries such as mining and ranching, not to speak of small-scale agriculture, require detailed study. Surprisingly little investigation of the coffee industry has been carried on as yet, despite its importance in nineteenth-century Nicaragua.

The deplorable absence of statistical data and private correspondence and records severely limits the opportunities for research in nineteenth-century Nicaragua. But foreign archives, travelers' accounts, and Nicara-

12. See for example Pedro Joaquín Cuadra Chamorro, *La reincorporación de la Mosquitia* (León, Nicaragua, 1964; first pub. in 1944); and Max H. Williams, *Gateway through Central America: A History of the San Juan River–Lake Nicaragua Waterway, 1502–1821* (La Paz, Bolivia, 1976).

13. José Salomón Delgado, "Nicaragua: unidades de producción más importantes durante el período de los 30 años conservadores (hacienda tradicional y otras y la mano de obra)" (n.p., n.d.), mimeo.

14. Ilva Hernández, "Nicaragua: estructura económica social y política del régimen de Zelaya, 1893–1909," thesis (Universidad de Centro América, 1978); José Santos Quant, "La revolución liberal en la historia económica de Nicaragua," thesis (Universidad de Centro América, 1975). See also Alberto Lanuza Matamoros, "Estructuras socioeconómicas, poder y estado en Nicaragua, de 1821 a 1875," thesis (Universidad de Costa Rica, 1976).

guan government publications have been utilized to produce acceptable
political and diplomatic histories; they can as well reveal many secrets of
Nicaraguan social and economic history.

The end of over forty years of Somoza family rule and the assumption
of power by the Sandinista Liberation Front (FSLN) produced an outpour-
ing of interest in Nicaragua's past, present, and future. Much of what was
published during the revolution was polemical in nature, designed to serve
as propaganda for one side or another, and of limited value to historians.[15]
More recent publications include memoirs of individuals who participated
in some of the major events of the period.[16] While subject to obvious bias,
these do provide considerable source material for academic researchers.
Collections of documents have appeared in both English and Spanish,
providing additional information for analyzing the Nicaraguan revolution.[17]

This surge of interest has not yet produced a corresponding increase in
serious works on earlier aspects of twentieth-century Nicaragua. There is
still no comprehensive history of modern Nicaragua.[18] Little work has
been done on the periods between the first and second United States interventions (1913–26) or the 1936–70 period. At least for English-speaking
scholars, the social history of Nicaragua remains virtual virgin territory.
The overall impression is one of considerable work in selected areas, notably the periods of United States intervention and the last few years, with
almost total neglect of other important aspects.

A number of problems confront any potential researcher into Nicaraguan history. The 1931 Managua earthquake destroyed much of the nation's records, leaving major gaps in available documentary material. Further destruction resulted from the 1972 earthquake and the 1978–79 civil
war. Perhaps the most tragic historical loss from the latter was the wanton

    15. Anti-Somoza publications are legion and appeared throughout the hemisphere. Typ-
ical is Jaime Galarza Zavala, *Nicaragua: Tiempo de fusiles* (Cuenca, Ecuador, 1978). For
pro-Somoza propaganda, see the publications of the Washington, D.C.–based Nicaraguan
Government Information Center.
    16. See J. A. Robleto Silas, *Yo deserté de la Guardia Nacional de Nicaragua* (San José,
Costa Rica, 1979); Francisco Urcuyo, *Solos: Las últimas 43 horas en el bunker de Somoza*
(Guatemala, 1979); and Mons. Miguel Obando y Bravo, *Golpe sandinista* (Managua,
1975).
    17. Sergio Ramírez M., ed., *El pensamiento vivo de Sandino* (San José, Costa Rica,
1974); Pedro Camejo and Fred Murphy, eds., *The Nicaraguan Revolution* (New York,
1979).
    18. Richard Millett, *Guardians of the Dynasty* (Maryknoll, New York, 1977) perhaps
comes closest to a full, modern history, but its focus on the military and on United States
influence leads to a neglect of social and economic aspects.

destruction of the entire plant of *La Prensa,* Nicaragua's leading news-paper. This resulted in the irreparable loss of photographic and documen-tary archives.

Despite the shortage of archival materials, there are numerous areas where diligent research and careful analysis could produce important new insights regarding twentieth-century Nicaragua. Studies focusing on the second intervention and the conflict with Sandino are already quite nu-merous and in some cases of high quality.[19] There is need for a full biog-raphy of the founder of the Somoza dynasty, Anastasio Somoza García.[20] While probably not warranting a full biography, Luis Somoza Debayle, the eldest legitimate son of Somoza García, would provide excellent ma-terial for an article, for his effort to liberalize the dynasty deserves further analysis. Finally, a biography of Emiliano Chamorro, twice president, co-signer of the Bryan-Chamorro Treaty, and leader of Nicaragua's Conserv-ative party till his death in the mid-1960s, would provide fascinating in-sights into the course of twentieth-century Nicaraguan politics.[21]

Other important contributions could be made by studying the history of the Nicaraguan Conservative party. Of even greater value would be a study of *La Prensa,* longtime organ of the Conservative party and the Chamorro family, which emerged in the 1970s as the most visible symbol of internal opposition to the Somoza family.[22]

A definitive history of the Frente Sandinista de Liberación Nacional (FSLN) is essential to understanding contemporary Nicaragua.[23] Several hurried studies of the fall of the Somoza dynasty have already appeared in Spanish, and numerous others are being prepared in English.[24] There

19. The best available studies in English are Neill Macaulay, *The Sandino Affair* (Chi-cago, 1967); and William Kammen, *A Search for Stability: U.S. Diplomacy Towards Nic-aragua, 1925–1933* (Notre Dame, Indiana, 1968). In Spanish see Gregorio Selser, *Sandino: General de los hombres libres* (Buenos Aires, 1958).

20. Ternot MacRenato, "Anastasio Somoza: A Nicaraguan Caudillo," M.A. thesis (Uni-versity of San Francisco, 1974) covers the general's career up to 1936.

21. General Chamorro's serialized autobiography was published in consecutive issues of Nicaragua's *Revista conservadora del pensamiento centroamericano* beginning with that journal's initial issue (August 1960).

22. See Ralph Lee Woodward, Jr., "Dr. Pedro Joaquín Chamorro (1924–1978), the Con-servative Party, and the Struggle for Democartic Government in Nicaragua," *SECOLAS Annals,* 10 (March 1979): 38–46.

23. Some material on this subject can be found in Humberto Ortega Saavedra, *50 años de lucha Sandinista* (n.p., 1978). Ortega has since become Nicaragua's minister of defense and is a member of the FSLN National Directorate.

24. In Spanish see Julio López C., et al., *La caída del Somocismo y la lucha Sandinista en Nicaragua* (San José, Costa Rica, 1979); Victor Morales Henríquez, *Los últimos mo-mentos de la dictadura Somocista* (Managua, n.d.); and Roger Mendieta Alfaro, *El último marine: la caída de Somoza* (Managua, 1979). Thomas Walker, ed., *Nicaragua in Revolu-*

should be, however, enough material here to occupy researchers for years to come. One area where additional studies will certainly be needed will be the role of other Latin American nations, notably Panama, Venezuela, Costa Rica, and Cuba, in the fall of Somoza. Studies of the role of business groups and of the churches would also be useful.

There are other topics in the area of Nicaraguan international relations which offer fertile ground for future study. The long-standing conflict between the Somozas and President José Figueres of Costa Rica certainly falls into this category.[25] Somoza family activities in Central America, including their ties with the military in neighboring nations, their investments in other parts of the region, and their role in regional organizations, deserve study. Perhaps the most fruitful focus for such research would be an examination of Nicaragua's role in the Central American Common Market. But the most intriguing aspect of Somoza family international activity—their connection with anti-Castro Cubans—would be difficult and perhaps even hazardous to study. Considerable information is, of course, available on Nicaraguan participation in the abortive Bay of Pigs invasion of 1961, but documentation of later activities would be difficult indeed. At the least, such a study will probably not be possible for several years.

While the internal history of the U.S. interventions in Nicaragua has been well studied, there are international aspects of this subject which deserve additional attention. Richard V. Salisbury has provided valuable insights into Costa Rican reaction to these events, but the impact on other area nations is less well documented.[26] The response in El Salvador would be of considerable interest, especially given the Salvadoran role in opposing U.S. intervention at the 1928 Pan-American Conference in Havana. On a related note, the rise and decline of United States interest in a naval base on the Gulf of Fonseca merits further examination.

Nicaraguan economic history has received relatively limited attention from North American scholars. The best work has been done by Larry Laird, Richard Lethander, and Harry Strachan.[27] Scholarly studies in

tion (New York, 1981). Studies are being completed for publication by Richard Millett and Ambassador Mauricio Solaún. Thomas Walker is editing a volume on the Nicaraguan revolution to be published by Praeger in 1981.

25. Material on the Costa Rican side of this dispute can be found in Charles D. Ameringer, *Don Pepe* (Albuquerque, 1978).

26. Richard V. Salisbury, "U.S. Intervention in Nicaragua: The Costa Rican Role," *Prologue* (Winter 1977): 209–17.

27. Larry K. Laird, "Technology versus Tradition: The Modernization of Nicaraguan Agriculture, 1900–1940," Ph.D. dissertation (University of Kansas, 1974); Richard W. O. Leithander, "The Economy of Nicaragua," Ph.D. dissertation (Duke University, 1968); Harry W. Strachan, "The Role of Business Groups in Economic Development: The Case of Nicaragua," D.B.A. dissertation (Harvard, 1972).

Spanish are also scarce, with much of the available material being written from a Marxist perspective.[28] Much more work needs to be done in this area. Histories of individual industries, companies, and exports are almost totally lacking. Since agriculture forms the basis for the Nicaraguan economy, additional research in that field would be of special value.

Excellent material on banana production in Nicaragua can be found in Thomas Karnes' history of the Standard Fruit Company.[29] Systematic studies of the more important coffee, cotton, and cattle industries development remain to be done. One subject for a truly indefatigable researcher would be the transformation of Nicaraguan agriculture in the post-1940 period with the steady rise of cotton, cattle, and sugar as export crops. Such work would require some detailed examinations of land titles and a search for available data on crop production and land usage over the past forty years in order to ascertain the extent of conversion to export crops, the growth of land concentration, and the impact of these changes upon inflation and demographic patterns. Before the fall of Somoza, any such study would probably have been impossible; even now it would be difficult and tedious at best, but the results, both for an understanding of Nicaraguan history and for a broader view of the impact of modernization upon small, dependent economies, would be most beneficial. Also worthwhile would be studies of the history of the major agricultural associations, such as the Nicaraguan Coffee Association.

Individual company studies should also prove useful. A study of the Bragman's Bluff Lumber Company, for years the most important enterprise on Nicaragua's northeastern coast and a leader in calls for American military protection, would be especially welcome. This also applies to studies of the American mining companies in Nicaragua. Studies of transportation in Nicaragua are also needed.[30]

Virtually no serious work has been done on Nicaraguan labor history. While organized labor has played a limited role in Nicaragua, some as-

28. The best available work is Jaime Wheelock Román, *Imperialismo y dictadura* (México, D.F., 1975). Wheelock is currently Nicaragua's minister of agriculture and a member of the FSLN's National Directorate.

29. Thomas Karnes, *Tropical Enterprise: The Standard Fruit and Steamship Company in Latin America* (Baton Rouge, 1978).

30. For accounts of the history of transisthmian transportation in the twentieth century, see Max H. Harrison, "San Juan River–Lake Nicaragua Waterway, 1502–1921," Ph.D. dissertation (Louisiana State University, 1971); and Thomas A. Bailey, "Interest in a Nicaraguan Canal, 1903–1931," *Hispanic American Historical Review,* 16 (February 1936): 2–28. Interesting examples of the historical studies which might be done on other aspects of Nicaraguan transportation are provided by J. Fred Rippy, "State Department Operations: The Rama Road," *Inter-American Economic Affairs,* 9 (Summer 1955): 17–22; and Roger W. Peard, "Bull Cart Transportation in the Tropics," *Marine Corps Gazette,* 15 (February 1931): 29–30, 47–49.

pects warrant further study, such as the interaction between the Somozas and the labor movement, especially during World War II. Foreign influences on Nicaraguan labor, especially those of the AFL-CIO, are of considerable importance. A related topic would be a history of social welfare and labor legislation in Nicaragua.

Nicaraguan social, cultural, and intellectual history has been almost totally neglected. The major exception to this rule is in the area of literary history, as considerable attention has been paid to Nicaraguan poetry. Most of what is available in this area has been produced by students of literature rather than history and concentrates on analysis or on the biographies of a few selected figures.[31] The history of education in Nicaragua also remains to be written. A study of university development would be especially welcome, given the crucial role which university students played in the development of the FSLN and the fall of Somoza.[32]

Some work has also been done on Church history, but much more attention could be devoted to this area.[33] The emergence of both Roman Catholic and Protestant church leadership as significant factors in the struggle against the Somoza dictatorship demonstrated the value of such studies. The role of foreign missionaries, Catholic as well as Protestant, is of vital importance in the development of the Nicaraguan churches and education. An examination of the history and impact of missionary movements would provide insights into foreign influences on Nicaraguan society, as well as adding to our understanding of the nation's religious history.[34]

Local and regional rivalries in Nicaragua have made local histories of special importance. A somewhat-dated history of Managua and a series of popularized monographs on Nicaragua's various departments have been published.[35] There is also a Ph.D. dissertation on Nicaraguan historical

31. Rubén Darío, of course, has received the most attention. For examples of studies of other writers, see Paul W. Borgeson Jr., "The Poetry of Ernesto Cardenal," Ph.D. dissertation (Vanderbilt University, 1977); and José Calatayud Bernabeau, *Manolo Cuadra* (Managua, 1968).

32. Some information on this subject is contained in Sergio Ramírez M., *Mariano Fiallos, biografía* (León, Nicaragua, 1971).

33. Some information on recent Roman Catholic church history can be gleaned from Mons. Donald Chávez Núñez, *Una ventana abierta* (Managua, 1974). For Protestant activities on the Atlantic coast, see Karl A. Mueller, *Among Creoles, Moskitos and Sumos: A Survey of the Moravian Mission from 1847–1930* (Bethlehem, Pennsylvania, 1932).

34. Valuable archival resources for the history of Protestant activities in Nicaragua can be found in the American Baptist Archives at Colgate-Rochester Seminary, New York, and in the Moravian Mission Archives at Bethlehem, Pennsylvania. The latter also contain material on German missionary activities.

35. Gratus Halftermeyer, *Historia de Managua* (4th ed. Managua, 1965). The monographs on various departments were written by Julián N. Guerrero and Lola Soriano and published in the 1960s as the "Colección Nicaragua" by the Banco Nicaraguense. A unique

geography, which is quite useful.[36] Further studies of local history are needed, especially those relating to the Atlantic coast. This traditionally isolated and neglected region contains most of the nation's black and Indian population, providing material for important cultural as well as regional studies.[37]

Despite the problems posed by the paucity of archival resources and the turbulence of political change, opportunities for research in recent Nicaraguan history are obviously considerable. The new revolutionary government seems anxious to encourage such studies, especially those which contribute to an understanding of the national cultural heritage or those which support their view of foreign responsibility for much of Nicaragua's current problems. The problem will be to avoid concentration on the few glamour areas—the U.S. interventions and the career of Sandino, the crimes of the Somoza dynasty and the recent revolution—and to investigate other areas which have hitherto been largely neglected.

Critical analysis is needed of questions such as why the Somoza dynasty could endure so long. Central to this question is an examination of the Somoza family's relations with Nicaragua's domestic oligarchy, and their ability to manipulate U.S. policy and public opinion is also important. Analysis of their relations with Congress and with the media might prove as revealing as the traditional approach of studying formal diplomatic interaction. Of equal value would be evaluations of economic linkages between the Somozas and their foreign and domestic allies. Finally, overall interpretations of the political, social, and economic results on a country under forty-two years of one family's rule and the effects of the end of this rule on the entire region will provide abundant opportunities for arguments for generations of scholars.

It is difficult to predict how long the current flood of research on Nicaragua will last or how solid its results will be.[38] It is hoped that some of the scholarly interest generated will outlast the political popularity and journalistic sensationalism, eventually producing careful, well-researched

type of local history is Ann Gonover Carson's as-yet-unpublished manuscript of the history of the 1931 and 1972 Managua earthquakes.

36. David R. Radel, "An Historical Geography of Western Nicaragua: The Spheres of Influence of León, Granada and Managua," Ph.D. dissertation (University of California, Berkeley, 1969).

37. For a popularized description of this region see Laszlo Pataky, *Nicaragua Desconocida* (Managua, 1956). A more scholarly approach is James R. Taylor, Jr., "Agricultural Settlement and Development in Eastern Nicaragua," Ph.D. dissertation (University of Wisconsin–Madison, 1968).

38. In this regard it might be noted that the 1980 Latin American Studies Association Meeting had more presentations on Nicaragua than all the meetings of the association during the 1970s. See also R. L. Woodward, comp., *Nicaragua* (Oxford, 1983).

material. At the very least, those who labor in the vineyards of twentieth-century Nicaraguan history will no longer feel so alone, nor find it as necessary as before to try to justify to colleagues and students why this tiny nation is so fascinating and so revealing of the entire history of United States relations with the smaller nations of this hemisphere.

9   Costa Rica
Charles L. Stansifer and John P. Bell

In 1947 Watt Stewart complained that Costa Rican historians tended to neglect the twentieth century in favor of the colonial period and the nineteenth century.[1] The Revolution of 1948 changed all that. Now the interest in the years preceding and following the Revolution of 1948 is so high that the nineteenth century is the relatively neglected century, and historical knowledge of the nineteenth century has not kept pace with the new questions that are being asked, especially about social and economic developments.

Within the traditional political history, the most obvious need is for a single-volume synthesis of the entire national period which would incorporate recent research. Two books, long out-of-date but regularly reprinted, pretend to fill the void. First is Ricardo Fernández Guardia's *Cartilla histórica de Costa Rica* (28th ed., San José, Costa Rica, 1957; 1st ed., 1909), a bare political narrative with heavy emphasis on the nineteenth century used as a textbook in secondary schools. Second is *Historia de Costa Rica* (13th ed., San José, Costa Rica, 1974; 1st ed., 1947) by the Chilean-trained historian Carlos Monge Alfaro, who died in 1979. Like *Cartilla histórica,* Monge's text emphasizes the nineteenth century. Because of Monge's interest in economic geography, his book has more economic flesh on the political bones than Fernández Guardia's. Still, it is inadequate as an explanation of the relationship between political and economic developments. An older history by Francisco Montero Barrantes, also deserves recognition as a pioneering synthesis of nineteenth-century Costa Rican history.[2] Not unexpectedly, his emphasis falls on political and military events, almost to the exclusion of social and economic develop-

1. Watt Stewart, "Historians and History Writing in Costa Rica," *Hispanic American Historical Review,* 27 (August 1947): 599.
2. Francisco Montero Barrantes, *Elementos de historia de Costa Rica* (2 vols., San José, Costa Rica, 1892–94).

ments. Religious matters, for example, enter the narrative only when there is a church-state conflict.

The lack of a one-volume synthesis of Costa Rican history is all the more surprising when one realizes that, in comparison with the other Central American countries, the Costa Rican documentary and monographic infrastructure is reasonably sound. Through the steady efforts of fulltime historians like Rafael Obregón Loría and Carlos Meléndez Chaverri and through the cooperation of institutions like the Archivos Nacionales, the Universidad de Costa Rica, and the Editorial Costa Rica, documentary publications of the critical periods of the nineteenth century are available. Volumes in the Biblioteca Patria series, currently being published by the Editorial Costa Rica, are especially useful. The single most important publication in this series for the purposes of this essay is Carlos Meléndez, *Documentos fundamentales del siglo XIX* (San José, Costa Rica, 1978). Education, agriculture, and international relations are well covered, although the focus is on domestic political events. Also, long before the Biblioteca Patria series got underway, government-sponsored historical commissions undertook to publish documents of the first years of independence and the years of the Guerra Nacional (1857–60).[3]

There are chronological gaps in the documentary publications. For example, so-called uneventful periods such as the decades of the 1840s, 1860s, and 1890s are deserving of more attention, especially the attitudes of Costa Rica's leaders in political ideology and economic development. A long-range collection of presidential messages would help historians in search of continuity. An inventory of nineteenth-century newspapers and broadsides published in Costa Rica would be a stimulus to further political research. A new collection of treaties and foreign agreements perhaps would call attention to the need for research on the evolution of Costa Rica's foreign policy.

On the basis of the availability of nineteenth-century public documents and archival material, a number of historians have brought several nineteenth-century Costa Rican figures to life. Meléndez' *Dr. José María Montealegre,* Stewart's study of Minor C. Keith, and Chester Zelaya's work on Rafael Francisco Osejo stand as excellent models.[4] Still needed are biographies of such prominent political figures as Juan Rafael Mora, Tomás Guardia, and Bernardo Soto, religious leaders such as Bishop Ber-

---

3. For example, *Documentos históricos posteriores a la Independencia* (San José, Costa Rica, 1923). Many additional documents may of course be found in the *Revista de los Archivos Nacionales*.

4. Carlos Meléndez, *Dr. José María Montealegre* (San José, Costa Rica, 1969); Watt Stewart, *Keith and Costa Rica* (Albuquerque, 1964); Chester Zelaya, *El Bachiller Osejo* (2 vols., San José, Costa Rica, 1971).

nardo Augusto Thiel, and medical leaders like Carlos Durán. As an indication of the dimension of the need for biographical studies, one might list the eighteen prominent nineteenth-century Costa Ricans officially designated as *beneméritos de la patria*. Of these eighteen only two or three have received full biographical treatment.[5] Costa Rica's Ministerio de Cultura, Juventud y Deportes has begun a biographical series called *¿Quien fue y qué hizo?*, which has renewed interest in a number of Costa Rica's leading politicians and men of letters, but the quality of these studies is uneven. Lack of collections of private papers hampers the work of biographers, but subjects worthy of study are numerous, and archival records of major figures are ample and underutilized.

In the field of collective biography, Angela Acuña de Chacón, Rafael Obregón Loría, and Luis Felipe González Flores have led the way. Acuna's massive *La mujer costarricense* (2 vols., San José, Costa Rica, 1969–70), although lacking in methodology, both illustrates the importance of the subject of women in Costa Rican history and suggests hundreds of individuals suitable for further study. Obregón's *Los rectores de la Universidad de Santo Tomás de Costa Rica* (San José, Costa Rica, 1955) casts much light on that institution, and González Flores' painstaking account of important foreigners in Costa Rica in the nineteenth century is one of the few studies of its kind in Central America.[6] These works suggest other possible collective biographies: church leaders, businessmen, teachers, scientists, newspapermen, etc.

Specific aspects of the nineteenth century have been studied by Costa Rican scholars. One thinks of Sáenz Maroto on agriculture, González Flores on education, Blanco Segura on religion, Láscaris on ideas, Soley Guell on economics and finance, Bonilla on literature, Peralta on constitutions, among others.[7] These are admirable works for the times in which they were written, but as a group they suffer from inadequate attention to documentary sources, slack methodology, and poor monographic base. Unfortunately, the tendency has been for these works to be reprinted,

5. See Guillermo Solera Rodríguez, *Beneméritos de la patria* (2d ed., San José, Costa Rica, 1964).

6. Luis Felipe González Flores, *Historia de la influencia extranjera en el desenvolvimiento educacional y científico de Costa Rica* (San José, Costa Rica, 1921).

7. Alberto Sáenz Maroto, *Historia agrícola de Costa Rica* (San José, Costa Rica, 1970); Luis Felipe González Flores, *Historia del desarrollo de la instrucción pública en Costa Rica* (2 vols., San José, Costa Rica, 1945–61); Ricardo Blanco Segura, *Historia eclesiastica de Costa Rica* (San José, Costa Rica, 1967); Constantino Láscaris, *Desarrollo de las ideas filosóficas en Costa Rica* (San José, Costa Rica, 1965); Tomás Soley Güell, *Historia económica y hacendaria de Costa Rica* (2 vols., San José, Costa Rica, 1947–49); Abelardo Bonilla, *Historia y antología de la literatura costarricense* (2 vols., San José, Costa Rica, 1957–61); Hernán G. Peralta, *Las constituciones de Costa Rica* (Madrid, 1962).

when what is needed is a rigorous reexamination of these aspects of Costa Rican history. González Flores' work on public instruction, which carries the story only to 1884, badly needs revision and extension. A perusal of Sáenz Maroto's encyclopedic annals of agricultural history leads to hundreds of suggestions for detailed study. Also, those particular aspects which have previously been neglected, such as science, medicine, and specific industries, ought to be investigated.

It is not surprising that local and regional history is not well developed in Costa Rica. The dominance of the Meseta Central and its four principal cities (San José, Alajuela, Heredia, and Cartago) is such that the ill-defined and lightly populated outlying regions are bound to be neglected. A project of the Universidad de Costa Rica and the national association of municipalities to document and reconstruct local histories has borne little fruit to date. Rigorous accounts of Puntarenas, San Isidro del General, and Siquirres, just to name a few of the historically important but relatively neglected municipalities, would help provide a national perspective of Costa Rican historical development. Jeffrey Casey Gaspar's *Limón, 1880–1940: un estudio de la industria bananera en Costa Rica* (San José, Costa Rica, 1979) is an example of what can be done.

Costa Rican historians' neglect of the four Meseta cities does cause wonder. There is not a single comprehensive study of any of these cities. Occasionally, a devoted native son attempts to rescue at least the prominent personalities of one of these cities from oblivion as Luis Dobles Segreda did for Heredia, but Dobles Segreda himself would have admitted that his labors were lacking in comprehensive and systematic methodology.[8] In view of San José's rapid transition from village capital to leading city of the republic in the nineteenth century, one would expect a great deal of interest in the social and economic aspects of its development, as well as in the manifestations of the regional struggle for power. But San José and its sister cities still await their chroniclers. Despite all the worldwide fanfare and recognition given to urban history in recent years and despite the current preoccupation with the problems of the exploding growth of Latin American cities, Costa Rica's metropolis and its regional centers and communities remain largely to be discovered by historians.

Apart from urban history the exploration of the social and economic history of nineteenth-century Costa Rica is well under way. Samuel Stone's book, *La dinastía de los conquistadores: la crisis del poder en la Costa Rica contemporánea* (San José, Costa Rica, 1975), has a contemporary message, as indicated in the title, but a major contribution of the book rests on the detailed revelation of the linkage between the economic

---

8. Luis Dobles Segreda, *La Provincia de Heredia* (Heredia, Costa Rica, 1935).

power of the nineteenth-century coffee elite of Costa Rica and their political power. Other studies such as those of Lowell Gudmundson, Meléndez and Duncan, and Carlos Araya focus on racial and social stratification.[9] These contributions deserve to be followed up and expanded, because many gaps have been left. Surprisingly little research has been done on specific immigrant groups—Jamaicans, Germans, Italians, Chinese, Nicaraguans, to name the most readily visible groups—and on their assimilation into Costa Rican life. Microstudies of interest groups, business enterprises, individual ranches (or *fincas*), labor unions, foreign colonies, and other groups and institutions are also needed to establish a firm base for generalization about Costa Rica's social and economic history.

Despite considerable expansion of sociological research in recent years on population, family life, and women, little of this research has been concerned with origins or nineteenth-century developments. Studies of nineteenth-century household economics do not exist. The role of women and parental attitudes toward children are known, for the most part, through extrapolation of current data, anecdotal history, and *costumbrista* accounts; no serious study of this topic in the nineteenth century has been undertaken. Social mobility, land tenure patterns, internal migrations, and fertility are other socioeconomic studies that are yet to be undertaken for nineteenth-century Costa Rica.

The pace of historical research in Costa Rica has intensified steadily during the last generation. With the advent of professional historians such as Rafael Obregón Loría, Carlos Meléndez, and the late Carlos Monge Alfaro and the increasing emphasis on research in the School of History of the University of Costa Rica (UCR), the resources for research have greatly increased. With great dedication these professional historians spawned a generation of historians, which is presently preparing a remarkably large and able group of young researchers, many of them interested primarily in the twentieth century. Yet despite the definitely upbeat ambience, with professional historians and their concerns present not only in San José but also in regional centers such as San Ramón, Turrialba, and Liberia, as well as at the Universidad Nacional in Heredia, much remains to be done, because this professionalization is so very recent.

Even in those areas where important work has already been done, such

9. Lowell Gudmundson, *Estratificación socio-racial y económica de Costa Rica, 1700–1850* (San José, Costa Rica, 1978); Carlos Meléndez and Quince Duncan, *El negro en Costa Rica* (San José, Costa Rica, 1972); Carlos Araya Pochet, "La minería y sus relaciones con la acumulación de capital y la clase dirigente de Costa Rica, 1821–1841," *Estudios sociales centroamericanos*, 5 (May–August 1973): 31–64.

as the decade of rapid change and reform from 1940 to 1950 and the formation and development of the National Liberation party, there are fascinating aspects which remain largely unexplored. A good example of this is the revolutionary period itself, which, with its innate drama and obvious impact, has attracted more research than any other decade. Yet while a whole generation of Costa Rican leaders, the "generation of 1948," were thrust on the national scene, incisive studies concerning their development as leaders and the organizations that nurtured them have yet to appear. Even the now-famous Center for the Study of National Problems, which so many have touched on in studies of that period, awaits researchers who will answer such fundamental questions as: Who were all the members? Were they truly all or mostly middle-class urban dwellers? What correlation existed between being a member of the center (*centrista*) and being a bank employee? Did *Surco*, its principal publication, express a clear ideological position? How were the center and its works financed? Even some very prominent leaders' roles in the pre-1948 period are largely unknown or known in very little detail. Of particular interest in this regard are Daniel Oduber, Rodrigo Facio, Gonzalo Facio, and Luis Alberto Monge. All have exerted great influence since 1948, but little is known regarding their activities between 1940 and 1948 and particularly during 1947–48.

Much of the published material written by the revolutionaries and by the progovernment press prior and subsequent to the revolution refers to a terrorist group within the ranks of those preparing the revolt, but there is no detailed account or analysis of its activities. How did the group organize and acquire expertise? Who directed it and to what ends? Did it finance itself or receive outside support? Charles Ameringer's *Don Pepe* provides some leads, but the topic merits deeper research. Similar largely unexplored topics include the Costa Rican Anti-Communist League, the electoral alliance between the National Republican administrations and the communist Popular Vanguard party, and the Popular Vanguard itself.

Definitive studies have yet to be written about Rafael Angel Calderón Guardia and Licenciado Teodoro Picado Michalski and their administrations. An in-depth analysis and overall interpretation of their social legislation would represent a significant contribution. Sound studies have been made of some aspects, such as Mark Roseberg's work on the Social Security system, but there is much yet to be done in regard to the labor code, the introduction of social guarantees to the constitution, the electoral reforms, and progressive income and property taxes.

Although José Figueres is one of the best-known leaders in contemporary Latin America and has been the subject of three full-length biographies and numerous shorter treatments, a need remains for further research on several periods of his career such as on his activities during the crucial prerevolutionary years, particularly outside Costa Rica. What political plans did he have at the time of his exile, and why was he alone sent into exile? What, in very specific terms, did he accomplish while in exile? Although this obviously was a key time in his evolution as a political leader, little is known about it, and even Ameringer, for this particular period, had to rely heavily on the same material that Figueres had provided Castro Esquivel.

Although a great deal has been written about the 1948 rebellion, too little attention has been given to the government forces. Did Calderón mobilize labor confederation forces?

The Nicaraguan exiles' role in the uprising in support of Figueres' National Liberation Army has been dealt with adequately in several studies, but this is not the case regarding the Nicaraguan government's role. Was Anastasio Somoza García interested in assisting the Costa Rican government to suppress rebellion or simply in preventive measures against the Nicaraguan exiles who planned to use postrevolutionary Costa Rica as an operational base for an attack on the Somoza regime? There is ample evidence that the Picado government received aid and offers of aid from Somoza. What needs further research are questions such as how extensive was this assistance, what form did it take, what conditions were acceptable and which not to Picado and/or Calderón? A particular episode which warrants special attention is the Nicaraguan National Guard's seizure of Villa Quesada (now Ciudad Quesada) in the last stages of the civil war. What motivated Somoza, and did he act with or without the American and Costa Rican governments' cognizance? Was this movement directly related to the unusual stopover by the Caribbean Legion under the command of Horacio Ornes and Ludwig Starke in Altamira (near the Nicaraguan border) enroute to seize Puerto Limón on the Caribbean coast? Such an indirect route seemed to be openly provocative to Somoza.

Although many topics of the period of the revolution remain largely unexplored, even more research is needed concerning the eighteen-month regime which followed the peace agreement negotiated during April 1948. No systematic study of Costa Rica under the Founding Junta of the Second Republic has yet been published despite frequent reference to it in many general works as the crucible for the formation of modern Costa Rica. There is a near void regarding even the most provocative facets of that period, such as the junta's two most decisive and significant acts—the bank nationalization and the abolition of the armed forces. The few works which deal with the bank nationalization tend to be political statements either justifying or condemning it on ideological grounds. What is needed

are studies which analyze the banking structure before and after nationalization from national and international perspectives, as well as research in
detail regarding the relationships among the banks, bank employees, directors, creditors, and credit seekers both during the armed uprising and
the eighteen months of the junta. At the UCR and the National University,
the researcher will find theses on which to build regarding the disbanding
of the army. The obvious link between the revolution and Costa Rican
demilitarization consisted in the fact that the military forces, though
miniscule and largely nonprofessional, nonetheless were employed by the
National Republican administrations to suppress dissent and to hamper the
proper functioning of the electoral process. It is not surprising then that in
the heat of victory the revolutionary junta should abolish the armed forces.
However, this, as well as other aspects concerning Latin America's only
demilitarized society, merits intensive research and illumination.

There are many related topics particularly worthy of study. One of the
more intriguing ones is the interrelationships among the United States
government's support to and influence on the revolutionaries, the Rio
Pact, the long-standing hope of the United States that a depoliticized constabulary force could be a stabilizing factor (e.g., forces created in Nicaragua, Panama, Haiti, and the Dominican Republic during interventions),
and the demilitarization under American auspices of Japan during the
same time. In these regards particular attention should be given to proving
or disproving that from the beginning Figueres and the National Liberation movement consciously saw themselves as endowed with a special
mission—to serve as a model or example for the rest of Latin America.

The junta, despite being ideologically sympathetic to organized labor,
sustained a fundamentally conflictive relationship with the labor movement, reflected in the assassinations at the Codo del Diablo and in the
incarceration and purge of labor leaders by the junta. The key to this
conflict resides in the close identification by organized labor with Calderón Guardia and/or the Vanguardia Popular. Even though Benjamín Núñez, Figueres' minister of labor, had considerable support and a sound
reputation among the working classes, the junta found itself frequently at
odds with elements within the labor movements, and the National Liberation party (PLN) continued to experience great difficulties with labor
throughout the next generation. These conflictive relations during the
junta regime and subsequent PLN governments are fertile fields for inquiry.

The groups united against the National Republican–Popular Vanguard
coalition split into two principal orientations, those favorable to Figueres
and the junta and those who preferred Otilio Ulate, the president-elect.

Ulate had reluctantly accepted the junta when he signed the Ulate-Figueres Pact on the eve of the transfer of power from the defeated National Republican government to the junta. The pact, however, marked the beginning of the end of the united opposition and the initiation of a sometimes acrimonious and fierce but generally benign rivalry between Figueres and Ulate, which persisted throughout the following quarter-century of Costa Rican political life. The Figueres-Ulate Pact itself and the subsequent rivalry merit more than the perfunctory glance they have been given to date. An interesting approach would be to cover the period from the emergence of Figueres and Ulate as the outstanding opposition leaders after the death of León Cortés through their on-again, off-again collaboration until the plebiscite in the 1953 election, which would have permitted an Ulate candidacy in the next presidential election had the PLN not chosen to ignore its results. Such a study might be extended to include Ulate's alleged complicity in the Calderónist invasion from Nicaragua in 1955 and ultimately the electoral coalition of Ulate's Unión Nacional with Calderón Guardia and other anti-PLN forces.

Several related topics which touch on the division among the anti–National Republican forces during the junta's reign need further research. The most significant is the defeat of the Social Democrats, who were identified with the junta's program and orientation in the election of the constituent assembly, and the consequent jettisoning of the junta's draft constitution in favor of mere reform of the 1871 constitution rather than the bold break with the past, which the name Founding Junta of the Second Republic suggests. This rift occurred again in the congressional elections in October 1949, over which the junta presided but in which its followers were clearly defeated by those of Ulate. There was conflict even within the junta, which culminated in the *cardonazo,* an attempt at a barracks revolt led by the junta's minister of public security, Edgar Cardona. As an early member of the revolutionary inner circle and the "terrorist group," Cardona's dramatic separation brought out into the open a long smoldering dispute over the junta's economic policies and the discord between the Costa Rican military leaders and their Caribbean-exile allies.

The manifold relationships between the junta and the defeated National Republicans and Vanguardists presents yet another fertile field for research to which far too little attention has been given. These relationships involve the efforts by the junta to suppress these still popular parties, to curtail their political futures, and to punish their members for real and imagined offenses committed while in power. The primary source material from the special courts created by the junta to try the "offenders" from the old regime offer a rich lode of primary material awaiting researchers, which should result in new insights into the revolutionary decade.

The most dramatic aspects of the reaction by those vanquished in 1948 took the form of two unsuccessful armed invasions, both organized in Nicaragua—the first in December 1948 and the second in 1955. Although both have published works dedicated to them, neither has been fully and objectively analyzed historically.

The National Liberation movement, first during the junta and later during the presidencies of José Figueres, Francisco Orlich, and Daniel Oduber, made extensive use of autonomous entities or institutes as means to provide essential social services and economic development. These organizations revolutionized many facets of Costa Rican national life during the last generation. Yet despite the wealth of archival material, which the institutes themselves maintain, they remain largely unexamined by historians. The breadth of the institutes is wide, ranging from housing and urban planning through electrification and communications, to tourism, insurance, and agrarian reform. The source material is rich and the theme has expanding significance for Costa Rica with the triumph of a social democracy, which has found this mix of socialism and capitalism very appropriate to its aspirations.

After this extensive look at the revolutionary decade with projections into the generation dominated by the figures which the revolution brought to the fore, it should be apparent that, even in that most intensely investigated decade of the Costa Rican past, much remains for further study, reflection, and analysis. If this is true for the revolutionary decade, it is even more so for the decades between 1900 and 1940. For although the sources are rich and abundant they have received proportionately less attention.

A professional sensitivity among social scientists and humanists, at least in part attributable to the ethos of the revolutionary decade and its aftermath, has inspired increasing concern for social, economic, and demographic history. The demographic history project at the National University and Héctor Pérez's UCR economic history project represent good examples of this new direction. For the outside researcher this means increased intellectual and material infrastructure on which he or she can draw.

There are a multitude of promising themes to investigate, only a few of which can be mentioned here. An area of particular concern to many contemporary scholars is social mobilization. Social movements such as cooperatives, labor unions, and benevolent societies, most of which have economic motivation as well, have until quite recent years received very little attention by researchers. Enough work has now been done to define these movements in Costa Rica back to the turn of the century and even earlier.

In economic history the topics to be researched are many, diverse, and quite important. Carolyn Hall's work on coffee could serve as a model for similar efforts dealing with other basic products such as sugar, bananas, beef, and cacao. The role of foreign investment has hardly been touched. Many of the areas in which autonomous entities now operate were at one time linked to foreign investment, and these linkages warrant investigation. Another significant topic awaiting study involves the Niehaus interests and La Victoria industrial-agricultural cooperative. The Niehaus family's extensive holdings and economic operations, particularly sugar, along both the Atlantic and Pacific slopes, were intervened and some expropriated as those of enemy aliens—Germans—during World War II. The family's enterprises and their development in and of themselves merit a monograph. Also of interest is the evolution of La Victoria, the development of the Inter-American Agricultural Center at Turrialba, and other uses made of the expropriated properties.

There are other viable and influential cooperatives in Costa Rica which should be studied either collectively or individually. The Dos Pinos milk producers' dairy processing and distributing cooperative has not only been a commercial success over the years but has had enormous impact on the consumption patterns and nutritional and health standards of the Costa Rican population as it extended its area of marketing to include most population centers in the nation. The airplane repair and refurbishing cooperative proved so successful that it came to serve not only Costa Rica's needs but those of customers in many other nations, including the United States. The cooperative movement and many of its components are important in understanding Costa Rican economic and social history in the twentieth century.

On the banana industry many topics come to mind such as the United Fruit Company and the evolution of the banana trade, which was already flourishing at the beginning of the century; the problems it solved and those it engendered with the development of its English-speaking enclave on the Atlantic coast; "the zone," its expansion and shift to the Pacific slope in the Quepos and Golfito region, and its subsequent development of the African oil palm. The African oil palm provided the raw material for the development of the production of an industrialized vegetable oil for human consumption. An intriguing history could be written of Numar, the leading firm in that new industry, its initiation, development, impact on the national economy, and relationship to United Fruit. Bananas in Costa Rica, however, involve more than the United Fruit Company and its successors. There have been interesting experiences with cooperatives. Independent producers have always existed. The Standard Fruit Company (now part of Castle and Cooke, Inc.) came into the nearly abandoned banana zone along the Atlantic coast in the post–World War II period with successful new approaches to marketing.

Costa Rica, particularly since World War II, has followed a policy of agricultural diversification, modernization, and industrialization, which along with its more traditional pursuits has allowed it to enjoy long-term, sustained economic growth with an ever increasing standard of living expressed in terms of per capita real income. This has been achieved despite Costa Rica's having one of the highest rates of population growth in the region for a number of years (this high rate, however, has now been brought under control). The economic success of Latin America's most stable democracy truly merits extensive research and publication. This consistent economic growth is all the more noteworthy when one considers that twentieth-century Costa Rica has not prospered from a mineral boom of any kind; agriculture has been its mainstay throughout the years, and its growth has been through increased agricultural production, through extending agricultural frontiers, and through improving techniques for growing, storing, processing, and distributing its product. The activities of the National Production Council (CNP) are of particular note in this regard.

An integral element in Costa Rica's contemporary economic development has been its multifaceted approach to opening up the entire national area through transportation. Again there are rich resources for researchers. The whole sweep of road-building projects has yet to be even chronicled other than in administrative reports. The approach has been one of tying the country together rather than one of grandiose projects from the capital to the ports, and most twentieth-century administrations have contributed to the development of the highway network. In recent years, with most of the basic network in place, more spectacular projects such as highways to the Juan Santamaría airport and to the new port of Caldera have been undertaken. A more specific topic, and one which breaks with the generalization above, is the building of the Pan-American highway. The route necessitated spectacular engineering as well as financial feats. The many ramifications of this program should make it a highly stimulating research project.

The history of petroleum, passing from state monopoly to private enterprise to a new, more sophisticated monopoly under an autonomous institute named Recope, could serve as a case history of a distinctly Costa Rican approach to economic activity. Costa Rica, which has never been a petroleum-producing country, now has an integrated industry, with Recope importing crude, refining it, and marketing the refined products.

Of significance in both the social and economic history of Costa Rica is the phenomenal rise of *La Nación*. The daily newspaper, with by far the largest circulation in Costa Rica and perhaps in Central America, entered a crowded field in 1946. Its success was nearly immediate, and it is now an arbiter in national politics and a force to be reckoned with in all aspects of national life.

A fascinating topic in social history, which has hardly been touched on, is the question of minorities in Costa Rica. Some work has been done, and other work is in progress concerning the black population centered in Puerto Limón. Little, however, has been written about the influential Jewish community, the Lebanese, the large Nicaraguan population, the large number of Latin American refugees, the increasing number of Americans, or the stable and ever more influential Chinese population. An indication of the general acceptance of immigrants in democratic Costa Rica can be deduced from the fact that many recent presidents were not from old stock but rather descendants of immigrants, including such men as Orlich, Figueres, Oduber, Cortés, and Picado. Picado's mother was Polish, and both of Figueres' parents were recent arrivals from Spain.

The history of Costa Rica's international affairs is still largely unwritten. Its bilateral relations with the Central American nations, the United States, and Mexico are of particular interest. In the postrevolutionary period Costa Rica has been very active in international organizations and in fostering multilateral solutions to American and international problems.

Costa Rica in the twentieth century is a vital and rewarding field for historical research. The resources are there and the atmosphere is propitious. In the context of the hemisphere, Costa Rica is thoroughly Latin American, yet its stability, democracy, and steady progress remain in sharp juxtaposition to its neighbors, whether large or small, populous or not, prosperous or not. In this context, expanding historical study will contribute both to understanding a significant if small nation and to illuminating the essential differences between Costa Rica and the rest of Central America and Latin America, which should lead to greater understanding of the whole region as well.

10   Panama
The Search for a National History
Sheldon B. Liss

While popularizers have produced numerous imaginative and graceful narratives about the quest for an interoceanic passageway and the Canal-building epic, the majority of academics who have dealt with Panama have usually written dull and pedantic articles and books on aspects of United States relations with that country, and have overlooked the history of the people and institutions which have existed under the legal jurisdiction of the Republic of Panama. There exists no substantial scholarly general history of Panama in English.

United States scholars who have delved into the history of the area appear at times obsessed by the idea of chronicling every detail of their nation's involvement in Panama. Of course, volumes on the Canal and those detailing Yankee intervention in the Isthmus sometimes sell well in the United States.[1] On the other hand, an excellent book surveying the social and cultural history of Panama, if it were to be written, might not have a large enough market to warrant publication. Individuals working on specialized aspects of Panamanian national history must produce works that appeal to a readership extending beyond just those interested in the isthmian nation, or resist succumbing to the temptation of writing books. It is understandable that historians in the United States prefer to concentrate on "major" countries such as Argentina, Brazil, or Mexico or on the colonial era, but it is inexcusable that they frequently overlook the national history of Panama in general books on Latin America and in more specialized topical or institutional studies. At best they treat Panama in a cursory fashion in amorphous and usually sketchy chapters on Central America.

Panama has a national identity, which historians have yet to characterize adequately. Most of the books and articles on Panama that this author has reviewed over the past decade have been mediocre or esoteric and not very useful to even the historian specializing in Latin America. How might the

---

1. For example, *The Path Between the Seas: The Creation of the Panama Canal, 1870–1914* (New York), a fine book by David McCullough, was promoted by Simon and Schuster in 1977. Also, the writer's *The Canal: Aspects of United States–Panamanian Relations* (Notre Dame, Indiana, 1967) has sold five times better than the average university press book and continues to sell despite being outdated, overly ethnocentric, and representing retrograde thinking.

many deficiencies in the field of Panamanian history be overcome? What areas need further exploration and explication? How can new techniques in historical research and social science skills be applied to Panama's history? Subsequent paragraphs deal primarily with the twentieth century, but they are written with the thought that a need exists for a solid English-language treatment of the 1821 to 1903 period of the prenational history of Panama.[2]

Despite the fact that most historical writing about Panama pertains to international diplomacy and the Canal, by no means have those areas been thoroughly investigated. There exists no exhaustive study of how United States policy toward Panama has been formulated. How Panama has devised and conducted its foreign policies and the relationship between its domestic and international postures remain unknown, as do the country's positions on international jurisprudence. For instance, because of its unusual location with respect to the Atlantic and Pacific oceans and the Caribbean Sea, has Panama over the years abided by or made original contributions to international codes of maritime or commercial law?[3]

Unable to defend itself militarily from attacks amounting to more than border skirmishes and having its geographical center occupied by the western hemisphere's most powerful state, with whom it has conflicted frequently, Panama has to a great extent depended upon diplomacy for survival. Nevertheless, the country's policies concerning the resolution of international discord, or how much it has relied upon arbitration or looked to the United States to provide protection from other nations, remain largely unknown.

Historians refer to Panama as the Hub of the Americas, but they have not probed more than superficially into the country's relations with its neighbors—in particular with Colombia from which it seceded[4]—or with other Latin American states, or into its roles vis-à-vis the rest of the world or international polities. For instance, in the United Nations and the Organization of American States, what stands has Panama taken on human rights, colonialism, nuclear proliferation, disarmament, or collective security? Within international organizations, has Panama followed the lead

2. For the colonial era see Rubén Darío Carles, *220 Años del período colonial en Panamá* (2d ed., Panamá, 1959); for the 1808–21 period, see Isidro A. Beluche M., *Independencia y secesión de Panamá* (Panamá, 1965); for 1821–1902, see Luis Martínez Delgado, *Panamá, su independencia de España, su incorporación a la Gran Colombia, su separación de Colombia, el Canal interoceánico* (Bogotá, 1972).

3. For some of the unique aspects of Canal and Canal Zone law, see Wayne D. Bray, *The Common Law Zone in Panama: A Case Study in Reception* (San Juan, Puerto Rico, 1977).

4. For a Colombian point of view on the separation, see Eduardo Lemaitre, *Panamá y su Separación de Colombia* (Bogotá, 1971).

of other Latin American nations, been independent, or subservient to the
United States or other major powers? Then too, what dichotomies have
existed between the public stances taken on foreign affairs by Panama's
ruling elites and the private attitudes held by the nation's general populace? For example, over the past three decades Panama's government has
made few statements about the socialist world, while simultaneously socialism has gained many new adherents in the country. Perhaps some insights into this situation could be found by examining the history of official and unofficial relations between Panama and the Soviet Union, China,
and Cuba from the beginning of the cold war to the present. Then too,
comprehensive histories of Panama's international relations, politics, and
economics, written from socialist perspectives, might prove illuminating.[5]

Undoubtedly, most historians of Latin America know the name of Phil-
lippe Bunau-Varilla and of his chicanery pertaining to the 1903 separation
of Panama from Colombia. But do they know about the history of ideas
in the Central American nation, or of the domestic and international philosophies which have been important there? How many Latin Americanists in the United States have read the writings or know about the accomplishments of Panama's nineteenth-century statesman-jurist Justo
Arosemena, the father of his country's twentieth-century constitutional
thought?[6] Even the few scholars who have worked on the history of Latin
American ideas have tended to overlook such Panamanian contributors to
the intellectual life of the hemisphere. Have thinkers such as Arosemena
added to a distinct Panamanian way of looking at the world?

The extent to which the contours of Panamanian history have been
shaped by the interaction of the philosophies of the nations and multinational businesses which have dominated isthmian trade remains unknown.
An objective historical interpretation of the effects of international economics upon the nation's social and political life might also disclose how
vital Panamanian control of the Canal is to the country's development. A
study of the evolution of what social scientist Herbet de Souza calls enclave dependency[7] would shed light on the power relationships which
have guided Panama and clarify the historical links between the nation's

5. Three works partially accomplish this task: Thelma King H., *El problema de la sobe-
ranía en las relaciones entre Panamá y los Estados Unidos de América* (Panamá, 1961);
Anteo Quimbaya, *Problemas históricas de actualidad: por qué el Canal de Panamá debe
ser y será de los panameños* (3d ed., Bogotá, 1964); and Rubén Darío Souza, et al., *Panamá, 1903–1970: nación-imperialismo; fuerzas populares-oligarquía; crisis y camino revolucionario* (Santiago, 1970).
6. See Justo Arosemena, *El estado federal de Panamá* (Panamá, 1972); and Adolfo A.
Benedetti, *El pensamiento constitucional de Justo Arosemena* (Panamá, 1962).
7. Herbet de Souza, "Economic Structure of Panama: Enclave Dependency," in *Panama:
Sovereignty for a Land Divided* (Washington, D.C., 1976), 35–37.

colonial subservience, its economic problems, and its government's inability to provide a great deal of political freedom and social justice to many of its citizens.

A number of the aforementioned hypothetical studies would be enhanced by the application of quantification techniques. By employing measurement tools, one could assess the impact of world trade on Panama, or evaluate Panama's fiscal policies in order to establish more concrete ideas about national social and economic development and the way it has affected various classes. Statistically based studies could tell more about the role of labor on the Isthmus. They might promote better understanding of how the importation of thousands of unskilled black workers from the British West Indies to work on Canal construction and the failure to return many of them changed the racial and cultural composition of the new republic and added to its social problems. Sufficient data exist to assemble a fascinating account of how immigration patterns affected organized and unorganized rural and urban labor, race relations, and the growth of Panamanian nationalism. Studies of this type might eventually lead to the construction of a "people's" history, written from the bottom up rather than from the top down, as have been the majority of histories about Panama, whether done by natives or foreigners. Such works would open up further possibilities for the study of modernization or the impact of urbanization on the Isthmus. Then too, Panama City as a focal point for international banking and commerce, Colón with its free-trade area, and the Canal and Canal Zone would make excellent laboratories for research on the function of urban centers as special enclaves in national history.

For more traditionally oriented academics, many other research opportunities exist. Institutional studies, such as those relating to the military or the Church need to be done for Panama. Authoritarianism of diverse types, inherited from Spain and Colombia and perpetuated in the young republic, provides a fertile field for scholarly endeavor. Does periodic control by Panama's military, the Guardia Nacional, represent a basic expression of, or a fundamental cause of, political instability? To what extent has Panama or the United States benefited or been hurt by the fact that since 1903 the Isthmus has been an armed camp? Has the continuous existence of considerable United States firepower in the nation given rise to the subversion of democratic processes in the country, or has it contributed to a modicum of stability? A study of the interaction between United States military and diplomatic leaders on the Isthmus, such as Canal Zone governors and ambassadors, and Panama's ruling elites might provide a better understanding of the neocolonial relationship that exists between the two countries. Also, an analysis of the disparities between what Panama's leaders tell their constituents and what they say to their Yankee counterparts might help explain the degree to which responsibility for conditions leading to anti–United States sentiment on the Isthmus rests with Panamanians.

From its authoritarian Spanish and colonial origins, through its subsequent political conservatism under Colombia, to its present liberal advocacy of total national sovereignty and elimination of dependence upon the United States, the Roman Catholic church has exercised considerable influence in Panama. Vatican, Spanish, Colombian, and Panamanian archives contain copious materials on local, national, and international matters, and deal with such varied topics as Church diplomacy, conflicts between civil and common law, domestic politics, and land reform. Parish records, in conjunction with local governmental sources, and studies of communities, done primarily by anthropologists, could serve as the bases for regional histories.[8] Such studies, if started at the colonial era, would tell from land-ownership patterns much about the evolution of economic power and its relationship to political power and social control in Panama.

At this juncture, scholarship on Panamanian history has not attained a high level of maturity. Very few substantial works exist—more are done by Panamanians than by United States historians—and many historical approaches have been neglected. For example, it is amazing to find so few biographies or published memoirs in Panama's personalistic society. Perhaps now, before all of the original builders and shapers of Panama perish, historians should interview them. Why not start a tradition of oral history, from which would emerge diverse scholarly works? At the same time, while some recent Ph.D.'s search for new worlds to conquer, others might translate into English some of the pioneering histories by Panamanians.[9]

Good history has three levels: the first masters facts and chronology, the second analyzes causal relationships, and the third theorizes. Most of the books about Panama belong to the first category, some articles reach the second plateau, and the third level has rarely been attained by historians. Exponents of traditional archival research, as well as synthesizers with a more cosmic approach, are confronted by many new challenges in the history of this nation, which from its inception has existed under unique circumstances.[10] Scholars might begin to draw upon existing case studies,

8. A good model is Ernesto J. Castillero Reyes, *Chiriquí: ensayo de monografía de la provincia de Chiriquí* (Panamá, 1968).

9. For example, Ricaurte Soler, *Formas ideológicas de la nación panameña* (San José, Costa Rica, 1972); and Ornel E. Urriola Marcucci, *Dialéctica de la nación panameña, período republicano* (Panamá, 1972).

10. Although it deals primarily with United States–Panamanian relations, Walter LaFeber's *The Panama Canal: The Crisis in Historical Perspective* (New York, 1978) is an

both empirical and theoretically oriented, dealing with other Latin American or Third World states, and possibly even interdisciplinary in nature, as bases for comparative analyses to help think through and write a national history of Panama.

11 Central American International Relations
Kenneth J. Grieb

The field of Central American international relations is a proverbial terra incognita. It is more than an unexplored wilderness in which scholars have failed to tread—it is a wilderness whose very existence is unknown to most scholars, including specialists in Latin America, international relations, and even inter-American relations.

That this subject continues untouched reflects the development of scholarship dealing with Latin America and foreign policy, as well as the general lack of attention to Central America. Historically, scholarship dealing with international relations in the Latin American area has focused overwhelmingly on the interaction between the colossus of the north and the other countries of the hemisphere. Although there has been a recent effort, at long last, to examine the foreign policies of the Latin American nations in and of themselves, this trend has had scant effect on the study of Central America. Instead, those works constituting the vanguard of the new thrust focus on the larger countries of South America and Mexico. In part this reflects the size of the isthmian republics. It also mirrors the tendency of scholars to ignore the smaller states, for even Latin American specialists often fail to pay sufficient attention to the isthmus, devoting few pages to it in general works.

The vast majority of the scholarly works dealing with international affairs in Central America focus on North American policy toward the isthmus. Written predominantly from the perspective of the northern colossus, they emphasize its concerns, such as the Canal and the importance of the isthmus in international commerce. Virtually the only exceptions are studies dealing with British policy in the area. Hence nearly all present literature views the nations of this area almost exclusively as the objects of the policy of the great powers. Thus dependency continues even in historiog-

---

excellent, compact but comprehensive, synthesis containing more analyses of internal Panamanian politics than other books by scholars from the United States.

raphy, with studies which are externally oriented and which consider the region and its nations important only when part of something larger and when involved in affairs which are primarily external in origin and consequence. The existing literature focuses on the disputes among the great powers which happen to occur in or involve Central America, rather than the disputes of the isthmian states themselves. Because of these circumstances, the imaginative scholar can find an almost unlimited range of topics awaiting treatment.

What is needed initially is simply an effort to understand the Central American view of the world, something which is virtually nonexistent in current literature. This requires the scholar to adopt the perspective of these republics, which of course entails utilizing their documents and publications. Such a venture into uncharted documents and neglected sources will yield a rich reward. Even relatively obvious and commonplace items, such as the Central American's reference to the three Americas—North, South, and Central—are virtually unknown among Latin American specialists dealing with other portions of the region. It is a phrase that reveals a great deal about the isthmian outlook, indicating as it does the region's central role as a vital link in the hemisphere. In fact, the definition of the term Central America is another obvious yet neglected aspect, for in the Central American mind the term encompasses only those areas that were part of the original Spanish captaincy general of Guatemala, which therefore excludes Panama. The latter, which is the focus of much Yankee attention on the area, is an outsider, having been part of the viceroyalty of New Granada rather than of New Spain. That even such basic factors escape the attention of scholars indicates the need for research in this area, and the potential impact of such investigation upon prevailing views of the hemisphere and the interaction among its states.

Viewing the world from a Central American perspective requires focus on the individual republics of the isthmus and the complex interaction among them, which can be considered as a case study of the problems of relations among the Latin American republics and, for that matter, all of the world's smaller nations. As with any other state, relations with one's neighbors must be paramount. Hence the world of Central American international relations focuses first and foremost on the isthmus itself. Relations with the region's major powers constitute the next priority. These include Mexico, the largest state bordering directly on the region, and the United States, the area's dominant power. Of secondary importance are relations with the rest of the Caribbean, including Panama, Colombia, and Venezuela, and the island republics, especially Cuba and the Dominican Republic. Next in importance are Europe, a distant focus since colonial times, and South America, especially the states of the Pacific Coast, whose links to Europe pass through Central America and the Canal. The Atlantic states of South America are of less significance, save in the realm of inter-American affairs, because their contacts with Europe make them more remote from the isthmus. The rest of the world appeared on the horizon only in the 1950s and 1960s. Hence the view from Central America is quite different, not merely from that of North America, but also from that of Mexico or the South American nations. The implications of this perspective require study. In this sense an approach from the Central American viewpoint would serve to illuminate even aspects of interaction with the United States that have been examined from the perspective of the northern colossus. Such questions as that of Belize, which appear peripheral to the rest of the globe, constitute to the isthmus the major foreign-affairs issue in the world, and the difference in perspective is one of the factors rendering the issue's solution difficult.

Analysis of the interaction among the isthmian republics and the rivalries which constantly split the region is the outstanding need in the area of Central American international relations. The situation of several small states relatively close to each other renders it easy for each to influence the others and inevitable for exiles to seek bases in neighboring states. The result is a volatile situation in which domestic and foreign policies are scarcely separable, intervention and attempts to influence events across borders are commonplace and to a certain extent mandated by self-defense, and in which events in any one nation inevitably affect its neighbors. To this one must add the aspects of ill-defined and remote borders, poor transportation facilities, and isolated pockets of population, which due to the terrain and the limited transportation facilities are in actuality quite remote from each other despite the proximity of borders. All these factors contribute to a complex and intensive interrelationship that makes diplomacy a part of all endeavors.

A regional balance of power constitutes a basic part of this situation, despite the fact that it remains almost unknown outside the isthmus. The rivalries date back to colonial days and are affected by such factors as economic development, population, and the actions of external powers. Guatemala and El Salvador, the largest nations by population, are the great rivals, constantly seeking to influence Honduras and Nicaragua. Costa Rica, whose center of population is quite removed from the northern vortex, responds by emphasizing its uniqueness and seeking to remain aloof from the quarrels of its compatriots, often to the point of adopting a quasi-isolationist line. All are highly nationalistic, yet periodically support universalist ambitions or exile groups.

Although the breakup of the original federation shortly after independence has been studied and the current of federalism has been assumed in scholarship relating to the region, its implications in the sphere of international relations have been virtually ignored. For the fact that federalism remains as an ideal has all too often provided the ambitious with a tool. Throughout the nineteenth century, dictators strongly entrenched in their own states have embraced the cause of federalism as a banner to serve their aspirations by attempting to restore union through conquest. On the other hand, exiles have often proclaimed themselves federalists, as a means of securing support in neighboring states to oppose the regime that forced them to flee their homelands. The degree to which the cause has been utilized for political expedience has not been closely examined by scholars. The rivalries and the various border disputes also served to emphasize international law and juridical proceedings, which constitute another fruitful area for investigation. The Central American contribution to international law has been considerable, and the early efforts toward the establishment of international juridical bodies in the region offer some of the primary examples of such endeavors in the world, illustrating the problems, pitfalls, and prospects.

Central American links with Panama, and—prior to Panamanian independence—Colombia, constitute another unexplored field. The entire process by which Panama, associated with Central America in the Yankee mind, has become increasingly involved in isthmian affairs and less of an outcast provides an illuminating case study, with considerable implications in the realms of psychology, culture, literature, etc., as well as in the more obvious aspects of diplomacy and economic development.

The role and ambitions of Mexico in the isthmus constitute an important and virtually unexplored aspect. Studies of this complex tie would provide considerable insight into Mexican foreign policy as well as into Central American affairs, with implications in the cultural realm. This approach would also provide an entirely new perspective on relations among the Latin American nations, their rivalries, and their own ambitions, which at times closely parallel those of the imperialists on a smaller scale. The fact that Mexico was compelled by the presence of a larger power (the United States) to take a back seat in what it regards as its own natural sphere of influence, adds a vital dimension to an understanding of Mexican outlook and its reaction to the northern colossus. It is also illuminating to realize that to some of the Central American nations, particularly Guatemala, Mexico is the "colossus of the north." These perspectives add a considerable dimension to an understanding of broader hemispheric relations.

Other aspects awaiting study include Central American relations with the Caribbean, South America, and Europe. Through the mid-nineteenth century, relations with Europe were the most important, given the British efforts to control the region due to its importance for transportation, and the fact that Europe provided virtually the sole source of development capital during that time. The change in the region's balance with the rise of the United States and the resulting confrontation between the North Americans and the British, though already studied from the point of view of the great powers, still awaits examination from the perspective of Central America. The implications of this shift for these nations constitute another fruitful avenue of approach. Ties to the other regional states vary with the era. For example, links to Venezuela have recently become more important, because of that nation's new-found ability to finance projects on the isthmus. The importance of and proximity to Cuba constitute another factor. The significance of ties to the Pacific Coast states of South America remains unexplored.

As indicated elsewhere in this volume, resources are ample, yet limited. The greatest problem is the absence of scholarly studies of the individual countries and regimes, which compels the scholar to construct his own context in order to be able to focus on the diplomatic events with an understanding of the domestic situations. Yet ample literature by contemporaries exists, and although biased, it nonetheless provides considerable information. One of the frustrations which the scholar will encounter is the fact that the interchange between the nations has been limited by transportation problems and intense nationalism. The result is that each respective national library and university focuses strongly on its own nation to the virtual exclusion of its neighbors, with collections invariably lacking books and particularly periodicals from across the border. Hence the researcher must visit all countries involved. Although documentary resources are limited by destruction and scarcities, significant collections exist. The resources of the United States Department of State constitute an important source, for although written from the North American perspective, they do furnish a continuous and extensive record, which provides ample information about interisthmian relations and the reactions of these states to U.S. actions if the researcher makes an effort to discover these aspects and to allow for biases. As such, these records constitute a valuable source regarding events on the isthmus, as well as American actions there. The key is imaginative use of the documents.

Hence the enterprising scholar will find a rich, interesting, and challenging field in the realm of Central American diplomacy, and whatever the topical or period interests, will have little trouble identifying a subject that is important and unexplored. It offers a vast opportunity to the enterprising investigator, and work on these topics would greatly strengthen existing knowledge of Latin America and international relations as a whole.

12 Quantification and Central American History

Miles Wortman

Two hundred years ago, the Spanish Bourbons undertook a reformation of the two-hundred-year-old governing structure of Spanish America. Officials trained in the latest sophisticated techniques of the Enlightened court were dispatched to the New World to ascertain the condition of the realm, its wealth, military posture, and the state of bureaucratic and ecclesiastical institutions. Data were compiled that reported colonial populations by caste and age distribution. Fiscal information was recorded in intricate tables that showed income from tribute, sales and trade taxes, and tobacco and liquor monopolies. Commercial documents detailed the number of cattle, agricultural and mineral production, and imports and exports for each colony. These figures were analyzed in Spain and further compressed into beautiful charts, bordered by dark black curlicues, red crests, green leaves, and other embellishments. Some of the attractive tables were so detailed that data were crammed into small columns on pages that had to be folded four times to fit into large folio books.

Fascinated with the possibility of a well-ordered universe, describable and reformable according to scientific principles, the Enlightened empire, indeed the world, was thought reducible to a series of dark-inked tables drawn by professional scribes. Manuals were compiled in Madrid and circulated throughout the empire establishing a common standard for the reporting of data, such as tithe and tax income or tributaries, that could be understood and further condensed, columnated, and analyzed in Madrid. The manuals, by the way, laid the basis for record keeping in independent Spanish America, influencing the shape of government and tax policy for the next 150 years.

The Bourbons differed from previous regimes by their faith that numbers reflect conditions of well-being and of "progress" and by their assumption that government could effect remedies through scientific means. Earlier governments had sought knowledge of fiscal receipts (how much was coming in? was it an increase or not?), but the Bourbons thought the numbers accurately portrayed social conditions.

Today the heirs of the Enlightenment make similar assumptions. They

87

use the computer and sophisticated accounting practices, which seem to offer an image of reality. The tables are not as beautiful as those of our forefathers, but they do have a certain attractiveness, because they come out of the machine well-ordered and definitive.

There are problems with quantification. Some are inherent in historical knowledge and others peculiar to Central America. Quantitative historians are not without their biases. The questions they ask, the data they choose, and the data that are available, all skew the input and therefore the resulting studies. Historians may, from time to time, be able to gather sufficient data from monasteries to speculate on population and family structure in a particular area, or from the sale of manors to debate the rise of a middle class, or, closer to home, from the sale of corn at colonial Latin American government granaries to analyze shortages, hoarding, and inflationary trends. They can understand some tendencies in Hispanic American fiscal policies on the basis of time series on tax income. However, quantitative history is not a science; it is a tool that can supplement other methods of investigation.

Quantification depends upon sufficient and valid data. The researcher must determine the validity of data like any historical fact. Further, he requires a sufficient amount of data reported in a consistent system over a long period of time without significant variations. Quantification does not provide short cuts to explaining obscure periods or answering difficult historical problems; the good cliometrician must use numerical data in addition to all other available historical evidence.

These problems are particularly troublesome for Central American historians. Colonial authorities did not make and maintain records with the diligence, complexity, and skill of the wealthier viceregal centers, where data were none too well recorded either. *Alcaldes mayores* were more interested in amassing wealth than in reporting accurate head counts to the Crown. Each bureaucrat had a different method of reporting; almost all generalized and based their calculations on those of their predecessors. There were diligent officials, but their efforts were frequently mitigated by custom. After 1765, royal legislation was enacted to bring tributary records into the same system as that of Mexico, but the decrees were resisted by colonials. "Modern" bookkeeping practices such as double-entry were introduced but failed because of a lack of training of bureaucrats. In the nineteenth century, the dissolution of Central America into independent states eliminated centralized government supervision of record keeping in most areas at the very moment that internecine warfare combined with natural disasters to destroy much documentation.

The fiscal records of Central America illustrate both the problems and uses of these data.[1] Taxation in Central America is well documented in records in Seville and Guatemala. But bookkeeping practices across the three-hundred-year colonial period varied so greatly that comparison is difficult. Until the 1730s, much royal income and outflow were hidden, collected, and spent before reaching the treasury, and thus not reported. Much time can be consumed unraveling the complicated mazes of seventeenth-century bookkeeping practices before elaborating firm data. Then, in the turbulent era of the Bourbon Reforms, administrative structures and accounting practices were juggled so frequently that the meaning and significance of taxes may often be lost or at best hidden. Finally, there remains the problem of tax evasion. How much taxation did merchants avoid through bribery, fraud, or contraband trade? And what government officials were financed by traders, involved illegally in commerce themselves, or just inefficient or inept? What role did the Church have in trade with its tax-free status?

After the Bourbon Reforms of 1763, fiscal data were reported regularly, but they still do not necessarily constitute an accurate index of economic activity in different regions. Under the system of "tax farms," collection was licensed to individuals or municipalities until 1786; their amounts often remained stable despite fluctuations in the economy. The Guatemalan Cabildo, for example, controlled sales-tax collections from 1728 onward. It, in turn, farmed out the tax. The government treasury assumed direct control of the tax in 1763, but continued the licensing process to the interior until the intendency reforms of 1786. The effect was to guarantee a stable amount of fiscal income. The data, however, do not provide any measure of economic trends.

Troy Floyd, Manuel Rubio Sánchez, and Robert S. Smith pioneered in the use of fiscal and commercial data to research indigo and silver production after 1765.[2] Still, much investigation needs to be done. Fiscal records in the AGI and the AGCA can reveal the intricate relation between the

1. See Miles Wortman, *Government and Society in Central America, 1680–1840* (New York, 1982), "Bourbon Reforms in Central America, 1750–1786," *The Americas,* 32 (1975): 222–38, and "Government Revenue and Economic Trends in Central America, 1787–1819," *Hispanic American Historical Review,* 55 (1975): 251–86.

2. Troy Floyd, "Bourbon Palliatives and the Central American Mining Industry, 1765–1800," *The Americas,* 18 (1961): 103–25, "The Guatemalan Merchants, the Government, and the Provincianos, 1750–1800," *Hispanic American Historical Review* 41 (1965): 90–110, and "The Indigo Merchant: Promoter of Central American Economic Development, 1750–1808," *Business History Review,* 39 (1965): 466–88; Manuel Rubio Sánchez, *Historia del añil o xiquilite en Centro América* (2 vols., San Salvador, 1976); Robert S. Smith, "Indigo Production and Trade in Colonial Guatemala," *Hispanic American Historical Review,* 39 (1959): 181–211.

new fiscal system and the expanding Central American trade. But there are pitfalls to be avoided. In some areas, all tax income was sent to the central treasury, and then bureaucratic salaries were sent back to the collection houses; in other areas, salaries were deducted before remitting monies to the central treasury; still, in other areas, salaries were paid from one fiscal revenue, tobacco for example, whereas elsewhere they were paid from tribute. In Nicaragua, some funds were sent directly to support the military fortress at the Río San Juan; their receipts do not show up on the general account ledgers. Income from tobacco was often, in reality, from ecclesiastical missions that the Crown ordered invested in tobacco production. But it appears as tobacco receipts. Tobacco monies were often sent to the mines for the purchase of silver. The complexities are endless.

The Bourbon chroniclers provided data from many areas of the economy. Documents in Guatemala and Seville show not only the sale of mercury for mining and the payment of the royal fifth, but the names of the miners and merchants involved in these transactions as well. The royal fifth (*quinto*), of course, cannot be calculated as 20 percent of mineral production. Usually it was 10 percent, although the rate varied widely.[3]

The same can be said of the sales tax. After the direct collection of *alcabala* began in 1786, the amount of taxation varied from region to region. However, *guías* (tax receipts) reveal how much was traded legally and by whom.

Shipping registers available in Seville[4] provide an interesting if partial view of the types of commodities exported from and imported into Central America. The size of the trade and the relative value of the goods can be compared easily over the course of the late eighteenth century. Manifests detail the names of merchants involved in Guatemala and in Seville, the origin of goods (i.e., from which province in Salvador indigo shipments were derived), and purchase prices along the trade route.

Another valuable source of data is the ecclesiastical archives. As Christopher Lutz has shown, the Church keeps important information on *parroquial* population, births, and baptisms, as well as interment records.[5] Of particular value are the *visitas* of bishops that have been, until now, kept secreted from the public view. Records of sodalities or confraternities reveal how much local wealth was protected from state taxation, where religion was strongest, and where idolatry was practiced.

3. Floyd, "Bourbon Palliatives"; and see the diverse mining reports in AGI, Audiencia de Guatemala, 234, 236, and 243.

4. Libros de registro in the AGI, Contractación.

5. Christopher Lutz, *Historia sociodemográfica de Santiago de Guatemala, 1541–1773* (Antigua, Guatemala, 1982).

The most important and most underused source of information for colonial history are the *protocolos* (or notary records) existent in the AGCA. Business transactions, wedding contracts, and testaments are all available in these volumes. A diligent researcher could compile almost a two-century time-series of inter- and intracolonial traffic by examining the multivolume notary records.

Second, the notaries certified the sale of any property, be it a farm, townhouse, or slave. Full descriptions were given of the condition and value of each, their encumbrances, and, in many cases, their histories (a sort of title-search). Since most land away from the capital had no value in itself, the buildings and cattle are described with the value of each, as well as are the number of Indians assigned to labor on the farms traditionally. Again the potential is great.

The registration of marriage contracts (with dowries) and testaments in the notary records provide a source of analysis of the movement of families, the wealth of men and of women, as well as the power of each, and, again, the changes in fortunes of different families. How many offspring entered the clergy? Whom did they marry, and which partner brought how much wealth into the family? The relationships between urban families with large rural holdings and those involved solely in trade, and the inter-marriages between these groups as well as with newly arrived men from Mexico, Peru, or Spain are particularly fascinating. Sizes of families, and, in some cases, infant mortality are provided here. The historian can compile this complex information, analyze, and correlate it, create time-series and see, indeed, if generalizations can be reached. Which families rose or declined? Why? How? What was the influence of outsiders? The possibilities are endless.

Finally, the protocolos provide a register for the sale of slaves, to the cities for labor and artisanal work and to the countryside for overseer and fieldwork. Notary records describe the age, sex, and condition of each slave, his or her history and abilities, and, finally, the sale price. The relationship between the number of slaves held, their value, and more general economic trends throughout the colony can be correlated to describe the fluctuations in the fortunes of the slave-holding class.

The protocolos have a few weaknesses. Some volumes and years are missing, and some testaments discuss codicils that exist "elsewhere." Nevertheless, it is possible to create time-series for notable families and for slaves over long periods of time.

The problem of population in Central American history certainly seems, on its face, to be the one that quantification could best address in both the colonial and national periods. Compare, for example, the outstanding works by Christopher Lutz and Murdo MacLeod:[6] Lutz used monastic, church, and government archives to research the population of Santiago de Guatemala throughout its colonial existence. He discerned a continuous growth in this urban center from the sixteenth until the late eighteenth century. MacLeod, on the other hand, used creative research techniques in other Central American urban settlements (León, Salvador, Nuevo Segovia, Granada, and others) and reached dissimilar conclusions. By analyzing testaments, he ascertained a general flight to the countryside from the cities in the seventeenth century. But Lutz says the population of Santiago grew. Does this contradict MacLeod? Not necessarily, for in the colonial epoch the distinction between the countryside and city was vague and record keeping differed from place to place. A member of a church in Guatemala could live on his farm to survive but have his children's births as well as his own death recorded in the city. On the other hand it is quite possible that there existed a difference in life patterns between the smaller *villas* of interior Central America and the bureaucratic and government center in Santiago de Guatemala.

A similar problem occurs in tracing the tendencies of Indian populations in the seventeenth and eighteenth centuries. There are large volumes—some in fragments—in the AGCA that detail from four to eight head counts for the Guatemalan and Salvadoran regions.[7] These are supplemented by tribute lists (quite detailed for the central Guatemalan regions) in the AGI.[8] Some lists detail the heads of households and the numbers of children, but others are vague and list only heads of households. Some suspiciously list the same figures that were reported thirty years earlier. Frequently towns listed, say, in 1680, are missing in 1720. Corruption by government officials either inflated the number of tributaries (to give the official a larger income from the percentage he derived or to win favor with the Crown) or depressed it (the official pocketing the difference). The total income the Crown received from Indian tribute through the entire seventeenth century rose in Central America, doubling and then tripling through the period. This occurred not because of a general rise in population but rather because of the pressure exerted by the Crown upon officials to maintain or increase fiscal income.

Later on, from the mid-eighteenth century onward, the "scientific" Bourbon officials provided more detailed information. The best example

6. Lutz, *Historia sociodemográfica;* Murdo MacLeod, *Spanish Central America: A Socioeconomic History, 1520–1720* (Berkeley, 1973).

7. Diverse documentation is listed under *tributos* in the AGCA catalogue.

8. Tribute lists from the central Guatemalan region are available in AGI, Contaduría, 975–77.

in Central America is Pedro Cortés y Larraz' visita and inspection of the diocese of Guatemala that detailed population and local wealth.[9] It is an impressive work: the original *legajos* in the AGI provide excellent material, but here again difficulties arise. The figures given are frequently rounded off, as if estimates were provided the cleric. In some areas, Cortés y Larraz divides population by race—Indian, mestizo, *ladino*, or creole—in some, by family size in such a specific manner as to tantalize the reader. The definition of ladino is unclear. How many Indians "escaped" their status by putting on Spanish clothing or by migrating to the city? How many "Spaniards" were, in reality, mestizos?

The data from other areas outside the Guatemalan diocese are more inexact. Cortés y Larraz only visited Guatemala and Salvador. Other visitas occurred in these other areas, but they are rough estimates of population, often rounded off.

After the 1770s, population figures become more prevalent, censuses were taken in 1795, 1805, in 1825 to ascertain political representation, and in 1835 in Guatemala for fiscal and voting purposes. Still, these figures are rough estimates. Most are inflated and rounded off. Some Guatemalans copied the original figures provided by Cortés y Larraz. Indeed, the influence of the cleric continued in some areas into the late nineteenth century.[10]

Through the nineteenth and into the twentieth century, the same problems persist. Censuses were compiled in Guatemala in 1880, 1893, 1921, and 1941, but none were well organized or detailed. The first modern censuses were taken in 1950 and again in 1964.[11] These detail population by town, province, sex, age, race, and distribution, and analyze such trends as migration, urbanization, infant mortality, literacy, schooling, language, clothing, and religion. No demographic study can be attempted without first examining these reports. They illustrate, for example, how population grew at a rate of between 1.1 and 1.7 percent, averaging 1.3 percent between 1778 and 1950, and at 3.1 percent between 1950 and

9. Pedro Cortés y Larraz, *Descripción Geográfico-Moral de la Diocesis de Goathemala*, 2 vols., Vols. 20 y 21: Biblioteca 'Goathemala' (Guatemala, 1958); and Santiago Montes, *Etnohistoria de El Salvador: Cofradias, Hermandades y Guachivales*, Vol. 2 (San Salvador, 1977). These two works publish large extracts of the visita. The complete document is in the AGI, Audiencia de Guatemala, 948.

10. See R. L. Woodward, Jr., "Crecimiento de población en Centro América durante la primera mitad del siglo de la independencia nacional: investigación reciente y estimados hasta la fecha," *Mesoamérica*, 1 (1980): 216–31.

11. The 1950 and 1964 censuses are published in multivolume series by the Dirección General de Estadística, Ministerio de Economía in Guatemala.

1964.[12] Between 1950 and 1964 the Indian became a minority for the first time since the conquest. Accompanying these reports are detailed analyses of the economic life of the nation, emphasizing agriculture by illustrating the concentration and types of landholding and the types of agricultural production. In all, these 1950 and 1964 censuses are the most complete statistical collections ever assembled. They show the type of data needed for quantification but which, unfortunately, is absent for most of Central America's history.

Finally, the most important but most complicated research in colonial Central American history remains to be done on prices. What was the effect of the fluctuations in the export trade upon the cost of life—corn for the Indian, wheat for the Spaniard? How did local economies react in the seventeenth century when trade with Europe declined and then in the eighteenth when it boomed? Indigo merchants talk of prosperity in the late eighteenth century, but Cortés y Larraz reports poverty among indigo farmers. Joaquín Pardo gives a cursory report on food prices in Guatemala City in his survey of *cabildo* reports.[13] Floyd provides the price of cattle at Guatemalan fairs.[14] A more careful and specific analysis of victual and land prices over a larger period and area is essential.

But where can the scholar find the information? Some tax *guías* report the prices of commodities. Protocolos provide some information on land prices. The historian must dig. The records of church construction and of military expenditures in the eighteenth century, for example, provide some data on wages, food costs, and the prices of construction material. So too do the figures given in documents concerning the consolidation of church debts in 1803.

The nineteenth century and independence period destroyed centralized

12. The 1964 census lists the reported populations of Guatemala: in 1778—396,149; in 1880—1,224,602; in 1893—1,501,145; in 1921—2,004,900; in 1940 "adjusted"— 2,400,000; in 1950—2,790,868; and in 1964—4,287,997. The genealogical society of Utah (the Church of Jesus Christ of the Latter Day Saints) has microfilmed parish and civil records in Guatemala (6,541 rolls), San Salvador (1,358 rolls), and Costa Rica (697 rolls). Also see T. T. Veblen, "Native Population Decline in Totonicapán, Guatemala," *Association of American Geographers Annals,* 67 (1977): 484–99; L. D. Jones, "Levels of Settlement Alliance Among the San Pedro Maya of Western Belize and Eastern Petén, 1857–1936," in *Anthropology and History in Yucatán,* ed. G. D. Jones, 139–89 (Austin, 1977); R. Wasserstrom, "Population Growth and Economic Development in Chiapas, 1529–1975," *Human Ecology,* 6 (1978): 127–44; L. Gudmundson Kristjanson, *Estratificación socio-racial y económica de Costa Rica, 1700–1850* (San José, Costa Rica, 1978); and H. Pérez-Brignoli's forthcoming study on "Demografía histórica del Valle Central de Costa Rica."

13. Joaquín Pardo, *Efemérides para escribir la historia de la Muy Noble y Muy Leal Ciudad de Santiago de los Caballeros del Reino de Guatemala* (Guatemala, 1944).

14. Floyd, "Guatemalan Merchants."

administration in Central America. Attempts to maintain the high standards of record keeping the Bourbons had established were thwarted by
warfare, the flight of bureaucrats, and the xenophobic reactions of local
families against any national authority (one of the chief issues of the
1827–29 civil war was the refusal by interior regions to report tobacco
receipts to the federation's central offices in Guatemala). The only areas
where records exist are in some church archives.

For the anarchic years of the mid-nineteenth century, most figures on
commerce derive from the reports of foreign consuls or travelers. But
these are unreliable for quantification; most consuls had an interest in attracting the attention of the home country. Information on imports and
exports, foreign investment, agricultural production, and prices can be
discerned from newspapers, the libraries of central banks, and the archives
of the Ministries of Finance. But many figures are guesses; some were
used to impress foreigners, others repeated old figures verbatim.[15]

In the twentieth century, data become more available and reliable. Material available from central banks' libraries can detail, for example, the
flow of investment in Central America, national productivity, and the effects of exports upon national economies. Enormous amounts of information, machine readable at that, are available from the Direcciones Gen-
erales de Estadísticas of the five Central American nations, the Banco
Centroamericano de Integración Económica, the World Bank, the Export-
Import Bank, and the United Nations or United States aid agencies.

In sum, quantification is a useful tool, particularly for Central American
colonial history, where other data may be lacking; it is especially valuable
for raising questions more orthodox historical approaches overlook.[16]

15. Primary documents are available under the country's name in the British Public Rec-
ord Office and in the Archives du Ministre des Affaires Etrangères in Paris. See the travel-
ers' accounts and accompanying documentation of: Jacobo Haefkens, *Viaje a Guatemala y
Centroamérica,* trans. from the Dutch by Theodora J. M. Van Lottum (Guatemala, 1969);
George A. Thompson, *Narrative of an Official Visit to Guatemala* (London, 1829); E. G.
Squier, *Travels in Central America* (2 vols., New York, 1853); Auguste Myionnet Dupuy,
Deux ans de sejour dans l'état de Nicaragua 1850, 1851, 1852 (Paris, 1853); and Pablo
Levy, *Nótas geográficas y económicas sobre la Republica de Nicaragua* (Paris, 1873). Also
see the manual printed by the government for foreigners, *Guía de forasteros de Guatemala
para el año 1853* (Guatemala, 1853).

Excellent secondary studies on nineteenth-century economic history are Ciro F. Cardoso,
"Historia económica del café en Centroamérica: siglo XIX," *Estudios sociales centro-
americanos,* 4 (1975): 9–55; and Thomas Herrick, *Desarrollo económico y político de
Guatemala durante el periodo de Justo Barrios, 1871–1885* (Guatemala, 1974).

16. For further information on quantification in Latin American history, see the works
of Herbert S. Klein, "Structure and Profitability of Royal Finance in the Viceroyalty of the
Rio de la Plata in 1790," *Hispanic American Historical Review,* 53 (1973), 440–69; John

13   Central America
Military History and Guerrilla Warfare
Neill Macaulay

Central America has seen its share of armed conflict. Indigenous forces have defended their turf against incursions by isthmian neighbors, and they have been engaged, on one side or another, in the struggles of great powers—Spain, Britain, and the United States—for hegemony in this strategic region. To date, the military historiography of Central America has dealt more with great power struggles for empire than with local or intraregional warfare. Among the favored topics are the Spanish conquest, corsair and buccaneer raids, fortification and Spanish colonial defense strategy, the Anglo-Spanish wars of the eighteenth century, the postindependence civil wars that destroyed the federal republic, the filibuster wars of the 1850s, the United States military intervention and native resistance in the twentieth century.

While there are a few studies of the military as a social and political institution, these focus on twentieth-century developments. Lacking are institutional studies of the colonial militia and the effects of the late eighteenth-century military expansion on the course of political and social change in the independence and federation periods. Twentieth-century rural insurgency and guerrilla warfare have received fair coverage, and there are a few studies of nineteenth-century antecedents, but little historical research has been done on the sociology or psychology of armed conflict on the isthmus—although social scientists have studied contemporary

---

J. TePaske, "Quantification in Latin American Colonial History," in *The Dimensions of the Past: Materials, Problems and Opportunities for Quantitative Work in History,* ed. Val R. Lorwin and Jacob Price, 431–50 (New Haven, 1972), and "Recent Trends in Quantitative History: Colonial Latin America," *Latin American Research Review,* 10 (1975): 51–62; and the forthcoming works of TePaske and Klein. Also see Peter H. Smith, "Quantification and Latin American History," *Historical Methods Newsletter,* 6(1973); and William P. Mc-Greevey, "Recent Materials and Opportunities for Quantitative Research in Latin American History: Nineteenth and Twentieth Centuries," *Latin American Research Review,* 9 (1974): 73–82. For a good guide to the use of the computer, see Edward Shorter, *The Historian and the Computer: A Practical Guide* (Englewood Cliffs, New Jersey, 1968). David Herlihy's "Computer-Assisted Analysis of the Statistical Documents of Medieval Society" in *Medieval Studies,* ed. James M. Powell, 185–212 (Syracuse, 1976) applies quite well to colonial Central America.

conditions, principally in Guatemala. The nineteenth century's legacy of institutionalized violence has yet to be fully assessed. The proportion of the population directly involved in nineteenth-century military operations and the social and economic consequences of conscription and the requisitioning of supplies are yet to be determined. As time enhances perspective, recent events like the neo-Sandinista guerrilla campaign in Nicaragua, the uprisings in El Salvador, and the "Soccer War" between Honduras and El Salvador will become likely topics for historical investigation.

The major military events in Central America from pre-Columbian times to 1842 receive summary treatment in Pedro Zamora Castellanos, *Vida militar de Centro América* (Guatemala, 1924). The same ground is covered in José N. Rodríguez, *Estudios de historia militar de Centro América*, which extends the survey through the first two decades of the twentieth century. Also, the standard general histories of Central America published in the nineteenth and early twentieth centuries devote much space to military events, as do most histories of the individual republics. A compendium of the campaigns fought by Salvadoran troops is provided by Gregorio Bustamante Maceo, *Historia militar de El Salvador* (San Salvador, 1935). A similar work for Costa Rica is Rafael Obregón Loría, *Conflictos militares y políticos de Costa Rica* (San José, Costa Rica, 1951). For the Guatemalan military since independence, General Zamora Castellanos has contributed an institutional history, *Nuestros cuarteles* (Guatemala, 1932), which concentrates on such matters as recruitment, training, organization, and command structure.

Accounts of the subjugation of the Indians of Central America and Panama by Spanish force and of the internecine combat among the conquerors are found in the early chronicles, in biographies of the conquistadores, and in a few monographs. Pedro de Alvarado tells his own story in *Account of the Conquest of Guatemala* (trans. and ed. S. J. Mackie, New York, 1924). The best biography of Alvarado is Adrián Recinos, *Pedro de Alvarado: conquistador de México y Guatemala* (México, 1952). The military feats of other conquerors are detailed in Pedro Álvarez Rubiano, *Pedrarias Dávila: contribución al estudio de la figura del gran justador, gobernador de Castilla del Oro y Nicaragua* (Madrid, 1944); Rafael Heliodoro Valle, *Cristóbal de Olid: conquistador de México y Honduras* (México, 1952); and Carlos Meléndez, *Hernández de Córdoba: capitán de conquista de Nicaragua* (Managua, 1976), and *Juan Vásquez de Coronado: conquistador y fundador de Costa Rica* (San José, Costa Rica, 1966). Also, for Costa Rica, there are Victoria Urbano, *Juan Vásquez de Coronado y su ética en la conquista de Costa Rica* (Madrid, 1968); and Ricardo Fernández Guardia, *History of the Discovery and Conquest of Costa Rica* (New York, 1913). For Honduras there is Robert S. Chamberlain, *Conquest and Colonization of Honduras, 1502–1550* (Washington, D.C., 1953). For the seventeenth-century campaigns against the Indians of the Petén district, Zamora Castellanos has edited and published the contemporary account of Juan de Villagutierre Soto Mayor, *Historia de la conquista de la provincia de el Itzá* (Guatemala, 1953). Like the Lacandón of the Petén, the Cuna Indians of Darién resisted the Spanish throughout the colonial period. One phase of the Spanish-Cuna struggle is the subject of Manuel Luengo Muñoz, "Génesis de las expediciones militares al Darién en 1785–86," *Anuario de estudios americanos* (Sevilla), 18 (1961): 333–416.

The operations of corsairs, buccaneers, pirates, and other sea-borne interlopers in Central America in the sixteenth and seventeenth centuries are discussed in Pedro Pérez Valenzuela, *Historia de piratas: los aventureros del mar en la América Central* (Guatemala, 1936). The most useful buccaneer accounts are Alexandre Esquemelin, *The Buccaneers of America* (various eds.); Lionel Wafer, *A New Voyage and Description of the Isthmus of America* (Cleveland, 1903); and Raveneau de Lussan, *Raveneau de Lussan, Buccaneer of the Spanish Main and Early French Filibuster in the Pacific: A Translation into English of his Journal of a Voyage into the South Seas in 1684 and the Following Years with the Filibusters* (trans. Marguerite E. Wilbur, Cleveland, 1930). The devastating attack by Francis Drake on Nombre de Diós in 1572 and his dying attempt to take Portobelo in 1596 are described in J. S. Corbett, *Drake and the Tudor Navy,* (2 vols., London, 1898). Henry Morgan's 1671 cross-Panama raid is featured in E. A. Cruikshank, *The Life of Sir Henry Morgan* (London, 1935).

The Spanish response to corsair and buccaneer attacks included abandoning some coastal towns and fortifying others, as shown in Pedro Pérez Valenzuela, *Santo Tomás de Castilla: apuntes para la historia de las colonizaciones en la costa atlántica* (Guatemala, 1955); Carmelo Sáenz de Santa María, "El castillo de Santa María en la entrada del Golfo Dulce," *Anales de la Sociedad de Geografía e Historia* (Guatemala), 39, 104(1956): 24–38; Pedro Zamora Castellanos, "El castillo de San Felipe," *Anales de la Sociedad de Geografía e Historia,* 3 (1926): 281–93; and Mariana Rodríguez del Valle, "El Castillo de San Felipe del Golfo Dulce," *Anuario de estudios americanos,* 17 (1960): 1–103.

The Bourbon accession to the Spanish throne and war with England gave new impetus to fort building in the eighteenth century, as is shown in Sofonías Salvatierra, "Los castillos en el reino de Guatemala," *Anales de la Sociedad de Geografía e Historia,* 14 (1937): 156–68; and Roberto Trigueros Bada and Mariana Rodríguez del Valle, "Defensas estratégicas de la capitanía general de Guatemala," *Revista conservadora del pensa-*

miento centroamericano (Managua), 21, 105(1969): 1–48. The most extensive treatments of the great fortress at Omoa are José A. Calderón Quijano, "El fuerte de San Fernando de Omoa," *Revista de Indias* (Madrid), 3 (1942): 515–48, and 14 (1943): 127–63; and Juan Manuel Zapatero, "Del castillo de San Fernando de Omoa, antigua audiencia de Guatemala," *Revista de Indias,* 13 (1953): 277–306. San Juan river fortifications are discussed at length in Roberto Trigueros Bada, "Las defensas estratégicas del río de San Juan de Nicaragua," *Anuario de estudios americanos,* 2 (1954): 413–513. Eighteenth-century Spanish and British military operation on the Caribbean coast, from Belize to Costa Rica, is described and analyzed in Troy Floyd, *The Anglo-Spanish Struggle for Mosquitia* (Albuquerque, 1967). Captain Edward Vernon's capture and destruction of Portobelo in 1739 are discussed in volume 1 of H. W. Richmond, *The Navy in the War of 1739–48* (3 vols., Cambridge, 1920) and in "Admiral Vernon at Portobelo: 1739," ed. James F. King, *Hispanic American Historical Review,* 23 (1943): 258–82.

While Allan J. Kuethe deals with Panama in *Military Reform and Society in New Granada, 1773–1808* (Gainesville, 1978), little has been written on the social or political implications of the raising of militia units in Central America in the late colonial period. Some light is shed on the organization and training of Spanish colonial forces after 1765 in José A. Calderón Quijano, "El ingeniero Simón Desnaux y su proyecto de academias militares en América," *Revista de Indias,* 6 (1945): 635–50. Insignia, uniforms, and flags of the colonial troops are described and pictured in Raoul Gérard, "Heráldico, banderas y uniformes de la capitanía general de Guatemala en los siglos XVI and XIX," *Anales de la Sociedad de Geografía e Historia,* 24 (1949): 226–42.

Unfortunately, there is no adequate biography of Matías de Gálvez, the captain general who mobilized the newly organized militia in 1779 and deployed them with considerable success against the British enemy. Sketches of Gálvez' career are provided by Carlos Martínez Durán in "La vida y obra de Matías de Gálvez," *Anales de la Sociedad de Geografía e Historia,* 9 (1932): 14–30; and Angeles Rubio Argüelles, "Reflejos de la vida de un malagüeño ilustre, Matías de Gálvez," *Anales de la Sociedad de Geografía e Historia,* 30 (1947): 119–35. Gálvez's northern offensive was halted in 1782 at the Río Tinto by British and Mosquito Indian troops, who began a counteroffensive by capturing and massacring a Spanish garrison; this incident is detailed in José A. Calderón Quijano, "Un incidente militar en los establecimientos ingleses en Río Tinto (Honduras) en 1782," *Anuario de estudios americanos,* 2 (1945): 761–84. In the south, Gálvez' forces lost and recovered Fort Imaculada on the San Juan river; prominent in the fighting on the British side was young Captain Horatio Nelson, whose most distinguished biographers, Robert Southey (*Life of Nelson,* various eds.) and Alfred Thayer Mahan (*Life of Nelson,* various eds.), devote only a few pages to their hero's exploits in Central America.

While there was no war for independence in Central America, revolutionary conspiracies and scattered armed uprisings prepared the way for separation from Spain in 1821, according to Arturo Valdés Oliva in *Centro América alcanzó la libertad al precio de su sangre* (Guatemala, 1965). Also, Spanish shipping and ports on both coasts of the isthmus were attacked by privateers with letters of marque from insurgent governments in South America or Mexico. Héctor Humberto Samayoa Guevara examines some of these operations in "Presencia de Hipólito Bouchard en Centro América," *Antropología e historia de Guatemala,* 19 (1967): 75–83, and in *La presencia de Luis Aury en Centro América* (Guatemala, 1965). The memoirs of one of Aury's officers, Augusto Codazzi, are the basis of Andrés Soriano Lleras, "Episodios de la independencia de Guatemala," *Universidad de San Carlos,* 1 (1970): 113–47.

The voluminous literature on Central America's declaration of independence and subsequent adherence to the Mexican Empire sheds little light on the role of the colonial armed forces in these events, although an indication of the importance of the military establishment is conveyed in Carlos Meléndez and José Villalobos' brief biography of a Costa Rican officer, *Gregorio José Ramírez* (San José, Costa Rica, 1973). The problems faced by the Mexican military expedition in Central America are discussed by its commander in Vicente Filísola, *La cooperación de México en la independencia de Centro América* (2 vols., México, 1911).

Memoirs, apologia, partisan accounts, and a few scholarly studies provide information on military operations in the many-sided civil wars of the federation period. Military matters are treated at length in the memoirs of General Miguel García Granados, *Memorias* (4 vols., Guatemala, 1952), and in most biographies of General Francisco Morazán. Data on the composition of Morazán's forces and their military performance are given in José Tomás Calderón, *El ejército federal de la República de Centro América* (San Salvador, 1922). Adam Szászdi's study of the adventures of a Napoleonic veteran in Central America, *Nicolás Raoul y la república federal de Centro América* (Madrid, 1958), affords valuable insights into the warfare of the federation period.

The rural insurgency that put Rafael Carrera into power in Guatemala and doomed the federation is examined in a number of works, including Pedro Tobar Cruz, *Los montañeses* (Guatemala, 1959); Keith Miceli, "Rafael Carrera: Defender and Promoter of Peasant Interests in Guatemala, 1837–1848," *The Americas,* 31 (1974): 72–95; and Ralph Lee Woodward, Jr., "Social Revolution in Guatemala: The Carrera Revolt," in *Applied*

Enlightenment: Nineteenth Century Liberalism, ed. Margaret Harrison and Robert Wauchope, 43–70 (New Orleans, 1971).

All the Central American republics were involved to varying degrees in the war against the forces of William Walker. The best study of this episode is William O. Scroggs, *Filibusters and Financiers* (New York, 1916). Supplementing but not superseding Scroggs are more recent works, like Rafael Obregón Loría, *La campaña del tránsito, 1856–1857* (San José, Costa Rica, 1956); Ildefonso Palma Martínez, *La guerra nacional: sus antecedentes y subsecuentes tentativas de invasión* (Managua, 1956); Virgilio Rodríguez Beteta, *Transcendencia nacional e internacional de la guerra de Centro América contra Walker y sus filibusteros* (Guatemala, 1960); J. R. Dueñas Van Severen, *La invasión filibustera de Nicaragua y la guerra nacional* (San Salvador, 1962); and Albert Carr, *The World and William Walker* (New York, 1963). Firsthand accounts include William Walker, *The War in Nicaragua* (Mobile, 1860); William V. Wells, *Walker's Expedition to Nicaragua* (New York, 1856); Peter Stout, *Nicaragua: Past, Present and Future* (Philadelphia, 1859); and Charles Doubleday, *Reminiscences of the Filibuster War in Nicaragua* (New York, 1886). Clinton Rollins, *With Walker in Nicaragua* was translated as "Con Walker en Nicaragua," *Revista conservadora del pensamiento centroamericano,* 21, 103(1969): 1–47, with notes by Arturo Ortega; but Alejandro Bolaños Geyer has exposed Rollins as a fictitious invention of Henry Clinton Parkhurst in *El filibustero Clinton Rollins* (Masaya, Nicaragua, 1976).

Economic development in Central America in the late nineteenth century did not curtail isthmian warfare. In fact, two of Central America's most development-minded chiefs of state, Justo Rufino Barrios of Guatemala and José Santos Zelaya of Nicaragua, were among the region's most persistent military adventurers. Barrios' campaigns are covered in Paul Burgess, *Justo Rufino Barrios* (New York, 1926); and in C. D. Rubio, *Biografía del General Justo Rufino Barrios* (Guatemala, 1935). While there is still no comprehensive study of Zelaya, the Nicaraguan general-president's own *La revolución de Nicaragua y los Estados Unidos* (Madrid, 1910) provides some details of his last campaign, particularly in regard to the capture, court-martial, and execution of soldiers of fortune Cannon and Groce. Zelaya's sometime ally, Policarpo Bonilla of Honduras, has a biography: Aro Sanso, *Policarpo Bonilla* (México, 1936). One Honduran general of the Bonilla period was a U.S. citizen and former banana company employee, whose exploits are the subject of Hermann B. Deutsch, *The Incredible Yankee: The Career of Lee Christmas* (London, 1931).

In 1900, during Colombia's Thousand Days War, the province of Panama was invaded by a band of Liberal exiles from a base in Nicaragua. The story of the expedition is told by its leader, Belisario Porras, in *Memorias de las campañas del istmo: 1900* (2d ed., Panamá, 1973); and by one of his lieutenants, Ignacio Quinzada, in "Memorias: apuntamientos para la historia de Panamá, 1868–1922," *Lotería* (Panamá), 10, 114(1965): 69–96. Porras' invaders were supported by guerrilla forces, organized in Panama and led by the Indian Victoriano Lorenzo, the subject of Rubén D. Carles, *Victoriano Lorenzo: el guerrillero de la tierra de los cholos* (2d ed., Panamá, 1966). Documents relating to Lorenzo's guerrilla tactics, and the atrocities his forces were accused of committing, are presented in Horacio Clare, Jr., "Detención provisional de Victoriano Lorenzo," *Lotería,* 11, 130(1966): 69–79. Other works on Lorenzo, who was executed shortly before Panama was declared independent in 1903, include Franklin Raymores, "¿Quién fué Victoriano Lorenzo?" *Lotería,* 13, 150(1968): 82–96; and J. Conte Porras, "Victoriano Lorenzo y la Guerra de las 1000 Días como antesala de la independencia," *Lotería,* 16, 189(1971): 55–68.

For the 1922 border conflict between Panama and Costa Rica, there is J. Conte Porras, "Reflexiones en torno de la guerra de Coto y de las primeras demandas panameñas para reformar el tratado del canal," *Lotería,* 16, 192(1971): 19–34, which blames the United States for provoking the fighting. An eyewitness account of the Coto War is provided by Mercy Morgan de Abrahams, "Reminiscencias de la guerra de Coto: la Cruz Roja chiricana," *Lotería,* 13, 149(1968): 10–37. The 1925 uprising in Panama of the Cuna Indians, instigated by a Yankee adventurer, is discussed in Richard Chardkoff, "The Cuna Revolt," *The Americas,* 22 (1970): 14–21. There is no comprehensive historical study of the United States–trained Panamanian National Guard, which has ruled the country since 1968.

Aside from Panama, the isthmian republic which has been most affected by foreign military intervention is Nicaragua. The United States Marines battled native forces in two Nicaraguan campaigns, in 1912 and in 1927–32. This combat and the marines' "peace-keeping" activities in the intervening years are discussed in Bernard C. Nalty, *The United States Marines in Nicaragua* (Washington, D.C., 1962), a monograph published by U.S. Marine Corps Historical Branch. Other useful publications of the Historical Branch include regimental histories (the Fifth and Eleventh Marines fought in Nicaragua) and bibliographies, e.g., *U.S. Marines in the Dominican Republic, Haiti, & Nicaragua: A Bibliography of Published Works and Magazine Articles* (Washington, D.C., 1958) and *An Annotated Bibliography of the U.S. Marines in Guerrilla Type Actions* (Washington, D.C., 1962). Articles published since 1949 are indexed in the *Air*

University Index to Military Periodicals (Maxwell Air Force Base, Alabama). The best Central American military journal, which regularly publishes historical articles, is Guatemala's *Revista militar.*

Central American sources for the 1912 Nicaraguan conflict are few, but the 1927–32 struggle generated a large body of literature. Guerrilla General Augusto C. Sandino was a prolific letter and manifesto writer, and his writings have been reproduced in works of both friends and foes. The most extensive of these are Anastasio Somoza García, *El verdadero Sandino* (Managua, 1936); Gustavo Alemán Bolaños, *Sandino, el libertador* (México, 1952); and Gregorio Selser, *Sandino, general de hombres libres* (2 vols., Buenos Aires, 1959). These are among the sources of Neill Macaulay, *The Sandino Affair* (Chicago, 1967).

The Nicaraguan military establishment, founded by the U.S. Marines in 1927–32, is the subject of Richard Millett's excellent institutional study, *Guardians of the Dynasty* (Maryknoll, New York, 1977). An earlier work, valuable for its comparative aspect, is Marvin Goldwert, *The Constabulary in the Dominican Republic and Nicaragua: Progeny and Legacy of United States Intervention* (Gainesville, 1962). Central America's most successful guerrilla movement of the 1960s and 1970s, the Frente Sandinista de Liberación Nacional, is analyzed from a radical perspective in a report of the North American Congress on Latin America, *Nicaragua* (New York, 1976). Since the rebel victory in 1979, a number of first-hand accounts have appeared, including J. A. Robleto Siles, *Yo deserté de la Guardia Nacional de Nicaragua* (San José, Costa Rica, 1979), and Anastasio Somoza Debayle, *Nicaragua Betrayed* (as told to Jack Cox, New York, 1980).

A former Sandinista officer who died in the 1932 revolutionary attempt in El Salvador is the subject of Jorge Arias Gómez, *Ezbozo biográfico: Farabundo Martí* (San José, Costa Rica, 1972). That revolutionary movement and its bloody repression by the Salvadoran armed forces are dealt with in Thomas P. Anderson, *Matanza* (Lincoln, 1971). Some military aspects of the 1948 Costa Rican revolution are covered in John Bell, *Crisis in Costa Rica* (Austin, 1971); and Miguel Acuña, *El 48* (San José, Costa Rica, 1975). The 1948 revolution supposedly abolished the Costa Rican army, but since then the country's police have been converted into a new military establishment, according to John Saxe-Fernández, "The Militarization of Costa Rica," *Monthly Review,* 24 (1972): 61–70. An institutional analysis of the Honduran military is provided by Steve C. Ropp, "The Honduran Army in the Socio-Political Evolution of the Honduran State," *The Americas,* 30 (1974): 504–28. There is no similar study of the Salvadoran armed forces, although a number of works deal with Salvadoran military operations in the 1969 "Soccer War" with Honduras.

The most comprehensive of these are Luis Lovo Castelar, *La Guardia Nacional en campaña: relatos y crónicas de Honduras* (San Salvador, 1971); and José Luis González Sibrián, *Las 100 horas: la guerra de legítima defensa de la República de El Salvador* (San Salvador, 1973). Honduran views are found in Marco Virgilio Carías and Daniel Slutzky, *La guerra inútil* (San José, Costa Rica, 1971). The most objective account is Thomas P. Anderson, *The War of the Dispossessed: Honduras and El Salvador* (Lincoln, 1981).

Some research has been done on the Guatemalan military since 1944. The political role of the military is discussed in Jerry L. Weaver, "Las fuerzas armadas guatemaltecas en la política," *Aportes* (Paris), 22 (April 1969): 133–46, and "The Political Elite in a Military-Dominated Regime," *Journal of Developing Areas,* 3 (1969): 373–88. Military group solidarity, education, and attitudes are analyzed in Richard N. Adams, "The Development of the Guatemalan Military," *Studies in Comparative International Development,* 4 (1968–69): 91–109. Of limited value is Augusto Acuña, *La Escuela Politécnica y su próximo centenario* (Guatemala, 1973), a superficial history of the Guatemalan military academy.

The Guatemalan rural insurgency of the 1960s, led by ex–army officers, is the subject of a number of works, including Eduardo Galeano, *Guatemala: Occupied Country* (New York, 1969); Donn Munson, *Zacapa: The Inside Story of Guatemala's Communist Revolution* (Canoga Park, California, 1967); and Adolfo Gilly, "The Guerrilla Movement in Guatemala," *Monthly Review,* 16 (1965): 1–41. Biographical data on the commander of the Cuban-backed guerrilla faction are provided in *Turcios Lima* (La Habana, 1968). The reaction of the United States military to guerrilla threats in Guatemala and other Central American countries is examined in John Saxe-Fernández, "The Central American Defense Council and Pax Americana," in *Latin American Radicalism,* ed. Irving L. Horowitz, Josué de Castro, and John Gerassie (New York, 1969).

With Lyle N. McAlister, *The "Fuero Militar" in New Spain, 1764–1800* (Gainesville, 1957); Christon I. Archer, *The Army in Bourbon Mexico, 1760–1810* (Albuquerque, 1977); and Allan J. Kuethe, *Military Reform and Society in New Granada, 1773–1808* (Gainesville, 1978), Central America is bracketed geographically by studies of the Spanish military reforms of the late eighteenth century. Sources exist, in the Archive of the Indies in Seville and in the Spanish National Archives in Simancas and Segovia, as well as in various Central American depositories, for an investigation of the impact of military reform on the Kingdom of Guatemala. Such a study should indicate whether Central American society was "militarized" like that of late colonial Mexico, or whether the military reforms had minimal effects, as Kuethe perceives to have been the case in most of New Granada. Postindependence developments suggest that the Mexican experience was closer to that of Central America. While a comprehensive study of the evolution of Central American military institutions in the nineteenth century would be difficult at this time, case studies are feasible for those localities where there are generally adequate archival resources.

On the eastern fringes of Central America and Panama, excellent opportunities exist for studies in military-cultural history, on the order of Nelson Reed, *The Caste War of Yucatán* (Stanford, 1967). The military accomplishments of the Sambo-Miskitos of Honduras and Nicaragua and the Cuna Indians of Panama are no less impressive than those of the Yucatecan Maya. Oral tradition and foreign records (e.g., those of the Admiralty and War Office in London) would be among the principal sources for studies of the military organization and operations of the Miskitos and the Cuna.

United States military and diplomatic archives provided essential documentation for Richard Millett, *Guardians of the Dynasty: The Guardia Nacional de Nicaragua* (Maryknoll, New York, 1977). The same depositories offer material for a comparable study of Panama's National Guard. While the armed forces of the other isthmian republics were not established under North American tutelage, all have been closely tied to the U.S. military since World War II. With the declassification of most official U.S. records from the 1940s and 1950s, studies of the transformation of the Central American armed forces under the impact of U.S. military aid and training missions are now possible.

14 The Archivo General de Centro América
Christopher H. Lutz and Stephen Webre

The most important depository of historical records in Central America is the Archivo General de Centro América (AGCA) in Guatemala City. It is also one of the best organized and most thoroughly catalogued documentary collections of its size anywhere. The AGCA shares a large, modern downtown building with the Biblioteca Nacional. Two blocks from the Palacio Nacional, the archive is within easy walking distance from government offices, hotels, *pensiones,* restaurants, bookstores, and other necessary services. It is open from 8:00 A.M. to 4:30 P.M., Monday through Friday.

The principal guide to the resources of the AGCA for the colonial and early national periods is the immense *fichero* (or card catalogue) in the main reading room.[1] The fichero is essentially an alphabetical subject-matter index to the documentation and is the fruit of three decades of selfless application on the part of José Joaquín Pardo, director of the old AGG[2] until his death in 1964. This detailed catalogue is an extremely welcome aid, but the researcher should be aware that Pardo's notions of topical significance and those of today's social and economic historians may not always coincide. It requires not only some familiarity with the fichero but also a fairly agile imagination to determine under precisely which of several possible headings a particular type of document is likely to appear.[3]

One of the most valuable features of the fichero is the extensive *índice onomástico* (or name file). This index cross-references much of the catalogued documentation by the names of individuals. By looking up the name of a particular individual (especially among elites), the researcher can normally expect to find a substantial (although seldom complete) listing of the available documentation (such as *nombramientos, probanzas, residencias, testamentos*) concerning his life and career. Also extremely useful is the detailed indexing of *cédulas* and other royal dispositions to be found in the various drawers labeled "Legislación."

While the fichero is indeed a magnificent tool, a few words of caution seem warranted regarding its use. An individual ficha will often contain a quite detailed and explicit description of its document's contents—so detailed and explicit, in fact, that even highly reputable historians have from time to time succumbed to the temptation to consult only the ficha and not the document itself. Such a practice can have embarrassing results, however, as there are just enough errors in the fichero to make it a dangerous gamble. Further, while the detailed catalogue makes it possible to solicit individual documents (*expedientes*) with some certainty, the researcher is often well advised to call the entire *legajo*.

1. There are no detailed published descriptions of the AGCA or its holdings. The reader may wish to refer to Ernesto Chinchilla Aguilar, "Documentos existentes en el Archivo General de la Nación," *Anales de la Sociedad de Geografía e Historia de Guatemala,* 39 (1966): 443–515, which does little more than describe the contribution of Pardo and explain his classification system, or to the never-completed *Índice de los documentos existentes en el Archivo General del Gobierno* (Guatemala, 1936). The archive itself has published a *boletín* sporadically over the decades. See also Sidney Markman, *Colonial Central America: A Bibliography* (Tempe, Arizona, 1977), 239–318.

2. Prior to 1968, the AGCA was known as the Archivo General del Gobierno (AGG) and is cited as such in many studies.

3. Subject headings can be quite broad (such as "Tributos," "Tierras," or "Ayuntamientos," with more specific subheadings), or they can be quite narrow (such as "Hipódromo del Norte" or "Matanza de Perros").

Pardo's vast cataloguing project encompassed virtually all of the AGCA's colonial materials. Because Guatemala was the administrative, demographic, and economic center of the Spanish Audiencia de Guatemala (a territory comprising the present Mexican state of Chiapas, part of Yucatán at various times, and the republics of Guatemala, El Salvador, Honduras, Nicaragua, and Costa Rica), the archive's colonial holdings are of potential use not only to historians of Guatemala but to specialists interested in other parts of the isthmus as well. It should be emphasized, however, that the bulk of the documentation pertains to the province of Guatemala (which, until quite late in the colonial period, included the territories which constitute the present-day republics of Guatemala and El Salvador), and there is relatively less material from the more remote provinces (see Table 14.1). What is more, while there are many conquest-period items in the AGCA, and extensive runs of certain types of documentation from the sixteenth and seventeenth centuries (such as cédulas, probanzas, *cabildo* books of Santiago de Guatemala, notarial registers, and scattered records of civil and criminal proceedings), the collection's greatest strength is the Bourbon period. The investigator concerned with the earlier centuries will find much of interest in the AGCA, but should anticipate the need to supplement his research in the Archivo General de Indias in Seville.

Among national-period materials (documents with a *B* prefix in Pardo's classification scheme), the early independence era is fully as well catalogued as the colonial period (*A* prefix), but coverage begins to weaken as the nineteenth century progresses. There are virtually no twentieth-century fichas. The inadequacy of the catalogue for the modern period creates the impression that the archive is weak in this area. Quite the contrary is true. While there are more than twelve thousand legajos of

Table 14.1. AGCA Colonial Period Holdings by Province[a]

Province	Legajos
Guatemala	8,328
El Salvador	1,231
Nicaragua	1,054
Honduras	969
Chiapas	699
Costa Rica	97
Yucatán	11

Source: Information supplied by AGCA staff.

[a]According to the formal division of documents, Guatemala and El Salvador are separate in the Pardo classification system, even though they formed a single province until quite late in the Spanish period. It should be noted also that many materials dealing with outlying provinces, such as remittances to the Real Caja in Santiago de Guatemala, are to be found in documents belonging to the province of Guatemala.

colonial-period materials, as opposed to only slightly more than four thousand legajos of catalogued national-period materials, the AGCA also holds nearly forty-five thousand numbered but still uncatalogued legajos of postindependence papers and many, many more that have not even been numbered (see Table 14.2).[4]

The AGCA is a functioning public-records depository and regularly receives consignments of papers from government ministries and their dependencies. These documents are filed according to agency of origin (including defunct entities such as the Ministerio de Fomento), and while there are no public catalogues, the archive staff maintains some guides (for example, detailed indices to criminal records) for its own reference and is generally pleasant and efficient in responding to requests. The prospective researcher should be aware that the records of certain "sensitive" ministries (specifically Guerra and Relaciones Exteriores) are open to scholars only upon special authorization by the government. In addition to papers produced by the organs of central government, some attempt has been made to centralize the inactive records of local jurisdictions. As a result, there are among the AGCA's holdings scattered *bultos* of municipal and departmental materials. Again, there is no public guide to these potentially valuable documents and the researcher will have to inquire and probe.[5]

A valuable complement to the AGCA's manuscript holdings for the national period is the *hemeroteca* (or periodicals) section, located on the building's first floor. While the collection of ephemeral and periodical material (newspapers, gazettes, magazines, bulletins, and *hojas sueltas*) for the nineteenth century is extensive, there are many lacunae, even for official publications. The researcher whose topic deals with Guatemala since 1870, and especially since the 1890s, however, will find generally good runs of most periodicals published in the republic. The hemeroteca's director has undertaken a cataloguing project to index periodical articles according to topic, place-names, and personalities (both as subject and author). While the fichero is far from complete, it is well enough along to

4. Virtually no cataloguing has taken place in the fourteen years since Pardo's death. Only recently has cataloguing of nineteenth-century documents resumed at the archive. In addition, a team of cataloguers from the Universidad de San Carlos de Guatemala was at work in 1978 assembling a fichero for the Liberal period (1885–1920) materials. It was planned that, when complete, this catalogue would be located at the Escuela de Historia on the university's main campus in Zona 12 and open to any researcher who wishes to consult it.

5. The researcher will sometimes find uncatalogued colonial materials (particularly from the eighteenth century) among these papers. The AGCA staff has indices (by *municipo*) for the following departments: Alta Verapaz, Escuintla, Izabal, Jutiapa, El Petén, Quezaltenango, El Quiché, Sacatepéquez, San Marcos, Santa Rosa, Sololá, and Suchitepéquez.

Table 14.2. Uncatalogued Material in the AGCA

Category	Period	Approximate number of shelf-stands of material
Ministerios		
Agricultura y Caminos	20 C.	5
Communicaciones y Obras Públicas	from ca. 1930	3
Economía e Inspección General del Trabajo	20 C.	½
Educación Pública	20 C.	7
Fomento	19 & 20 Cs.	2
Gobernación y Justicia	19 & 20 Cs.	6
Guerra (Defensa)	19 & 20 Cs.	4
Hacienda y Crédito Público	19 & 20 Cs.	½
Público	19 C.	½
Relaciones Exteriores	19 & 20 Cs.	6
Salud Pública (Hospitales)	19 & 20 Cs.	1½
Sanidad Pública	20 C.	2
Tesorería	n.a.	1
Trabajo	20 C.	6
Departamentos y Municipios		
Alta Verapaz (also called "Cobán")	19 & 20 Cs.	4
Baja Verapaz	19 & 20 Cs.	1
Chimaltenango (San Martín Jilotepeque only)	19 & 20 Cs.	½
Chiquimula	19 & 20 Cs.	1
Escuintla and Jutiapa (especially San Francisco de Zapotitlán)	19 & 20 Cs.	14
Guatemala (department)	19 & 20 Cs.	2
Guatemala (municipality)	20 C.	1
Huehuetenango	19 & 20 Cs.	2½
Izabal	20 C.(?)	2
Jalapa	19 & 20 Cs.	1½
Petén, El	from early 19 C.	1
Quiché, El	19 & 20 Cs.	2
Sacatepéquez	19 & 20 Cs.	3½
San Marcos	19 & 20 Cs.	2
Santa Rosa	from late 19 C.	1
Sololá	19 & 20 Cs.	1
Suchitepéquez (Mazatenango and Chicacao only)	20 C.(?)	3
Totonicapán	1823–1950	2
Miscellaneous		
Administración de Rentas	20 C.	1
Banco de Occidente	20 C.	1½
Boletines Oficiales	1831–37	1
Café, Oficina Central del	20 C.(?)	1
Congreso, Poder Legislativo	19 & 20 Cs.	1½
Correos, Dirección General	19 & 20 Cs.	3
Estrada Cabrera, secretaría particular del Presidente Manuel	1890–1917	1
Juicios criminales y civiles (by department and year)	19 & 20 Cs.	50
Pasaportes	19 & 20 Cs.	undetermined
Penitenciaría de Guatemala	19 & 20 Cs.	undetermined
Policía Nacional	1900–46	undetermined
Protocolos notariales	19 & 20 Cs.	18
Registro Cívico o Electoral	from 1947	4
Tarjetas de embarque y desembarque de pasajeros	20 C.	undetermined
Tipografía Nacional	1923–46	½
Turismo	20 C.	4

Source: Unpublished report prepared by María Teresa de la Peña of the Archivo Histórico Nacional, Madrid, under the auspices of UNESCO, ca. 1970.

be of considerable value. Periodicals are also catalogued alphabetically by title and chronologically by date of first appearance. The AGCA possesses a *biblioteca* section as well, but it is poorly catalogued and its holdings limited.

The archive's photocopying service is expensive and of erratic quality. Microfilming facilities are normally restricted to institutional use, although "semiofficial" arrangements can sometimes be made in slack periods. Scholars have in the past been permitted to photograph documents with their own equipment. There are, as a general rule, no restrictions on the copying of materials; one may assume that any manuscript which may be called and consulted may also be copied. A microfilm copy of the entire colonial holdings of the archive has been made for McMaster University. (See p. 160 below.)

The researcher need make no prior arrangements to work in the AGCA, although a letter of introduction and a courtesy visit to the director are considered polite gestures. Inquiries should be addressed to the director, Archivo General de Centro América, 4ª. Avenida entre 7ª y 8ª Calles, Zona 1, Guatemala, Guatemala, C.A.

15   The Biblioteca Nacional and Hemeroteca Nacional of Guatemala
Ralph Lee Woodward, Jr.

Although the Guatemalan Biblioteca Nacional dates from 1880, until recently it contained few books or major collections of primary sources. A small manuscripts division included the correspondence of historian Antonio Batres Juáregui and some additonal, uncatalogued, nineteenth-century items. The Valenzuela Collection also includes important rare books and a large assortment of *hojas sueltas*. Recently, however, this depository has acquired the library of Juan José Arévalo, consisting of more than fifty thousand volumes. These include many works on Guatemala and the other Central American states, but also much from South America and other parts of the world. In addition, the library has a huge collection of uncatalogued, mostly ecclesiastical works dating from the fifteenth to the nineteenth century, which were confiscated from the religious orders expelled during the administration of Justo Rufino Barrios. The National Library is located in the same building as the Archivo General de Centro-América, facing 5ª Avenida between Calles 7ª and 8ª in

Zona 1, on the Central Plaza. It is open from 8:00 A.M. to 4:30 P.M. daily. There is a card file index next to the circulation desk in the main reading room.

Located on the second floor of the Biblioteca Nacional, but an autonomous institution, the Hemeroteca Nacional is the creation of its dedicated director, Rigoberto Bran Azmitia. It contains a fine collection of Guatemalan newspapers and other periodicals of the nineteenth and twentieth centuries, and therefore represents one of the most important historical depositories in the country. Something of Bran Azmitia's dedication and plan for the Hemeroteca may be found in his *Vida y misión de una hemeroteca, panorama del periodismo guatemalteco: 1965* (Guatemala, 1967). The hemeroteca is usually open the same hours as the library, but the researcher should understand that its administration is entirely separate.

16   Guatemalan Ecclesiastical Archives
Hubert J. Miller

The Archivo de la Curia in Guatemala City is a very rich depository, but because of limited accessibility scholars have not been able to utilize the resource adequately.[1] The depository is located in the Palacio Arzobispal, next to the cathedral on the central plaza of the capital. It consists of two small rooms, one of which houses colonial documents, and the other, national-period sources. Another room is available for the researcher to consult documents, which are brought to him by the archivist.

Since research is not permitted in the depository rooms, indices and guides are indispensable to facilitate the search for desired materials. The collection is well organized, and certain sections of the collection contain their own indices. Even where no index is available for a specific section,

1. From 1959 to 1960 the author used the collection under a Smith-Mundt Student Exchange grant. A second opportunity arrived in August of 1977 to revisit the archive. These visits provide the basis for a survey of the contents of the collection and some practical advice to scholars who may be interested in utilizing this depository. Special recognition is in order for Dr. Arnulfo Martínez, Director of the Division of Inter-American Affairs and International Education at Pan American University, who helped obtain a grant from the Committee on International Education of the Border States University Consortium on Latin America. At the same time a word of gratitude belongs to the late Mario Cardinal Casariego and Archivist Augustín Estrada Monroy, whose help greatly facilitated the author's work, as well as to his graduate student, Armando Alonzo, who assisted in surveying the collection.

the material is chronologically filed. For instance, the largest collection containing marriage records covers the period from 1670 to 1977. All the *tomos* are arranged in chronological order, and therefore the researcher can quickly select the needed tomo(s). In the case where sections are indexed, the investigator will find a very convenient system for locating needed documents. An example of an index entry in this area reads as follows: "Doc. #427, August 16, 1871—Copia de un oficio al Presidente Provisorio, acerca de la expulsión de los PP. Jesuítas de país." Unfortunately, not all sections are indexed.

In view of the fact that El Salvador until 1842 belonged to the Diocese of Guatemala, the collection also houses documents from that state. On the other hand it lacks material for the Petén, which was under the ecclesiastical administration of the bishop of Yucatán until 1863. Records are present from that date forward. In 1921 the Diocese of Quezaltenango was formed, and consequently records for this region extend only to that date.

The following résumé will give the reader some idea as to both the size of the depository and the type of documents. The section devoted specifically to colonial topics contains 26 tomos on religious congregations; 44 *legajos* of parish records; Church records treating clerical licenses and dispensations; royal decrees (1539–1821); 63 volumes of *diezmo* records (1675–1810); 4 legajos of *limpiesa de sangre* (1780–1807); census records of 285 pueblos (1803–13); 2 volumes of pontificals (1595); 1 volume of records covering chaplaincies, convents, ecclesiastical courts, slaves, last wills and testaments, correspondence, ecclesiastical statutes, *confradías,* civil government affairs, Church inventories and clerical census data (1620–1821); and several tomos of *actas capitulares,* which currently are closed to the public with the exception of tomos 1 and 5. The actas are the official minutes of the ecclesiastical *cabildo.* The first tomo treats the founding of Antigua and the fifth one, the transfer of the colonial headquarters from Antigua to Guatemala City. In the national section can be found the Larrazábal Collection, which consists of 68 tomos of ecclesiastical and civil edicts from 1808 to 1848. In addition there are 10 tomos of vicar reports from various pueblos from 1844 to 1854. The most interesting and significant records for this period are in the official and private correspondence collection, which is very well indexed and consists of 298 legajos from 1821 to 1913. A third category containing documents relating to both the colonial and national era includes 17 volumes of seminary census data for the years 1600–1807 as well as other seminary records for the period from 1740 to 1853. Other collections are 57 tomos of pastoral visits (1670–1916) and 143 legajos of confirmation records. The largest collection is the 601 legajos of marriage records (1670–1977). In addition there are a few miscellaneous items such as a collection of rare books containing baptismal, marriage, and burial records for the colonial era. A most interesting work is a handwritten biography of an early nineteenth-century nun. The handwriting is a work of art.

There is also a collection of colonial musical compositions. The archivist indicated that this was a recent find and was in the process of being identified and indexed. It will eventually be housed in the music depository section of the Archivo de la Curia.[2]

During the late 1960s the late Mario Cardinal Casariego adopted tighter security measures, including the prohibition against microfilming, photographing, and xeroxing. The announced schedule for work in the depository is as follows: Monday through Saturday from 9:00 A.M. to noon; and Monday through Friday, 3:00 P.M. to 5:00 P.M. The exception is Thursday, when the depository is closed. Because of other commitments, the archivist is not always available during these times without prior appointment, since his position is unsalaried. Furthermore the work schedule is subject to change because of religious and civic holidays, as well as seasonal celebrations such as the Christmas holidays through January 6, the Feast of the Epiphany. It is recommended that a person desiring to utilize the collection first contact the archivist, Augustín Estrada Monroy, at 2ª Calle 7–74, Zona 9, Guatemala. His telephone number is 31–53–80. A letter of introduction to the head of the Archdiocese of Guatemala can help in expediting matters.

Although not part of the Archivo de la Curia, there is a useful but small depository of less than a hundred legajos or volumes known as the Archivo de la Parroquia del Sagrario[3] in the rectory of the cathedral. Permission to use the archive can be sought from Rev. Edgar J. Castro Pineda, who serves as rector of the cathedral and chancellor of the Archdiocese of Guatemala. He can be reached in the chancellor's office in the Palacio Arzobispal on Monday, Tuesday, Wednesday, and Friday from 9:00 A.M. to noon. One must submit a letter of introduction and an explanation of one's project. At the first meeting, an appointment to begin actual work in the archive can be made. Rev. Castro will also prove helpful in explaining the organization of the archive.

The documents in the Archivo de la Parroquia are shelved in large le-

2. The reader who may wish more information on the music collection is advised to consult Robert Stevenson, *Renaissance and Baroque Musical Souruces in the Americas* (Washington, D.C., 1970), 50–64. Unfortunately, the section treating Guatemala is somewhat dated by recent finds. Alfred Lemmon (of the Historic New Orleans Collection) has used the collection recently, and has noted that several items have changed since Stevenson wrote his description. First, the location of the archive has changed, and second, the division of the *archivo musical* into more than one section has occurred. For instance, the sixteenth-century volumes are now kept with the Museo del Arte Religioso, whereas the other volumes are kept with the archivo musical proper.

3. Again, the author is very much indebted to Mr. Lemmon for this section on the Archivo de la Parroquia del Sagrario.

gajos (or bound volumes) according to subject matter and year. Each legajo has a number by which it can be cited. The various classifications consist of *bautismos* (including both *españoles* and *gente ordinario*), *matrimonios, defunciones, entierros, padrones, archcofradía,* and *ynventarios*. The time period covered ranges from the seventeenth to the nineteenth century, and mainly concerns the daily life in the cathedral parish. Obviously some of the information in this collection is a duplication of what can be found in the Archivo de la Curia, such as vital statistics and inventories of cathedral property.

The parish archive can serve a variety of scholars. Genealogists will be interested in the legajos containing bautismos, matrimonios, and defunciones. Demographers may profitably utilize the entierros, since the cause of death is often given in addition to other vital statistics. Particularly valuable in this respect is volume 14, *Libros de entierros de la parroquia rectoral del Sagrario desde el año de 1816 hasta el de 1870.* A word of caution, however, is in order, since the judgment on the cause of death was not always rendered by an expert. Art historians will find the ynventarios, as well as the archcofradía volumes, helpful in shedding light on the artistic treasures of the cathedral. Music historians will discover excellent information in the same volumes to supplement the music holdings of the Archivo Musical de la Catedral and the Museo del Arte Religioso. Especially valuable is tomo 13, *Ynventario de las alajas de Sacristía* (dated September 15, 1704) and tomo 63, which contains archcofradía documents from the second half of the eighteenth century. The versatility of the collection is attested to in the five large archcofradía volumes which span more than two hundred years and illuminate topics such as ceremonial life and the organization's land holdings in Chiquimulilla.

Unfortunately no photocopying services are available in the cathedral parish archive. However, permission for photographs can be obtained.

In summation the Archivo de la Curia is extremely valuable not only for national Church history but also for many other aspects of Guatemalan history. In addition the cathedral parish archive can provide helpful sources for the study of cathedral activities and the people who worshipped there. Scholars utilizing these collections can expect great rewards for their efforts.

17   Other Depositories of Historical Materials in Guatemala

Stephen Webre and Christopher H. Lutz

Except for those depositories described elsewhere in this guide, the documentary resources in Guatemala are little known and little used. Especially important are the substantial but heretofore largely neglected manuscript holdings of parish and municipal archives across the country. Parish archives in Guatemala offer tremendous potential for the study of demographic history, as well as other aspects of local social and economic history, but vary greatly in the quantity of materials and dates covered, as well as the state of conservation—the latter depending upon a variety of factors, including local climatic and seismic conditions, the tenure of priests, and more recent efforts to care for archival materials.[1] A growing number of Guatemalan parish archives are being microfilmed by the Genealogical Society of Utah and are thus being made available to researchers in the United States and elsewhere.[2] Admission to a parish archive often requires a letter from the local bishop.

The father of the AGCA, Joaquín Pardo, sought to preserve Guatemala's municipal archives by accessioning these materials to the national archives. Pardo's plan was largely successful—although, unfortunately, the materials in the AGCA remain uncatalogued—but the researcher still should not overlook municipal depositories, since some towns never responded to Pardo's call for consolidation, and many, especially in predominantly indigenous areas, retained in local hands items considered vital to the protection of ethnic identity and control over lands. Specific examples of useful municipal archives would include Antigua, whose *armario* contains documentation especially rich for nineteenth-century developments

---

1. Comprehensive dates for parish archival holdings throughout Guatemala are given in *Guía de la iglesia en Guatemala* (Guatemala, n.d.). Some of Guatemala's minor ecclesiastical archives are described in Lino Gómez Canedo, *Los archivos de la historia de América: período colonial* (2 vols., México, 1961), Vol. 1, 366–71. A new, more thorough edition of this important guide is presently in preparation. Some systematic surveying of local archives, both parish and municipal, has been carried out over the years in the southeastern departments and along the Salvadoran and Honduran frontiers by a team of researchers under the direction of Professor Lawrence Feldman of the University of Missouri's Museum of Anthropology.

2. See the description of the Utah Genealogical Society microfilm collection, pp. 167–69 below.

in the town and its surrounding valley. Another important highland town, San Martín Jilotepeque, has abundant local resources. Anthropologists and historians continue to "discover" early postconquest *títulos* and other important documents long protected by members of different Mayan communities.

Another major resource as yet largely unappreciated is the depository of land records known as the Registro de Propiedad Inmueble (14 Calle at 9 Avenida, Zona 1, Guatemala City; hours: Monday through Friday, 8:00 A.M. to 4:30 P.M.). Handwritten indices of property owners by department guide the researcher to specific *libro, folio,* and *finca (urbana* or *rústica)* numbers. Since *municipios* are also listed in one column in the departmental indices, it is possible to trace land transactions within smaller jurisdictions as well. The registro in Guatemala City covers only the departments of central and eastern Guatemala. For land records for the departments of Quezaltenango, Suchitepéquez, Retalhuleu, El Quiché, Sololá, Totonicapán, and Huehuetenango, the researcher must consult the Segundo Registro de la Propiedad in the city of Quezaltenango.

Like the Civil Registry, which produced a documentary explosion when it replaced parish registers as the basis of record keeping on vital statistics, the Property Registry is a product of liberal administrative reforms of the late nineteenth century and is thus strongest for that period to the present. Until recently, however, the registro in Guatemala City also maintained a historical section—known officially as the Archivo de la Escribanía del Gobierno y Sección de Tierras—which contained extremely valuable land documentation, dating back in some cases to the very early eighteenth century. These materials have now been incorporated into the AGCA, where they can be consulted in the "Sección de Tierras," whose *paquete* numbers can be identified in the *Indice de los expedientes que hasta la fecha corresponden al Archivo de la Escribanía del Gobierno y Sección de Tierras* (Guatemala, 1944).

The largest collection of notarial registers in Guatemala is in the AGCA, where one will find virtually all the extant colonial *protocolos*[3] and virtually complete holdings for the twentieth century. For the nineteenth century, however, many runs are broken; the missing volumes can often be found in the Archivo de Protocolos de la Corte Suprema, in the new court building located in the Civic Center on 7ª Avenida at the southern end of Zona 1. Twentieth-century holdings of this archive are dupli-

3. Colonial notaries whose registers are preserved in the AGCA are listed along with dates and *legajo* numbers in Jorge Luján Muñoz, *Los escribanos en las Indias occidentales y en particular en el reino de Guatemala* (2d ed., Guatemala, 1977), Apéndice 1.

cated in the AGCA. Notarial documentation for Guatemala for all periods is abundant and almost completely unworked.

The scholar interested in newspaper sources will find the country's two major *hemerotecas* described elsewhere. He should also be aware that Guatemala's most prestigious daily, *El Imparcial,* maintains a "morgue" famous for its completeness and organization. This depository is doubly important when one considers that, just as in other Latin American countries, much fine Guatemalan historical writing has appeared exclusively on the literary page of *El Imparcial.* The "morgue" of *El Imparcial* clips and indexes other newspapers as well.

The location of printed materials, especially secondary sources, in Guatemala can often be more difficult than finding original manuscript materials. There are, however, several specialized libraries of possible interest to the historian. Among the most important are:

Academia de Geografía e Historia, 3ª Avenida 8–35, Zona 1. Formerly known as the Sociedad de Geografía e Historia, this is one of the best and most complete collections in the country, numbering some twenty-five thousand to thirty thousand volumes. The collection of journals is particularly important. Unfortunately, it is not catalogued.

Instituto de Antropología e Historia, Museo de Bellas Artes, Parque Aurora, Zona 13. Tel. 31–0902. This library is partially catalogued and is particularly strong in Guatemalan history and archaeology. The collection received an extremely valuable donation of materials from Mrs. Matilda Geddings Gray in the 1940s; there is a published catalogue of these items.[4] Otherwise, this library is weak in serials and has many gaps, especially among more recent publications.

Instituto Indigenista de Guatemala (Biblioteca de Antropología), 6 Avenida 1–22, Zona 2. Tel. 2–2532. This collection is less useful than those cited above but still merits consultation, especially for topics dealing with indigenous society and culture.

Centro Nacional de Información, Dirección General de Estadística (DGE), Edificio América, 8ª Calle 9–55, Zona 1. Hours: Monday through Friday, 8:00 A.M. to 4:30 P.M. Tel. 8–2587. This small, but extremely valuable collection contains complete holdings of government statistical publications for the past two decades, although holdings appear to be less comprehensive for earlier periods. Here the researcher will find published

4. *A Collection of Books Pertaining to the Archaeology, Ethnology & Anthropology of Mexico, Guatemala and Central America—with Particular Reference to Guatemala: Presented by Matilda Geddings Gray to the Museo Nacional de Antropología de Guatemala* (San Francisco, 1948).

copies of all national censuses from the so-called Second Census (1880–81) to the Eighth (1973), with the exception of the Primera Parte (two volumes) of the Fourth Census (1921).[5] In addition to its own publications, the DGE's library collects statistical publications from other Guatemalan agencies and institutions, as well as from other Latin American countries and regional and international organizations.

Centro de Investigaciones Regionales de Mesoamérica (CIRMA), 5ª Calle Oriente, no. 5, Antigua. Hours: Monday through Friday, 8:00 A.M. to noon, and 2:00 to 6:00 P.M.; Saturdays, 8:00 A.M. to noon. Located in the colonial city of Antigua, this well-catalogued collection is particularly strong for recent publications and current national and international serials in history, anthropology, archaeology, and the social sciences. It also includes material on southern Mexico, Belize, and El Salvador.

In addition to those collections noted above, there are a number of other public and private libraries the researcher may find useful. The library of the Faculty of Humanities of the National University of San Carlos in Zona 12, has a good reputation in letters and philosophy. The best organized library *system* in the country is that operated by the Banco de Guatemala, the most important branch being the one in the bank's main office in the Civic Center in Guatemala City. Also worthwhile for certain highly specialized topics is the collection of rare colonial and early national imprints known as the Museo del Libro Antiguo, located in the old university building in Antigua.[6] Connections made at any of the above-mentioned institutions may direct the researcher to one of Guatemala's fine private libraries, which tend to be highly specialized, reflecting the owners' individual tastes.

Finally, the scholar whose work requires maps should visit the Instituto Geográfico Nacional (Avenida de las Américas 5–79, Zona 13). Particularly valuable is an excellent series of topographical maps available at $1.00 (U.S.) a sheet. Due to changes in local political conditions, maps of different areas of the republic are often restricted.

5. The authors were informed that the missing part of the Fourth Census can be found at the Biblioteca Nacional. The "first" Guatemalan census (1778) is available only in manuscript in the AGCA, A3-Leg. 1749–Exp. 28130.

6. Strongest for ecclesiastical and religious materials. See Manuel Reyes Hernández, comp., *Catálogo del Museo del Libro Antiguo: Impresos guatemaltecos de la época colonial* (Guatemala, 1971).

18   Belize
Theresa Armstead-Fairweather
and Ralph Lee Woodward, Jr.

The National Archives are now established at 22 Santa Maria Street, Belmopan. The building provides an air-conditioned stack area, a repair room, and a work/reading room.

The bulk of the records held by the archives consists of the superintendents', lieutenant governors', and governors' correspondence. These date from the late 1700s to the early twentieth century and are still being indexed. Until this index is completed, users may well have to dig for material they are interested in.

The archives also hold:

Many of the colonial secretary's minute papers, dating from the late nineteenth century to the late 1920s. These have been briefly listed.
Some records of the British settlement on the Mosquito Shore, dated from 1776–89. These have been indexed.
Some papers from the Stann Creek and Toledo district officers. These have been briefly listed.
A stamp collection, incomplete prior to 1974, complete thereafter.
Several Supreme Court records, briefly listed.
Certified copies of ordinances, listed.
A small picture collection.

The archives are open to the public during office hours from Monday through Friday, and the staff will be more than pleased to conduct a preliminary survey of available material on a specific subject for users who find it difficult to reach Belmopan.

The Belize Institute for Social Research and Action (BISRA) at St. John's College has become an important center for Belizean studies. The small but growing BISRA library is becoming a respectable depository for Belizean historical research, both published and unpublished, and recently an ecclesiastical archive has been established. The nucleus of this archive is the Jesuit records of Belize, but other documents are also being acquired. Encouraging serious study of Belizean history, BISRA can offer researchers advice and assistance in pursuing specific projects. St. John's College is located on a modern campus at the northern edge of Belize

119

City. Arrangements should be made in advance for using this collection, for hours are irregular.

The Central Library in Belize is located in the Bliss Institute, on the south side of the mouth of Haulover Creek in the center of Belize City. It is principally a national public library, auditorium, and exposition center, but a small room on the second floor houses the National Collection, the most important public depository of published materials on Belize in the country. It also contains a few unpublished works and a great many mimeographed government reports, although it is by no means a complete collection. The collection's newspaper holdings are especially important, at least for the twentieth century. Catalogues of the collection have periodically been published by the library, the most recent of which is a *Bibliography of Books on Belize in the National Collection* (Belize, 1977). Although this collection is far from being a comprehensive collection of Belizean historical materials, it holds much that will be of use to historical researchers. The room is well lighted and (for Belize, equally important) well ventilated, and the staff is most helpful. It is open daily during normal working hours.

There are a few other public and private libraries in the country, mostly in Belize City, which may contain significant historical materials, but as yet there has been little coordinated effort to identify such materials. Church records are available for some parishes, among which those of St. John's Anglican Cathedral should be the richest. In Belize City and Belmopan some government offices have small libraries and records that may be open to historical researchers, but little survived Hurricane Hattie of 1961. The Supreme Court Law Library may be especially helpful. Anyone doing historical research in Belize will probably find it helpful to contact Richard Buhler at St. John's College. Also essential to the researcher in Belizean history is the *Belize* volume in Clio Press's World Bibliographical Series (Oxford, 1980), compiled by Ralph Lee Woodward, Jr.

19   Honduran Archival Resources[1]
Thomas Schoonover and
Kenneth V. Finney

For the first time, it might be possible to confirm or reject the hunches and guesses that have passed for Honduran history, because of two recent alterations in Honduran archives: the decision of the Archivo Nacional de Honduras to order and classify its large collection of national-period documentation, and the decision of the Ministerio de Relaciones Exteriores to transfer its archives to the Palacio Legislativo. Implementation of these decisions should significantly benefit the serious historian, although in the foreseeable future work in Honduran history will still demand both patience and imagination. While serious problems remain, considerable documentation is available. The Honduran National Archive is less ample than Guatemala's and not nearly so well organized as Costa Rica's, but Honduras is significantly better endowed with historical documentation than either El Salvador or Nicaragua.

The Archivo Nacional is open Mondays through Fridays from 7:30 A.M. to 3:30 P.M., and the staff is very helpful. Photocopy service is available. A researcher should write prior to visiting the archive and bring a copy of a letter of introduction from his or her university or research institute.

The present archives date from 1880, when they were moved with the government from Comayagua to Tegucigalpa. Much documentation was lost, especially in the 1873 civil war and resulting fires. Antonio R. Vallejo assembled the archives in the late nineteenth and early twentieth centuries. His staff bound most of the documents and classified them by an elaborate formula. With the death of Vallejo in 1914, most of this work fell into disarray. The Vallejo *fichero* is no longer useful, since most of the covers have fallen off volumes, titles have disappeared, and volumes are no longer in their original order. Many volumes, in fact, have fallen completely apart and are now just separate pages.

What has evolved since Vallejo is a chronological organization of the documents under the direction of Julio Ponce Valeriano. Generally, holdings for the colonial period and first two decades of independence are well

1. The authors of this essay wish to acknowledge the collaboration of Marcos Carías Zapata, Ralph Lee Woodward, Jr., Julio Ponce, and Mario Argueta in the preparation of this essay. Researchers may also find helpful the Instituto Panamericano de Geografía e Historia guide, *Guía para investigadores de Honduras* (México, 1977).

organized. But only about two-thirds of the colonial documentation, contained in 128 indexed boxes, were included in the UNESCO microfilm project.[2] Ponce is preparing a complete index of the colonial materials for publication by the archive. A team from the University of Texas at Arlington Library has just completed microfilming the colonial documentation and intends to microfilm the independence period as well.[3]

The postindependence documents are arranged by decades and ministries: Hacienda, Gobernación, Relaciones Exteriores, Fomento, Guerra, Militar, Instrucción Pública (Educación Pública), Justicia, and the Congreso (Asamblea) Nacional. In addition there are sections of records for Tesorería, Intendencias, Gobernadores Políticos, Aduana, Gobiernos Municipales, Dirección de Rentas, Universidad Nacional de Honduras, Factoría de Tabacos, Policía Nacional, and Telegramas. Some idea of the relative volume of this material is suggested by the approximate shelf space it occupies:

    1821–29— 26 linear feet
    1830–39—120 linear feet
    1840–49—180 linear feet
    1850–59—186 linear feet
    1860–69—100 linear feet
    1870–79— 93 linear feet
    1880–89— 63 linear feet
    1890–99—166 linear feet
    1900–06—153 linear feet

In addition, there are sixteen *legajos* of telegram copies from the late 1880s and early 1890s and nine bundles of the raw census data forms (filled out) for the 1895 census. An additional valuable holding of the Archivo Nacional, separate from the official section, includes private papers of President Marcos Aurelio Soto (1876–83)—5 linear feet; President Luis Bográn (1883–91)—13 linear feet; and President Policarpo Bonilla (1893–99)—23 linear feet. These collections contain correspondence, copybooks, printed material, and miscellaneous items. Most holdings end in 1903, although a considerable volume of twentieth-century documentation exists in the archive, almost all of which is unsorted.

2. *Documentos microfotografiados por la Unidad Móvil de Microfilm de la UNESCO,* 100 reels (n.p., 1958). See also Instituto Panamericano de Georgrafía e Historia, Comisión de Historia, *Honduras: guía de los documentos microfotografiados por la Unidad Móvil de Microfilm de la UNESCO* (México, 1967).

3. Copies of these microfilms will be available at cost or on interlibrary loan. Contact Dr. John Hudson, Director, Library of the University of Texas at Arlington, Arlington, Texas 76019.

Julio Ponce is also supervising the ordering of a significant collection of late nineteenth- and twentieth-century Honduran newspapers. On the fourth floor of the Archivo Nacional the recently organized and as yet unbound newspapers begin in 1877 and contain six runs for the 1877–1900 period and very extensive holdings of twentieth-century newspapers. Moreover, the collection of bound newspapers is significant. In addition to *La Gaceta,* the official newspaper, which exists in substantial part for the years 1841 to 1883 and is complete for the period from 1883 to the present, the *hemeroteca* on the second floor has important bound holdings of thirteen newspapers published between 1877 and 1900. The bound collection of twentieth-century newspapers is quite full and varied. Also involved in this project is the ordering of journals, *memorias, informes,* and other government publications, numbering about thirty-five thousand items. This collection contains much Honduran and Central American material and dates back to the turn of this century. While the bound material is sorted, the lack of an index and the necessity of shelving the bound material sideways and flat do not permit easy use of the government publication collection.

The Archivo Nacional has also recently begun to survey historical materials in other sections of the country, most notably in Gracias and Olancho.

Another major archive in Honduras, which has now become accessible for research, contains the material previously held in the Ministerio de Relaciones Exteriores. It is now located on the fifth floor of the Palacio Legislativo in Tegucigalpa. To obtain admission one should write to the Ministerio de Relaciones Exteriores and also the Departamento de Estudios Territoriales y Asesoría, 4º piso del Palacio Legislativo, Tegucigalpa (D.C.). This archive is open only by permission, reportedly sometimes difficult to obtain, from 9:30 A.M. to 5:00 P.M., Mondays through Fridays. Photocopying is available in the building. Since Mario Argueta is involved in the labor of classifying and cataloguing this collection, it would be advisable to write him at Collección Hondureña, Sistema Bibliotecario, Universidad Nacional Autónoma de Honduras, Tegucigalpa, in order to inquire regarding the relevant materials for any precise research project. The Relaciones Exteriores archive was moved in the last months of 1977, and the organization and classification have proceeded well. Although there are a few volumes with documents dated before 1890, the Relaciones Exteriores archive has significant holdings only beginning in the 1890s. Containing bound volumes of correspondence, it has series of both diplomatic and consular materials regarding Honduran relations with Europe, the United States, South America, and other Central American countries from the 1890s to 1951. Of special interest are the extensive series of correspondence of the ministry with domestic Honduran political units, as well as the Secretarías de Estado and Ministries of Interior, Hacienda y Crédito Público, Guerra y Marina, Fomento, Obras Públicas, Agricultura, and Instrucción Pública. Total Relaciones Exteriores documentation amounts to about a thousand bound volumes and between seventy-five and eighty-five cubic feet of unbound manuscript materials.

Materials from other archives in or near Tegucigalpa can supplement the generous amount of documentary sources in the Archivo Nacional and the Archivo de Relaciones Exteriores. The Archivo del Juzgado de Tegucigalpa contains documents dating back into the colonial epoch, but permission must be obtained from the Corte Supremo before working there. The Archivo del Consejo del Distrito Central also contains records dating back into the colonial period. The Archivo de la Dirección General de Minas contains registry and other documents concerning mining concessions for the last half of the nineteenth and the twentieth centuries. The holdings of the Archivo del Ministerio de Hacienda y Crédito Público date principally from the 1950s, but some things from earlier times are being gleaned from what was described as a large mass of documents in storage that will soon be burned! This depository also has a complete set of *La Gaceta* and is intending to microfilm it. Although this archive is not well set up to accommodate investigators, it is open to the public during normal working hours. Other public offices in Tegucigalpa that are open to researchers include the Registro de Propiedades, Dirección de Estadística y Censos, and the Instituto Nacional Agrario. All should yield important data. The Archivo del Congreso apparently has available only printed materials from 1900 to the present, but the personnel there claim that they have a considerable body of material in storage, and, after moving to larger quarters, they intend to have their whole collection open to researchers.[4]

Parish archives have record books of births, baptisms, marriages, and deaths, although little has been done to organize such materials. The archive at the Cathedral of Tegucigalpa has an important collection of these records, which is being indexed now by the Instituto Hondureño de Antropología e Historia. The archives of the cathedral in Comayagua, some sixty miles from Tegucigalpa, possess a large body of colonial material, which has unfortunately suffered considerable deterioration from insects and storage conditions. The cathedral archive's nineteenth-century collec-

4. The Archivo Nacional staff, however, were skeptical about the Archivo del Congreso containing nineteenth-century materials, and to date scholars have not yet probed this potential source. Archivists of the city stated that the soccer stadium has several large rooms full of documents from the Ministerio de Educación Pública, but this possibility remains unconfirmed.

tion is extensive and in much better physical condition. Julio Ponce has a descriptive list of the *bultos,* legajos, and *libros* in the Comayagua cathedral archives, which should be consulted before undertaking a trip to Comayagua. This list will inform the researcher of what is available; but physically locating the desired documents is still difficult, since the archive is not catalogued. While in principle the cathedral archives are open, it has in fact been difficult for scholars to obtain permission to consult them. The most advisable procedure would be very early in a researcher's project to write to the archbishop at the cathedral in Tegucigalpa, describing the research project and the kinds of materials he or she would like to consult.

There are five public research libraries in Honduras containing important historical materials. The library of the Archivo Nacional and the Biblioteca Nacional are both useful; they are in the same building complex as the Archivo, but independently operated. The third research library in Tegucigalpa is that of the Banco Central, which also has archival holdings. The library of the Universidad Nacional Autónoma de Honduras has recently initiated a Colección Hondureña. It is now a significant research library for Honduran history, but suffers the disadvantage of a location far from the archival centers in downtown Tegucigalpa. Worthy of mention is the card index for periodical literature in this library. Running to an estimated 12,500 entries, this fichero is a convenient guide to Honduran periodical literature, catalogued by author, title, and subject. Finally, there is the new library of the Instituto Hondureño de Antropología e Historia. Located just below the Casa Lozano, which houses the National Museum, the IHAH is rapidly developing a good collection. This institution is also most cooperative in helping foreign scholars find lodging and make useful contacts for their research. The emergence of these collections renders most of Honduran history from the colonial era until the World War II era subject to monographic examination.

20   Local Archives in Danlí and Yuscarán
Marcos Carías Zapata

History majors at the Universidad Nacional Autónoma de Honduras take a seminar on Honduran history in which, under the direction of a professor, they undertake research in archives situated outside Tegucigalpa. The object of the seminar is to achieve a more intimate understanding of the country, considering its history from a broader perspective than that obtained in the capital alone. At the same time, this has required evaluation of the condition of several documentary sources and cooperation in preserving them with institutions such as the Archivo Nacional and the Instituto Hondureño de Antropología e Historia. Two of these seminars have been conducted in Danlí in 1978 and in Yuscarán in 1979.

In both Danlí and Yuscarán the most extensive and important documentary collections have been found in the respective municipalities. The municipal archives of Danlí are classified chronologically, a task which was carried out on the initiative of a local amateur historian. The archive at Yuscarán was completely abandoned in a damp storeroom. Now it has been provided with a better location, and the documents have been classified in packages comprising thirty-year periods. The Instituto Hondureño de Antropología e Historia has begun a very detailed classification, building an index that covers from the end of the eighteenth century to 1870. Documentation prior to 1876 is fragmentary, but after 1876 it improves considerably both in volume and in organization of the data. The documents contain correspondence between local authorities and the central government and between the various agencies of local authority, dispositions of the municipal government, participation in local activities of different social groups, and since 1876 much demographic and economic statistical information. There is also material on education. The experimental studies carried on by the university have been oriented toward the social composition of these localities at the beginning of the present century.

Since Yuscarán is a department capital, it was hoped that there would be good documentary sources in the Gobernación Política. That archive was organized in a manner similar to the municipal archive, but successive fires and lack of care have left fewer records than at the municipality.

Parish archives have preserved their books in good condition. These include registers of births, baptisms, etc., although not in very great quantity.

The judicial archives in Danlí and Yuscarán remain disorganized and in a high degree of deterioration; they contain documents such as wills, land records, and juridical litigation.

21　El Salvador
Italo López Vallecillos,
Ralph Lee Woodward, Jr.,[1]
and Thomas Schoonover

Historical materials in El Salvador have been less well preserved than in most other Central American states. There are, nevertheless, several important depositories, and there have been some important recent efforts to improve the care and cataloguing of historical records. The most serious losses occurred as a result of the earthquake and accompanying fires in 1889, in which most of the Salvadoran government's records, as well as the Archivo General de la Federación Centroamericana (1821–40) and the Archivo de los Protocolos were destroyed.

Various ministry archives developed during the subsequent years, but not until 1948 was the Archivo General de la Nación reestablished, located in the new National Palace in downtown San Salvador. Understandably, this depository holds only a very few colonial and nineteenth-century records before 1889, but its holdings for the twentieth century are much stronger, if not completely organized. In addition, some microfilmed material has been acquired from earlier periods.[2] The National Archive also has a small library and some runs of newspapers, principally from the twentieth century. The materials in this archive, although sparse, are reasonably well organized and easily accessible. The personnel are courteous and helpful, but no photocopying machines are available. Records from the ministries are deposited in the archive within thirty years of their dates, but are not necessarily immediately open to the public. All documents are open to the public after seventy-five years, in accordance with the standards of the International Council of Archives, to which El Salvador is a signatory.

Ministry archives may yield additional materials upon consultation with specific ministries, most notably the Foreign Ministry, which also maintains an excellent library on international relations and diplomacy. Photo-

---

1. This essay was written by Professor Woodward, based on his own research experience in El Salvador, but greatly assisted by a questionnaire survey of archives and libraries in El Salvador conducted by Professor López and by Professor Schoonover's "Primary Research Materials in El Salvador on the 19th-Century," *The Americas,* 31 (January 1975): 360–62.

2. A UNESCO project microfilmed most of the AGN in the late 1950s.

127

copying is available at the Foreign Ministry, located on the road to Santa Tecla at Km. 6.

The library and archives of the Asamblea Legislativa, located in the Centro de Gobierno, contains records of El Salvador's legislative bodies, including committee papers, which are organized alphabetically by year. It is a major collection for the legislative history of the country, with published and manuscript records dating back to its foundation in 1875. This depository also publishes the *Recopilación de Leyes* for El Salvador every five years. Photocopying service is available.

Founded in 1870, the Biblioteca Nacional of El Salvador is a major source of printed materials for the late nineteenth and twentieth centuries. The library holds, either in original or microfilm copies, a large collection of newspapers from 1847 to the present, although there are few if any complete runs. Although by law all works published in El Salvador are to be deposited in the National Library, in practice this has often been ignored. Nevertheless, this is the most important single library in El Salvador and is especially useful for the publications of government ministries and other agencies. The library is located near the center of the city on Calle Delgado and 8ª Avenida Norte. Well-organized libraries in the Banco Hipotecario and the Banco Central are valuable supplements to the holdings of the Biblioteca Nacional.

Another major collection, principally of printed materials, is found at the Biblioteca Especializada del Museo Nacional David J. Guzmán, located in the western part of the city, near the Foreign Ministry, at Avenida La Revolución, Calle San Benite, in front of the Feria Internacional. Organized in 1883, this library has collected a large volume of Salvadoran and other Central American newspapers, periodicals, and books, especially on archaeology, history, linguistics, and anthropology. It has few long runs of newspapers, but does have a large volume of assorted printed materials, including several volumes of broadsides and political ephemera, more or less well catalogued. The library is divided into three sections: the Biblioteca, containing about three thousand volumes; the Hemeroteca, with about five hundred periodical titles; and Periódicos, containing about seven hundred volumes of newspapers, separate from the Hemeroteca principally for reasons of space. The collection includes a fairly large number of colonial publications, as well as some manuscripts, most notably the private correspondence of Gerardo Barrios (1860–63). There is also a significant collection of maps, pamphlets, and illustrations. The collection of illustrations, principally relating to archaeology, also includes 350 photographs of "illustrious personages of El Salvador." Publications of this library of interest to historians include the *Boletín Bibliográfico Trimestal, Anales del Museo Nacional David J. Guzmán, La Cofradía,* and the *Compilación Trimestral de Indices de Publicaciones*

Periódicas. The library is open to the public Monday through Friday from 8:00 A.M. to 12:20 P.M. and from 1:00 P.M. to 4:00 P.M.; photocopy service is available.

The universities of El Salvador do not have especially impressive libraries by North American or European standards, yet they can be useful for historical study. The Biblioteca Central Universitaria of the Universidad de El Salvador dates from 1887, when it was separated from the Biblioteca Nacional. It contains important collections of nineteenth- and twentieth-century printed materials, including the very fine Edwin Shook Collection of Archaeology and History. In addition, there are near complete runs of *La Gaceta, El Constitucional,* and the *Diario Oficial.* Photocopy service is available in this library. The Dr. Luis Edmundo Vásquez Library of the university's School of Medicine may be of some interest to students of the history of medicine in El Salvador. Organized in 1920, this library includes a collection of French medical texts dating from 1770, as well as other medical volumes and periodicals. A photocopy machine is available. The library of the Universidad Centroamericana José Simeón Cañas, located on its modern campus on the southwestern outskirts of San Salvador, dates only from 1965 and thus is limited in its holdings. It does, however, contain basic reference works in Salvadoran history, as well as a good collection of newspapers published from 1847 to the present and a collection of doctoral dissertations. Working conditions are pleasant, in a well-lighted building, with photocopying facilities.

An important private collection of Salvadoran books and manuscripts is the Biblioteca Dr. Manuel Gallardo, located on Avenida Manuel Gallardo 1–6, in Santa Tecla. Organized in 1930 by Dr. Miguel Angel Gallardo, this is a well-organized library, which is open to scholars. It includes a great many personal papers, not only of Salvadorans, but also of Guatemalans. Most of these papers date from the nineteenth century, although some of the collections include a few colonial items. A photocopy machine is available, and there are also microfilm readers for microfilmed collections. The collection includes good runs of *La Gaceta, Diario Oficial, La Prensa Gráfica,* and *El Diario de Hoy,* as well as the publications of the Ministry of Education.

Another small but important archive in San Salvador is the Archivo Eclesiástico, located in the archbishop's palace. It contains manuscript and published materials, including correspondence between bishops and the churches, reports by the bishops of visits through the parishes, records of the Cathedral of San Salvador, correspondence between bishops and the government, reports on construction of churches, and other ecclesiastical records. In addition, this archive has a good collection of Salvadoran periodicals, both Catholic and government.

Another rich source of uncatalogued documentation is in the parish and municipal archives of Sonsonate, Izalco, Nahuizalco, Santa Ana, Dulce Nombre de María, San Miguel, San Vicente, and perhaps elsewhere. Records of births, baptisms, marriages, and deaths were maintained in the churches from 1540 to 1872. In addition, these archives probably contain a wealth of other information on their individual localities. Municipal records have hardly been noticed in El Salvador, and there is a need for a survey of what is available. Other important sources for Salvadoran history are the property registers established in the seat of each department, as well as the civil registries for births, marriages, and deaths recorded there since 1872. The Registro Civil for San Salvador is maintained in good order and has photocopy service.

This brief survey highlights only the most obvious sources available for Salvadoran history. A thorough survey of manuscript materials remains to be done. At the same time, the paucity of Salvadoran materials need not discourage the potential historian, for it should be remembered that the Archivo General de Indias and the Archivo General de Centro América contain much Salvadoran material for the colonial and early-independence periods, and that printed materials, notably government newspapers of the nineteenth century, not only for El Salvador but also for the other Central American states as well as diplomatic correspondence, contain much still largely untapped data on El Salvador before the twentieth century.

22   Nicaragua
Charles L. Stansifer

In Nicaragua the student of history faces formidable obstacles. There are few libraries or archival depositories of any kind, and those that exist are poorly equipped and poorly organized. Natural disasters have taken a heavy toll of Nicaraguan historical materials. Earthquakes and fires have destroyed many records and books, and neglect and lack of funds have made it difficult to make what is left accessible. As an indication of the difficulties awaiting the researcher, there is not a single depository in the country with a complete collection of the *Gaceta Oficial*. In Nicaragua it is difficult to determine what laws were passed, let alone the political rivalries and hidden motivations behind the scenes. Still, with care in the selection of topic and perseverance in the search for sources, research on Nicaraguan topics can be realized.

The Archivo General del Gobierno, established by presidential decree in 1863, remained a dependency of various ministries until 1896, when

President José Santos Zelaya established it as a separate entity, the Archivo Nacional. One of the great Nicaraguan historians, Jose Dolores Gámez, who was a member of Zelaya's cabinet, was a prime mover in this effort to preserve for students the record of the country's past. Unfortunately, the disastrous civil wars of the twentieth century, combined with the earthquake and fire of 1931, left the country virtually without an archive. Besides the newspaper collection, all that remained in the archive were seventy packages of correspondence from departmental *jefes políticos* to various ministries. It is evident, however, that many of the documents survived, as some material from the National Archive later turned up for sale. Beginning in the 1940s, some effort was given to the preservation of documents and newspapers, but not until 1959 was a comprehensive archival law passed and a systematic effort begun to reorganize the archives. After 1959 the Nicaraguan government put considerable resources into the microfilming of the records of other countries which pertained to Nicaragua. This last effort was brought to a halt by the devastating earthquake of December 1972, which left archival work rather low on the list of national priorities. Following the Sandinista revolution of 1979, the archive was reorganized as the Archivo General de la Nación under the Ministry of Culture.

The national archive has a modest collection of nineteenth- and twentieth-century periodicals. Even the most recent ones are so deteriorated that each use could easily be the last. Fortunately, all newspapers up to 1940 have been microfilmed. Collections of the *Gaceta Oficial* (240 volumes) and of the *memorias* of the various ministries are incomplete.

As for correspondence and official records of the ministries, few documents exist. What is available has to do primarily with public education and *gobernación,* the two ministries which have been most responsive to the law requiring them to deposit their records in the archive. For lack of space few of the ministries have handed over documents more recent than 1940. This was disastrous because, although the quarters of the national archive suffered little damage from the earthquake of 1972, practically all of the ministries were destroyed. It can be said that virtually no Nicaraguan documentation after 1940 is located in the archive. The microfilm of foreign materials dating from 1500 to 1900 on Nicaragua is preserved.

There are no recent guides or indices to the holdings of the archive. In 1977 the archive did publish a reprint of an index to the Land Section of the archive, which was originally published in 1904. It is not clear, however, if any of the documents referred to still exist.

In one respect the earthquake of 1972 was a blessing. After the disaster, money was obtained for the construction of a new National Cultural Center, including new quarters for the national archive. In the tiny alcove atop the National Palace, the archive had no room to expand and almost no place to work. As of June 1977, the national archive occupied its new site in the National Cultural Center, which is located in Colonia Dambach opposite Candelaria Park. Although space is still very limited and budgetary support weak, the archive is well maintained, and an attitude of service has been established. The archive is open to the public Monday through Friday, 8:00 A.M. to 4:00 P.M., and Saturday mornings. The new director, historian Jorge Eduardo Arellano, has begun publication of a *Boletín del Archivo General de la Nación.*

Fire destroyed the old National Library and all but seventy-six hundred of its books in December 1972. Perhaps the most severe loss was the main part of the Rubén Darío Collection, which contained many first editions and also some of the books Darío consulted in the 1880s when he worked in the library. The remainder of the Darío Collection was put on exhibition, with accompanying catalogue, in February 1978. With practically no acquisitions budget, the library has made little recovery since the disaster. Scattered copies of the *Gaceta Oficial,* of newspapers, and of government memorias exist, but essentially the National Library is a small collection of gifts from foreign governments. Some 690 books by Nicaraguan authors were saved from the fire.

The most ambitious effort in the country to preserve and collect Nicaraguan materials is undoubtedly the Instituto Histórico Centroamericano, located on the campus of the Universidad Centroamericana on the outskirts of Managua. The building housing the collection was severely damaged by the earthquake of 1972, but few books or documents were lost. Now the collection is housed in a building alongside the modest university library. Of the twenty thousand volumes in the book collection, perhaps one-half pertain to Central America and a sixth to Nicaragua. The periodical collection is separate and probably contains another ten thousand items, divided into official periodicals (including memorias) and unofficial periodicals. Father Alvaro Argüello, the founder and director of the institute, believes that the collection of memorias is the most complete in the country, but only a few of these date to the nineteenth century. The earliest memoria of foreign relations, that of 1850, is in the collection. The institute's collection of the *Gaceta Oficial,* plus most of the periodical runs, are well bound and in good condition. Many of the Central American books in the book section are also well bound. The institute has some scattered correspondence of governmental officials in the nineteenth and twentieth centuries.

No guides or catalogues to the collection of the Instituto Histórico Centroamericano are available. Since the destruction of the building in the earthquake of 1972, the staff has had to give highest priority to boxing and preserving the material. All the bound items are now reshelved. They are arranged according to country and not by any library system. Cataloguing and rearranging of the collection were scheduled to begin in 1978.

For the past twelve years the library of the Banco Central has made a substantial effort, far beyond the expected, to collect Nicaraguan materials relating to the country's economy and natural resources. The library aims to collect Nicaraguan imprints and all books and dissertations relating to Nicaragua that have been completed outside the country. Memorias dating to the nineteenth century are available, although widely scattered, plus recent official reports and studies of government agencies and private and professional organizations.

The bank's high-rise building in downtown Managua had to be abandoned after the earthquake of 1972. Offices are scattered throughout the outskirts of the city. The library is housed in temporary quarters along with other bank offices near the Lotería Popular in the Plaza de Compra area on the road from Managua to Masaya. Another service of the Central Bank Library is the publication of the *Boletín Nicaragüense de bibliografía y documentación* and the *Boletín bibliográfico*. The former contains bibliographical studies and articles on Nicaraguan political and literary figures and occasionally describes primary sources on Nicaragua in other countries. The latter lists the library's acquisitions.

Through its publication program the Banco de América has done much to distribute information about Nicaragua and Central America. The recent purchase of the Alejandro Bolaños Geyer Collection of nineteenth-century Nicaraguan materials, centering primarily on the William Walker era, makes this library an important stop for the investigator. The Banco de América is easy to locate; it is an eighteen-story, gleaming white tower in the heart of what once was downtown Managua.

Although few other possibilities for historical research in Nicaragua exist, some comments may be made to guide the determined student. Libraries and archives at the municipal building in León, at the Universidad Nacional Autónoma de Nicaragua, and at the *curia metropolitana* may be consulted. The latter contains many of the scarce Nicaraguan colonial documents. No survey has been made of church archives in Nicaraguan cities, but they do exist. Some private collections can supplement what is available in the public depositories mentioned above. It might also be pointed out that the *Revista conservadora del pensamiento centroamericano,* a remarkable journal for any country let alone one so poor in resources as Nicaragua, contains a mine of material for the student in Nicaraguan history. At present, it contains reprints of hundreds of out-of-print books, articles, pamphlets, handbills, and newspapers. As for newspapers, anyone interested in early nineteenth-century Nicaraguan history would do well to consult the *Catálogo de la exposición: Treinta años de periodismo en Nicaragua, 1830–1860,* published in 1971 by the Instituto Histórico Centroamericano. In addition to discussing the background of each newspaper, the compilers list the locations of copies.

23   Costa Rica
Richard V. Salisbury
and Charles L. Stansifer

Founded in 1881 by León Hernández, the Archivos Nacionales serve as a depository for the various ministries of the Costa Rican government.[1] The archival holdings for the Ministries of Gobernación, Fomento, Hacienda, Educación, Guerra-Marina, and Relaciones Exteriores are extensive. A well-organized set of *ficheros* greatly facilitates investigations in areas represented by these ministries. Other ministries such as Justicia, Salud, Trabajo, Cultura, and Ganadería are also represented. The holdings of these ministries, however, are termed incomplete by personnel of the archives. In addition to these ministries, various autonomous agencies such as Seguridad Social and the Instituto Costarricense de Electricidad also send documentation to the National Archives. Although the ministries and other agencies of the government are supposed to transfer their documents to the archives after a thirty-year period, this rule is infrequently observed. In many instances documents are sent to the archives well before the expiration of the thirty-year limit, and in other instances it is clear that documents over thirty years old are not transferred at all.

The archives are divided into four sections: Administrative, Legislative, Juridical, and Historical. Lawyers, legislators, and government officials use the first three sections for data on specific cases. Of major interest to historians is the Historical Section, which is divided into the following subsections: Colonial Era, Municipal Archives (up to 1850), Map Archives, the National Campaign of 1856–57, Autographed Letters, and Foreign Relations.

The Foreign Relations Subsection includes boxes of diplomatic docu-

---

1. Arthur E. Gropp, *Guide to Libraries and Archives in Central America and the West Indies, Panama, Bermuda, and British Guiana* (New Orleans, 1941), 29, contains the most extensive discussion of Costa Rican archives and resource depositories in English up to now. See also *El Archivo Nacional: Su creación, legislación y organismos internacionales* (San José, Costa Rica, 1975); *Indice de los protocolos de Cartago* (6 vols., San José, Costa Rica, 1909–30); and Ligia María Estrada Molina, *La investigación histórica y los Archivos Nacionales* (San José, Costa Rica, 1964).

ments, which date from the early years of the national period to 1955. The boxes contain folders bearing the following designations: Foreign Legations, Foreign Governments, Foreign Consuls, Costa Rican Legations, Costa Rican Consuls, International Conferences, Special Missions, and other miscellaneous categories. Material in the folders includes diplomatic and consular correspondence, press clippings, government publications, and abundant miscellaneous material. Because Costa Rica relied infrequently on permanent legations, even in Central America, the Special Missions box assumes importance for relatively mundane matters. The Foreign Relations Subsection also contains the following special collections: Limits with Panama (52 boxes), the League of Nations (22 boxes), the Central American Court of International Justice (8 boxes), and the Manuel María de Peralta Collection (55 boxes). The Peralta Collection contains correspondence, press clippings, and various government publications gathered by Peralta while he served as Costa Rica's representative in Europe from 1886 to 1929. The Costa Rican mission in Europe was accredited to France (where Peralta spent most of his time), Belgium, Spain, Germany, Switzerland, and the Holy See. Documentation on Costa Rica's border dispute with Colombia is included as well as Peralta's files as the head of the Costa Rican consulate in Paris.

It is good to point out that the Foreign Relations Subsection contains much material on Central American international relations. In view of the weakness of the documentary collections in other isthmian states, the Costa Rican materials must be considered of importance to students of the other Central American republics. Reports of Costa Rican diplomats and agents not only shed light on international isthmian relations but on internal matters as well. Material on the Independence period and on the Guerra Nacional is extensive, reasonably well indexed, and relatively untouched by serious investigators of social and economic history.

Much documentary material from the archives has been reproduced in the *Revista de los Archivos Nacionales*. One of Costa Rica's leading historians, Ricardo Fernández Guardia, founded the *Revista* in 1936 while he was director of the National Archives. Continued under the able direction of Jorge Volio and José Luis Coto Conde, the *Revista,* which is readily accessible in many libraries in the United States, is a useful guide to the materials in the archives. Unfortunately, only four single issues have appeared since 1964.

The Costa Rican Foreign Ministry maintains both an archive and a library in the Casa Amarilla, the building originally constructed for the use of the Central American Court of International Justice. A lengthy and extensive reorganization process, not to speak of sensitivity to research on controversial topics, renders the archive difficult of access, but it undoubtedly contains much valuable material for the post-1955 period.

The Costa Rican Biblioteca Nacional, the largest library in the country, has an excellent collection of Costa Rican secondary works, journals, and newspapers. Completed in 1972, the National Library affords the researcher adequate space and facilities and ready access to probably the largest collection of secondary materials on Costa Rica in existence. The card catalogues are divided into sections that relate to secondary books on non–Costa Rican subjects and on Costa Rica (divided into author and subject categories) and a section that relates to material found in *La Gaceta Oficial,* various Costa Rican newspapers, and journals. The file of Adolfo Blen, which is maintained in the National Library, contains a massive bibliography of pamphlets, periodicals, books, and even newspaper articles on Costa Rica for the 1830–1912 period.

The most valuable collection in the National Library is the newspaper collection. It contains complete runs of the most important San José newspapers and an assortment of provincial and short-lived topical periodicals. This unique collection is deteriorating under increasingly heavy use but is yet to be microfilmed.

Due to the efforts of a number of pioneer scientists in the late nineteenth century, an excellent library on tropical science and agriculture was established in the Museo Nacional. It includes ethnographical and archaeological publications. Henri Pittier, a Swiss geographer who lived in Costa Rica for approximately fifteen years and who was primarily responsible for the founding of the Instituto Físico Geográfico in 1888, and Anastasio Alfaro, for many years director of the National Museum, were instrumental in building this collection. Pittier's and Alfaro's correspondence, as well as that of collaborating Costa Rican and foreign scientists, form the nucleus of an excellent collection of primary material, useful for the study of the scientific and economic development of Costa Rica, particularly during the years of the museum's greatest activity (1880–1914).

Occupying a new building since 1969, the Library of the University of Costa Rica is easily the finest university library in Central America. It is located in the heart of the university's campus in San Pedro de Montes de Oca, a suburb of San José. This rapidly building collection of Costa Rican secondary materials and Costa Rican imprints is particularly strong in government *memorias,* presidential messages, and published official documents, but it is also growing in books and periodicals privately published in Costa Rica. Publications of the Department of Publications and the university press are also to be found in the university library. In addition to the central library, individual schools and facilities of the university also have libraries. The *Tesis de grado* series, published annually by the University of Costa Rica, lists the numerous theses in history and other fields.

Two special collections of the university's Institute of Central American Studies deserve special mention. These are the extensive clippings and other data on Costa Rican municipalities and the Franco Cerutti Collection. The municipal collection has been assembled in cooperation with the Instituto de Fomento y Asesoría Municipal for the purpose of writing the histories of Costa Rican towns and cities. The Cerutti Collection is an extraordinarily diverse collection of Central Americana, particularly of the nineteenth century. Although its strength is in the other Central American countries, especially Nicaragua, and in historical literary themes, many of the items touch on various aspects of Costa Rican history.

The Biblioteca de Congreso, which is located in the Congress building and is used primarily as a reference tool by members of the Costa Rican Congress, has a small collection of journals, books, and newspapers, although it offers little that is not available in the National Library.

The Biblioteca del Banco Central has recently taken on the responsibility of collecting materials for research on the national history and economy. Emphasis is on economic development and financial matters, but the collection also includes cultural and literary publications. The library, which is well arranged and catalogued, has three principal sections: Economics, Costa Rica, and Costa Rican Authors. An extensive collection of the country's principal newspaper, *La Nación,* as well as a few other newspapers and periodicals, is also available.

The library of the Instituto Centroamericano de Administración Pública (ICAP) has established a research library of small proportions and with a special focus on public administration (this term, however, is interpreted broadly). Founded in 1953, ICAP is located in the Schyfter Building, which is across the street from the Central Bank.

A very small collection of secondary materials is available at the National University in Heredia. The National University was founded in the early 1970s. Although no rival to any of the libraries previously mentioned, the National University Library bears checking for special subjects such as diplomacy, labor, and oceanography, which have been chosen for special emphasis by the university.

The Office of Tropical Studies, a consortium of United States and Costa Rican universities, maintains its headquarters at the University of Costa Rica. Its library contains secondary material on scientific subjects and reports and papers (many unpublished) of North American and other scientists who have done research in Costa Rica. Although the emphasis of these materials falls heavily on biology, studies on sociological, anthropological, geographical, and historical subjects are included.

As an agency of the Associated Colleges of the Midwest, the Tropical Science Center is a research center for students and faculty who are working on independent projects. In twenty years of operation the library of the center has accumulated scores of unpublished research reports in a wide variety of fields.

Formerly the Interamerican Institute of Agricultural Sciences, the Centro Agronómico Tropical de Investigación y Enseñanza at Turrialba, maintains one of the finest collections on tropical agriculture in the hemisphere. Although focused on agricultural production, the center's graduate program has produced scores of studies in related fields—communications, sociology, anthropology, and others—on rural life in Costa Rica. These and other studies of Costa Rica are available in modern facilities in a pleasant rural setting. Furthermore, the Library and Documentation Service has for several years published a bibliography and documentation series, which is admirable in its comprehensiveness.

The Liceo de Heredia, a secondary school in Heredia, has a modest collection of nineteenth-century Costa Rican newspapers. Of the twenty-five newspapers represented, the earliest is the *Crónica* of 1858, the latest, *Actualidades* of 1916.

The best collection of maps of Costa Rica is available at the National Geographic Institute located on the Plaza González Víquez. Topographic maps and published studies on population distribution and natural resources are available to the public, and other detailed and specific maps and reports are available to scholars.

The Escuela Interamericana de Educación Democrática (EIDED) is located at La Catalina, on the volcanic slope above Alajuela. Founded by José Figueres in the 1950s, EIDED now contains a conference and convention center, a school, and a library. It is the best place to consult the school's own considerable list of publications, but it has a good collection on Costa Rican politics and history as well.

For specific research projects many other agencies or institutions in addition to those mentioned above might prove useful. Many of the government ministries and agencies maintain specialized libraries and are receptive to researchers. For material relating to the role of the Church in Costa Rica, one should consult the Archive of the Metropolitan (see Archivo de la Curia Metropolitano). Autonomous agencies, hospitals, orphanages, and schools are well worth looking into for specific subjects. The library of the Centro Cultural Costarricense Norteamericano could be helpful.

Unfortunately for biographers and historians the papers of most Costa Rican executives and prominent public figures are in private hands. Access, of course, depends on agreement between the investigator and the family or individual in possession of the papers. The papers of Julio Acosta (president from 1920 to 1924), which are held by the Revollo-Acosta family, have been used by researchers. Surviving papers of Ricardo Jiménez (president from 1910 to 1914, 1924 to 1928, and 1932 to 1936), presently in the hands of the Vargas-Genet family, have been utilized by some Costa Rican scholars.

Other private collections belong to historians who have been generous to investigators. The private biographical archive of Professor Rafael Obregón Loría of the University of Costa Rica contains extensive data on virtually every prominent (and not so prominent) Costa Rican of the nineteenth and twentieth centuries, and has been used by many historians and biographers. Another well-known historian and professor of the University of Costa Rica, Carlos Meléndez, has been equally generous with his excellent collection of government publications and secondary materials.

24   Panama
Gustavo Anguizola

The various book depositories and the National Archives of Panama house a good deal of primary-source material, much of it still unworked. Selection and cataloguing of primary and secondary sources in Panama have not been easy tasks because of the absence of trained personnel in the public institutions. Panama did not have its first trained librarian until the 1950s, with the arrival of Galileo Patiño as head of the National Library. Since centralism has characterized Panama's history, all the most important historical depositories are located in Panama City. But many family papers, including those of this author, are still in private hands and not open to the general public.

The Biblioteca Nacional, formerly known as the Columbus Memorial Library, is the largest library in Panama. As the doyen of the isthmian libraries, it accumulated a wealth of information dating from the colonial age and the decades of the Colombian occupation. Its holdings include:

Collections 1–10, a very important series of newspapers, dailies, weeklies, monthlies, and quarterlies printed in Panama since 1891. These publications are catalogued by periods, monthly and yearly, and include newspapers ranging from *La Estrella de Panamá*—still publishing—to the short-lived *El Agricultor* (1911–14).

Collections 11–16, which contain all the numbers of Panama's official *Gazette* from November 1903 to the present time.

Collections 17–21, which include several editions of geographic studies relating to the physical configuration of the Isthmus, as well as all volumes of Angel Rubio's *Diccionario Geográfico de Panamá*.

Collections 22–302, which include volumes and documents of several histories of Panama and Central America, written by many authors from the time of Rodrigo de Bastidas (1502) to the present. Of particular interest are the volumes dealing with rural life in Panama, as well as the different opinions on Panama's endemic problem—the Canal Question.

The Simón Bolívar Library of the University of Panama is a new institution enriched by the addition of several private collections:

Collection 1, theses by university graduates on variegated themes;
Collection 2, bulletins of Panama's Academy of Letters;
Collection 3, bulletins of Panama's Academy of Letters;
Collection 4, the entire library of one of the cofounders of the university, Octavio Méndez Pereira, dealing with his travels, diplomatic missions, eductional and political activities, plus many rare books.
Collection 5, the private library of Panama's first professional historian, Enrique Arce. It contains editions of a myriad of Latin American newspapers, learned treatises from Hispanoamericanists, and considerable Colombian history.
Collection 6, the library of President Belisario Porras, plus his political and diplomatic correspondence.
Collection 7, some of the papers and books of Juan Antonio Susto, Panamanian diplomat, son-in-law of President Porras, and first director of the National Archives.
Collection 8, materials relating to the War of 1000 Days and the activities of the Indian populist leader Victoriano Lorenzo.

Other important collections at this institution deal with education in Panama, the Costa Rica boundary dispute, religious missions, physical education, the historic town of Natá de los Caballeros, the fire fighters of Panama City, early exploration, Panama's literature, the National Institute, the hospitals of Panama, and the historiography of Panama.

The Library of the University of Santa María la Antigua is principally a depository of secondary sources written by native authors and dealing with isthmian history. Among its collections, however, is the correspondence of General Tomas Herrera. Other collections not completely catalogued deal with Panama's role in Latin America, laws prevalent among some of the Indian tribes of the Isthmus, social problems in the ghettos of Panama, the history of architecture in the Isthmus, and a long list of biographies of Panamanians from the nineteenth century to the present. Also, there is a collection on the early inhabitants of the Isthmus, and all copies of the yearly bulletin of the ecclesiastical dioceses of Panama City.

The National Archives are the depositories of all the official documents gathered from the colonial period to the present time. Of interest to the researcher are the collections of memorias printed by the different government departments during each administration, beginning with the separatist junta of 1903 and the Mensajes Presidenciales addressed to the legislature from time to time by the chief executives. The archives hold natal records, transferred from the provinces to the capital after 1920. The archives house census data, particularly since 1940, when the first scientific study of this nature was made in Panama. There is also material on the social and health conditions of the Spanish Main, and unpublished manuscripts pertaining to the activities of those engaged in the search for the *cinchona*, which included the Panamanian José López Ruiz. Two other important collections in the archives are devoted entirely to Panama's secessionist movements from Spain and Colombia, and to the real estate deeds and transactions conducted by the different notaries in Panama City from 1821 to the 1940s.

Most of the collections in the library of the normal school of Santiago de Veraguas contain secondary-source material and duplicate the public libraries of Panama City. A number of items on its shelves have to do with the history of educational systems and pedagogical methods, especially those modeled after the Chilean format.

The libraries of the Instituto Nacional and the Escuela Profesional once rivaled the Columbus Memorial Library in number of volumes and quality of works, but this is no longer so because of the continuous raiding of its shelves by the National University Library. Perhaps the most important item in the library of the National Institute is the collection of *Antorchas*, the official yearbook of that institution, dating from its foundation to the present time.

In addition, the ratification of the new Panama Canal Treaties—under which part of the Canal Zone has been placed under the jurisdiction of the Panamanian government—has transferred to Panama a new depository for the study of isthmian history: the American-staffed library at Balboa Heights. Its holdings should not be overlooked by any researcher interested in delving into the history of the Canal and all phases of its administration, from its construction to now. The library's collection of photographs and files of administrative records are invaluable, but the final disposition of this material is at present uncertain because of a dispute over whether to transfer these items to the Smithsonian Institution in Washington, D.C., or to leave them in Panama.

25 Mexico
Kenneth J. Grieb

The researcher seeking information regarding Central America will find that Mexican archives and libraries contain considerable resources, especially for the colonial era and diplomatic topics in the national period. Nearly all are located in the capital. Mexico has been a major destination of isthmian exiles, and their revealing broadsides and propaganda published in Mexico are often found in Mexican libraries.

The most valuable holdings are in the Biblioteca Nacional de México, which in 1979 moved from the downtown area to the campus of the Universidad Nacional Autónoma de México (UNAM); the Library of the Pan-American Institute of Geography and History, somewhat more remote on Ex-Arzobispado in Zona 18, whose collection is somewhat broader than those of the purely Mexican depositories; and the principal university libraries at UNAM and El Colegio de México, both located at the southern edge of the metropolitan area. Those working on the ethnohistory or archaeology of Mayan culture will also find much of value at the Instituto Nacional de Antropología e Historia in the Museo Nacional de Antropología in Chapultepec Park.

The largest and most valuable newspaper collection is the Hemeroteca Nacional de México, which joined the library in moving from its downtown location to the new Unidad Cultural on the university campus in 1979. Like the library it offers virtually full-day operation on weekdays and Saturdays. Although this institution is dedicated primarily to the collection of domestic newspapers, the Central Americanist would do well to consider it as a resource, for Mexican papers frequently report events in Central America. In addition, exile pronouncements of individuals and groups who have sought refuge in Mexico often appear in that country's press. As such, the Mexican press constitutes an important source regarding political propaganda related to the isthmus, as well as for providing contemporary reporting from a neighboring country that is far more interested in the isthmus than is the North American press. An additional newspaper collection, which is especially strong for the nineteenth century, is located in the Ministry of Hacienda offices in the National Palace.

Documentary collections in Mexico are easily the most valuable resources available to the Central Americanist in that nation. While such holdings consist primarily of the records of governmental domestic agencies as in any nation, there is considerable overlapping and interlocking of interests between Mexico and Central America. Since the two areas were encompassed in colonial days in a single viceroyalty with its seat in Mexico City, most depositories containing documentation relating to the colonial era are of interest to Central Americanists and constitute important supplements to the collections contained in the Archivo General de Centro América in Guatemala City. After independence, the interaction between the isthmian republics and their larger northern neighbor continued to be extensive, rendering Mexican archival collections relating to diplomacy and the executive branch especially valuable for students investigating interaction between the nations, border disputes, refugee activity, and the Belize question. The dispatches of Mexican diplomats in Central America contain descriptive reports of domestic political events in Central America and provide analysis of these events from a Latin American viewpoint. They also provide information regarding Mexican ambitions and actions in the isthmus, another aspect of the region that has been largely overlooked by scholars.

The Archivo General de la Nación contains the principal collection relating to the colonial period. This institution has moved several times recently, but has finally settled in its own building, the Antiguo Palacio de Lecumberri, making the collections more available and allowing the excellent staff to devote its energies to organizing and cataloguing the collections instead of moving them. The colonial period is well indexed and readily accessible. Guides and card catalogues exist for some sections, and a knowledgeable and helpful staff will provide assistance in other areas. The Archivo Histórico de Hacienda also contains valuable materials regarding the colonial period, including the archives of the hacienda section of the viceregal government. Catalogues and a guide exist but have their limits, and the researcher should have exhausted the secondary sources and be well along in his research before consulting the documents in this depository.

In the modern period, the most valuable collection for Central Americanists is the Archivo de Relaciones Exteriores, located at the Ministerio de Relaciones Exteriores at the Plaza de Tres Culturas, Santiago Tlatleloco. Recently furnished with modern and expanded quarters, the archive offers pleasant working conditions and a diligent staff, which has greatly expanded the card catalogue. Despite inevitable gaps, the researcher should be able to locate the extensive material housed in this archive through the catalogue, using some imagination regarding headings, since they vary with the eras involved. The Archivo General de la Nación also contains considerable material for the national period in Central America, particularly in the Ramo Presidencial, which contains the papers of the presidents or their secretariats. All regimes are not represented, and the volume of the records varies greatly, but extensive documentation is available for many. Those working in the nineteenth century will find most useful the Porfirio Díaz Papers at the University of the Americas in Puebla and the Benito Juárez Archive, located in the Biblioteca Nacional in the capital. The biblioteca also contains a collection of Francisco Madero Papers.

The various depositories have differing hours, and the researcher would be well advised to check on these in advance, particularly because of recent changes in the government workday. In general, however, most are open weekday mornings, beginning about 8:30 or 9:00 through the noon hour, and also sometime during the afternoon. Increasingly there is a tendency to function through the midday break, closing early in the afternoon, although this system is not yet employed in all depositories. Hours are generally shorter than those for North American archives. All of the depositories have card catalogues, though their extent, detail, and comprehensiveness can exhibit considerable variance. The researcher should plan on spending his initial day consulting with the director and appropriate staff members, for they can be very helpful, and often such efforts provide the only means of becoming current on the extent of the collection and the availability of finding aids.

Outside the capital researchers may find useful material in the state archives of Chiapas and Yucatán.

26   The Library of Congress
John R. Hébert

The research material on Central America available in the collections of the Library of Congress is especially rich and covers the entire range of Central America's written history. Pertinent items are located in the general collections of the library and in several special format divisions: Manuscript, Serial, Prints and Photographs, Geography and Map, General Reading Rooms (its Microform Reading Room), Music, Hispanic Law, Rare Book and Special Collections, and the Hispanic Division. The researcher should be aware of the existence of these possible sources of relevant material in order to utilize the collections effectively. The Hispanic Division provides reference assistance to those engaged in serious research; a visit to that division will hasten the orientation of the uninitiated scholar to the library's many resources.

The strength of the library's varied Central American materials lies in primary works relating to the republics of the region and their international relations in the past two centuries. Most prominent are documents and descriptions of the several regional attempts at federation, travelers' reports, and the proposals of diverse efforts to construct railway and ship routes across the isthmus.

The general collection of the library in the fields of the humanities and the social sciences is extensive. Luis Dobles Segreda's six-thousand-piece collection of writings on Costa Rican life and culture serves as an excellent example of its depth. Broad holdings of journals of scholarly institutions, development organizations, and literary societies, plus representative numbers of general information serials, augment monographic works. The files of official gazettes for each country from the 1860s to the present are practically complete; scattered holdings for the earlier period of the republics are valuable because of their rarity. Among nineteenth-century titles are the *Gaceta Oficial* (Panama, 1876–96), *La Gaceta* (Tegucigalpa, 1876–1900), *La Gaceta* (Managua, 1851–1900), and the Guatemalan gazettes, *Boletín Oficial* (1831–39), *Gaceta de Guatemala* (1841–71), and *El Guatemalteco* (1873–1900).

The Manuscript Division possesses the papers of Ephraim George Squier (Nicaragua, Honduras, 1849–1850s), Philippe Jean Bunau Varilla (Panama, 1884–1940), George W. Goethals (Panama, 1890–1927), W. C. Gorgas (Panama, 1885–1909), Nicaraguan Canal Construction (1887–1913), and the microfilm file of the British Foreign Office Papers on Panama (1803–1906).

The library's outstanding collection of nineteenth- and twentieth-century Central American newspapers includes extensive holdings of the most important current dailies for each capital, e.g., *La Nación* and *La República* (San José), *El Dairio de Hoy* and *La Prensa Gráfica* (San Salvador), *El Imparcial* and *Prensa Libre* (Guatemala), *La Epoca* and *El Día* (Tegucigalpa), *Novedades* and *La Prensa* (Managua), and *La Estrella de Panamá* and *Panama American* (Panama City). Steven Charno's *Latin American Newspapers in the United States Libraries: A Union List* (Austin, 1968) and *Newspapers in Microform, Foreign Countries, 1948–72* (Library of Congress, 1973, and its supplements) are useful guides to the newspapers.

The collections of the Prints and Photographs Division are strongest in photographic materials of Panama and the Panama Canal, although twentieth-century photographs of locations throughout the region are also among the collections. A unique photographic print and color slide collection, the Archive of Hispanic Culture, contains a large number of photo-reproductions of the fine and folk arts and noteworthy architecture of Central America.

The Geography and Map Division's treasure trove of maps and atlases of the region is concentrated in the national period. It includes detailed topographic and thematic maps, city plans, maps and supplemental cartographic data for various isthmian canal proposals, national and thematic atlases, and a number of manuscript maps. Among colonial-period materials are small-scale maps or plates from European atlases and photostatic copies of original manuscripts in Spanish and otner European archives. The maps prepared by Ephraim George Squier for his ship canal and railroad proposals for Nicaragua and Honduras in the mid-1800s and a number of eighteenth-century manuscript maps of the Caribbean coast of Central America are especially noteworthy.

Microfilm, microfiche, and other microforms, other than those contained in the Newspaper and Current Periodicals Room and the Manuscript Division, are found in the collections of the Microform Reading Room. Among Central American items are 101 reels of microfilm of materials in Panama's Biblioteca Nacional, Archivo Nacional, and the national university library; included in the film are the *Gaceta Oficial* of Colombia (1854–60), *Gaceta de Panamá* (1878, 1880–81, 1883, 1887–99), and the archive's Sección Jurídica (Panama, 1825–85).

Central American legal materials have been routinely collected by the library and maintained by the Law Library. The staff of the Hispanic Law Division is especially versed in the relatively complete collection of codes, constitutions, and other legal materials found in the library. The division prepares and maintains the *Index to Latin American Legislation;* this publication will appear eventually in computerized form.

The Hispanic Division, established as a center for the study of Hispanic culture, maintains several useful bodies of material for Central American specialists. The division's pamphlet file, containing primarily twentieth-century material, and its reference collection provide researchers with many necessary finding aids, bibliographies, biographical dictionaries, collection guides, and other tools. The Archive of Hispanic Literature on Tape is a unique collection of recordings of outstanding twentieth-century poets and writers from the Hispanic world; Central American representatives include Juan José Arévalo and Miguel Angel Asturias (Guatemala), Ernesto Cardenal and Pablo Antonio Cuadra (Nicaragua), and Joaquín Beleño and Ricardo J. Bermúdez (Panama). The basic *Handbook of Latin American Studies* is compiled in the division. The Panama collection of the former Canal Zone Library Museum was transferred to the Library of Congress.

The Library of Congress contains a wealth of research materials related to Central American culture. The key to the discovery and use of these materials lies in an awareness of the diversity of the many special collections and services offered by the institution.

27   The Bancroft Library
Murdo J. MacLeod

The Bancroft Library at the University of California, Berkeley, has long been a center of importance for the study of colonial Latin America. Its Mexican collections are strong and varied. Central American materials are much less numerous, but there are many items of interest and importance. The best and most recent guide to Central American materials in the Bancroft Library is George P. Hammond, ed., *A Guide to the Manuscript Collections of the Bancroft Library,* Vol. 2, *Mexican and Central American Manuscripts,* Bancroft Library Publications, Bibliographical Series (Berkeley and Los Angeles, 1972).

Researchers should note that not all microfilms are reported in this guide. In at least one case the films of colonial documents from Central America left to the Bancroft by former graduate students upon completion of their Ph.D. dissertations have not yet been catalogued. Reference librarians will usually know the whereabouts of such films.

28   The Newberry Library
Stanley M. Hordes

The Newberry Library, 60 West Walton Street, Chicago, is a free, privately supported, noncirculating reference and research library. While the Newberry's holdings are strongest in the areas of European and United States history, it also contains a considerable amount of valuable research material of interest to Latin Americanists in general and to Central Americanists in particular.

The bulk of the Central American holdings can be found in the Edward E. Ayer Collection,[1] a large body of primary and secondary material concerning the exploration and colonization of the Americas, collected by Ayer around the turn of the twentieth century. While the Ayer Collection includes published works on Central American history, the heart of the collection consists of a number of manuscripts dating from the sixteenth through the nineteenth century and dealing with a variety of topics ranging

---

1. Some general histories and travel accounts may be found among the general Newberry Library holdings in the Main Reading Room on the second floor.

from travel accounts to the miscellaneous papers of Alejandro Marure.
Ruth Lapham Butler's *A Checklist of Manuscripts in the Edward E. Ayer
Collection* (Chicago, 1937) includes the following entries of interest to
scholars of Central America:

1025—Albrizzi, Carlo. Lettra del Gesuita Carlo Albrizzi [a suo padre].
Quito, May 4, 1756. 20 pp.

1030—Alvarado, Pedro. Algunas noticias de la Conquista, y batalla que
Dn. Pedro Alvarado ganó en el Pinar de Quesaltenango [*sic*] . . . May 13,
1524. 21 pp.

1054—Caravero, Francisco. Testmento cerrado de Francisco Caravero,
abierto en Panamá. June 26, 1556. 34 pp. mutilated.

1056—Casas, Bartolomé de las. Historia de las Yndias. (Nineteenth-
century copy.) 5895 pp.

1057—Casas, Bartolomé de las. Historia de las Yndias. Libro segundo
(sixteenth-century copy). 392 pp.

1074—Cozar, Prudencio de. Diario de lo ocurrido en la Toma, y destrucción de la Ysla Roatan . . . al mandado del Mariscal de Campo Dn. Matías de Gálvez, Presidente y Capitan General del Reyno de Guatemala.
Truxillo, March 24, 1782. 13 pp.

1079—Dios Gonzáles, Juan de. Reconocimiento Que se manifiesta por el
adjunto plan de la Provincia de Yucatán y parte de la Costa de Honduras
desde punta de Castilla pasando por el Oeste, y Cavo de Catocha hasta la
Ysla de Fris o Presidio del Carmen . . . February 18, 1766. 51 pp.

1100—Guatemala, Catholic church. Sobre el Auto de Cofradias, y guachivales de 5 de Diz. de 1741 . . . Guatemala, April 14, 1744. 46 pp.

1100.5—Gutiérrez y Ulloa, Autenio. Estado General de la Provincia de
San Salvador en Guatemala. 1814. 118 pp.

1104a—Honduras, 1826–31. Document concerning Indian slaves emancipated and compensated for by the British government in 1836. Belize,
Honduras, 1826–31. 24 pp.

1113—La Gasca, Pedro de. Letter to Pedro Hernández Paniagua. Panamá, October 14, 1546. 1 p.

1116—León, Nicolás. Ensayo de una historia general del Estado de Chiapas. 674 pp.

1119—León Cardona, Juan de. Documentos sobre la casa de León Cardona. Nueva Goathemala, August 13, 1783. 35 pp.

1126—Luthereau, Jean Guillaume Antoine. Décoration de premiere
classe . . . Grey-Town, May 1, 1857. 1 p.

1127—Luthereau, Jean Guillaume Antoine and Charles de Villery. Histoire des Républiques Centro-Américaines, ou Grey-Town devant
l'Europe, 1858. 203 pp.

1131—Marure Papers. Miscellaneous papers of Alejandro Marure. The earliest, dated from 1779 to 1786, are copies of treaties, conventions, and accounts of military affairs. For the period 1800–76, the documents concern political affairs; forty-one letters dating from 1823 to 1876 include correspondence of Marure and his associates. All of these concern the domestic affairs of Guatemala. The majority of the papers relate to the period 1810–50. 1,028 pp.

1262—Journal de notes. No. 2 (Copán). Notes et traditions no. 2, recueillies d'apres les auteurs espagnoles et indigenes de l'Amérique Centrale, sur l'origine de sa premiere civilization laquelle prit naissance dans l'Yucatan et las Chiapas. 136 pp.

As alluded to above, the Ayer Collection contains a body of secondary works and journals that complement the manuscripts very well. Heavily weighted toward Guatemala and Costa Rica, this section includes a large selection of nineteenth- and early twentieth-century travel accounts as well as the major synthetic histories written by Central American authors. Periodical holdings in the Ayer Collection are unbalanced in favor of Guatemala; seven journals from Guatemala are represented (including the *Gazeta de Guatemala* from 1797 to 1804), while Honduran and Costa Rican periodicals number three each, Salvadoran journals, two, and Nicaraguan and Panamanian publications, one each. Regretably, there is no periodicals file, and the researcher must leaf through the entire catalogue of the Ayer Colection in order to locate each journal entry. The Newberry has no Central American newspapers.

The Ayer Collection materials may be consulted only in the Department of Special Collections, located in the Rare Book Room on the first floor.

Admission to the Newberry Library is by card, available at the information desk on the first floor. To obtain such a card, researchers are asked to fill out a registration form and to present positive identification. The staff, both in the Main Reading Room and in the Rare Book Room, are extremely knowledgeable of the materials under their care and are available for consultation. The Newberry is open Tuesday through Thursday from 9:00 A.M. to 9:40 P.M., and on Friday and Saturday from 9:00 A.M. to 5:40 P.M.

29   The Latin American Library of Tulane University
Ralph Lee Woodward, Jr.

Tulane's Latin American Library contains one of the largest collections of published materials on Central America anywhere in the world. It contains an especially large number of published works dating from the colonial period and the nineteenth century, but the collection has continued to add current publications and includes most contemporary periodicals from Central America. The Guatemalan holdings are especially large, but there is excellent coverage of the other states as well, including Chiapas and Yucatán. The library has an extensive collection of nineteenth-century Central American newspapers, pamphlets, political *hojas sueltas,* and major collections of laws and decrees. United States, British, and some other European diplomatic and consular correspondence with Central America is available on microfilm. A photographic archive has been established recently within the Latin American Library, which already includes a large number of Central American photographs. Among the manuscript collections are the papers of E. G. Squier, a collection of papers of Francisco Morazán, the business and family records of Erwin Paul Dieseldorf (a German coffee planter in Guatemala), the Captain C. I. Fayssoux Collection of William Walker Papers, the Chiapas Collection of decrees, laws, and government and ecclesiastical documents and manuscripts (1822–1916), a collection of climatology records of the St. Josephs Meteorological Observatory in Belize (1887–1931), the personal correspondence of Lewis Hanke, the correspondence of Nicaraguan President Joaquín Zavala, and a microfilm copy of the Libro Verde, containing publications, broadsides, etc., from the early nineteenth century and other rare materials from the Archivo General de Centro América. Some of the manuscript collections, including a number of Louisiana personal and business collections relating to Central America, are located in the Special Collections Division of the Tulane Library, across the hall from the Latin American Library.[1] The Latin American Library is also a major depository of materials on Central American archaeology and ethnology. The library's card

---

1. See William E. Meneray, comp., *A Brief Guide to the Manuscripts Section of the Special Collections Division, Tulane University Library* (New Orleans, 1977).

catalogue has been published by G. K. Hall.[2] Photocopying services are available, and visiting scholars are most welcome. For inquiries contact Director, Latin American Library, Tulane University, New Orleans, Louisiana 70118. The Latin American Library is located on the fourth floor of the Tulane University Library, Newcomb Place, on the Tulane campus in uptown New Orleans. Additional Central American material is located in the Tulane Law School and Business School libraries, also on the uptown campus. An important collection of materials relating to tropical medicine is located in the Tulane Medical School Library, 1430 Tulane Avenue, in downtown New Orleans.

30   The Department of Archives and Manuscripts of Louisiana State University
Ralph Lee Woodward, Jr.

This depository contains a number of collections of potential interest to Central Americanists. These include cacao plantation records (1736–97), Guatemalan merchant records (1812–21), the papers of Frans Blom and the Middle American Research Institute of Tulane University, correspondence of Louisiana businessmen and politicians with Central Americans on a wide range of topics, various manuscripts of both an official and unofficial nature from nineteenth-century Guatemala, a collection of Guatemalan cartoons (1930–31), manuscripts relative to confederate exiles in Costa Rica, Belize, and Honduras, and manuscripts relating to William Walker and other filibustering expeditions in the 1850s. For a complete list of these collections, see Brian E. Coutts, "An Inventory of Sources for the History of Latin America in the Department of Archives and Manuscripts, Louisiana State University, Baton Rouge, Louisiana," Department of Archives and Manuscripts (Baton Rouge, 1977), mimeographed.

2. *Catalog of the Latin American Library of the Tulane University Library, New Orleans* (9 vols., Boston, 1970); *First Supplement* (2 vols., Boston, 1973); *Second Supplement* (2 vols., Boston, 1975); *Third Supplement* (Boston, 1978).

31 The Joseph Byrne Lockey Collection University of California at Los Angeles Library
Mario Rodríguez

The Lockey Collection at UCLA includes four boxes of Central American diplomatic correspondence, notes, and other research materials. An inventory of the material follows:

Box 1—Central America   *Number of items*
  Central America (Guatemala, Nicaragua,
    British Honduras, etc.), 1837–38   27
  Central America, 1839   16
  Central America, 1840   32
  Central America, 1841   68
  Central America, 1842   23
  Costa Rica, 1848–49   5
  Costa Rica, 1862–65   9
  Costa Rica, 1847–58   45
  Dispatches and instructions (miscellaneous), 1858–64   20
  Diplomatic representatives, British, to Central America, 1825–34   43
  Guatemala, Honduras, Salvador; Squier Mission:
    Letters on Confederation, 1842–67   25
  Honduras, 1863–1925   42
  Interoceanic railroad, 1857   2
  Manuscripts—Central America, n.d.   2

Box 2—Central America
  Miscellaneous, 1849–56   19
  Mosquito Indians, Treaty of 1843 with   1
  Mosquito King, 1848–50   3
  Newspaper, 1849–61   13
  Nicaragua (Dispatches)—Privateering—William
    Walker—Filibustering to 1866, 1855–66   24
  Nicaragua (note), 1855–64   20
  Notes, 1839–55   35
  Notes (miscellaneous), 1830–64   35
  Transit, n.d.   3

152

Box 2—Central America (continued)	*Number of items*
Treaties, British, with Central American nations, 1849–95	9
Alston, Francis B., 1859	1
Barrundia, 1854	1
Beelen, Fred A., 1854	1
Berendt, D. C., 1876–78	2
Borland, 1853	3
Buchanan, 1856	2
Bulwer, H. L., 1850–51	29
Cass, Lewis, 1857–59	3
Castlereagh, Viscount, 1817	1
Chatfield, Fred, 1847–51	25

Box 3—Central America	
Christie, W. W., 1848–49	5
Clarendon, 1854–57	8
Clarke, 1849	2
Clayton, John M., 1849–56	5
Crampton, John F., 1848–56	27
Dallas, 1856	19
Gliddon, 1855–56	5
Holland, G., 1859	5
Keeler, David M., 1849–50	4
Malmesbury, 1852	2
Marcy, William L., 1855–56	8
Marcoleta, T. de, 1856–57	2
Napier, 1857	2
Norton, Charles E., 1849	5
Norton, Charles E., 1851	5
Norton, Charles E., 1852	7
Norton, Charles E., 1853–54	15
Norton, Charles E., 1861–66	9
Ousley, 1858	3
Palmerston, 1846–51	23
Russell, 1853	2
Sanford, 1856	2
Savage, 1853–54	3
Squier, E. George, 1849–50	9
Squier—Bibliography	1
Squier—Clippings, 1850–59	15
Squier—Summary	4
Squier, E. George, to C. E. Norton, 1851–64	21

Box 4—Central America	*Number of items*
Walsh, Robert M., 1852	1
Whelpley, James D., 1849–51	2
White, J. L., 1849–53	11
Wyke, 1852–59	11
Duplicates (State Department), 1849–57	38
Correll, Ruth E., *The Mission of Ephraim George Squier to Central America* (n.p., n.d.), copy of term paper in typescript, 22 pp.	1

32   The University of Florida Libraries
Irene Zimmerman

The University of Florida Libraries have comparatively extensive holdings of materials for the study of Central American history and related fields. The card catalogue of the Latin American Collection (LAC) lists approximately eighty-four hundred volumes under official entries and subject headings. Of these, up to 10 percent are specifically listed as "(name of country)—History," but most of the other categories (e.g., "Foreign Relations," "Social Conditions," etc.) eventually become history. Of other headings which read in the reverse order—e.g., "Art," "Education," "Geology," "Music," etc., with subdivisions by country—there is no easy way to make an estimate, but Latin American materials surely number fewer than a fourth as many as those listed under the countries' names. The related field of literature totals approximately twenty-five hundred volumes of Central American literature. The UF Libraries have made a conscious effort to acquire Central American materials (including Ph.D. dissertations) second only to those from and about the West Indies, as a part of the Caribbean specialty undertaken at midcentury.

Among noteworthy materials are long runs of periodicals, such as possibly the only complete set of the monumental *Repertorio americano,* founded, edited, and published in San José by Joaquín García Monge from 1919 to 1959. From Guatemala there is an even longer run of the valuable *Anales de la Sociedad de Geografía e Historia,* founded in 1924 and still appearing. Panama is represented by its incomparable *Lotería, organo de la Lotería Nacional de Beneficencia,* long edited by historian Juan Antonio Susto and in its third *época* still a unique source of information about the history, international relations, and culture of that isthmian country. University journals, archival and statistical bulletins, *revistas* published by official agencies, and independent periodicals have been consistently acquired from all six countries.

Of official gazettes, the Latin American Collection has on microfilm the Costa Rican *La Gaceta* from 1949 through 1969 and the Honduran *La Gaceta* from January 1949 through 1968—all that are so far available. In the same general category is a Costa Rican *Colección de leyes, decretos, acuerdos, y resoluciones,* from 1824 to 1953, plus incomplete holdings from 1954 to 1967.

Census data are another type of official publication of interest to historians. The earlier holdings, in more or less complete form, are as follows: Costa Rica, 1864, 1888, and 1927; El Salvador, 1930; Guatemala, 1893 and 1921; Nicaragua, 1920; Panama, 1940. The earliest for Honduras is 1950, from which date the LAC should have records of the extensive midcentury Census of the Americas and presumably all other Honduran censuses since that time. The originals are backed up by the microfilm edition of the International Population Census project sponsored by the University of Texas, covering, in its first series, all censuses from 1945 to 1967. Also, the Data Bank, located in the nearby graduate studies building, has a great deal of valuable census data, notably from Costa Rica, on tape.

The Map Library, recently instituted, aspires to collect Latin American maps as comprehensively as possible. The Central American countries are well covered by topographic series at 1:250,000, and most countries, including Costa Rica, El Salvador, Guatemala, and Honduras, are covered by detailed topographic maps at 1:50,000. Thematic (special subject) maps are being obtained for these countries on geology, land use, population, soils, etc. As a result of a unique project commissioned by the University of Florida, the Map Library has an unpublished blueprint reproduction of Costa Rican census maps, detailed to the smallest census division. Data were provided by the Dirección General de Estadística y Censos, Sección Cartografía Censal.

Of newspapers on microfilm, the most noteworthy holdings are a series listed as "Panama Newspapers," representing the *Panama Star and Herald* from May 1919 to August 1949, plus incomplete holdings through March 1951. Subscriptions are maintained to the microfilm editions of two newspapers, *El Imparcial* (Guatemala City) from 1964 and *La República* (San José) from 1962.

The Rare Books and Manuscripts Department has a limited number of papers relating to Ephraim George Squier (1821–88), which are listed in the union catalogue. They include correspondence (1842–74) regarding the Anthropological Association and manuscripts regarding travels and descriptions of Central America. The LAC holds most of his important publications. Also held by the Rare Books and Manuscripts Department is the "Central American Collection of 34 Broadsides," covering 1768– 1904, contained in a single box (38 × 24 cm.). Several nineteenth-century Guatemalan periodicals and gazettes provide fragmentary records.

G. K. Hall has published the *Catalog of the Latin American Collection of the University of Florida Libraries, Gainesville, Florida* (13 vols., Boston, 1973), plus a *Supplement* (7 vols., 1979).

33   The University of Kansas Libraries
Charles L. Stansifer

The University of Kansas Libraries began the systematic collecting of Central American materials in the 1950s. Two decisions made in that decade have had a lasting impact on the development of a significant corpus of Central American research materials. The first was the establishment in 1958 of an exchange relationship between the University of Kansas and the Universidad de Costa Rica. The agreement, which has been renewed every five years since, specifically provides for a program of exchange of publications. The second decision was the promise of the University of Kansas, under the Farmington Plan of 1958, to concentrate on collecting Costa Rican materials. Acquisitions personnel at the University of Kansas Libraries have invariably followed the policy of acquiring any publication about Costa Rica and any Costa Rican imprints since that date.

Several special collections provide variety and depth to the Costa Rican holdings. Purchase in 1964 of the Jorge Lines Collection, which contains over a thousand items, was an important step forward in filling in out-of-print items, especially in the fields of anthropology, literature, politics, and history. The Lines Collection is also strong in periodical literature. An extensive collection of Costa Rican maps, painstakingly located by Albert E. Palmerlee during preparation of his book, *Maps of Costa Rica: An Annotated Cartobibliography* (Lawrence, Kansas, 1965), is housed in the Map Library of Spencer Library on the University of Kansas campus. Because of the Costa Rican bibliographical work of Larry K. Laird, who recently donated his Latin American holdings to the University of Kansas, the libraries' holdings on Costa Rican bibliography are exhaustive. A small, unprocessed collection of Tobías Zúñiga Montúfar's materials— scrapbooks, letters, and public documents—augments the Costa Rican collection. Frequent acquisitions trips and regular communications with Costa Rican publishers, including the many Universidad de Costa Rica departments, book dealers, and scholars, are responsible for extending these special holdings into a truly comprehensive Costa Rican collection.

Recognizing the importance of the Central American Common Market and the historical ties of Costa Rica with the other four Central American republics and Panama, the University of Kansas Libraries' collection policy also has aimed at Costa Rica's neighbors. Purchase of the eighteen-thousand-item Ernesto Alvarado García Collection in 1966 and the William Griffith Collection in 1982 enriched the Central American holdings, especially on Honduras, El Salvador, and Guatemala. Alvarado García gave particular attention to twentieth-century Central American periodical literature and Griffith to nineteenth-century Guatemalan ephemera.

Building on the strengths of the blanket Costa Rican purchase policy and the Lines and Alvarado collections, the University of Kansas Libraries have attempted to augment the Central American collections by acquisition of government and university publications. Publications of the six public universities of Central America and Panama and Ministry of Education reports are especially well represented. Because of direct involvement by the University of Kansas faculty in the work of the Consejo Superior de las Universidades Centroamericanas, the libraries' holdings of their publications are nearly complete.

A total of 565 titles are included in the list of Central American periodicals in the Kansas collection. Approximately one-third of these are Costa Rican. Many of the titles on the list represent only fragmentary holdings, but major Central American periodicals, such as the principal publications of the historical and geographical societies, are nearly complete.

34   Latin American Collection
University of Texas at Austin
Thomas Niehaus

The Nettie Lee Benson Latin American Collection at the University of Texas has a very strong collection of Central American books, periodicals, and manuscripts. The published works can be found listed in the *University of Texas Library, Austin. Catalog of the Latin American Collection* (31 vols., Boston, 1969), plus three supplements of sixteen additional volumes, up to 1975.

The most important Central American collection in the library is the Arturo Taracena Flores Library, which was acquired in the early 1960s.[1] It is a collection of Guatemalan materials on all topics, covering the period 1820–1963. It contains approximately five thousand books, ten thousand pamphlets, nine thousand *decretos,* and numerous broadsides. There are also thirty linear feet of uncatalogued manuscripts. Nettie Lee Benson has determined that the Taracena Flores Library contains more Guatemalan imprints (3,000) for the period 1821–1900 than does Gilberto Valenzuela's four-volume *Bibliografía guatemalteca* (2,739 imprints). She also indicates that the number of twentieth-century imprints outnumbers those of the nineteenth century.

Taracena Flores did not limit himself to any certain subject in his book collecting. His purpose was to obtain all Guatemalan imprints. The collection has more religious works than any other subject, but that reflected the nature of publishing in Guatemala. There is enough material, for instance, for a detailed study of famous Guatemalan preachers and the religious and social content of their sermons. The following selective list of topics indicates the wide scope of the collection: political pamphlets, medical tracts, agriculture, poetry, short stories, alcoholics, almanacs, textbooks and elementary school primers, government documents, railroads, and army publications. There are about 280 items under "Guatemala. Laws, statutes, etc." Many are from the late nineteenth century. A few are pre-1850. Most are twentieth-century laws up to 1969. Worthy of special mention are the many items on border disputes in Central America. There are also many "little journals," published by religious social action groups, labor unions, teachers colleges, civic and political associations, medical associations, social clubs, and art organizations. Taracena Flores assembled in single packages all types of information about individual Guatemalans. This includes newspaper clippings, broadsides, speeches, programs, and photos.

Of special interest are the photographs in the collection, numbering about four hundred. Almost all are in the *carte-de-visite* format, i.e., small, mass-produced photos that were used as a sort of calling card. Most are of politicians, bishops, and preachers, all taken in the late nineteenth and early twentieth centuries. There are thirty-one photos of Guatemalan bishops and priests, many with biographical sketches written on the backs, and twenty-five photos of Guatemalan politicians and other leading persons, many also with biographies.

The card catalogue in the Benson Latin American Collection contains eleven drawers devoted exclusively to the Taracena Flores Library.

---

1. Nettie Lee Benson, "The Arturo Taracena Flores Library," *Library Chronicle* (Austin), 7, 4(Spring 1964): 37–39.

35   Yale University Libraries
Lee Williams

The Latin American Collection of Yale University Libraries is a general collection, covering the humanities and social sciences for all countries from Mexico to the south, including Central and South America and the Caribbean Islands. It is dispersed throughout the library system. With such an arrangement it is difficult to focus on geographical coverage in the many subject areas where books may be classed. The inventory in Table 35.1 will give some idea of Yale's Central American holdings.

In addition to these volumes acquired in the routine course of developing the overall collection of Latin American material, the library has a special collection of Central American material known as the Lindley and Charles Eberstadt Collection on the Central American Federation. It contains 961 local imprints of original historical sources, recording the life and times of the Central American Federation from its foundation in 1825 through its dissolution in 1838, and of its individual components—the Republics of Costa Rica, Guatemala, Honduras, Nicaragua, and El Salvador—on through the 1860s. The imprints record presses from Agua Caliente, Antigua, Cartago, Chinandega, Chiquilala, Cojutepeque, Comayagua, Granada, Guatemala, León, Managua, Mazatenango, Quezaltenango, Salamá, San Cristóbal, San Fernando, San José, San Salvador, San Vicente, Sonsonate, Tegucigalpa, Totonicapán, and Yuscarán. The collection ranges over such topics as the rebellion, depredations, assassinations, dictatorships, exploration, topographical surveys, literature and freedom of the press, trade and commerce, the Nicaraguan canal, counterfeiting and banking, education, agriculture, and industry and labor, and it comprises official documents, private reports, constitutions, laws, treatises, and proclamations.

Table 35.1. Number of Titles

	Literature	History	Economics	Law	Total
Costa Rica	200	300	125	50	675
Guatemala	100	375	125	25	625
Honduras	50	200	100		350
Nicaragua	200	300	75	5	580
Panama	100	750	200	10	1,060
El Salvador	100	250	100		450
Central America		150			150
					3,890

159

In 1981 the Latin American Collection acquired Franco Cerutti's Central American Library, consisting of ten thousand items. One third of the Cerutti Library was made up of Nicaraguan imprints, with extraordinary strength in serial publications, both periodicals and newspapers, from the nineteenth and early twentieth centuries. In addition there are over four hundred pamphlets from nineteenth-century Nicaragua with broad coverage of the activities of the times. Approximately one third of the Cerutti Library was composed of publications from Costa Rica, mostly from the twentieth century. The final third contained books from Guatemala, El Salvador, Honduras, Panama, and Belize.

The Historical Manuscripts Collection of the Sterling Memorial Library has a collection of records relating to the Kingdom of Mosquito (Nicaragua) (1820–47), including minutes of the Council of State.

36   Microfilm of the Archivo General de Centro América at McMaster University
Paul McDowell and
Ralph Lee Woodward, Jr.

Under a grant from the Donner Canadian Foundation of Toronto, the McMaster University Library has acquired a microfilm copy of the documents in the Archivo General de Centro América, a total of five to six million pages of documents resulting in 3,925 reels of microfilm. The library is now in the process of compiling a detailed-content summary of the archives for interested scholars. There is as yet no complete index of the holdings, but further information on this important microfilm collection and other Central American holdings in the Division of Archives and Special Collections at McMaster may be obtained by writing the Special Collections Librarian, Mills Memorial Library, McMaster University, 1280 Main Street West, Hamilton, Ontario, Canada L8S 4L6. The telephone number is (416) 252–9140, ext. 4781.

37   Records of North American Firms Doing Business in Central America
Thomas L. Karnes

For at least two decades the historian of modern Latin America, irrespective of ideology, has found it necessary to make some allusion to the presence and operations of North American corporations. Whether defending or assaulting these companies, the writers almost unanimously ascribe primary importance to them. Some critics have woven elaborate themes explaining how the growth of the corporations came about and what they have done to hold back the progress of Latin America and other developing regions of the world. If the writers are specific, they usually refer to the mining, fruit, or utilities companies with broad generalizations gleaned from some particular event and then offer a hypothesis or two. Shrinking the canvas to Central America makes little difference; the small size of those nations and their nearness to the United States seem to indicate that the power of the multinational should be all the greater.

Notwithstanding this attention, however, the researcher who would go beyond models and theories is in trouble, and the search for support of these hypotheses can prove most frustrating. Some of this is reflected in the secondary literature. A search through a score of the more popular text books on Latin America found only one which included the word *dependency* in the index, and not a single index contained the word *multinational* or any resemblance of that expression. From Charles C. Griffin's *Guide to the Historical Literature* and the *Bibliography of United States–Latin American Relations Since 1810* by Trask, Meyer, and Trask, to the latest catalogue on "Economics, Business, and Finance" of the Arno Press, the coverage of United States business in Central America is virtually ignored. One outstanding exception must be noted; a dozen approaches to the United Fruit Company have been essayed, generally making Unifruco the *bête noire* of the Central Americanist. But otherwise the detailed operations have yet to be related.

The times seemed propitious in 1979 to make a survey of corporations (restricted in this case to Central America) to ascertain the degree of availability of business materials and to determine what needs still exist for future research. A questionnaire was sent to 299 firms which, according to a number of guides and directories, did business of one sort or another

161

in Central America.[1] No attempt was made to distinguish between companies with vast landholdings and those with little more than a postal box for mail-order transactions, although such distinction might prove useful if it could be accomplished.

The questionnaire explained its purpose as trying to improve the scholars' understanding of the impact of American business upon Central America. The specific items asked included: (1) Did the corporation maintain any sort of archive of the Latin American phase of its business? (2) Could serious scholars obtain permission to use any of the materials? (3) Where was the archive located? (4) Would the respondent give a description of the size, nature, and regulations concerning use of the collection? Room was provided for further comments.

Fifty-five firms, or 18 percent, responded, and, of these, fifteen declared that they did maintain something in the nature of an archive, open to the scholar, ranging from a file drawer or two to a few rather imposing libraries.

By way of comparison it might be interesting to refer to Warren Dean's *Latin American Research Review* article of 1968.[2] Dean had a larger base to operate from, since he was surveying all of Latin America not just Central America, but his results were similar. His questionnaire went to 681 corporations, and 152 of them, or 22 percent, replied, compared with the author's response rate of 18 percent. Both are fairly good returns for mail surveys. Thirty-seven of Dean's respondents declared their willingness to let serious researchers use their files under certain circumstances; this amounts to just under 6 percent of his mailings. The author's 15 out of 299 amounts to 5 percent for Central America. The first obvious conclusion is that the passage of ten years has made slight difference in the attitude of corporations toward the opening of their records to the historian.

Some other conclusions are less simplistic. The questionnaire was deliberately brief to keep from intruding too much on the time of the respondents; even so, a note of testiness crept into many of the replies. Using the self-addressed envelope supplied with the questionnaire, a number of officers scribbled replies that were of little more use than if the questionnaire

1. Most useful for this author's purposes was the *Directory of American Firms Operating in Foreign Countries* (8th ed. rev., New York, 1975). A disconcerting number of corporations, including some very large ones, have moved since the directory was published and left no forwarding address. So, at least, said the post office. Many other firms denied doing any business at all in Central America, in spite of the author's guides.
2. Warren Dean, "Sources for the Study of Latin American Economic History: the Records of North American Private Enterprise," *Latin American Research Review,* 3 (1968): 79–86.

had been thrown away. Some of the larger, more public relations-conscious corporations gave the author paternal lectures about the frequency with which the academic world solicits the business world for information. One manufacturer of a soft drink that is surely a household word, declared that it answers no surveys at all from faculty, but sent a colorful advertisement for the author's very own.

At the risk of obtaining a smaller response, a longer letter of explanation might have been useful, for some replies indicated a misunderstanding of the purposes of the questionnaire. A few officers, in fact, seemed to consider worthless the very kind of documentation that the historian most seeks, presumably feeling that an elaborate library or archive was essential for the historian. However, others were quite at home with the questions, even having brochures printed which explain the precise rules governing the use of their archives.

The following corporations, all doing business in one or more Central American states, indicated their willingness to cooperate with scholars, at least to the extent of answering inquiries and attempting to make materials available:

Allied Chemical Corporation
Box 1053
Morristown, New Jersey 07960
A collection of business books, journals, specialty reports on textiles and chemicals is available. It can be used on special request within the library. There is very little on Latin America.

American International Underwriters Corporation
102 Maiden Lane
New York, New York 10005
General office files regarding insurance operations of their Latin American offices are available.

The Chase Manhattan Bank
1 Chase Manhattan Plaza
New York, New York 10015
The bank has specific policies for the use of their substantial archives. Write for their published statement of these regulations.

Cutler Hammer
4201 North 26th Street
Milwaukee, Wisconsin 53216
Contact Lorenzo Christie, General Manager, San José, Costa Rica, for the company's activities in all of Central America.

Deere and Company
John Deere Road
Moline, Illinois 61265
Scrap books and confidential reports are available. Requests for use are processed individually by the company archivist.

Eastman Kodak Company
343 State Street
Rochester, New York 14650
Materials are classified, but inquiries may be directed to the company's Historical Information Specialist, Corporate Information Department.

Eli Lilly and Company
Indianapolis, Indiana 46206
There is little material available on international operations. Requests are handled individually by the company archivist.

Firestone Tire and Rubber Company
Akron, Ohio 44317
There are some twenty-five hundred square feet of archives, including clippings, photographs, and information about the company in Latin America. Most of the material is classified, however.

Gerber Products Company
445 State Street
Fremont, Michigan 49412
The company is now organizing an international archives in Fremont. It contains clippings and pictures back to about 1931 in Latin America.

Gulf Oil Company–Latin America
Box 340910
Coral Gables, Florida 33134
The company has no central archives for Latin America alone; records are widely scattered. The company will consider specific requests and will rule depending on the nature of the request.

International Engineering Company, Incorporated
220 Montgomery Street
San Francisco, California 94104
This company is new to Guatemala, El Salvador, and Nicaragua. It will consider specific requests.

International Harvester Company
401 North Michigan Avenue
Chicago, Illinois 60611

Permission may be granted. Write to Director of Public Relations for rules governing their policies.

Kraft, Incorporated
Kraft Court
Glenview, Illinois 60025
Kraft will consider requests for permission, but the librarian considers Latin American materials to be very skimpy.

Texaco, Incorporated
2000 Westchester Avenue
White Plains, New York 10650
Past company publications, annual reports, magazines, and official photographs are available for study.

Wells Fargo Bank
420 Montgomery Street
San Francisco, California 94104
Materials about economic conditions in certain countries and relations with governments and customers are available. Most are confidential, but written requests will be considered.

Since none of the companies gave carte blanche for use of their archives, are the returns of any value? Just as a sort of control, the author included in the survey a corporation whose archives he had personally used. The reply to the questionnaire was firmly negative. That strange response merely helps to demonstrate that no organization, no matter how well it thinks of the academic world, is likely to announce that its records are open to one and all. Scholars should be grateful that certain corporations operating in Central America think seriously enough about the historical value of their records to put them aside with someone in charge for safekeeping, and under certain circumstances to let other people, equally concerned and responsible, use them for research.

These companies should be treated with the same understanding that researchers give to governmental archives—especially those foreign. At the very least, a courteous letter of introduction followed up by a personal visit with a list of specific research problems that the company might reasonably be expected to help solve would be valuable. Scholars have no right to expect a broad warrant to search the premises, or to ask for a detailed calendar of the contents. They can get nowhere without cooperation, and that can come only with the development of mutual respect and confidence based upon behavior and attitudes over some period of time.

Meanwhile, historians can do a double job of selling. While trying to prove their individual worth, they can do their bit for the profession.

There are many corporations with assets in the hundreds of millions, whose records are scattered over several nations, even continents, to the degree that no one in the firm knows what exists or where. Frequently the company executives themselves are unable to take advantage of these mines of information. Corporation administrators are geared to the streamlining or actual destruction of records rather than to their use. Since investment in Central America is a relatively recent thing, the memories of old-timers are often the best record of why a particular packaging failed in one nation or why a certain chemical worked in one republic and not another. The historian can help demonstrate that an archive is valuable incidentally to the historian but directly to the corporation for administrative as well as public-image needs. One multinational estimates that its archives have saved it ten million dollars in settlements. Another declares that its *marketing* people use the archives far more frequently than any other group of people.

Without question the most cordial responses came from those firms who had the services of a librarian or archivist. They understood the needs of the historian, just as they made clear the value and limitations of the company's records.

The comments cited above about the different company archives came from the respondents themselves and with some examination are quite suggestive. Most of them at least can provide the researcher with a run of the annual reports. There are photographs, scrapbooks, and even correspondence available, and *mirabile dictu* most of the material will be printed, not handwritten.

The odds are not impossible that one or more of these companies would tolerate or encourage the production of a history of its Central American activities; the problem is one of persuasion and selling. Any historian who has ever received a research grant should know how to do that. But the other possibilities are limited only by the historian's imagination.

Some research can be accomplished without cooperation from the corporation, of course, for since New Deal days a great deal of information has been a part of the public record, but not a great amount of research worth attempting can be done without the company's help. Annual reports, for example, are public, but try getting a complete run of them from anyone but the company officers. Unless the day comes when all private records must be opened to the public, the historian must have the assistance of the corporation. Getting that assistance is a task whose time has come.

38 The Genealogical Society of Utah
Shirley A. Weathers

A description of the microfilm holdings of the Genealogical Society of Utah represents for some a correction of misconceptions and for others an introduction to an archive seldom used by historians of Central America. Undoubtedly, many are aware of the existence of this archive, formulated for and dedicated to the sole purpose of aiding individual Mormon church members in tracing their genealogies as part of their religious responsibilities. However, this motivation, unique among the archives discussed in this *Guide,* offers to the academic community a U.S. depository of materials otherwise found only in foreign archives. Particularly historians with an interest in the fields of demography and social and cultural history can benefit from utilization of this collection, which consists of over seven thousand hundred-foot rolls of filmed manuscripts.

This description will concern itself only with Central America, because, to date, filming projects have not begun in any part of the Caribbean. Likewise, only Guatemala, Panama, El Salvador, and Costa Rica will be discussed in detail, since archives within present-day Nicaragua, Honduras, and Belize have not been opened to filming.

Vital statistics are one type of document placed high on the society's priority list, being defined by policy-makers as "of genealogical significance." Therefore, parish registers (consisting of baptismal, marriage, and burial records) form a sizable portion of the Central American collection. Thus far, the only country where filming of parish registers has been completed is Panama. The earliest dated records of this type for that country is 1707, the latest 1973, although the majority most usually span dates from approximately 1850 to 1950.

Guatemalan records of the same type are not nearly so complete—an estimated 38 percent have been filmed. Materials for most parishes begin within ten years of their establishment dates (the oldest of those filmed being the early seventeenth century). Only one parish register extends to dates past 1936; many terminate during the nineteenth century.

El Salvador is the only other country of Central America from which filmed parish registers have been acquired. An estimate of parishes completed is 15 percent. Dates covered are the eighteenth through the early twentieth century.

Also of genealogical significance are vital statistics produced by civil

167

authorities—civil registers (consisting of birth, marriage, and death records). Only Guatemalan filming is significant (approximately 84 percent complete); civil registers for Costa Rica and El Salvador are sparse as yet, although projects are ongoing in all three countries. Those films in the society's possession date approximately from 1870 to 1940, with a few scattered exceptions.

A major part of the Central American collection is a 2,700-roll copy of documents in the Archivo General de Centro América. These films reflect the enormously varied contents of that archive from the sixteenth through the twentieth century. Among the types of records available are civil and criminal court records of the eighteenth and nineteenth centuries; Fiscalía investigations of *limpieza de sangre, hidalguía, real concesiones,* and other types of documentation relating to individuals' honors and titles; wills and probate records from throughout the captaincy general (the early sixteenth century) to the 1820s; records of the Audiencia de Guatemala (1808–22); a wide variety of land records from the sixteenth to the nineteenth century; nineteenth-century census records; *pensiones* and *reales cédulas,* seventeenth century to 1821; marriage records and litigation, seventeenth to the nineteenth century; notarial records (1508–1917); Dirección General de Estadística records, including *padrones* and tribute information for all parts of the former captaincy general from 1599 through 1877; government documents, including passport records, 1579 to the twentieth century; account books (1688–1815); military records (1895–1903); scattered records of municipal councils and correspondence; *Real Hacienda* (1636–1833); an index of the archives of the municipality of Guatemala (1578–1878); baptismal records (1694–1880); and a small number of burial records for Guatemala (1871–1920). A complete and detailed description of the portion of the archive held by the society, as well as a roll-by-roll catalogue, is contained in Shirley A. Weathers, "Bibliographic Guide to the Collection from the Archivo General de Centro América," Number 8, in *Finding Aids to the Microfilmed Manuscript Collection of the Genealogical Society of Utah,* ed. Roger M. Haigh (Salt Lake City, 1981).

Two sizable collections pertaining to the former captaincy general of Guatemala but not filmed at the Archivo General include the following: (1) Archivo General de la Diócesis de Chiapas (420 rolls), containing Church records including parish records, business matters, wills, censuses, titles, royal decrees relating to ecclesiastical matters, chapel and convent records, and records of the ecclesiastical *cabildo,* sixteenth to the nineteenth century; (2) Archivo General y Público de la Nación—Proceso del Santo Oficio de Méjico (1522–1820), containing microfilm copies of volumes 1–1551 of the Inquisition's records of activity throughout New Spain. Information includes accusations, testimonies, inventory lists of confiscated goods, lists of deportations, and genealogies of processed persons. An index to the contents is included.

Utilization of the society's collection can be aided by an awareness of the cataloguing system. The volume and speed of acquisition of film has forced cataloguers to rely almost entirely on reports by camera operators in the preparation of card entries as to the contents of films. This amounts to a reproduction of the cataloguing system in use at each archive where filming is done. For records residing in well-organized depositories, this practice presents no problems; however, the practice used by others—that of bundling records without careful perusal by adequately trained personnel—can lead to inaccurate accounting of contents, and even inadequate description of record types. These kinds of errors go undiscovered and are transferred onto catalogue cards at the society.

Another related problem is vagueness of some card catalogue designations. Prior to 1968, cataloguers in the Latin American section of the society attempted to ascertain the meanings of the originally filmed volume headings and translated them into English. Due to a lack of familiarity with record types generated within religious and civil bodies in the region, a significant number of cases can be found where the actual nature of the contents was misconstrued. Moreover, this procedure increased the chances of similar types of documents appearing under several different English names in the card catalogue, depending on the degree of expertise of the cataloguer or even on the particular dictionary consulted by various individuals. Having recognized the problem, the society attempted to rectify it in 1968 by preparing cards for subsequently acquired films in Spanish. However, the majority of pre-1968 cards have not been changed.

A researcher interested in utilizing the society's holdings can proceed either by traveling to Salt Lake City, or by making use of various branch libraries throughout the country, normally affiliated with a local church of Jesus Christ of Latter Day Saints (Mormon). Although it is obvious that the use of an interlibrary loan facility requires time for the transport of the desired materials, it must be noted that few films from the Central American collection are immediately available at the main library. Films are stored in a vault in their negative state until such time as a request is filed for printing a positive copy. Two weeks are required for this process. Nevertheless, it is hoped that this description of the materials and organizational procedures of the archive will encourage researchers to avail themselves of this rich collection. One may correspond directly with the Genealogical Society at 50 E. N. Temple, Salt Lake City, Utah 84105. A useful précis of Guatemalan documentation and where to find it is the Genealogical Society's *Major Genealogical Record Sources in Guatemala,* Ser. H, No. 1 (n.p., 1970).

39   Spanish Archives
William L. Sherman and
Thomas M. Fiehrer

In his 1969 confessions of a researcher in the period of the Spanish republic and civil war, historian Gabriel Jackson marveled at the rare personal qualities of the peasants he encountered during his sojourn in Spain in the 1950s. The stoic dignity with which the masses endured the poverty of the post–civil war era inspired Professor Jackson "to write the best history of which [he] was capable."[1] The results have been two very fine works on the Middle Ages[2] and the republic and civil war. The archives were another matter: "Their effective use would have to wait for a thoroughgoing change of regime."[3] With the passing of Franco, that change has, of course, transpired, and researchers in medieval, colonial, and modern materials enjoy considerable freedom to lose themselves in Spain's numerous depositories, and to ponder the grandeur of Hispanic civilization as revealed in a seemingly infinite manuscript record.

Of particular interest are those holdings and materials derived from the centuries of Spanish colonial society and economy in the Central American isthmus. Like the rest of the Latin American region, Central America is presently undergoing a series of discreet national liberations from the constraints of economic colonialism. Part of this historic struggle involves rewriting, but in most instances writing for the first time, systematic studies of the colonial societies and of the nineteenth-century experiment with various modes of liberalism. For several decades the quality and quantity of scholarly or "scientific" works treating the evolution of Middle American society have increased dramatically. Key sources for this ongoing exploration of the past (and their concomitant development of a new sense of identity in the present) are to be found in the masses of colonial material preserved in peninsular archives. There the multitude of modern nation states whose origins lay in the three centuries of Spanish imperialism will generally find sufficient data to reconstruct their respective pasts and to explain many of the anomalies in the present day.

The richest trove of materials emanating from nearly a half millennium

1. Gabriel Jackson, *The Historian's Quest, a Twenty-Year Journey into the Spanish Mind* (New York, 1968), 18.
2. Gabriel Jackson, *Spain in the Middle Ages* (Princeton, 1978).
3. Jackson, *Historian's Quest,* 187.

of expansionary activity in Africa, America, and the Pacific is housed in the Casa Lonja in Seville, where the Archivo General de Indias (AGI) has represented a sort of Mecca, training ground, and highly personal adventure for historical and other researchers since its establishment in the late eighteenth century. The AGI is indispensable to nearly any serious study of practically any conceivable topic or discipline related to Spain's overseas history. Situated among monuments of Spain's rich past (the Christian cathedral, the Moorish Alcázar, and the old Jewish quarter of Santa Cruz), the AGI opens onto an avenue leading to the river Guadalquivir and the New World.

Construction of the building (the old Casa de Contratación), in the architectural style of Juan de Herrera, began in the 1580s, when Seville prospered as the entrepot of the Indies. But it was not until much later— by which time Cádiz had superseded Seville as the most important port— that the structure became the archive. Although colonial documents had been catalogued since the sixteenth century, not until the 1780s was don Juan Bautista de Muñoz, the *cronista de Indias,* commissioned to organize an archive specifically for papers concerning the American colonies. The actual transfer of documents began in 1785. With its large salons, imposing stairways, and spacious courtyard, the building was a fitting choice for the treasures it was to house.

The scholar beginning investigation in the AGI will find a fertile field for the history of colonial Central America. In addition to 3,392 maps and plans of the Spanish colonies, the archive has a total of almost forty thousand *legajos,* arranged under sixteen divisions (*secciones*) according to different subject categories. It is practically impossible to determine the precise number of legajos with Central American content, but the investigator can gain some idea of the quantity and variety of documentation from the few representative examples that follow.

Section	*Number of legajos*
Audiencia de Guatemala	973
Justicia:	
Autos apelados ante el Consejo (1534–82)	55
Autos visto ante el Consejo (1528–72)	11
Escribanía de Cámara (*pleitos, residencias, visitas,* and *comisiones*)	50
Contraduría:	
Registros de ida, Honduras (information on cargos, including	
books, as well as names of passengers)	22
Naos que vienen flotas o en conserva de Honduras (1591–1690)	37
Naos que vinieron sueltas de Honduras (1604–1778)	19
Other categories	30

Papeles de Correos (Guatemala, 1768–1822)   12
Papeles de Estado (Guatemala, 1787–1820)   3

These legajos by no means represent all the Central American colonial documents in the AGI, and all secciones should be consulted with care. Researchers unfamiliar with the holdings of the archive are strongly urged to study some of the various publications that examine the nature of the documentation before actually commencing research in the archive. Such groundwork is extremely helpful in defining the scope of one's project, and it avoids wasting valuable time in the archival research itself.

Services offered by the archivo include efficient microfilm service as well as competent research assistants and copyists. In recent years facilities of comfort have been added for the convenience of scholars. Traditional appointments and the customary courtesy of the staff further enhance a pleasant *ambiente*.

In addition to photographic copies and microfilm holdings in various depositories in the United States, recent projects have extended the availability of AGI materials in this country. Specifically, a cooperating group of researchers that includes members of the AGI, the University of Pennsylvania, and the American Philosophical Society has reproduced about seventy thousand pages of sixteenth-century documents relating to the Audiencia de Guatemala. Moreover, astonishing news was made public recently that Mexico has arranged to microfilm the entire holdings of the AGI! Still, the colonial historian should make every effort to spend at least a few months working with the original documents in their natural historical setting. The rewards of the experience help to compensate for the eyestrain and premature graying of the paleographer.

Of the several guides available, the following are recommended for their helpful details: José María de la Peña y Cámara, *Archivo General de Indias de Sevilla: Guía del Visitante* (Madrid, 1959); Lino Gómez Canedo, *Los archivos de la historia de América* (2 vols., México, 1961); VI Congreso Internacional de Minería, *Documentos existentes en el Archivo General de Indias, sección de Guatemala,* Vol. 6 (León, España, 1970).

Several lesser depositories in Spain also contain Central American sources, and a number of these house unique collections.[4] The two largest holdings of American material outside Seville are the Archivo General de

---

4. Among the basic guides, Gómez Canedo, mentioned above, is the most useful. Others include: Vicente Cortés Alonso and Federico Udina Martorell, *Guía de los archivos estatales españoles* (Madrid, 1977); Jesús Larios Martín, *Catálogo de los archivos españoles en que se conservan fondos genealógicos y nobillarios* (Madrid, 1960); Luis Sánchez Belda, *Guía del archivo histórico nacional* (Valencia, 1958); and Julian Paz, *Catálogo de manuscritos de América existentes en la biblioteca nacional* (Madrid, 1933).

Simancas and the Archivo Histórico Nacional, the former in Old Castile, the latter in the capital. Simancas is located on a windswept, arid plain some ten kilometers from the one-time capital Valladolid. The archive is housed in the castle of the village of Simancas. Old guidebooks suggest that researchers may find residence here, but lately accommodations in the village have evaporated. There is, however, a convenient bus service from Valladolid. Documents were preserved here from the earliest American exploits of the Castilians, and many remain despite the transfer of substantial materials to Seville in 1785.

In the Archivo General de Simancas, Central American data may be found in secciones 9, 20, 21, and 25. Sección 9, Secretaría de Guerra (siglo XVIII), includes *serie* 41, legajos 6393–951, covering roughly the years 1783–1802, and serie 50, Hojas de Servicio, legajo 7269, covering the period 1789–99. Lastly, this section contains serie 51, Revistas de Ynspección, legajos 7299–300, covering the years 1787–1800. These deal with administrative and often military matters. The Hojas de Servicio contain considerably detailed biographical information on military and civil functionaries. Each record indicates (with occasional inconsistency or omission) data such as place of origin (not necessarily birth), age, promotions, rank, and, most interesting, an evaluation of the subject's ability (*talento*) made by his superior.

Sección 20, Dirección General de Rentas, serie 20, legajos 568–80, concerns "free trade" between Spain and the Indies from 1778 to 1795, including Central American data. Sección 25, Secretaría de Hacienda, contains fragmentary records of *asientos* in the slave trade for the years 1732–39, 1760, and 1761. Some of these records refer to agriculture and port construction in Central America. Under the heading "Guerra," this section also contains Hojas de Servicio, taken from serie 50 of sección 9 and catalogued by surname. Sección 9 further offers a collection of materials added to the archive in 1844. Listed as legajos 5589–7327 under the heading "Guerra Moderna," these materials pertain to the last third of the eighteenth century. Serie 41 deals with Guatemala from 1783 to 1802; and serie 49, called Generalidad de Indias, holds miscellaneous data on Central American subjects from the period 1769–1800.

Lastly, the Estado subdivision includes two legajos treating Scottish activity in the Panama region toward the end of the seventeenth century.

The Archivo Histórico Nacional (AHN) (founded in 1816) is located in the complex of the Consejo Superior de Investigaciones Científicas at Serrano 15, a bit to the northeast of downtown Madrid. The archive is enhanced by the nearby library and *residencia*, where rooms and meals are available in the company of scholars from every part of the peninsula. Of central importance to Central American researchers are secciones 2, Ordenes Militares; 3, Estado, and 8, Consejos Suprimidos. The first contains the *pruebas,* (or proofs) of lineage, old Christian ancestry, nobility, legitimacy, and honor that accompanied petitions for admission to the military orders of Alcántara, Santiago, Calatrava, and St. John of Jerusalem (Malta). Worthy of careful study, these materials illuminate untold mysteries concerning the bases of status, nobility, patronage, and family alliance in eighteenth-century Spanish society. Among the personalities whose pruebas appear are several who left their mark on administration and society in the isthmus. These papers offer rich detail of the criteria of social stratification and genealogy as to the civil and military bureaucracy.[5] Estado (sección 3) contains general administrative papers of colonial officials, illustrative of foreign relations, diplomacy, war, and defense. The legajos occasionally include drawings, sketches, *planos* of topography, waterways, fortifications, etc. The Central Americam material may be tedious to ferret out, for it is often subsumed under more inclusive headings such as "New Spain." There are twenty-two legajos of reports of functionaries from 1704 to 1833. Consejos (sección 8) holds proceedings of the Council of the Indies, including reports of colonial functionaries and their residencias. This collection offers a nucleus of Guatemalan and regional residencia proceedings, including those of seven *audiencia* presidents, one regent, three *oidores,* one *fiscal,* eleven governors, six *alcaldes mayores,* and two secretaries. These materials are dense, verbose, and repetitive in their elaboration of lengthy standard-form prefatory material. But the essence of colonial administrative processes, problems, tensions, and accommodations is dramatically set forth in the testimonies, charges, and countercharges therein recorded. Outgoing functionaries were often charged with offenses, requiring the state to supply contrary testimony. Here the level of control and conflict may be accurately discerned, as well as the socioethnic makeup of communities and whole regions. They further suggest the mechanics of the law and the detailed operation of a cumbersome administrative machinery, which seems so incongruous in remote, slightly developed, agrarian societies.[6]

A very heterogeneous and less-known collection, the Archivo General Militar, and specifically the section Servicio Histórico Militar, is located

5. See the comprehensive study of M. A. Burkholder and D. S. Chandler based on collateral materials from the AGI: *From Impotence to Authority, the Spanish Crown and the American Audiencias, 1687–1800* (Columbia, Missouri, 1977); on pruebas and their origins see L. P. Wright, "The Military Orders in 16th and 17th Century Spanish Society," *Past and Present,* 43 (May 1969): 34–70. See also José Tudela de la Orden, *Los manuscritos de América en las bibliotecas de España* (Madrid, 1954).

6. See María del Carmen Pescador del Hoyo, *Documentos de Indias, siglos XV–XIX: Archivo Histórico Nacional* (Madrid, 1954).

at Ventura Rodríguez Street, Madrid. As the section's name suggests, these materials originate in military jurisdictions, and generally contain data on strategy, defense, and the militarization of the colonies in the Bourbon century.[7] The documents are catalogued in geographical order, preceded by capital letters. Sección E indicates the Americas, followed by twelve subdivisions by country. Sección B includes materials on Central America, which run from signatures 6.713 to 6.827. Many of the records here are copies of originals in the AGI. Several signatures include analyses of the defense posture of the isthmus during the wars with England. There is a valuable section of *mapas y planos* with drawings of the ports and the new capital site, discussions of mobilization prospects, descriptions of the militia forces, and characterizations of the imagined enemy. Several maps show the audiencia in its entirety.[8] There is also a small library arranged haphazardly. Some shelves contain bound manuscript collections or treatises on military matters in the colonies, which could prove invaluable to certain research interests. Microfilming is possible. And no colonial researcher should miss "Descripción del reyno de Guatemala," written by the engineer Luis Díaz Navarro in 1769 (signature 1–11–1).

The next depository in order of importance, and the most interesting for its variety of materials, is the Archivo General de la Marina, located at Montalbán 2, overlooking the Cibeles and the post office in downtown Madrid. Also known as the Museo Naval, this collection is unexcelled in the breadth and variety of its offerings. A tremendous variety of unconventional sources is housed here, although most pieces appear to be fragments of more extensive collections. Heterogeneous documents have been bound together, occasioning considerable excitement and frustration. A card catalogue is available for the location of manuscripts, generally by region, but research here is haphazard, since some materials are as yet unorganized. Central American data are dispersed throughout many of the bound manuscript reports of travel, economic patterns, trade reforms, and Indian revolts.

A thoroughly fascinating though incompletely organized body of materials, many of them anonymous but bearing the mark of Bustamante or Malaspina, is the Colección Malaspina (manuscript numbers 175 and 279–80). Included are numerous poignant observations and interviews with prominent colonial officials by members of Malaspina's party, which

7. I. Christon Archer, *The Army in Bourbon Mexico, 1760–1810* (Albuquerque, 1977); and Leon Campbell, *The Military and Society in Colonial Peru, 1750–1810* (Philadelphia, 1978) are recent works that explore this theme.

8. An example of the uses of these materials is Troy S. Floyd, *The Anglo-Spanish Struggle for Mosquitia* (Albuquerque, 1967).

departed Spain in July of 1789 and returned from a voyage around the world in May of 1792.[9] Many of the pieces are clearly copies. Of central interest is a loosely contained collection of *grabados y dibujos,* made by the four Spanish artists who accompanied the *Descubierta* and the *Atrevida* and their Italian navigator on this scientific expedition–reconnaissance mission to the Pacific. These include detailed and occasionally incomplete sketches, some in color, of the Indians of coastal South America and the Andes, Central America, and North America to Nootka Sound and Vancouver.[10] There are also a few drawings of Central American ports and their inhabitants.

The fifth holding of manuscript sources relating to Central America may be located in the department of manuscripts in the Biblioteca Nacional on the Castellana thoroughfare in Madrid. Here are over three dozen items on seventeenth- and eighteenth-century isthmian life, ranging from monasteries and convents to the dealings of the Justiani Chaverri family, Genoese merchants of social prominence and economic significance in the region.[11] Although the catalogue lists only thirty-seven documents that refer directly to Central America, they represent a variety of subjects and span the sixteenth through the eighteenth century.[12]

In the Biblioteca del Palacio Real is a valuable collection of materials derived from the eighteenth-century office of the Secretaría de Gracia y Justicia. The American-related items have been catalogued by Jesus Domínguez Bordona (1935),[13] and include the bulk of the monumental Muñoz Collection, brought here in 1817 from the Real Academia de Historia, and the original manuscript of Fuentes y Guzmán's *Recordación Florida,* written in 1690 and published in 1882–83. A number of lesser documents of Central American interest are also inventoried.

9. Studies in English of this phenomenal expedition are limited to occasional periodical literature. In Spanish see: Pedro Novo y Colson, *Viaje político-científico alrededor del mundo de Malaspina, 1789–1794* (Madrid, 1885); Ramón Manjarres, *En el mar del sur; expediciones españolas del siglo XVIII* (Sevilla, 1916); Carlos Divito Arias, *Las expediciones científicas españolas del siglo XVIII* (Buenos Aires, 1959); and Bonifacio del Carril, *La expedición Malaspina* (Buenos Aires, 1961).

10. A dissertation by María García Sotoca, which analyzes a large sample of the paintings and drawings of the expedition, is available in the archive to assist researchers. See also, Henry Raup Wagner, "The Diary of Thomas Suria, a Painter with the Malaspina Expedition," *Pacific Historical Review,* 5 (1936): 232–36.

11. Murdo MacLeod, *Spanish Central America: A Socioeconomic History, 1520–1720* (Berkeley, 1973), 188–89, 321, discusses this group.

12. The traditional guide is Julián Paz, *Catálogo de manuscritos de América existentes en la biblioteca nacional* (Madrid, 1930). See also, Federico Esteve Barba, "Notas para un estudio de los fondos relativos a América en la Biblioteca Nacional," *Revista de archivos, bibliotecas y museos,* 73 (1966): 245–70.

13. Jesus Domínguez Bordona, *Manuscritos de América* (Madrid, 1935).

The Biblioteca de la Academia de Historia at 43 León, Madrid, has been a key institution in the preservation and compilation of Spanish history since 1735. It conserves a number of collections and a manuscript index to the Fondo General de Manuscritos, which do not pertain to the great collections. Of interest here are Manuscript 11–4–3/848 with maps and descriptions concerning the Panama region (1761–85) and Manuscript 12–11–6.M.106 on ruins and volcanos in Guatemala in 1775. There is a catalogue to the Muñoz Collection, showing a number of Central American documents: letters of Alvarado and Cortés; a letter from the regent of the Audiencia de Guatemala; and a description of Panama in 1650.

The Archivo General y Biblioteca del Ministerio de Asuntos Exteriores is located at 1 Salvador Street within walking distance of the Plaza Mayor in Madrid. The documents of American origin derive largely from the office of Manuel Godoy, favorite of Charles IV and virtual head of the Spanish state in the turbulent 1790s. The papers came to the Secretaría de Estado y del Despacho Universal, which evolved after creole independence into the Ministry of Foreign Affairs.[14] Under the decimal classification system used here, one finds in sección 3, Ciencias Sociales, subheading 341 (Derecho Internacional), documents from the years 1534 to 1821, amassed to arbitrate a Honduran-Nicaraguan conflict over the Mosquito Coast in 1905. These are originals drawn from the AGI. In sección 9, Geografía, Biografía, e Historia, are papers from the notables of the Malaspina expedition mentioned above.

The Archivo-Biblioteca del Jardín Botánico in Madrid holds a remarkable series of writings by the scientific giants and sages of the late Spanish Enlightenment. Among these are the works of Mociño and Longinos, both of which treat, among other things, Middle American agriculture and thus indigo. Most colonial scientists resided in the jurisdictions of New Granada or New Spain, but several studied products of great economic importance to Central America.

In conclusion, specialists in the colonial history of Middle America will find a number of the manuscript holdings discussed of varying degrees of importance, depending on their particular areas of interest. Trade, agriculture, and militarization in the second half of the eighteenth century are referred to and, in a few cases, thoughtfully analyzed in the writings of the period. Some researchers will perhaps find at least some of these sources indispensable.

14. Miguel Santiago, "Los manuscritos del Archivo General y Biblioteca del Ministerio de Asuntos Exteriores," *Revista de archivos, bibliotecas y museos*, 74 (1967): 243–326.

40   Great Britain
Robert A. Naylor

Great Britain is a major source for archival materials dealing with Central America. England presented one of the earliest and most successful challenges to Spanish power in the Caribbean in the seventeenth and eighteenth centuries, achieved a position of preeminence on the Central American isthmus in the nineteenth century, and remained influential well into the twentieth century. The one indispensable tool for locating relevant materials on Central America in Britain is Peter Walne, ed., *A Guide to Manuscript Sources for the History of Latin America and the Caribbean in the British Isles* (London, 1973). This well-indexed work provides detailed descriptions of materials relating to Central America throughout Great Britain.[1]

British contact with the Kingdom of Guatemala prior to its independence in 1823 was sporadic and limited. British activities in the seventeenth and eighteenth centuries were restricted to buccaneering, woodcutting, contraband trade, and small-scale military ventures on the Mosquito Shore and in the Bay of Honduras along the isolated and relatively unimportant Caribbean coast of Central America. These furtive activities did not leave a clear historical trail behind them. The British incursions emanated from the British stronghold on Jamaica after 1655, and materials pertinent to Central America have to be gleaned indirectly from masses of

1. For a description of the collections of *printed* material pertaining to Latin America held by some three hundred libraries in Great Britain as of July 1973, along with information on admission, hours, copying, and lending policies, Bernard Naylor, Laurence Hallewell, and Colin Steele, *Directory of Libraries and Special Collections on Latin America and the West Indies* (London, 1975). The most extensive holdings are those of the British Museum Library, but, with the exception of Costa Rica, Central America is not as well covered as other areas. See Pascual de Gayangos, *Catalogue of the Manuscripts in the Spanish Language in the British Museum* (4 vols., London, 1875–93). The second best collection is in the Bodleian Library at Oxford, but, again, Central America is not one of the areas of specialization. The Latin American History collection of University College Library in London is one of the best in the United Kingdom. Research tools are the specialty of the Institute of Latin American Studies Library, University of London. The University of Essex Library is making extensive acquisitions of Central American publications for Guatemala, Honduras, Nicaragua, and El Salvador, and the Devon County Library of Exeter is specializing in collecting material on the history of Central America and the West Indies. See also Dean Kortge, "Centro América en los archivos británicos (siglo XIX)," *Estudios sociales centroamericanos*, 1, 3(1972): 206–10.

documents dealing primarily with the British West Indies. The results can be disappointing, since only occasional references to Central America may surface.

The major collections of documents on the West Indies for the seventeenth and eighteenth centuries are those of the Colonial Office and the Foreign Office deposited in the Public Record Office, London. Jamaican materials are found in the records of the Colonial Office. Any information prior to 1688 is filed under Colonial Papers, General Series, C.O. 1, when the British colonies in the New World were all lumped together. Beginning in 1689 relevant material was filed under the Original Correspondence of Jamaica, C.O. 137, with volumes 59–81 dealing almost exclusively with the Mosquito Shore. Some of the military affairs in Central America appear in the Supplementary Correspondence, C.O. 537, beginning with 1759. Of peripheral interest would be the Jamaican Sessional Papers, C.O. 140, beginning in 1661, and Miscellanea, C.O. 142, beginning in 1658.

Since the British maintained a foothold in Belize, information can be found in the first thirty volumes of the Original Correspondence of British Honduras, C.O. 123, starting in 1744. Spain's response to the British intrusions appear in the State Paper Office, Foreign Division, under Spain, S.P. 94 (1577–1780), 255 volumes, and in the Domestic Division under Miscellaneous, S.P. 9 (1463–1800), 265 volumes, the latter including materials on Central America. Later relations with Spain are in the records of the Foreign Office under Spain, F.O. 72, beginning in 1781. The 144 volumes of the Naval State Papers, S.P. 42 (1689–1782), including letters from the lords of the admiralty and naval commanders on naval affairs are another source for early Central American history. Occasional references turn up in the correspondence of the Board of Trade, filed under C.O. 323 (1689–1780) and C.O. 5 (1606–1807).

There are also relevant manuscripts in the British Museum in London, especially in the Sloane Collection. In addition, there are a variety of other relevant manuscripts in other British Museum collections listed in the Walne *Guide,* pages 57–123.

Outside the Public Record Office and the British Museum there exists a diverse assortment of individual documents on colonial Central America that are widely scattered in various collections throughout England. Walne identifies Central American materials in the Hobart Papers in the County Record Office in Aylesbury, Buckinghamshire; in the Pitt Papers and Cholmondeley Papers in the university library at Cambridge; the Grenville Papers in the care of G. G. Fortescue, Esquire, Baconnoc, Lostwithiel, in Cornwall; the personal papers of Admiral Sir William Parker in the National Maritime Museum, Greenwich, London; the libraries of the Royal

Commonwealth Society and the Bodleian Library at Oxford; the Finch
Papers of Lieutenant Colonel James Hanbury, Burley-on-the-Hill in Rut-
land; the Saumarez Smith Papers, Farnham in Surrey; the Marquess of
Lansdowne Papers, Bowood, Calne, in Wiltshire; and in ecclesiastical
records in London at the archive of the Bishop of London, in the Fulham
Palace Papers in the Lambeth Palace Library, and at the United Society
for the Propagation of the Gospel, 15 Tufton Street. The journals of the
United Society, dating from 1701, include letters and reports from Central
American missions, and the unbound Miscellaneous Papers (1701–1850),
class C/WI, include one box of papers on the Mosquito Shore (1769–85)
and British Honduras (1812–47). Additional material is located in the
Honduran Archives of the Royal Commonwealth Society Library in Lon-
don, and the Prerogative Court of the Archbishop of Canterbury, Somerset
House in London.

In Scotland, Walne indicates manuscripts on colonial Central America
in the Nisbet Papers and the Liston Papers in the National Library of
Scotland; in private papers deposited in the Scottish Record Office, H.M.
General Register House; and among the Laing Manuscripts in the university library, Old College, Southbridge, all in Edinburgh.

Walne also lists a very limited amount of manuscripts relating to colonial Central America in Belfast, Dublin, and on the Isle of Man.

For the national period of the nineteenth and twentieth centuries, the
archival material in Great Britain pertaining to Central America becomes
voluminous and is readily accessible because of the systematic way in
which it is organized. The major collections of documents on Central
America are those of the Foreign Office and the Colonial Office deposited
in the Public Record Office in London.

The correspondence in the Foreign Office from British diplomatic and
consular agents in Central America provides in chronological order a
wealth of information on just about every topic, and is the single best
source available. There are 367 volumes of general correspondence for
Central America and Guatemala, F.O. 15 (1824–1906). Material pertaining to all five of the Central American states up until the mid-nineteenth
century is filed under F.O. 15, after which time the correspondence deals
largely with Guatemalan affairs. There are 70 volumes dealing with Costa
Rica from 1848 to 1905 under F.O. 21; 71 volumes on Nicaragua from
1848 to 1905 under F.O. 56; 79 volumes on Honduras from 1856 to 1905
under F.O. 39; and 52 volumes on El Salvador from 1856 to 1905 under
F.O. 66. There are another 77 volumes on the Mosquito Shore (1844–95)
under F.O. 53, and additional material on the Mosquito Shore (1844–51)
is included in the supplement to General Correspondence filed under F.O.
97, volume 88.

Since Great Britain was at various times involved in controversies with other nations over Central American questions, considerable information can be extracted from the series on the United States, F.O. 5 (1793–1905); on Spain, F.O. 72 (1781–1905); on France, F.O. 27 (1781–1905); and to a lesser degree from the series on Mexico, F.O. 50 (1822–1905) and Colombia, F.O. 55 (1835–1905), twenty-four volumes of the latter dealing with Panama and the Nicaraguan canal, with additional information in the five volumes on Panama, F.O. 110 (1904–05).

After 1906 the Foreign Office correspondence is arranged in ten classes including Political, F.O. 371; Consular, F.O. 369, Commercial, F.O. 368; News, F.O. 395; and Treaties, F.O. 372. Each class is subdivided each year under countries or under subject headings, with the five Central American states appearing under the heading "Central America." With some exceptions, the records are open to inspection thirty years after their creation.

Also found in the Foreign Office records are the archives maintained by overseas embassies and consulates. Although much of this material is duplicated elsewhere, new material may surface that can prove valuable to the historian. For Guatemala there are 781 volumes (1825–1945) under F.O. 252, which also include consular dispatches from Nicaragua, El Salvador, and Honduras. There are also 6 volumes of letter books under F.O. 253 (1829–74), including 2 volumes of letters from the vice-consul at Chinandega in Nicaragua (1859–64). Additional general information is filed in the 20 volumes of Miscellanea, F.O. 254 (1803–73), which include Sir W. Gore Ouseley's special mission of 1857–59; Registers of Correspondence, F.O. 235; and the 7 files of the Quezaltenango Consulate, F.O. 659 (1891–1948). Correspondence from Tegucigalpa consists of 22 volumes filed under Honduras, F.O. 632 (1893–1912). Correspondence of the consulate in Managua in Nicaragua consists of 9 files under F.O. 809 (1931–33). There are also 29 files for El Salvador, F.O. 813 (1922–32); 205 volumes for Panama, F.O. 288 (1828–1936); and 12 files of correspondence between the San José consulate and the embassy in Panama, F.O. 654 (1922–24).

The Foreign Office also printed certain important political papers known as *Further Correspondence*. This series includes 11 volumes on Central America and the Caribbean, F.O. 533 (1947–57); and 294 volumes on South and Central America, F.O. 420 (1833–1941), of which 29 volumes are devoted almost exclusively to the Mosquito Shore. Additional material is filed in the 13 volumes of F.O. 461 (1942–56).

Since certain foreign secretaries played important roles in Central American affairs, their papers sometimes contain relevant information. Notable are the papers of Lord John Russell in the Public Record Office in

London, P.R.O. 30/22, containing correspondence on Central America between 1859 and 1865, and the Palmerston Papers in the British Museum and in the Broadlands Archives, c/o the National Register of Archives, Quality House, Chancery Lane, London. Of lesser importance for Central Americanists are the papers of the Earl of Clarendon, in the Bodleian Library, Oxford, where they can be used only with permission, and those of the Marquess of Salisbury in the library of Christ Church, Oxford.

The Colonial Office collections in the Public Record Office in London are another major source for information on Central America in the national period. With the British now firmly established in Belize, the Jamaican Correspondence, C.O. 137, can generally be dispensed with, since the relevant material will now appear under the Original Correspondence of British Honduras, C.O. 123, of which there are over 350 volumes for the period 1823–1943. In addition, for British Honduras there is a volume of Supplementary Correspondence, C.O. 537 (1872–98); 15 volumes of letters sent to British Honduras from the Colonial Office, C.O. 124 (1630–1872); 16 volumes of Acts, C.O. 125 (1855–1947); 42 volumes of Sessional Papers, C.O. 126 (1848–1945); 40 volumes of the government *Gazette,* C.O. 127 (1861–1945); and 117 volumes of Colonial Blue Books, Miscellanea C.O. 128 (1807–1943). There is also a series on the neighboring Bay Islands, consisting of 10 volumes of Original Correspondence, C.O. 34 (1852–61); 1 volume of Acts, C.O. 35 (1852–59); and 5 volumes of Blue Books, Miscellanea C.O. 36 (1855–59).

Other information on British Honduras appears in the Public Record Office in the 153 folders of Defense Schemes, Cab. 11 (1863–1914), filed under the Colonial–Overseas Defense Committee of C.I.D., Cabinet Office. Data on the regiments stationed in Belize can be found in volumes 1,875–929 of the War Office Monthly Returns, W.O. 17, for Honduras (1810–65). Reports relating to military lands, building, utilities, and services in British Honduras are included in the four boxes of War Office material filed under W.O. 130 (1886–1935). Volumes 503 and 504 in the War Office In-letters, W.O. 1, have some information on British Honduras for 1848–49. Limited information also appears in the 153 volumes of North America and West Indies Correspondence of the Admiralty, Adm. 128 (1810–1913) (prior to 1867 Central America was under the Jamaican sphere of operations). Accounts, correspondence, and the logbook of the *Honduran Packet* (1865–72) (C. 110/54: Hill) are among the Masters' Exhibits of the Judicial Proceedings in the legal records of the Chancery. It should be noted, furthermore, that deposited in the custody of Rhodes House Library in Oxford, under the Colonial Records Project, are development plans for British Honduras (1948–49) (C. W. L. Fishlock); the papers of Sir Eric Swayne, commissioner to British Honduras (1902–14);

reports on lands and railroads in British Honduras (1925–27); and an account of an expedition to the Cockscomb Mountains in British Honduras (1880–1900). Miscellaneous Correspondence in the library of the Royal Botanic Gardens, Kew, Richmond, contains various volumes on economic botany and plant collecting in Central America and British Honduras, for example, Central American Cultural Products (1856–1909) and British Honduras Cultural Products (1879–1913).

Trade between Central America and Great Britain since 1792 can be derived partly from the huge ledgers of the Board of Customs and Excise in the Public Record Office, London. Walne provides a detailed description of these voluminous records.[2] The records of the Board of Trade in the P.R.O. are of limited value for information on Central America. The In-letters, B.T. 1 (1796–1863), and Miscellanea, B.T. 6, are a confused mass of unsorted material. The reports under B.T. 6 and In-letters, B.T. 2 (1824–45), can usually be found in F.O. 15.[3]

Information on British companies operating in Central America can be derived in part from the files on all companies registering after 1856, maintained by the Board of Trade, Companies Registration Office, Bush House, Strand, in London. The Bancroft Library at the University of California at Berkeley has microfilmed the records of the companies operating in Central America. The files of companies that voluntarily dissolved are in the 31,740 boxes filed under the Board of Trade, Files of Dissolved Companies, B.T. 31 (1856–1948), in the Public Record Office in London.

Several hundred privately owned volumes of newspaper cuttings and letter books providing economic information on Central America are found in the archive of the Council of Foreign Bondholders, 17 Moorgate, London—an organization founded in 1868 to protect British holders of foreign government bonds. Walne's *Guide* lists, on pages 442–93, private business archives, not necessarily available to the researcher, perhaps only nine or ten of which include data on Central America.

The British Museum contains a great variety of documents on Central America in the national period, listed in Walne on pages 84–123. It also has a very good collection of Belize newspapers (1864–1913); and of the six known copies of the *Honduras Almanack,* published annually in Belize, those for the years 1826, 1827, and 1830 are in the British Museum.[4]

2. Walne, *Guide to Manuscript Sources,* 217–19. It is important to understand precisely what the customs and excise data provide the researcher. Suggested reading: Stephen Bourne, "The Official Trade and Navigation Statistics," *Journal of the Statistical Society in London,* 35 (1872): 196–217.

3. See Walne, *Guide to Manuscript Sources,* 251–55.

4. The remaining three copies of the *Almanack* for the years 1828, 1829, and 1839 are in the Royal Colonial Institute Library in London.

As with the seventeenth and eighteenth centuries, there exists outside the major collections a scattered assortment of individual documents pertaining to Central American developments in the nineteenth and twentieth centuries. Careful use of Walne's *Guide* will reveal a great many of these.[5]

There are various maps of Central America in the Public Record Office in London, and in the British Museum and the National Maritime Museum, Greenwich, London.

The foregoing introduces the researcher to the wealth of manuscript materials pertaining to Central America that are housed in British collections. Specific investigations could well carry the historian into collections not listed here, because, like gold, historical evidence is where you find it.

41   Other Western European Depositories
Thomas Schoonover

The material available in Western European archives (excluding Spain and Great Britain, treated in separate essays) for the study of European foreign relations with Central America and for important aspects of the internal history of Central America is abundant, rewarding, and generally easily accessible. Of the countries under examination in this essay, the German and French holdings are the most abundant and potentially most fruitful, followed by the holdings in Italy, Belgium, the Netherlands, and Scandinavia. Swiss and Austrian archives apparently yield little material for Central Americanists.

Germany

Students of Central America know that German archives should hold vast bodies of materials relative to Central America, because, beginning in the mid-nineteenth century, German colonists, businessmen, and diplomatic agents played an active and significant role in Central America. Fortunately, the German materials relevant to Central America escaped destruction in both world wars. Two aspects of German history have complicated the modern Central Americanist's quest to use this information. First, the

5. Not listed in Walne, however, are a few important published pamphlets related to the Poyais venture written by Bryan Edwards, Colonel G. A. Low, James Hastie, and Herman Hendriks, in volume 1, Central America, the Hume Tracts, University College Library in London. The difficulty the historian has locating related materials can be exemplified at this point by indicating that documents pertaining to the aftermath of this venture turned up in the Manuscript Division of the New York Public Library.

fact that Germany was not unified politically until 1871 means that the records of German economic and political involvement prior to 1871 are dispersed in the archives of various German states. Second, the fact that Germany and its archives were divided after World War II means that even the archival holdings for the period of German unification are dispersed.

In the German Federal Republic the largest body of material is held at the Politisches Archiv des Auswärtigen Amts (Political Archives of the Foreign Ministry) in Bonn, where it is divided into various series and subseries, the most rewarding of which is Abteilung 1A (Section 1A—the normal diplomatic correspondence). The place to begin a search of this archive or most any West German archive is in *Führer durch die Quellen zur Geschichte Lateinamerikas in der Bundesrepublik Deutschland* (Guide to the sources on Latin American history in the Federal Republic of Germany), comp. Renate Hauschild-Thiessen and Elfriede Bachmann (Bremen, 1972). However, while the Hauschild-Thiessen and Bachmann *Guide* is valuable, it serves only as an excellent indicator of sources and a general description of the main holdings of an archive. With regard to the Bonn Foreign Ministry holdings, it must be supplemented with microfilm publication T–322 of the U.S. National Archives, "A Catalog of Files and Microfilm of the German Foreign Ministry Archives, 1867–1920," which is also available in book form with the same title (Oxford, 1959), and the *Catalog of Files and Microfilm of the German Foreign Ministry Archives, 1920–1945* (3 vols., Stanford, 1962–66). The guides at the Foreign Ministry reveal materials in addition to those described in the Hauschild-Thiessen and Bachmann *Guide*. There are also quite a few collections of private papers of diplomats in the Bonn Foreign Archive. The collections of private archives continue to grow regularly.

Another rich source of material on Latin America is housed in the Bundesarchiv (National Archives) and divided among the chief depository in Koblenz and the depositories in Freiburg and Frankfurt. Koblenz holds the economic section of the Foreign Ministry archives, the Reichsfinanzministerium (Imperial Finance Ministry), Reichskanzlei (Imperial Chancellory), the Deutsches Auslands-Institut (German Foreign Institute), and some personal collections. All these materials will be useful for Central Americanists. The Bundesarchiv, Freiburg, possesses the army and navy records. The navy records are particularly interesting for Central Americanists, since they hold the richly rewarding reports and policy recommendations of naval officers who had contact with Central American countries. The Bundesarchiv, Frankfurt, possesses only material relative to the mid-nineteenth-century Frankfurt Parliament and a considerable number of private collections, some relative to Germany's foreign relations.

For the years after Central American independence and before German unification, the Staatsarchive (state archives) of some of those German states most involved in trade, shipping, and foreign affairs should be consulted. Foremost among Staatsarchiven are Hamburg, Bremen, Lübeck, Prussia, and Bavaria—the first three because of their commerce and navigation role in world trade, the latter two because they considered themselves to have a special role in Germany in influencing greater German growth and development, hence their desire to keep in touch diplomatically with areas of special interest to Germans. For special cases, other state archives might also require consultation. Once again, the Hauschild-Thiessen and Bachmann *Guide* is a good starting point, to be supplemented by the guides and experts at the Staatsarchiven themselves.

Finally, any German business archives, if they survived destruction in the last war, would offer valuable insights into German trade, investment, and other forms of political-economic involvement with Central America. The Staatsarchive of Bremen and Hamburg contain some business archives, particularly of shipping and import-export firms, some personal archives of businessmen involved in shipping and commerce, or of firms owning coffee plantations in Guatemala or elsewhere in Central America. Other useful sources of economic activity relative to Central America are the Commerz-Bibliotheken (commerce libraries) of Hamburg and Bremen. These libraries contain manuscript as well as printed primary materials relative to Germany's economic ties with Central America. The Stadtarchiv (city archive) of Frankfurt contains the archives of Frankfurt's Industrie- und Handelskammer (Chamber of Industry and Commerce), which holds very useful material relative to Central America. Much of the Frankfurt material comes from individuals and firms throughout Germany, writing the Frankfurt Chamber of Industry and Commerce to ask for its cooperative action in persuading the German Foreign Ministry to promote joint goals for developing or holding Central American, or general Latin American, trade or investment interests. In the 1880s the Siemens firm became interested in the Central American electrical industry—power, urban transit, urban lighting, and so forth. Siemens maintains a fine, publically accessible archive in Munich. Certainly other German firms possess useful material. Information regarding holdings and access to many firm archives is listed in the Minerva guide, *Archive im deutschsprachigen Raum* (2 vols., 2d ed., Berlin and New York, 1974).

It should be noted that many Prussian and some German imperial archives are now housed in the German Democratic Republic's (GDR) Deutschen Zentralarchiven (German Central Archives) at Potsdam and Merseburg. Access to these archives is uncertain but definitely worth an effort. A small amount of the Latin American material contained in the German Central Archives is available in the German Federal Republic.

The Institut für Sozial- und Wirtschaftsgeschichte, Universität Erlangen-Nürnberg, Findelgasse 7, Nürnberg, possesses microfilm copies from the German Central Archives of German consular dispatches from Latin America for the years up to 1850. In addition, the Bundesarchiv, Koblenz, possesses poor quality microfiche of the Reichskanzlei for the late nineteenth and early twentieth centuries. These records contain summaries of cabinet-level meetings and chancellory materials which could be of interest when specific matters about the strategic, transit, or economic rights of Germany in Middle America were directly or indirectly under discussion. There are several guides which are useful for making a preliminary decision about the research materials in the archives of the GDR: "Übersicht über die Quellen zu den lateinamerikanischen Staaten im Deutschen Zentralarchiv Potsdam" (Overview of the sources on the Latin American states in the German Central Archives at Potsdam) (typescript dated July 1960; photocopy in the library, University of California, Berkeley); Irmtraut Schmid, "Der Bestand des Auswärtigen Amts im Deutschen Zentralarchiv Potsdam" (The Records of the Foreign Ministry in the German Central Archive at Potsdam), *Archivmitteilungen,* 12 (1962): 71–79, 123–32; or, specifically for Central America, the bibliography of Hendrik Dane, *Die wirtschaftlichen Beziehungen Deutschlands zu Mexiko und Mittelamerika im 19. Jahrhundert* (Germany's economic relations with Mexico and Central America in the 19th century) (Köln, 1971), 229–32; and the recent Ministerrat der Deutschen Demokratischen Republik, Ministerium des Innern, *Übersicht über Quellen zur Geschichte Lateinamerikas im Archiven der Deutschen Demokratischen Republik* (Overview of sources to Latin American history in the German Democratic Republic archives) (Potsdam, 1971).

France

In Paris there are at least six research centers of potential utility to Central Americanists: the Ministère des Affaires Etrangères (MAE), Archives Nationales, Archives du Ministère de l'économie et des finances, Bibliothèque Nationale, Archives de l'Armée de la Mer, and archives of the Chambre de commerce et d'industrie. There is an excellent new guide to archival and research centers in Paris: Peter Klaus Hartman, *Pariser Archive, Bibliotheken und Dokumentationszentren zur Geschichte des 19. und 20. Jahrhunderts,* Band 1, Dokumentation Westeuropa (München, 1976).

The largest volume of information about Central America, in Paris as in other European countries, is in the archives of the foreign ministry (MAE). In Paris, these archives contain three large record groups relative to Central America. The section Correspondance Politique, Amérique

Central, consists of seventy-eight chronologically organized volumes of correspondence from the French minister, consul general, gérant, or chargé d'affaires during the period from 1823 to 1918. While this series contains the high-level diplomatic exchanges, a second section, Correspondance Consulaire et Commerciale, contains routine and commercial correspondence of French vice-consuls and consular agents. Most of the Central American consular material is found in the thirteen-volume Guatemalan series covering 1823–1901. However, supplementary material is found in a two-volume series on San José de Costa Rica (1872–1901), one volume on San Salvador (1833–43), nine volumes on Panama (1843–1901), and one volume on Colón (1876–1901). A third section, Mémoires et Documents, consists of special reports or studies, often from other departments or from special agents sent to Central America. Eight of the volumes in this section (numbers 29, 45, 47, 48, 68–71) contain special reports or studies on Central America in general or on the transisthmian Canal. The Correspondance Politique series contains the normal correspondence between the chief French diplomatic agent in Central America and the MAE, excluding matters of commerce and navigation. The commercial and navigation material is included in the Correspondance Consulaire et Commerciale. Since these two series were written by the same officials and only artificially separated by the foreign ministry bureaucracy in Paris, often the material found in these series is overlapping. Moreover, duplicates or copies were sometimes placed in the other series. Finally, the MAE archives possess a fourth series, the Papiers d'Agents, which are the official and semiofficial papers of former foreign ministry personnel, both those serving overseas and those serving in the Ministère des Affaires Etrangères. While there does not appear to be a specific collection of an agent who served in Central America, this body of material could yield important information on general policy formation and general French government attitudes toward the Central American and Caribbean areas with regard to French strategic, transit, market, raw material, and investment interests. For a more detailed guide to these archives, see Didier Ozanam, *Les Sources de l'histoire de l'Amérique Latine; Guide du chercheur dans les archives françaises. 1. Les Affaires étrangères, Cahiers de l'Institut des Hautes Etudes de l'Amérique Latine, no. 4* (Sources for Latin American History: Guide for the Researcher in French Archives. 1. Foreign Affairs, No. 4, Reports of the Institute of Advanced Studies of Latin America), no. 4 (Paris, 1963).

The archives of the Ministère de l'économie et des finances contain a considerable body of material on French trade, investment, and banking in Central America. Like all French archives, their collections are normally open only for the period before 1931. A guide to these archives,

Ministère de l'économie et des finances, *Archives Economiques & Financières: état des fonds au 31 mars 1976* (Economic and financial archives: State of the sources as of 31 March 1976) (Paris, 1976), offers detail on this material.

The Archives Nationales contain a variety of materials useful to the Central Americanist. The naval records (series BB^2, BB^3, and BB^4) offer large quantities of material about the Caribbean area, including the mainland Central American ports. The material in the Finance section and the Commerce and Industry section (both series F^{12}) offers primarily valuable trade and economic information about Central America's economy, but also about French economic ties to Central America. The MAE consular dispatches were often sent to the Finance Ministry for its information, comment, or action. These dispatches and the Finance Ministry's response are available in the Archives Nationales.

The archives of the French Chambre de commerce et d'industrie contain information relative to the trade, commercial, investment, and transit route interests of the French business sector and legislative lobbying activities in support of French economic ties with Central America. Finally, the Bibliothèque Nationale is valuable for its collection of printed materials and for its extensive holdings of private manuscript collections, mostly of aristocratic families and men of affairs, but includes some collections with documents about general international political affairs and international economic ties.

The archives of French ports should contain valuable manuscript collections. An example of the types of Latin American materials available in French port archives can be judged from Jürgen Schneider, *Handel und Unternehmer im französischen Brasiliengeschäft, 1815–1848: Versuch einer quantitativen Strukturanalyse* (Commerce and entrepreneurs in French trade with Brazil, 1815–1848: Attempt at a quantitative structure analysis) (Köln and Wien, 1975), based upon archival records from Le-Havre, Bordeaux, and Marseille.

Italy and the Vatican

The nineteenth-century Central American material at the Italian Archivo Storico del Ministero Degli Affari Esteri in Rome is scattered into no less than twelve separate record groups. To attempt to explain precisely to which record groups and which series and subseries one must go to find these materials would require several pages and a short course in Italian. Fortunately, two detailed guides exist for the nineteenth-century Italian Foreign Ministry archives. For the years until 1861, consult the guide to the Sardinian Foreign Ministry, *Le Scitture della Segretaria de Stato degli Affari Esteri del Regno de Sardegna* (The Correspondence of the Secre-

tary of State for Foreign Affairs of the Kingdom of Sardinia), Indici
dell'Archivo Storico, Vol. 1 (Roma, 1947), and for the period after 1861,
*Le Scritture del Ministero degli Affari Esteri del Regno d'Italia dal 1861
al 1887* (The Correspondence of the Minister of Foreign Affairs for the
Kingdom of Italy, 1861 to 1887), Indici dell-Archivo Storico, Vol. 6
(Roma, 1963).

The Catholic church, of course, preserves a large amount of documentation useful not only for religious history, but also valuable for social,
economic, and even political and diplomatic history. The archives of the
Vatican and the religious orders contain much material. Unfortunately,
these materials are scattered in no less than sixty-seven archives and libraries in Italy, mostly in Rome and the Vatican City. The despair the
researcher feels upon confronting the dispersal of Church records is partly
mitigated by the knowledge that a large, detailed guide exists to facilitate
the search: Lajos Pasztor, ed., *Guida dell fonti per la storia dell-America
Latina negli archivi della Santa Sede e negli archivi ecclesiastici d'Italia*
(Guide to the sources for the history of Latin America in the archives of
the Holy See and in the ecclesiastical archives of Italy) (Citta del Vaticano,
1970).

Belgium

Belgian documentation of interest to Central Americanists is located in the
Archives du Ministère des Affaires Etrangères in Brussels. These materials are dispersed throughout many collections, of which the most important are located in two main subsections: Catalogue par pays (Catalogue
by country) and Catalogue par matières (Catalogue by subjects). The most
interesting material is found in the Catalogue by subjects under various
subheadings. Consult Leone Liagre and Jean Baerten, eds., *Guide des
sources de l'histoire d'Amérique Latine conservées en Belgique* (Guide to
the Sources on Latin American History Preserved in Belgium) (Bruxelles,
1967) for the details of the holdings of this extensive body of material.
Other archives in Belgium hold material relative to Belgian relations with
Central America. The holdings of the Archives générales du Royaume,
Archives de l'Etat à Anvers, Archives de l'Etat à Gand, and the Musée
Royal de l'armée et d'histoire militaire are also described in some detail
in the Liagre and Baerten *Guide*.

The Netherlands

The Netherlands has recently published a *Guide to the Sources in the
Netherlands for the History of Latin America* (s'-Gravenhage, 1968),
which, although it describes the holdings well, in many cases cannot be
used for ordering materials at the Rijksarchieven in The Hague. Some of

the numbers used to identify record holdings in the *Guide* are insufficient to locate the records in the Rijksarchieven. The Rijksarchieven typescript guide, "Leezaal 13," can be used, however, to locate materials on Central America. These four bundles (with shortened titles) contain the vast body of material on nineteenth-century Central America: No. 3024, Correspondence Relative to Appointment and Dismissal of Dutch Consuls in Central America (1852–70); No. 3138, Correspondence on the Guatemalan-Dutch Friendship, Trade, and Commerce Treaty of 1856–58; No. 3501, Correspondence on the Costa Rican Trade Treaty (1850–54); No. 3517, Correspondence on the Nicaraguan Trade Treaty (1844–61). The titles and time periods cited in the guide are, however, not restrictive; they merely suggest the focus of the bundle's contents in terms of time and subject matter.

Scandinavia

Scandinavian archives contain material related primarily to significant Swedish interests in Central America. Relevant documentation is scattered in several archives, but Magnus Mörner, *Guía de fuentes para la historia de Ibero-América: Escandinavia* (Stockholm, 1968) is an adequate guide. See also *Scandinavian Studies on Latin America, No. 1: The Study of Latin American History and Society in Scandinavia; Reports Presented at a Conference Organized by the Institute of Political History, University of Turku, Finland, 3–4 September 1970* (Stockholm, 1973). Although some volumes, bundles, files, and folders are simply labeled Latin America or Caribbean, thus containing a variety of material, the principal items of interest to Central Americanists are in the Riksarkivet (National Archives) in Stockholm, in the foreign correspondence of the cabinet. The most useful items in the archives are volume 20 of Consular Correspondence, volumes 44, 106, 370, and 431 of Consular Reports, volume 13 of Special Relations and Reports, and the Annual Reports of Consuls at Guatemala (1884–1905) and Panama (1894–95). The National Archives also hold the extensive archives of the Swedish General Association of Exportation for the years from 1887 until the 1940s, which might prove to be a valuable source. Swedish consuls reported annually about their national shipping activity in foreign ports. These reports are located in the National Archives, in the archives of the Kammarkontoret (to 1891), and in the statistical section (after 1891). In addition, the Swedish Ministry of Foreign Affairs archives contain several record groups of interest to Central Americanists. The most important collection is Record Group 112, Central America, but Record Groups 6, 21, 22, and 114 also deserve attention. The material described in Mörner's *Guía* for Denmark's National Archive is disappointing. Mostly related to Panama, New Granada, or Colombia, the holdings listed seem thin and do not appear to reflect adequately Danish shipping or trade interests in Central America, based upon this author's collection of Central American trade and navigation research.

Switzerland

The Swiss archives in Bern contain a modest body of material on Central America, but for the most part it is of a routine nature. In Bestand Nummer 2—Politische Angelegenheiten (1848–95) (Record Group 2—Political Affairs)—there are nine boxes for Central American countries: Costa Rica, boxes 956 and 1466 (1865–74); Honduras, box 965 (1872); Nicaragua, boxes 972 and 1603 (1863–89); El Salvador, boxes 974 and 976 (1876–93); and Guatemala, boxes 960 and 1307 (1870–94).

Austria

The Austrian Haus-, Hof-, und Staatsarchiv in Vienna contains almost no material on Central America before the 1890s. In Record Group 38, Consul Reports, there are several brief routine notes from the Austrian consul general in Guatemala in the 1870s and 1880s. In Record Group 33, the United States, carton 125 is entitled, Recognition in Central and South America, 1847–1861, but holds only cursory mention of Central America. Since this archive suffered significant losses during World War II, it is possible that only this remnant of Austrian materials on Central America still exists.

In summary, there are valuable materials about Central America in the Western European archives under review in this essay, materials relevant not only to the political, diplomatic, trade, and navigation ties, but also other forms of economic, cultural, and strategic-military relations. Particularly the French and German archives, but also the Italian, Belgian, Dutch, and Scandinavian archives possess abundant materials. Generally, the published guides to these archives are adequate for initiating the design of a research project, while unpublished guides and research aides in the archives will extend and supplement the researcher's access to useful materials. The researcher considering the use of Western European archives should note that, while the traditional mining of Foreign Ministry archives usually leads to the most voluminous collections, use of other official archives in the finance, treasury, legal, and navy ministries may also produce important and sizable collections of rewarding documentation. For immigration as well as trade and navigation matters, port and other local archives are indispensable. Finally, nonofficial or quasi-official archives, whether private collections, business/firm archives, chambers of commerce, trade associations, or immigration societies, often contain materials of a kind which shed light on internal policy formation, the goals, and the objectives of the Western European countries as they sought to gain, in various forms, access to and influence in the political economies of Central America.

Generally, records in Western European archives are open until some legally fixed date in the twentieth century. Nevertheless, it is strongly recommended that a scholar should write an archive before traveling to Europe, explaining the nature of the projected research, stating the expected dates of the visit, and formally requesting permission to use the archives. A prospective researcher should also carry an original and several copies of a letter of introduction from his or her university or research institute and multiple prints of a recent photograph.

The Caribbean

42   Rural Land Use in the Caribbean

Gustavo A. Antonini and
Dianne K. Rocheleau

The Caribbean is a region which is clearly open to further rural land use research. Changes in the pattern and distribution of land use systems under varying socioeconomic, political, and technological conditions need to be more fully documented or explained. The marked spatial variation and the parallel historical evolution of the many distinct cultural, economic, and environmental systems might be more fully utilized as a research laboratory for the study of man-land relationships. Indeed, more Caribbean history could be explained better by analyzing the rule of land use processes and patterns on a regional scale. There is a substantial body of literature related to development planning and policy that could benefit from broader historical and regional studies of related land use issues. A review of existing literature indicates that there is still much to be done for analysis of rural land use in the Caribbean.

Rural land use as a field of study in the Caribbean is characterized by fragmented topical treatment as well as partial coverage of historical periods and geographical areas. The topic of rural land use is not the exclusive domain of one particular discipline, and in part, due to this fact, the topic lacks a cohesive theoretical framework, research methodology, and source material. This lack is complicated further by the heterogeneity of the subject matter and geographical area. By and large, the scope and content of rural land use research varies with each disciplinary focus and professional orientation. The national origin of the investigator, as well as the current sociopolitical milieu, appears to exert a strong influence on the content of rural land use studies. Taken as a whole, variability, rather than consistency in research objectives and emphasis, is the pervading characteristic of the literature surveyed.

This review focuses primarily on the last twenty years, reflecting a concern with contemporary research, though some earlier publications are selectively included because of their special empirical or methodological value. Furthermore, the more recent entries contain several studies included for purposes of either theoretical or methodological discussions, or as examples of rural land use research conducted in other similar world regions. Geographical coverage is limited to the Bahamas, the Greater and Lesser Antilles, and the islands of Caribbean coastal Central and South America.

197

There are three distinct approaches that characterize contemporary research in this field. The first consists of studies that are explicitly land use oriented, usually geographical or historical in content and methodology and often academic in scope. The second group includes the topic of rural land use as an adjunct to or a part of broader studies concerned with demography, anthropology, sociology, economics, and political science in the Caribbean. The regional and national rural land use surveys carried out over the past thirty years account for a third and substantial portion of the literature.

Many recent publications by geographers on rural land use in the Caribbean reflect a traditional focus, which includes descriptive regional inventories of settlement and rural land use and studies of landscape evolution. Recent innovative approaches include work on cultural adaptation in agricultural land use systems, the ecological impact of agricultural land use, spatial analyses of settlement, land use and marketing, and rural land use as a behavioral response to environmental perception.

Whereas earlier works emphasize the development and distribution of plantation agriculture and production systems associated with export crops, the focus of studies today is on subsistence agriculture and small-scale commercial food crop cultivation. Other increasingly familiar contemporary themes deal with rural development, environmental resource conservation, and landscape indicators of social well-being.

Descriptive regional studies contain extensive bibliographies of statistical documents, maps, and data sources, and serve as useful references by themselves. The proportion of factual and analytical content varies from a functional description of agricultural land use in Haiti to an encyclopedic account in the Bahamas. Such studies have been made of Barbados, Martinique, Guadeloupe, St. Vincent, and the Corn Islands.

Regional descriptions and histories can serve to supplement existing rural land use research. The general historical and geographical texts of the Caribbean contain abundant references to land use, which vary widely in quality. Helmut Blume places strong emphasis on rural land use and includes sections on agricultural regions and systems as well as agrarian social structure.[1] He includes a discussion of cultural landscape as well as population and settlement by country for the whole of the island Caribbean. While the other general descriptive works include some land use information and settlement history, it is doubtful that any equals the coverage of rural land use reflected in the Blume work.

Historical study of land use change in the Caribbean is the dominant

1. Helmut Blume, *The Caribbean Islands,* trans. Johannes Maczewski and Ann Norton (London, 1974).

theme of the University of California at Berkeley School of Geography. By and large, studies conducted within this paradigm proceed by historical description to reconstruct and account for the cumulative impact of successive cultural traditions on evolving land use systems and settlement patterns. The indigenous cultures of the pre-Columbian period may serve as a point of departure with subsequent analysis of the periods of discovery, colonization, and independence. The influence of Carl Sauer is preeminent in the Berkeley tradition of scholarship, with continuing emphasis on human ecology, demography, and economic history.[2] Indeed, such an approach is evident in much of the work dealing with human ecology and historical land use studies of the Caribbean conducted by geographers.

Over the past twenty years, landscape evolution has been the prevailing conceptual geographical framework for studies of the Bay Islands, Honduras, Jamaica, the Cayman Islands, the Haitian-Dominican borderlands, the Dominican Republic, Isla Fuerte, Colombia, St. Kitts and Nevis and other Lesser Antilles, southwest Haiti, Margarita Island, Venezuela, San Andres and Providencia, and other English-speaking islands of the western Caribbean.

Variations of the landscape-evolution theme are numerous. For example, Watts documents the impact of European settlement on the natural flora of Barbados, including forest clearance, purposeful introduction of food crops and commercial plants, as well as accidental introduction of noncultigens.[3] Alice Dyson presents a more contemporary treatment of land use in the Maracas–St. Joseph Basin, Trinidad, which includes a similar discussion of European settlement, land clearance, and the introduction of new agricultural systems.[4] Marlin Clausner, in a historical analysis of agrarian structure in the Dominican Republic, examines the evolution of institutions and attitudes which shape patterns of land ownership and rural land use.[5] His emphasis, however, is on social and institutional elements of landscape evolution and not on land use per se.

The Caribbean's maritime location is reflected by the combined study of land and water use. Most of these studies focus on turtling, fisheries, salt production, boat-building, or tourism. There are historical treatments of fisheries and rural land use, such as María Dolores García-Ramón's

2. Carl O. Sauer, *The Early Spanish Main* (Berkeley, 1966).

3. D. Watts, *Man's Influence on the Vegetation of Barbados, 1627 to 1800,* No. 4, Occasional Papers in Geography (Hull University, 1966).

4. Alice Dyson, "Land Use in the Maracas–St. Joseph Basin, Trinidad," in *Geography and the Tropics: Liverpool Essays,* ed. R. W. Steel and R. M. Prothero (London, 1964).

5. Marlin D. Clausner, *Rural Santo Domingo: Settled, Unsettled, and Resettled* (Philadelphia, 1973).

study of mariculture in Cuba.[6] She follows the Berkeley approach by tracing the sequential evolution of Cuban fisheries from prehistory to the present day in order to better explain the expansion of the industry before and
after the revolution.

Parallel to the landscape-evolution tradition is the use of a historical
approach in the study of attitudes, belief systems, and accompanying institutions related to environmental land use. Following David Lowenthal's
seminal work on environmental perception in the region,[7] others have attempted to relate cultural landscape evolution with land use and environmental perception. Recent studies cover Dominica, Trinidad, Tortola, and
a general discussion of fragmentation and the indigenous cultivator's perception of risk, hazard, and land tenure in a case study of Jamaica.

The region's tropical coastal location astride the hurricane belt undoubtedly has produced inestimable losses from tropical storm damage, yet
there is no study of the impact of natural hazards upon coastal land use.
The few bibliographic references found are limited to the study of the
occurrence and subsequent impact of hurricanes on St. Thomas. In this
case, Martyn Bowden analyzes the perception of such hazards by local
residents and documents the historical adjustments to the perceived hazards through archival research and interviews.[8]

While landscape evolution and related approaches portray people as the
dominant agent of change and the physical environment as the passive
recipient, recent studies in human ecology describe a more balanced interaction of people and land. Land use in this sense expresses varying forms
of cultural adaptation within a regional ecosystem. One such study of
early nineteenth-century Jamaica by Richard Ormrod examines the patterns of estate-based sugar planting and is an example of such an ecosystem approach.[9] The collapse and transformation of the sugar industry,
which occurred after emancipation, is used as an empirical foundation for
the observation of adaptive change in cultural ecosystems. For the reconstruction of these events, Ormrod depends upon archival records as well
as influences from the behavioral universe of contemporary Jamaicans.
This research sets a methodological precedent for the study of rural land

6. María Dolores García Ramón, "Recent Development of the Marine Fisheries in Cuba:
The Gulf of Batabano and the Port of Surgidero as a Case Study," M.A. thesis (University
of California, Berkeley, 1970).

7. David Lowenthal, "Caribbean Views of Caribbean Land," *Canadian Geographer*, 5,
2(Summer 1961): 1–9.

8. Martyn J. Bowden, *Hurricane in Paradise: Perception and Reality of the Hurricane
Hazard in the Virgin Islands* (St. Thomas, 1974).

9. Richard K. Ormrod, "Adaptation in Cultural Ecosystems: Early 19th Century Jamaica," Ph.D. dissertation (Pennsylvania State University, 1974).

use history in the Caribbean and offers useful information with respect to competition of subsistence and plantation agriculture.

An analysis of the Miskito Indian's subsistence ecology in eastern Nicaragua utilizes a similar cultural ecosystem framework. In this case, Bernard Nietschmann describes the nature of indigenous subsistence systems and their adaptability and resilience in the face of such potentially disruptive forces as population increase, rising expectations, and demands of foreign markets.[10] The methodology includes a rigorous accounting of household budgets, the agricultural system and its yield, seasonal and spatial availability of food, and total time and energy expended on productive activities.

The behavioral approach to land use and contemporary development of the tourist industry is exemplified by a study of Tortola, British Virgin Islands. Here, Christopher Howell relates carrying capacity, land use, and local attitudes to the selection of alternative modes of land development.[11] Rafael Yunen evaluates the impact of a tourism-development project on the town of Samaná in the Dominican Republic.[12] Based on questionnaire-survey research techniques, Yunen attempts to determine the degree to which the government's development project meets the objectives of the planners and the aspirations of local residents. The impact of tourism on land use and the competition for both land and water resources among tourism, fisheries, and agriculture in the island Caribbean have yet to be fully developed as topics of research.

An impact analysis of population and rural land use on soil erosion and reservoir siltation published in 1975 applies ecological-systems theory to study the carrying capacity of land in an upland watershed of the Dominican Republic.[13] The methodology combines elements of cartographic analysis and ecological energy modeling to evaluate changes in productivity as well as the relative amount and distribution of land in forest, coffee, pasture, and subsistence crops since 1948. In this case, sequential land use change is documented through interpretation of time series aerial photographs and survey data. The use of energy equivalent for labor, capital investments, and agricultural and forest productivity facilitates the com-

    10. Bernard Neitschmann, *Between Land and Water: The Subsistence Ecology of the Miskito Indians, Eastern Nicaragua* (New York, 1973).

    11. Christopher D. B. Howell, "Tourism in Tortola, British Virgin Islands: Perceptions Toward Land Carrying Capacity," Ph.D. dissertation (University of Florida, 1978).

    12. Rafael E. Yunen, "The Impact of a Tourism-Development Project on the City of Samaná, Dominican Republic," M.A. thesis (University of Florida, 1977).

    13. Gustavo Antonini, Katherine C. Ewel, and Howard M. Tupper, *Population and Energy, a Systems Analysis of Resource Utilization in the Dominican Republic* (Gainesville, 1975).

parison of natural, subsistence, and commercial land use in common terms. The study establishes a precedent in the Caribbean for the ecological analysis of complex land use patterns and provides a potential link with research traditions in spatial analysis and settlement theory.

The application of geographic settlement theory in the Caribbean builds on the paradigm of landscape evolution and allows for a more coherent overview of the settlement process. Such an approach is used in a historical analysis of settlement in the Bay Islands, Honduras. Based on previous theoretical works, Ian Watt developed a four-stage process in the description of settlement history of the Bay Islands.[14] This typology may be applicable to other Caribbean areas.

Other studies demonstrate the use of theoretical concepts and quantitative techniques in the study of Caribbean settlement patterns. Bonham Richardson uses spatial-analysis techniques to explain the location of land use and settlements in Trinidad and Guyana.[15] L. A. Eyre combines the methodology of population geography and spatial analysis with the theories of cultural adaptation and landscape evolution to explain population dynamics in Jamaica.[16] Specific case studies in Jamaica are analyzed within the larger context of man-land relationships. This study is primarily explanatory and includes specific historical information. A similar spatial-systems analysis is used by B. Floyd to evaluate the relationships among settlement patterns, rural markets, and agricultural land use in Jamaica.[17]

It is often necessary in rural land use research to compensate for the lack of a coherent body of theory and the scarcity of information by having recourse to studies in related social science fields. Much of the work in demography, population policy, and rural socioeconomic institutions provides empirical data and theoretical material relevant to rural land use research.

Social science publications of the 1960s reflect a growing interest in population policy. Aaron Segal, summarizing such policy research in the Caribbean for that decade, cites the growing need to relate population dynamics and distribution with land use processes and patterns, since the

14. Ian Watt, "The Historical Development of Settlement, Bay Islands, Honduras," M.A. thesis (University of Calgary, 1973).

15. Bonham C. Richardson, "Livelihood in Rural Trinidad in 1900," *Annals of the Association of American Geographers,* 65, 2(June 1975): 240–51.

16. L. A. Eyre, *Land and Population in the Sugar Belt of Jamaica,* Occasional Publication No. 1, Department of Geography, University of the West Indies (Kingston, 1970).

17. B. Floyd, "Planning for Rural Development in Jamaica: Spatial Systems Analysis," *Caribbean Quarterly,* 18, 1(March 1972): 5–11, "Agricultural Innovation in Jamaica: The Yallahs Valley Land Authority," *Economic Geography,* 46, 1(January 1970): 63–77, and "Rural Land Use in Jamaica," in *Essays on Jamaica,* ed. Dawn Marshall (Kingston, 1970).

policy trend is increasingly to look inward for answers to problems of internal migration, high energy inputs, and costly food imports.[18]

The government documents of census and mapping agencies provide a broad data base for combined time series analyses of population and land use. The combined use of population and land use maps with statistics is illustrated particularly well in recent demographic studies conducted in Jamaica[19] and Dominica.[20] Aside from providing insight into population as a variable affecting land use, the authors explicitly discuss rural land use, carrying capacity of the land, and competition between commercial and subsistence agriculture.

The concept of carrying capacity transcends simple linear relationships between land use and population, and includes considerations of environmental quality as well as cultural adaptation. This concept has been a major theme of human ecological studies in anthropology for many years, but it has not been utilized extensively within the Caribbean. A number of published works in this field, however, do incorporate discussions of carrying capacity, physical environmental characteristics and land use as a reflection of adaptive behavior. One such example is Hill's ethnography, which contains descriptive information on land use and tenure, agricultural practices, and local markets.[21] The methodology is eclectic and is heavily dependent upon personal interviews and informal observation. Historical accounts are based largely on oral history as relayed by local informants. For descriptions of settlement and development of land use practices and patterns over time, the same informants may well provide further information to interested researchers. Anthropological sources thus can be valuable both for the tangential discussions of land use as well as the biographies and lists of informants where identified. Ethnographies as well as economic and social anthropological studies can be useful.

Anthropological studies conducted within the ecological tradition are of interest to land use historians. Robert Werge's case study of cultural adaptation and agricultural development in the Dominican Republic is an example of such an approach in the island Caribbean.[22] He uses energy

18. Aaron Segal, ed., *Population Policies in the Caribbean*, (Lexington, Mass., 1975).

19. Colin G. Clarke, *Kingston, Jamaica: Urban Growth and Social Change (1692–1962)* (Berkeley, 1975).

20. J. P. Chardon, "La Population d'Une Petite Antille: La Dominique," *Geographie Antillaise*, No. 11, Groupe Universitaire de Recherches Inter-Caraibes, Etudes et Documents, Centre d'Enseignement Superior Litteraire (Pointe-à-Pitre, 1971).

21. Donald R. Hill, "England I Want to Go: The Impact of Migration on a Caribbean Community," Ph.D. dissertation (Indiana University, 1973).

22. Robert W. Werge, "Agricultural Development in Clear Creek: Adaptive Strategies and Economic Roles in a Dominican Settlement," Ph.D. dissertation (University of Florida, 1975).

analysis to evaluate farm productivity and concludes that labor productivity is highest under shifting cultivation as is total production efficiency, i.e., total output per unit input. Such conclusions are supported by other studies conducted both within and outside of the Caribbean. Taken as a whole, these studies indicate that optimization of land, labor, and capital inputs can occur in shifting cultivation and small-holder agriculture.

The ecological approach can be applied to historical studies of land use as well. Whereas the exact figures for a given land use in a specific time and place cannot be reconstructed, estimates of productivity for broad classes of land use are available in the literature. These estimates are adequate for purposes of a general analysis. Furthermore, the precedent for applying these concepts in a historical context is well established in studies of the pre-Columbian cultures of Mesoamerica and influence on current land occupants.[23] This methodology is useful also for comparing and evaluating land use systems which operate partially or completely outside of the exchange economy.[24]

Sociology, political science, and economics provide a wide range of information applicable to the study of rural land use in the Caribbean. A selective review of recent literature reveals widespread interest in issues of land tenure and agrarian reform, economic aspects of agricultural production, recent political changes and their impact on the agricultural sector, particularly in Cuba and Jamaica, and Caribbean regional integration. Discussions of the scale of landholdings and the means of organizing production and productivity of labor are common in journals and books alike. The literature on Jamaica, Cuba, and Guyana has a strong emphasis on land redistribution. The historical development of such programs is well documented in the Commonwealth Caribbean. Records in Jamaica extend from the Crown Island Settlement Scheme to the current Operation Land Lease in the bauxite areas. In Guyana, documentation of land distribution extends from the purchase of plantation lands through the postemancipation land sales to the recent consolidation of coastal landholdings by East Indian rice farmers.[25] By contrast, the literature on Cuba focuses primarily on the period from 1959 to the present.

Studies on Puerto Rico tend to emphasize urban problems or land use issues specific to the export-production sector, reflecting the effective urbanization of the island as a whole and the rationalization of the sugar industry. Hispañola and the Lesser Antilles currently receive less

23. William E. Carter, *New Lands and Old Traditions: Kekchi Cultivators in the Guatemala Lowlands* (Gainesville, 1969).

24. Roy A. Rappaport, "The Flow of Energy in an Agricultural Society," *Scientific American*, 225, 3(September 1971): 116–33.

25. Bonham C. Richardson, "The Rice Culture of Coastal Guyana; A Study in Location and Livelihood," Ph.D. dissertation (University of Wisconsin–Madison, 1970).

emphasis in the social science literature, though many works do include a country-by-country comparative analysis. Some recent work compares the planned, unplanned, and mixed economies of the Caribbean with respect to productivity of land and labor, and discusses implications for regional economic integration.

Existing material on rural land use in the Caribbean is diversified in content and methodology. Over the past twenty years, study topics have expanded to include subsistence and small-holder agriculture, the area covered has extended to include the Hispanic nations of Cuba and the Dominican Republic, and the time period now includes the contemporary scene of rapid economic development and rising expectations. During this period, the methodology has shifted from solely historical narrations of sequent occupance to include use of cartographic and quantitative analysis. There is also a marked trend in the use of location, settlement, and ecological-system theories.

The rural land use field offers a challenging research frontier in interdisciplinary studies. The unanswered research questions dealing with location, settlement, and carrying capacity are of mutual interest to historians and social scientists. An overriding concern with agricultural development coupled with a strong interest in decentralization, intermediate technology, food production, and rural market development suggests a potential role for land use specialists in studies of subsistence and small-holder agricultural systems.

There exists an untapped potential for historical research dealing with the analysis of both antecedent land use conditions prior to development projects and of completed and ongoing projects. The ad hoc responses of Caribbean small-holders and subsistence farmers to the environmental, technological, and economic exigencies of the past provide a living history of agricultural experimentation and innovation. The successful examples of adaptive strategy may be incorporated into development efforts, while the general historical perspective on land use can provide a better local orientation for planners.

An applied research focus implies a concomitant change in methodology and techniques of data analysis. The historical uniqueness of particular case studies should be described using standard land use nomenclature to facilitate later comparisons with other areas or other epochs. In this regard, use of Harold Wood's classification for the American tropics or the International Geographical Union system is advisable for purposes of comparison and generalization.[26]

26. Harold A. Wood, "A Land Use Classification for the American Tropics," a report prepared for the Natural Resources Unit, Pan American Union (Washington, D.C., 1976), and *Northern Haiti: Land Use and Settlement* (Toronto, 1963).

The use of complementary sources of information also is desirable. Whenever available, the use of aerial photographs is preferable to sole reliance on maps and archival records; such photography often includes information selectively deleted from maps.

The discussion of combined spatial and diachronic changes in evolving land use systems offers a dynamic perspective to individual case-study work and assists in the discrimination of normal versus exceptional land development. Such a combined historical-geographic approach can lead to limited extrapolations of carrying capacity and development with other areas previously mapped and described. The process is iterative and, it is hoped, will lead to formulating a theory of land use development in the Caribbean. The challenge is to standardize and summarize description by using quantitative and cartographic methods without sacrificing the historical case-study approach.

The development of a more unified research framework may provide further comparative-study opportunities that in turn can contribute to and draw upon a substantial body of theory and applied research in the history and development of small-holder agriculture. The recent work in West Africa includes studies of subsistence agriculture and small-holder commercial agriculture for local markets and export. Johannes Lagemann's work presents a valuable methodological example of integrating historical information and analysis into studies of carrying capacity and agricultural development.[27] The comparative context also can build upon similar natural ecologies, cropping systems, ethnic origins, and the broader patterns of colonization and dependency.

The successful development of applied and comparative research rests on the continued pursuit of theoretical lines of inquiry in spatial analysis, settlement, cultural adaptation, environmental perception, and regional ecology. The elaboration of new regional and historical land use models and the adaptation of site-specific models from other disciplines also are necessary to provide both theoretical norms and analytical tools. The research opportunities are abundant in both theoretical and applied aspects of the rural land use field. The needs vary from good historical description to development of computer simulation models. The frontier appears to be most suitable for interdisciplinary collaborative work in which geographers and historians can play a significant role.

27. Johannes Lagemann, *Traditional African Farming Systems in Eastern Nigeria: An Analysis of Reaction to Increasing Population Pressure* (München, 1977).

43   Exploitative Systems
Slavery, Commerce, and Industry
Richard B. Sheridan

Scholarship in Caribbean history in recent decades has been concentrated heavily upon the exploitation of the region. The last quarter century has seen the production of a number of important monographs, new methodological approaches, impressive quantitative studies, general syntheses, and growing interest in scholarly interpretation. Issues and debates have focused attention on the nature and profitability of the slave trade and slavery, the rise and fall of the planter class, the changing structure and methods of trade, shipping, and finance, the role of the West Indies in the growth of metropolitan economies, the relative importance of economic and humanitarian factors in slave abolition and emancipation, and labor and other problems in the transition from slavery to freedom. Reasons for the heightened interest in Caribbean economic history include the need to understand the background of the gap between rich and poor nations, the need for a new consciousness of the region's history and culture in an age of national independence, and the growing ability to meet these needs on the part of universities, libraries, archives, and local history societies in the region. Notwithstanding the substantial body of scholarly publication, rich fields of research materials have been overlooked or underutilized, and much scope remains for synthesis and interpretation.

Eric Williams' seminal study, *Capitalism and Slavery* (Chapel Hill, 1944), has had a continuing influence on West Indian historiography. Williams attacks the notion that the abolition of the slave trade and slavery had been due to the humanitarian agitation and propaganda of the British abolitionists. He maintains that the commercial capitalism of the eighteenth century developed the wealth of Europe by means of slavery and monopoly. However, the rise of industrial capitalists in the early nineteenth century produced hostility to slavery and the Atlantic slave trade, especially in the dynamic British cotton industry. By this time plantation slavery in the British West Indies had become vulnerable to attack by its enemies, who, under the banner of laissez-faire, organized a political

The author wishes to acknowledge the assistance in the preparation of this essay of Professors Stanley L. Engerman, Jack P. Greene, Woodville K. Marshall, Walter E. Minchinton, and Dr. B. W. Higman.

207

movement which destroyed the power of commercial capitalism and slavery.

Though Williams' book has gained favor among historians in the West Indies and West Africa, it has come under attack by certain historians in Britain and the United States. Roger Anstey claims that Williams uses evidence misleadingly and was not warranted in asserting that economic forces were predominant causes of abolition of the slave trade.[1] Anstey scales down Williams' estimates of the profits of the slave trade, regards the West Indian plantation economy as only marginally relevant to the process of capital formation in Britain, and maintains that abolition was motivated chiefly by the religious and humanitarian zeal of great numbers of Britishers.

After an extended period of research in the archives of Jamaica, R. B. Sheridan published an article entitled "The Wealth of Jamaica in the Eighteenth Century" (*Economic History Review*, 18, 2[1965]), which tends to support the Williams thesis. It presents statistical and other data, based chiefly on the sugar plantation economy of the island, which demonstrate that Jamaica was Britain's richest colony, both before and after the American Revolution. Sheridan estimates that from 8 to 10 percent of the income of the mother country came from the West Indies in the closing years of the eighteenth century. R. Keith Aufhauser has calculated that, on the eve of slave emancipation in 1834, slave capital in Barbados yielded a mean rate of return of close to 7 percent.[2]

On the other hand, R. P. Thomas and P. R. Coelho have criticized Sheridan's article, maintaining that the sugar colonies were, in practice, an economic drain on the mother country.[3] They contend that, owing chiefly to the high costs incurred by Britain in protecting and governing the colonies, together with the tariff protection given to colonial sugar over the foreign product, the income of Britishers would have been higher in the absence of the West Indies from the empire. In a rejoinder to Thomas,

1. R. T. Anstey, "Capitalism and Slavery: A Critique," *Economic History Review*, 21, 2(1968), "A Re-interpretation of the Abolition of the British Slave Trade, 1806–1807," *English Historical Review*, 87 (1972), "The Volume and Profitability of the British Slave Trade, 1761–1807," in *Race and Slavery in the Western Hemisphere: Quantitative Studies*, ed. Stanley L. Engerman and Eugene Genovese (Princeton, 1975), *The Atlantic Slave Trade and British Abolition, 1760–1810* (Atlantic Highlands, New Jersey, 1975), and "A Note on J. E. Inikori, 'Measuring the Atlantic Slave Trade: An Assessment of Curtin and Anstey,'" *Journal of African History*, 17 (1976).

2. R. Keith Aufhauser, "Profitability of Slavery in the British Caribbean," *Journal of Interdisciplinary History*, 5 (1974).

3. R. P. Thomas, "The Sugar Colonies of the Old Empire: Profit or Loss for Great Britain?" *Economic History Review*, 21, 1(1968); Philip R. Coelho, "The Profitability of Imperialism: The British Experience in the West Indies, 1768–1772," *Explorations in Economic History*, 10 (1973).

Sheridan argues that the colonies bore the major part of their governance costs, that tariff preferences were reduced substantially, and that the residual costs were more than compensated for by the indirect benefits of the sugar colonies to the empire.[4] That the objectives of mercantilist policy included both economic and noneconomic goals is a reality which Thomas apparently had ignored.

Stanley Engerman, reacting negatively to the Williams thesis, has calculated that the slave trade contributed only about 1 percent to the national income of Great Britain, while the sum of the profit from the slave trade and from the West Indian plantations was less than 5 percent of national income in the early years of the Industrial Revolution.[5] He admits, however, that his "static neo-classical model" cannot provide a favorable outcome for arguments such as those of Eric Williams.

In his monograph-length critique of the Williams thesis, Seymour Drescher investigates the "decline" thesis of British slavery,[6] which was first advanced by Lowell J. Ragatz. Drescher attempts to show that the slave system expanded down to the eve of abolition in 1807, and that the West Indies and Africa were among the most dynamic areas of British trade. Drescher supports the humanitarian thesis, maintaining that the antislavery movement was a spontaneous social movement, which imposed its attitude upon imperial politics. Unfortunately, his book is faulted by its Euro-centric bias. For example, Drescher denies that the black revolution in Haiti spread fear among British planters or that imported African slaves constituted "seeds of destruction."

Partly in reaction to the Williams thesis, Philip D. Curtin published a book-length quantitative analysis of the Atlantic slave trade, which sought answers to such questions as how many slaves were transported, from what parts of Africa were they obtained, and to what destinations in the New World were they delivered?[7] In particular, Curtin finds grounds to reduce the estimated total export of slaves from Africa to the New World by about one-half of previous estimates. J. E. Inikori examines the quantitative methods and data employed by Curtain and Anstey and finds that their estimates are substantially understated.[8]

4. R. B. Sheridan, "The Wealth of Jamaica in the Eighteenth Century," *Economic History Review,* 2d ser., 18, 2(1965); and "A Rejoinder," ibid., 21, 1(1968).

5. S. L. Engerman and E. D. Genovese, eds., *Race and Slavery in the Western Hemisphere: Quantitative Studies* (Princeton, 1975); S. L. Engerman, "The Slave Trade and British Capital Formation in the Eighteenth Century: A Comment on the Williams Thesis," *Business History Review,* 46 (1972).

6. Seymour Drescher, *Econocide: British Slavery in the Era of Abolition* (Pittsburgh, 1977).

7. P. D. Curtin, *The Atlantic Slave Trade: A Census* (Madison, 1969).

8. J. E. Inikori, "Measuring the Atlantic Slave Trade: An Assessment of Curtin and Anstey," *Journal of African History,* 17 (1976): 197–223.

Michael Craton is the author of a short history of British slavery, which includes much useful data and analysis on the organization and economics of the slave trade and plantation slavery.[9] R. B. Sheridan attempts to show how the Atlantic slave trade was influenced, both in Africa and the Caribbean, by changing agricultural systems, man-land ratios, demography, epidemiology, and systems of slavery.[10]

Slave plantation economies, with special reference to sugar, have been investigated by numerous writers. Two recent works by Carl and Roberta Bridenbaugh and Richard Dunn are concerned with the English West Indies in the seventeenth century.[11] In *No Peace Beyond the Line,* the Bridenbaughs maintain that all Englishmen went to the Antilles to get rich, worshipping Mammon all of the time and God only occasionally. In stocking their plantations with a vastly superior number of African slaves, they created an unprecedented situation with which they were ill-equipped to deal. Dunn, in his *Sugar and Slaves,* is more quantitative and analytical than the Bridenbaughs. He not only shows how the planters created a truly impressive sugar-production system, but also one of the harshest systems of slavery in Western history. Richard Pares's *A West India Fortune* is a classic account of the Pinney family's sugar plantation on the island of Nevis and their sugar factorage business in Bristol. Pares, along with Gabriel Debien, pioneered the use of family plantation papers. Other historians have used plantation records to reconstruct the story of individual planters and plantations.[12] In their *History of Worthy Park,* Craton and Walvin tell the remarkable story of a Jamaican plantation that has had a continuous existence since 1670 and has changed hands only three times.[13] Sheridan's *Sugar and Slavery* focuses on the organization and

9. M. Craton, *Sinews of Empire: A Short History of British Slavery* (Garden City, New York, 1974).

10. R. B. Sheridan, "Africa and the Caribbean in the Atlantic Slave Trade," *American Historical Review,* 77, 1(February 1972).

11. Carl Bridenbaugh and Roberta Bridenbaugh, *No Peace Beyond the Line: The English in the Caribbean, 1624–1690* (New York, 1972); R. S. Dunn, *Sugar and Slaves: The Rise of the Planter Class in the English West Indies, 1624–1713* (Chapel Hill, 1972).

12. J. H. Bennett, *Bondsmen and Bishops: Slavery and Apprenticeship on the Codrington Plantations of Barbados, 1710–1838* (Berkeley, 1958), "Cary Helyar, Merchant and Planter of Seventeenth-Century Jamaica," *William and Mary Quarterly,* 3d ser., 21, 1(1964), and "William Whaley, Planter of Seventeenth Century Jamaica," *Agricultural History,* 40, 2(1966); R. S. Dunn, "A Tale of Two Plantations: Slave Life at Mesopotamia in Jamaica and Mount Airy in Virginia, 1799 to 1828," *William and Mary Quarterly,* 3d ser., 34 (January 1977); C. Y. Sheridan, "Samuel Martin, Innovating Sugar Planter of Antigua 1750–1776," *Agricultural History,* 24, 3(1960), and "Planter and Historian: The Career of William Beckford of Jamaica and England, 1744–1799," *Jamaican Historical Review,* 4(1964); R. B. Sheridan, "Planters and Merchants: the Oliver Family of Antigua and London, 1716–1784," *Business History,* 13, 2(1971).

13. M. Craton and J. Walvin, *A Jamaican Plantation: The History of Worthy Park, 1670–1970* (London, 1970).

operation of the British sugar colonies in the emergent Atlantic economy from their first settlement in 1623 to the American Revolution in 1775.[14]

Foremost among planter and slave historians of the West Indies is Gabriel Debien, whose writings on the French islands extend over the course of the last thirty-five years and include a total of 168 publications to the year 1975.[15] Bad food and underfeeding, he finds, were the greatest evil of slavery, which led, in turn, to running away, theft, and harsh punishment. Debien's articles and monographs are based chiefly on family papers, including business correspondence and accounts. Elsa Goveia writes that his "use of private papers for illuminating the history of the slaves is undoubtedly his most important contribution to the historiography of French West Indian slavery."[16]

Elsa Goveia will be remembered for her publications and influence as a teacher and research director of West Indian history. Her *Slave Society in the British Leeward Islands at the End of the Eighteenth Century* (New Haven, 1965) is concerned not only with the slaves but with other elements of the wider society of which they were a part. Held together by principles of racial subordination and inequality, the slave society was characterized by excess numbers of slaves, a high dependency ratio, and costs of production which were inflated by debt, extravagance, absenteeism, and inefficiency.

Compared with Goveia, Orlando Patterson reaches quite different conclusions in his study of slave society in Jamaica.[17] He regards Jamaica as "a monstrous distortion of human society," chiefly characterized by "the astonishing neglect" and perversion "of almost every one of the basic prerequisites for normal living" (p. 9). Patterson's chief contribution is in describing the social institutions of the slaves and the various ways in which they resisted slavery. While Patterson focuses attention on the slave society of Jamaica, Edward Brathwaite investigates both the white and black segments of Jamaican society.[18] He views "white and black, master

---

14. R. B. Sheridan, *Sugar and Slavery: An Economic History of the British West Indies, 1623–1775* (Barbados, 1974).

15. Space limitations prevent listing the works of Gabriel Debien which begin with *Une Plantation de Saint-Domingue: La Sucrerie Galbaud du Fort (1690–1802)* (Cairo, 1941), and end in 1974 with *Les Esclaves aux Antilles Francaises (XVIIe–XVIIIe Siècles)* (Basse-Terre, Guadelupe, and Fort-de-France, Martinique, 1974).

16. Elsa V. Goveia, "Gabriel Debien's Contribution to the History of French West Indian Slavery," paper presented at the Third Annual Conference of Caribbean Historians, University of Guyana (April 1971), 46.

17. H. Orlando Patterson, *The Sociology of Slavery: An Analysis of the Origin, Development and Structure of Negro Slave Society in Jamaica* (London, 1967).

18. Edward Brathwaite, *The Development of Creole Society in Jamaica, 1770–1820* (Oxford, 1971).

and slave" not as "separate nuclear units, but as contributory parts of a whole," as "two cultures of people, having to adapt themselves to a new environment and to each other" (p. 307).

Cuban slavery and plantation economy have invited comparison with other slave societies. Following in the tradition of Frank Tannenbaum and Stanley Elkins, Herbert S. Klein published a comparative study of slavery in Cuba and Virginia.[19] Contrasted with the arbitrary power of slave-owners in Virginia, Klein contends that Cuban master-slave relations were tempered by the intervention of priests and public officials. Franklin W. Knight challenged the Tannenbaum-Elkins-Klein thesis by demonstrating that the greater proportion of Cuban slaves who were attached to sugar plantations were overworked, underfed, and prone to disease and premature death.[20] He faults writers whose comparative studies of slavery neglect equivalent stages of economic and social growth and exaggerate the influence of metropolitan institutions.

Slave demography, which was pioneered by George Roberts,[21] has become a vital field of research in recent years. Michael Craton contends that there was sustained progress toward a natural increase of the population, especially after the abolition of the slave trade.[22] On the other hand, B. W. Higman finds fault with the argument that the slave population was likely to increase because of a better balance of the sexes and a growing proportion of creole to African slaves.[23] Higman's contribution is to show how the patterns of fertility and mortality varied between urban and rural slaves, crop types, size of slave holdings, labor requirements, disease environments, and other variables. The results of Stanley Engerman's research suggest that the mortality experience of creole slaves in the islands may not have differed as markedly from that in the United States as did

19. H. S. Klein, *Slavery in the Americas: A Comparative Study of Virginia and Cuba* (Chicago, 1967).

20. F. W. Knight, *Slave Society in Cuba during the Nineteenth Century* (Madison, 1970).

21. G. W. Roberts, "Movements in Slave Population of the Caribbean During the Period of Slave Registration," in *Comparative Perspectives on Slavery in New World Plantation Societies,* ed. Vera Rubin and Arthur Tuden (New York, 1977).

22. M. Craton, "Jamaican Slave Mortality: Fresh Light from Worthy Park, Longville and the Tharp Estates," *Journal of Caribbean History,* 3 (1971), and "Jamaican Slavery," in *Race and Slavery in the Western Hemisphere: Quantitative Studies,* ed. Stanley L. Engerman and Eugene Genovese (Princeton, 1975).

23. B. W. Higman, "The Demography of Slavery in Jamaica, 1817–34," paper presented at the Third Annual Conference of Caribbean Historians, University of Guyana (April 1971), "The Slave Population of the British Caribbean: Some Nineteenth Century Variations," in *Eighteenth Century Florida and the Caribbean,* ed. Samuel R. Proctor (Gainesville, 1976), and *Slave Population and Economy in Jamaica, 1807–1834* (London, 1976).

the fertility rates. Compared with the United States, he finds a longer interval between births in the West Indies, which is thought to be a carryover from African sources.[24]

Trends in the writing of West Indian trade and shipping history include new quantitative data sources, refinements in data processing, use of family and trading-firm papers, histories of individual ports, colonies, regions, and comprehensive histories of interregional and Atlantic trade and shipping. The history of Port Royal, Jamaica, which was once the most powerful British center across the Atlantic, has been reconstructed.[25] Case histories of trading firms based on letter books and account books have been published.[26] Trade and shipping between North America and the West Indies in the age of the American Revolution have been analyzed.[27] For example, Shepherd and Walton have written a quantitative study of the maritime trade of the North American colonies, which contains much data and analysis of the important Yankee-Creole trade.[28] D. H. Makinson's monograph affords insight into the effects of world events upon the island of Barbados with special reference to its trade with North America.[29]

More information is needed on the nature and extent of West Indian trade, shipping, and finance after the American Revolution. Recent studies include those by Dookhan on war and trade from 1783 to 1815,[30] Drake on Liverpool's trade with Africa and the Caribbean,[31] Drescher on

24. S. L. Engerman, "Some Economic and Demographic Comparisons of Slavery in the United States and the British West Indies," *Economic History Review,* 2d ser., 29, 2(1976).

25. D. J. Buisseret, "Port Royal, 1655–1725," *Jamaica Historical Review,* 10 (1973); W. A. Claypole and D. L. Buisseret, "Trade Patterns in Early English Jamaica," *Journal of Caribbean History,* 5 (1972); Michael Pawson and David Buisseret, *Port Royal Jamaica* (Oxford, 1975).

26. Richard Pares, "The London Sugar Market, 1740–1769," *Economic History Review,* 2d ser., 9, 2(1956), "A London West India Merchant House, 1740–1769," in *Essays Presented to Sir Lewis Namier,* ed. R. Pares and A. J. P. Taylor (London, 1956), and *Merchants and Planters* (Cambridge, England, 1960); D. W. Thomas, "The Mills Family: London Sugar Merchants in the Eighteenth Century," *Business History,* 11 (1969).

27. Richard Pares, *A West India Fortune* (London, 1950), and *Yankees and Creoles: the Trade Between North America and the West Indies Before the American Revolution* (London, 1956); R. B. Sheridan, "The Plantation Revolution and the Industrial Revolution, 1625–1775," *Caribbean Studies,* 9 (1969).

28. James F. Shepherd and Gary M. Walton, *Shipping, Maritime Trade and the Economic Development of Colonial North America* (Cambridge, England, 1972).

29. D. H. Makinson, *Barbados, a Study of North American–West Indian Relations, 1739–1789* ('s-Gravenhage, 1964).

30. Isaac Dookhan, *A History of the Virgin Islands of the United States* (London, 1974).

31. Barry F. Drake, "Continuity and Flexibility in Liverpool's Trade with Africa and the Caribbean," *Business History* (Jamaica), 18, 1(1976): 85–97.

the trade in sugar, coffee, and cotton,[32] and Minchinton on the trade of Bristol and economic relations between metropolitan countries and the Caribbean.[33] Much more work remains to be accomplished on trade, shipping, and finance in the nineteenth century.

The transition from slavery to freedom in individual colonies and on a regional level has been a vital field of research in recent decades. Foremost among the historians of the transition is Douglas Hall, whose contributions to West Indian history and culture are manifold. In his *Free Jamaica,* he presents a detailed account of the island's economic development from 1838 to 1865.[34] He finds that while emancipation brought difficult problems it also unleashed a spirit of enterprise among all classes. The freedmen established interior towns, villages, and market places and came to constitute an important class of small farmers, peasants, and rural laborers. At the same time the sugar industry, though declining, was reorganized and brought under better management. Hall's study of five of the Leeward Islands illustrates some of the larger social, economic, and political problems of the period 1834–70.[35] He finds that the island's commitment to sugar production and an export-import economy in a period of secular decline led to a hardening of planter-labor relationships and class conflict, which culminated in the establishment of Crown colony government.

William A. Green attempts a new comprehensive assessment of the more than dozen Caribbean sugar colonies of Great Britain in the period from 1830 to 1865.[36] He is concerned with the relationship between colonial policy and the social and economic problems of slavery and emancipation. Green has also written on the apprenticeship period in British Guiana and the planter class.[37]

Knowledge of Guyanese economic history has been greatly enhanced by the recent publication of two scholarly monographs. Alan Adamson explains how the hegemony of sugar came about and how it affected Guy-

32. Drescher, *Econocide.*

33. W. E. Minchinton, *The Trade of Bristol in the Eighteenth Century* (Bristol, 1957), and "The Economic Relations between Metropolitan Countries and the Caribbean: Some Problems," in *Comparative Perspectives on Slavery in New World Plantation Societies,* ed. Vera Rubin and Arthur Tuden (New York, 1977).

34. Douglas Hall, *Free Jamaica, 1838–1865: An Economic History* (New Haven, 1959).

35. Douglas Hall, *Five of the Leewards, 1834–1870* (Barbados, 1971).

36. W. A. Green, *British Slave Emancipation: The Sugar Colonies and the Great Experiment, 1830–1865* (Oxford, 1976).

37. W. A. Green, "The Apprenticeship in British Guiana, 1834–1838," *Caribbean Studies,* 9, 2(1969), and "The Planter Class and British West Indian Sugar Production, Before and After Emancipation," *Economic History Review,* 26 (1973).

anese society in the nineteenth century.[38] He finds that sugar monoculture exacted high social costs as it turned from African slaves to indentured laborers from India and drove out nonsugar industries. While Adamson's book covers the period from 1838 to 1904, that of Jay R. Mandle spans the century and a quarter from 1838 to 1960.[39] Mandle searches Guyana's colonial past for the roots of its underdevelopment. He attributes the underdevelopment to policies which were designed primarily to repress the growth of all sectors of the economy which would compete with the sugar planters for scarce labor and drive up wage rates.

The rise of a black peasantry after emancipation has been a field of lively investigation in recent decades. In a series of important articles, Woodville Marshall breaks new ground in analyzing the origin and stages in the growth of a peasantry in the British West Indies.[40] By means of persistent effort, both on an individual and cooperative basis, numbers of peasants managed to secure an independent existence through cultivation outside the dominant plantation society and sugar economy. Marshall observes, however, that plantation control of basic agricultural resources has severely restricted the advancement of the peasants.

Many historians have been concerned with the indentured immigrants from India and elsewhere who, to a large extent, manned the plantations after emancipation. Abundant information about the recruitment, transportation, labor contracts, and economic and social effects of the migration has been supplied.[41]

38. A. H. Adamson, *Sugar Without Slaves* (New Haven, 1972).

39. J. R. Mandle, *The Plantation Economy: Population and Social Change in Guyana, 1838–1960* (Philadelphia, 1973).

40. Woodville K. Marshall, "Notes on Peasant Development in the West Indies since 1838," *Social and Economic Studies,* 17, 3(1968), "The Termination of the Apprenticeship in Barbados and the Windward Islands: An Essay in Colonial Administration and Politics," *Journal of Caribbean History,* 2 (1971), "Aspects of the Development of the Peasantry," *Caribbean Quarterly,* 18, 1(1972), and "The Establishment of a Peasantry in Barbados, 1840–1920," paper presented at the Sixth Annual Conference of Caribbean Historians, University of Puerto Rico, Río Piedras (1974).

41. I. M. Cumpston, *Indians Overseas in British Territories, 1834–1854* (London, 1953); H. Johnson, "Immigration and the Sugar Industry in Trinidad During the Last Quarter of the 19th Century," *Journal of Caribbean History,* 3 (1971); C. Kondapi, *Indians Overseas, 1838–1949* (Madras, 1951); K. O. Laurence, "The Evolution of Long-Term Labour Contracts in Trinidad and British Guiana, 1834–1863," *Jamaican Historical Review,* 5, 1(1965), and "Immigration into the West Indies in the 19th Century," in *Chapters in Caribbean History* (Barbados, 1971); G. W. Roberts, "Immigration of Africans into the British Caribbean," *Population Studies,* 7, 3(1954), and *The Population of Jamaica* (Cambridge, England, 1957); G. W. Roberts and J. Byrne, "Summary Statistics on Indenture and Associated Migration Affecting the West Indies, 1834–1918," *Population Studies,* 20 (1966); G. W. Roberts and M. A. Johnson, "Factors Involved in Immigration and Move-

Linking the past with the present is the "new" school of political economy which is associated with the Caribbean New World Group at the University of the West Indies. New World economists contend that although slavery has been formally abolished for about five generations, the basic structure of the plantation society is today very much like that of slave days. In his model of the pure plantation economy, Lloyd Best attempts to explain the dynamics of change in Caribbean and other similar societies.[42] He seeks to isolate the basic institutional, structural, and behavioral features which have served as a check on economic development. The interesting thing is that Best's model has been to a large extent inspired by Eric Williams' *Capitalism and Slavery.* Best finds modern counterparts to historical links between colonial and metropolitan economies that have perpetuated a condition of chronic commercial and industrial exploitation. George Beckford seeks to elaborate Best's model further to explain the dynamics of economic underdevelopment of plantation economies of the Caribbean and other Third World countries.[43] Beckford advances the hypothesis that the peasant sector of the economy has greater potential for growth than the plantation sector. Most remarkable is Beckford's assertion that the new foreign-owned multinational corporations, based on mining, manufacturing, and tourism, are operating essentially within the framework of the traditional plantation sector.[44]

To be sure, there are lacunae in the literature of Caribbean economic history, as well as material which has been overlooked or underutilized previously. Three recent studies point to new directions in writing the history of the slave trade and slavery. In *The Middle Passage,* Herbert S. Klein has used demographic and other quantitative data in his analysis of

---

ments in the Working Force of British Guiana in the 19th Century," *Social and Economic Studies,* 23 (1974); Judith Weller, *The East Indian Indenture in Trinidad* (Río Piedras, Puerto Rico, 1968); Donald Wood, *Trinidad in Transition: The Years After Slavery* (London, 1968).

42. Lloyd Best, "Outlines of a Model of Pure Plantation Economy," *Social and Economic Studies,* 17 (September 1968).

43. G. L. Beckford, *Persistent Poverty: Under-development in Plantation Economies of the Third World* (New York, 1971), and Beckford, ed., *Caribbean Economy: Dependence and Backwardness* (Mona, Jamaica, 1975).

44. Beckford, *Caribbean Economy;* Havelock Brewster, "The Social Economy of Sugar," *New World Quarterly,* Dead Season/Croptime (1969); J. Bryden, *Tourism and Development: A Case Study of the Commonwealth Caribbean* (Cambridge, England, 1973); Norman Girvan, *The Caribbean Bauxite Industry* (Mona, Jamaica, 1967), and "Multinational Corporations and Dependent Under-development in Mineral Export Economies," *Social and Economic Studies,* 19 (December 1970); Norman Girvan and Owen Jefferson, eds., *Readings in the Political Economy of the Caribbean* (Kingston, Jamaica, 1971), and *Foreign Capital and Economic Underdevelopment in Jamaica* (Mona, Jamaica, 1972).

the trans-Atlantic slave trade of all the major European powers.[45] Jerome S. Handler and Frederick W. Lange employ the methodologies of archaeology, history, and ethnography in their *Plantation Slavery in Barbados*.[46] Michael Craton delves beneath the conventional sources in an effort to discover the lives of the slaves in his handsomely produced book, *Searching for the Invisibile Man*.[47] He uses more than thirty slave lists from a plantation in Jamaica to provide biographical details for over thirteen hundred individual slaves. Moreover, he has interviewed ordinary country folk in search of modern perceptions of slavery and insights into the lives of slaves.

Much work remains to be done on the demographic and medical aspects of slavery. B. W. Higman is extending his work on the demography of slavery to the British Caribbean as a whole from 1807 to 1834, while Robert Fogel and Stanley Engerman are working with the slave registrations for Trinidad to see what can be said about fertility, mortality, physical growth, and occupations. R. B. Sheridan is studying the health and medical treatment of slaves with special reference to Jamaica. Though some progress has been made in discovering why slave deaths usually exceeded slave births, studies have been limited in time and place. The following are some of the questions that need to be answered. Prior to 1808, was it actually cheaper to buy new slaves from Africa than to encourage family life and reproduction on the plantations? How did the slave trade contribute to the morbidity and mortality of the slaves? How did the abolition of the slave trade effect the health and demographic performance of the slaves? Why was infant mortality so high? Can the insights from modern studies of malnutrition and children's diseases shed light on this question? Was the average slave's diet sufficient in quantity and quality? Did the amelioration laws contribute to better feeding and other improvements in the treatment of slaves? Did the European doctors who practiced in the West Indies tend to kill more slaves than they cured? Were the folk medical practices of the slaves more beneficial than European medical practices?

B. W. Higman believes that economic historians continue to be preoccupied with the external or institutional aspects of slavery. He thinks it is time to turn attention to the internal features of the system. "We need to

45. H. S. Klein, *The Middle Passage: Comparative Studies in the Atlantic Slave Trade* (Princeton, 1978).

46. J. S. Handler and Frederick W. Lange, *Plantation Slavery in Barbados: An Archaeological and Historical Investigation* (Cambridge, Massachusetts, 1978).

47. M. Craton, *Searching for the Invisible Man: Slaves and Plantation Life in Jamaica* (Cambridge, Massachusetts, 1978).

study further the differential allocation of slave labor to particular resource uses," he writes, "the functioning of the internal slave markets, the economic costs of deciding slave occupations on the basis of demographic principles, and the resulting regional inequalities in slave prices. Even more than this, we need studies of the domestic economy of the slaves themselves, their attitudes to resource allocation, to saving money and patterns of consumption."[48] Jack Greene suggests that "scholars could profitably do a series of micro studies of the socio-economic organization, ethnic composition, and labour environments in localities through court records, wills, inventories, tithable lists, etc. comparable for what is being done in community and regional studies of portions of North America."[49]

As noted, Gabriel Debien and Richard Pares pioneered the use of private plantation papers to illuminate the history of slavery and the plantation economy and society. Considering the numerous family papers which have come into the public domain during recent decades and the publication of guides to these and other records dealing with the British Caribbean colonies, it can be expected that monographs based on plantation papers will occupy a place of primary importance in coming years. Guides to archival materials have been published for individual family papers and for certain islands.[50]

Moreover, private papers can supply valuable data for ascertaining the profitability of plantation agriculture. Among the questions that deserve consideration, according to Walter Minchinton,[51] are the following: (1) How far was there a difference in profitability among different crops—among sugar and coffee and indigo, for example? How important were the differences in quality? (2) What effect did the size of plantation, equipment, quality of management, etc., have on profitability? (3) How important were variations between particular islands? (4) How far did location within a particular island affect the situation? (5) What shifts in long-run profitability occurred? (6) How did short-run fluctuations affect the profitability of a West Indian estate? (7) Did the presence or absence of the planter matter? Furthermore, were the profits abnormally large in the long run? What happened to them? Did they assist British industrialization, either directly or indirectly?

Much remains to be done on the economic history of the Caribbean region in the postemancipation era. From the vantage point of Barbados

48. B. W. Higman, "Economics of Circum-Caribbean Slavery," in Vera Rubin and Arthur Tuden, *Comparative Perspectives on Slavery in New World Plantation Societies* (New York, 1977), 143.
49. Letter from Jack P. Greene to the author.
50. Three sets of plantation papers are available on microfilm.
51. Minchinton, "Economic Relations," 571.

and the Cave Hill campus of the University of the West Indies, Woodville Marshall and his colleague, Frank Taylor, suggest the following topics and areas need investigation: (1) history of business houses: transnational combines as well as local conglomerates; (2) new industrial development in the region: oil, bauxite, tourism, telecommunications, transport, etc., particularly for the period after the late nineteenth century; (3) the minor staples: cocoa, coffee, citrus, bananas, rice, ganga; (4) migration during the late nineteenth and twentieth centuries: Panama and other parts of Central America, the United States, Aruba and Curaçao, the United Kingdom; (5) labor in the early twentieth century; (6) the fishing industry; (7) international trade: links with individual territories, scope and effect of trade agreements; (8) intraregional trade; (9) banking, insurance, and finance; (10) public sector policies; (11) history of economic thought in the region; (12) comparative economic history across the region. B. W. Higman suggests the need to study artisan skills and small-scale industry, using oral history and photographing techniques. Richard Lobdell's Ph.D. dissertation on the relationship between economic structure and demographic performance among the administrative parishes of Jamaica during the period 1891–1935 provides valuable methodological tools and far-ranging findings that promise to stimulate further work by economic historians. Briefly stated, Lobdell concludes that by contrast with plantations, "peasant organized production is more conducive to overall economic development because incomes are distributed in a more egalitarian fashion, because social stratification is less rigid and because political institutions are more responsive to local needs."[52]

In his monumental *From Columbus to Castro,* Eric Williams maintains that the whole history of the Caribbean can be viewed "as a conspiracy to block the emergence of a Caribbean identity—in politics, in institutions, in economics, in culture and in values." He believes "the future way forward for the peoples of the Caribbean must be one which would impel them to start making their own history, to be the subjects rather than the objects of history, to stop being the playthings of other people."[53]

52. Richard A. Lobdell, "Economic Structure and Demographic Performance in Jamaica, 1891–1935," Ph.D. dissertation (McGill University, 1975), 26.
53. Eric Williams, *From Columbus to Castro: The History of the Caribbean, 1492–1969* (London, 1970), 503.

44   Migrant Groups in the Caribbean
Marianne D. Ramesar

The current concern with ethnicity and immigrant "roots" in the United States is apparent also in the renewed interest in immigration history among Latin Americanists. In the Caribbean, the black consciousness of the 1960s was partly a resurgence of earlier black nationalism. These stirrings have reawakened similar identity consciousness among large minority groups like the East Indians and concern among the less numerous descendants of other immigrants like the Chinese and Lebanese.

"Migrant groups" are defined in this article as groups united by common ethnic links. These have shared the common experience of migrating virtually permanently from non-Caribbean territories into the Caribbean archipelago. All communities in the Caribbean have received stocks of immigrant groups under similar conditions since their control and settlement by European powers.

The introduction of immigrants in organized groups to provide unskilled plantation labor after the emancipation of the African slaves provides a common factor. These groups include: East Indians, Madeiran Portuguese, Free Africans, Chinese, Europeans and others, notably Javanese and Lebanese.[1]

General studies on migration embrace the immigration of several ethnic groups to a single territory. Some of the earliest are travelogues which reveal the reactions of foreign visitors fascinated by Caribbean exotics in the persons and characteristics of immigrants from diverse sources. There are also early accounts of the origins and process of migration, some of which deal with the organization of indentured immigration in the French colonial territories, including the Caribbean.[2] Much later Noel Deerr's *History of Sugar* (Vol. 2 [London, 1950]) includes chapters dealing with the introduction of plantation labor after emancipation: Europeans, Indians, and the Chinese coolie traffic to Cuba. The 1950s saw the publication of several general works, which include useful statistical and demographic data.[3]

1. G. W. Roberts and J. Byrne, "Summary Statistics on Indenture and Associated Migration Affecting the West Indies, 1834–1918," *Population Studies*, 20, 1(1966).

2. Lucien Castalumio, *Etude historique sur les origines de l'immigration réglementée dans nos ancieenes colonies de la Réunion, la Guadeloupe, la Martinique et la Guyane* (Paris, 1906); and also works by Pierre Lacascade (1907) and Pierre Guirald (1911).

3. M. J. Proudfoot, *Population Movements in the Caribbean* (Port of Spain, 1950);

With refreshing impartiality and sensitive insight, Donald Wood has dealt with the diverse groups which entered postemancipation Trinidad—Americans, Europeans, Indians, and Chinese—introducing each ethnic group into the main problem area of finding labor for the plantations.[4] K. O. Laurence has drawn on his extensive research to present a wide-ranging coverage of migration to the main receiving colonies—English, French, and Dutch, as well as Spanish Cuba.[5] Also in the 1970s Cornelius Goslinga presented a paper on "Immigration into Surinam, 1865–1939" (at the Fourth Annual Conference of Caribbean Historians, University of the West Indies, Mona, Jamaica [1972]), and David Lowenthal's book on *West Indian Societies* (London, 1972) includes chapters on the history and integration of ethnic minorities.

Early accounts of the organization of East Indian migration include an informative article by Arthur H. Hill, "Emigration from India" (*Timehri,* 3d ser., 6 [1919]), which considers recruiting, embarcation, obstacles to the traffic by some authorities and members of the public, and the plight of returning repatriates. Two biographical works on the careers of the pioneer Canadian missionaries in Trinidad furnish much firsthand information on the early reactions, work conditions, social attitudes, behavior, and adjustments made by the new arrivals.[6] All these are seen through the eyes of Victorian clergymen, singleminded in their mission of religious conversion and education despite resistence from some Hindus and Muslims and a few of their leaders.[7] Recent revisionist studies by Samaroo assess the impact of the missionaries' program;[8] and Ramesar analyzes the conflict experienced over the value of a Western education leading to upward ca-

G. W. Roberts, *The Population of Jamaica* (Cambridge, England, 1957), and "Immigration of Africans to the British Caribbean," *Population Studies,* 7, 3(March 1954); Douglas G. Hall, *Free Jamaica, 1838–1865: An Economic History* (New Haven, 1959).

4. Donald Wood, *Trinidad in Transition: The Years after Slavery* (London, 1968); also see Marianne Ramesar, "Patterns of Regional Settlement and Economic Activity by Immigrant Groups in Trinidad, 1851–1900," *Social and Economic Studies,* 25, 3(September 1976).

5. K. O. Laurence, *Immigration into the West Indies in the 19th Century* (Barbados, 1971).

6. K. J. Grant, *My Missionary Memories* (Halifax, 1923); Sarah E. Morton, ed., *John Morton of Trinidad: Journals, Letters and Papers* (Toronto, 1916).

7. Grant, *My Missionary Memories,* 66–67, 73; Marianne Ramesar, "The Position of the East Indians in Trinidad, 1890–1917," in *Social Groups and Institutions in the History of the Caribbean* (Río Piedras, Puerto Rico, 1975), 80.

8. Brinsley Samaroo, "Missionary Methods and Local Responses: The Canadian Presbyterians and the East Indians in the Caribbean," in *East Indians in the Caribbean: Colonialism and the Struggle for Identity,* ed. Bridget Brereton and Winston Dookeran (Millwood, New York, 1982); also see Idris Hamid, *A History of the Presbyterian Church in Trinidad* (Trinidad, 1980).

reer mobility for the descendants of immigrants, but with the consequent loss of traditional culture and ethnic identity.[9]

Tributes to the career achievements and the group's contribution to the economic development of the host country are contained in J. A. Luckhoo's article in 1919,[10] as well as in later centenary albums by Ruhomon and Kirpalani.[11] Dwarka Nath has expanded a similar undertaking into a full-fledged history.[12] Several short accounts assess the role of the Indian group as a work force.[13] Adamson and Mandle have written monographs analyzing the economic impact of immigration policies on the development of British Guiana.[14]

The nationalist movement in India inspired interest in overseas Indians, including those in the Caribbean, by Gangulee and Kondapi.[15] Recently Indian nationals serving as academics in Caribbean universities have investigated the development of the group in the Caribbean and cultural survivals among its descendants. Among these are J. C. Jha[16] and Singaravelou, a native of Pondicherry who published in 1975 an overview of the history and development of the Indians in Guadeloupe.[17]

Some themes of early articles have become the subject of weightier

9. Marianne Ramesar, "The Integration of East Indian Settlers in Trinidad after Indenture," *Caribbean Issues* 2, 3(December 1976): 62.

10. J. A. Luckhoo, "The East Indians in British Guiana from Their Advent to This Colony to the Present Time: A Survey of the Economic, Educational and Political Aspects," *Timehri,* 3d ser., 6 (September 1919).

11. P. Ruhomon, *Centenary History of the East Indians in British Guiana, 1838–1938* (Georgetown, 1946); Murli Kirpalani, et al., eds., *Indians Centenary Review, 1845–1945* (Port of Spain, 1945).

12. Dwarka Nath, *A History of the Indians in British Guiana* (2d ed., London, 1970).

13. Edgar L. Erickson, "The Introduction of East Indian Coolies into the British West Indies," *Journal of Modern History,* 6 (June 1934); Noel Deerr, "Indian Labor in the Sugar Industry," *International Sugar Journal* (London), 40 (March 1938); C. Y. Shephard, *Agricultural Labour in Trinidad* (St. Augustine, 1929); Howard Johnson, "Immigration and the Sugar Industry in Trinidad during the Last Quarter of the 19th Century," *Journal of Caribbean History,* 3 (1971).

14. A. H. Adamson, *Sugar Without Slaves* (New Haven, 1972); J. R. Mandle, *The Plantation Economy: Population and Social Change in Guyana, 1838–1960* (Mona, Jamaica, 1974).

15. N. Gangulee, *Indians in the Empire Overseas: A Survey* (London, 1947); C. Kondapi, *Indians Overseas, 1838–1949* (Bombay, 1951).

16. J. C. Jha, "The Background to the Legislation of Non-Christian Marriages in Trinidad and Tobago," in *East Indians in the Caribbean,* "The Indian Mutiny-cum-Revolt of 1857 and Trinidad (West Indies)," *Indian Studies Past and Present* 13, 4(July–September 1972), and "The Indian Heritage in Trinidad," in *Calcutta to Caroni: The East Indians of Trinidad,* ed. John La Guerre (Port of Spain, Trinidad, 1974).

17. Singaravelou, *Les Indiens de la Guadeloupe: Etude de géographie humaine* (Bordeaux, France, 1975).

monographs published by professional historians, especially in the English-speaking Caribbean. The unfolding of colonial policy is the core of I. M. Cumpston's detailed and thorough account of the early period of Indian-indentured immigration to the British colonies, including the Caribbean, where this labor was added to inputs of British capital and management expertise for the development of plantation colonies.[18] Judith Weller has examined the legislation on which the system was based, with some assessment of the correlation between regulations and practice.[19] But Weller's monograph has been roundly criticized by K. O. Laurence for evident breaches of professionalism.[20] Laurence shares with Weller the general conclusion that, despite the hard, narrow life of the indentured Indian immigrant, the imperial and Trinidad governments tried to make the system tolerable.[21] This is not the view of Hugh Tinker, who has made a "first attempt to provide a comprehensive study of the whole process of emigration from rural India across the seas to more than a dozen countries," including some in the Caribbean.[22] Tinker has written a full and thorough study based on a wealth of primary sources. In the process he concludes from the accumulated evidence that the indenture-migration system was a thinly disguised form of the slavery which it replaced, and that its abuses persisted because of the supine acceptance of the status quo by colonial officials.

The 1960s were the era of debate on the plural society and of ethnic conflict, especially in the British Caribbean. Local and foreign sociologists and cultural anthropologists who participated and published their research findings included M. G. Smith, Lloyd Braithwaite, and Allen Erlich, the Niehoffs and Klass, R. T. Smith, Jayawardena, Despres, Newman, and J. D. Speckmann on Suriname.

The historian's contribution to the assessment of intergroup relations tended to come later, during the 1970s. Ramesar has researched the socioeconomic position of Indians in Trinidad,[23] and Lesley (Key) Potter has

18. I. M. Cumpston, *Indians Overseas in British Territories, 1834–1854* (London, 1953).

19. Judith Weller, *The East Indian Indenture in Trinidad* (Río Piedras, Puerto Rico, 1968).

20. K. O. Laurence, Book review, *Caribbean Quarterly* 17, 1(March 1971).

21. K. O. Laurence, "The Development of Medical Services in British Guiana and Trinidad, 1841–1873," *Jamaican Historical Review,* 6 (1964), and "The Evolution of Long-Term Labour Contracts in Trinidad and British Guiana, 1834–1863," *Jamaican Historical Review,* 5, 1(1965).

22. Hugh Tinker, *A New System of Slavery: The Export of Indian Labour Overseas, 1830–1920* (London, 1974), xiii.

23. Marianne Ramesar, "The Impact of the Indian Immigrants on Colonial Trinidad Society," *Caribbean Quarterly,* 22, 1(March 1976).

studied their relations with the Afro-Guyanese.[24] Acheen and Tikasingh have surveyed nineteenth-century public opinion to determine attitudes concerning the Indian group in Martinique and in Trinidad, respectively.[25] Brinsley Samaroo has sought evidence of Afro-Indian solidarity in the common history of colonial exploitation in Trinidad,[26] and Brereton has traced the roots of mutual stereotyping and covert hostility to the plantation experience.[27] But John La Guerre urges the need for the awareness of persistent cultural diversity and the creation of policies to accommodate it.[28] Kusha Haraksingh, in a short book review (*Caribbean Issues*, 1, 1[April 1974]), advances the valuable viewpoint that race prejudice probably had roots not only in the attitudes learned from the colonial masters, but, in the case of the Indians, in traditional values and attitudes imported from India.

Since the 1960s there has been a spate of scholarly articles and a few monographs on the factors underlying the introduction of laborers from India and the administration of the indenture system. The historian has contributed an essential dimension to the understanding of questions which have only been partially investigated through surveys of present conditions. There is room for further research on the immigrants' prospects and fortunes after indenture, on their economic impact on territories other than British Guiana, and for monographs comparable to Gillion's *History of Indian Migrants to Fiji*.

One strong justification is the wealth of existing source material, both in metropolitan depositories and in Caribbean archives. There is a need to preserve as well as make use of abundant government records and rare newspapers, now threatened by neglect and decay in territories like Trinidad, and to use the methods of oral history to draw on the resources of the remaining survivors and early descendants of the original migrants.

The island of Madeira supplied the bulk of the Portuguese immigrants

24. Lesley (Key) Potter, "Population Trends in the Immigrant Communities: East Indians in Guyana, 1838–1920," *Actes du XLIIᵉ Congrès International des Americanistes*, Vol. 1 (Paris, 1977).

25. René Achéen, "Le problème de l'immigration indienne devant l'opinion martiniquaise dans les années 1882–1885," *Les Cahiers du Centre d'Etudes Regionales Antilles-Guyane*, 27 (1972); Gerard Tikasingh, "Toward a Formulation of the Indian View of History: The Representation of Indian Opinion in Trinidad, 1900–1921," in *East Indians in the Caribbean*.

26. Brinsley Samaroo, "Politics and Afro-Indian Relations in Trinidad," in *Calcutta to Caroni*.

27. Bridget Brereton, "The Foundations of Prejudice: Indians and Africans in the 19th Century," *Caribbean Issues* 1, 1(April 1974).

28. John La Guerre, "Afro-Indian Relations in Trinidad and Tobago: An Assessment," *Social and Economic Studies*, 25, 3(September 1976), and as ed., *Calcutta to Caroni*.

who were introduced as plantation laborers, especially into British Guiana. Here they formed an intermediate social group between the emancipated blacks and the dominant white planter group, from whom they were distinguished in census reports. Although small in number, their significance lay in their early abandonment of plantation labor and domination of the retail trade, especially in the rural areas. Two research papers analyze the factors which contributed to their upward mobility.[29] H. P. Jacobs has published an article on the Portuguese in Jamaica, and Ciski has worked on those in St. Vincent.[30] This remains a lightly tapped field for researchers.

An early article by Cruickshank describes the introduction of liberated Africans from the Sierra Leone depots and of independent Kroo-men from the (Liberian) coast to British Guiana.[31] Asiegbu's general study includes the Caribbean.[32] Like Cumpston's study, it reviews colonial policy, but it resembles Tinker's approach in its attempt to reach the "secret part of the official mind," exposing harmful complacency. A more recent monograph by Thomas surveys the experiment of voluntary African laborers for Jamaica.[33] There is renewed interest in researching African survivals in the Caribbean, and also the history of those Free African immigrants who entered the Caribbean after emancipation. This is one area in which the methods of oral history are being used, notably by Maureen Warner for Trinidad,[34] and by Monica Schuler for Jamaica.[35]

Next to the East Indians, the Chinese immigrants have most attracted the attention of historians, especially regarding experiences in Cuba,

29. K. O. Laurence, "The Establishment of the Portuguese Community in British Guiana," *Jamaican Historical Review*, 5, 1(1965); Brian Moore, "The Social Impact of Portuguese Immigration into British Guiana after Emancipation," *Boletín de estudios latinoamericanos y del Caribé*, 19 (December 1975).

30. H. P. Jacobs, "The Portuguese in Jamaica," *Bulletin of the Jamaican Historical Society*, 4, 16(December 1968); Robert Ciski, "The Vincentian Portuguese: A Study in Ethnic Group Adaptation," Ph.D. dissertation (University of Massachusetts, 1975).

31. J. Cruikshank, "Graham African Immigrants after Freedom," *Timehri*, 3d ser., 6 (1919).

32. Johnson U. J. Asiegbu, *Slavery and the Politics of Liberation, 1787–1861: A Study of Liberated African Emigration and British Anti-Slavery Policy* (London, 1969).

33. Mary Elizabeth Thomas, *Jamaica and Voluntary Labourers from Africa, 1840–1865* (Gainesville, 1974).

34. Maureen Warner, "Africans in 19th Century Trinidad," in the African Studies Association of the West Indies *Bulletin* No. 5 (December 1972), part 2 in Bulletin No. 6 (December 1973).

35. Monica Schuler, "The Experience of African Immigrants in 19th Century Jamaica," paper presented at the Fourth Annual Conference of Caribbean Historians, University of the West Indies, Mona, Jamaica (1972); also see Andrew T. Carr, "A Rada Community in Trinidad," *Caribbean Quarterly* 3, 1(1953).

where the treatment of these bonded laborers was particularly harsh and exploitative. Evidence of vast abuses in this human traffic were exposed in Campbell's early general work about receiving countries within the British Empire.[36] With reference to the history of the group in Cuba, Reckord's paper covers much the same period as Helly's.[37] Corbitt's monograph is a testament to the group's record of attrition as well as to the dogged persistence of its survivors.[38] There are several studies by Cuban authors not yet consulted by the author of this essay, as well as a bibliography on the overseas Chinese by Uchida, and articles on the Chinese in Suriname by Snelleman and Ankum-Houwink.[39]

Sir Cecil Clementi's book, *The Chinese in British Guiana* (Georgetown, 1915), remains a valuable source, supported by the official records and correspondence available to him in his position as government secretary. His previous experience as deputy colonial secretary in Hong Kong underlay his authoritative statements on the motivation, social customs, and work habits of Chinese migrants. Records of the achievements of prominent Chinese are also available in Horton's Souvenir Album on the thirtieth anniversary of the republic in 1941.[40] Lind includes important background information on the transfer of Chinese laborers from the Panama Railway to Jamaica and the relations between later migrants and the blacks in Jamaica.[41] Jacqueline Levy has presented a paper on the immigration history of this group and its eventual domination of the grocery trade.[42]

36. Persia Campbell, *Chinese Coolie Immigration to Countries within the British Empire* (reprint, London, 1971).

37. Mary Reckord, "Chinese Contract Labor in Cuba, 1847–74," paper presented at the Fourth Annual Conference of Caribbean Historians, University of the West Indies, Mona, Jamaica (1972); Denise Helly, "Immigrants Chinois à Cuba, 1847–1886," *Actes du XLIIe Congrès International des Americanistes,* Vol. 1 (Paris, 1977).

38. Duvon Clough Corbitt, *A Study of the Chinese in Cuba, 1847–1947* (Wilmore, Kentucky, 1971).

39. Juan Perez de la Riva, "Demografía de los culies chinos en Cuba, 1853–1874," *Revista de la Biblioteca Nacional José Martí,* 8 (1966); Pastrana Juan Jimenez, *Los chinos en las luchas por la liberación cubana, 1847–1930* (La Habana, 1963); Guillermo Tejeiro, *Historia ilustrada de la colonia china en Cuba* (La Habana, 1947); Naosaku Uchida, *The Overseas Chinese* (Stanford, 1960); J. Ankum-Houwink, "Chinese Contract Migrant Workers in Surinam between 1853 and 1870," *Boletín de estudios latinoamericanos y del Caribé,* 17 (Summer 1974); J. F. Snelleman, "Chineesche Immigranten in Surinam," *West-Indische Gids,* 2 (1920).

40. V. P. Oswald Horton, ed., *The Chinese in the Caribbean, Souvenir 30th Anniversary of the Chinese Republic, 1911–41* (Kingston, 1941); also see Lee Tow Yin, *The Chinese in Jamaica* (Kingston, 1957).

41. Andrew W. Lind, "Adjustment Patterns Among the Jamaican Chinese," *Social and Economic Studies,* 7, 2(June 1958).

42. Jacqueline Levy, "Chinese Indentured Immigration to Jamaica During the Latter Part of the 19th Century," paper presented at the Fourth Annual Conference of Caribbean Historians, University of the West Indies, Mona, Jamaica (1972).

Higman has written a valuable article on a preemancipation immigration project, which introduced a small group of Chinese males into Trinidad.[43] Great gaps persist in the history of the later influx of this group to Trinidad and the further movement of its members from British Guiana to Trinidad.

For the English-speaking Caribbean there has been little and late attention to the history of groups introduced from Europe as postemancipation laborers, or of people who found their way to the Caribbean while participating in the great intercontinental migration from Europe to the Americas. (This is in contrast to publications regarding the presugar European settlers in several colonies.) Douglas Hall has published articles on the introduction of German settlers to Seaford Town in Jamaica up to 1850.[44] Patrick Bryan documents the entry of white French emigrés from Haiti into plantation ownership and commerce in Jamaica.[45]

Most of the studies of Javanese immigration concern Suriname, in which this group only began to arrive during the 1890s. These studies include works by Ahrens, Kalff, Heemstra, and Azimullah, as well as a monograph by the anthropologist Malefijt, which offers some historical background.[46]

The Lebanese were another group of late arrivals who came voluntarily as families or individuals in search of security under the British flag, or from religious persecution by the Turks, or in search of adventure and fortune in the Americas. In 1970 an introductory article appeared, based on some oral evidence taken from the second generation of this group in Jamaica.[47] Bruijne has reported on a recent survey of the Lebanese in Suriname, and Nicholls on the role of the group in the Greater Antilles.[48]

Even a preliminary review reveals the paucity of research done on some migrant groups (for instance the free American blacks who entered Trini-

43. B. W. Higman, "The Chinese in Trinidad, 1806–38," *Caribbean Studies,* 12, 3(1972).

44. Douglas G. Hall, "Bountied European Immigration into Jamaica, with Special Reference to the German Settlement at Seaford Town up to 1850," part 1, *Jamaica Journal,* 8, 4(1974), part 2, 9, 1(1975).

45. Patrick Bryan, "Emigrés: Conflict and Reconciliation. The French Emigrés in Nineteenth Century Jamaica," *Jamaica Journal,* 3 (September 1973).

46. H. Ahrens, "Kolonisatie opparticulier land in Suriname met Javanem onder contract onder de thans geldende immigratie wetten," *West-Indische Gids,* 4 (1922–23); S. Kalff, "Javanese Emigrants in Suriname," *Inter-Ocean,* 9, 10(October 1928); J. Heemstra, "De Indonesiers in Suriname," *Indonesie,* 6 (1952–53); E. G. Azimullah, "Geshiedenis van de Javaanse bevolungsgroep," *Schakels* s–71 (1969); Annemarie de Wall Malefijt, *Javanese of Surinam: Segment of a Plural Society* (Assen, 1963).

47. Nellie Ammar, "They Came from the Middle East," *Jamaica Journal,* 4, 1(March 1970).

48. G. A. de Bruijne, "The Lebanese in Suriname," *Boletín de estudios latinoamericanos y del Caribé,* 26 (June 1979); David Nicholls, "No Hawkers and Pedlars: Levantines in the Caribbean," *Ethnic and Racial Studies,* 4, 4(1981).

dad) and on receiving countries. Material exists in official records and newspapers and in the private records of ethnic associations like those of the Chinese and the Portuguese. There are also human sources of oral information.

The recent attention to studies on the East Indians, on the other hand, may reflect more than their numbers and concentration. The literature on specific ethnic groups in the Caribbean goes back some seventy years and is fairly prolific concerning the Jews—a tiny minority. The relatively small number of studies on other ethnic groups suggests that they are seen as having become assimilated, or are perceived as marginal to Caribbean society, or their descendants—potential publicists—have lost the willingness to stake a determined claim for inclusion in the independent Caribbean, unlike their predecessors in the colonial empires.

The underlying need seems to be the assessment of the positive contribution of migrant groups to the Caribbean. Gordon Lewis, in his *Growth of the Modern West Indies*,[49] notes that "so far West Indian discussion has failed to identify with any clarity what functional role it wants minorities to play." The historian's contribution should help by determining the role which all of its minority and majority groups have already played.

45   Caribbean Integration
Thomas Mathews

The lack of success of both political and economic efforts at integration in the Caribbean may be the reason why there are very few studies on such efforts. However one might reflect that there also are few studies with depth and detail on the history of the League of Nations, or the founding and development of the United Nations, or for that matter the Pan American Union or the Organization of American States. Thus instead of success or failure, an alternative reason for this lack of studies might be the fact that an exceptional or uncommon interest is required to focus attention on a concept which usually runs counter to national or imperial concerns.

A study focusing on regional cooperation would presume to appeal to a regional audience with a common reason for being. If this community does not exist or is in the process of being formed, then the attention or

49. Gordon Lewis, *Growth of the Modern West Indies* (New York and London, 1968), 45.

interest in studying the process of integration will be very weak or non-existent. Thus the basic question is whether or not a Caribbean community or culture exists. This topic has attracted interest and has been explored fruitfully by anthropologists like Sidney Mintz, cultural historians like Richard Morse, and political scientists like Gordon Lewis. The generally accepted conclusion of these scholars, albeit outsiders to the Caribbean region, is that there are sufficient common elements within the region to justify the identification of a Caribbean community.

Just how strong this feeling of commonality within the Caribbean actually is can be debated. Furthermore, it would appear that the community spirit is not constant or necessarily steady in growth but waxes with the feeling of oppression and wanes with the surge of nationalism. The study of this process is lacking, and even the periods of fluorescence have not received much more than passing attention from one or two scholars.

Even in the studies of the region under the control of Spain, the attention of the colonial historian has been primarily on the development of this or that island. Thus there is more existing scholarship about the early history of Cuba or Puerto Rico than about the operation and development of the territory nominally under the jurisdiction of the Audiencia de Santo Domingo. Indeed there is only one very preliminary study of the first audiencia of the New World.

The military mind, like that of the strategist Admiral Mahan or the Spaniard Menéndez, comprehended the Caribbean as a unit and dealt with it accordingly, but very few historians have ventured to study the Caribbean from this point of view. Several historians have tried to trace the history of the Armada de Barlovento through the late sixteenth and most of the seventeenth centuries. The effort has not been much more successful than the armada itself and, although perhaps not as costly, certainly comparatively just as taxing. Again the problem with the armada and also the audiencia before it and the study of these regional entities is that local interests or national imperatives almost invariably prevailed over regional interests and concerns. Thus the audiencia gets tangled up in internal affairs of Santo Domingo and grossly neglects its regional responsibilities. The armada was diverted to the more pressing national effort to defend the flow of merchandise and minerals to and from Spain, thus leaving the region to muster its own defense.

The seventeenth century saw the rise of a truly broad Caribbean community, which ignored and even flaunted any national loyalties. Yet this anarchistic community of pirates has rarely received any serious attention from scholars. Juan Bosch wrote eloquently about the way of life of the *filibusteros* in Hispaniola, and Clarence Haring recognized the economic impact on the mercantile systems of this group of Caribbeanists, but others have only been intrigued by this or that attack on Spanish strongholds from Porto Bello to Veracruz.

With the movement for independence in the northern and southern continents of the New World, the history of the Caribbean is too often reduced to an appendage of one or the other of these struggles. As Lepkowski has pointed out, we know something about the impact of the ideas of Bolívar on Cubans, Dominicans, and Puerto Ricans,[1] but very little about the impact of the example of Toussaint L'Ouverture on the enslaved masses of the Caribbean. Alejo Carpentier in his historical novels has captured some of the regional feelings which united the Caribbean at this time of upheaval and crisis.[2] Lacking is a comprehensive study of all of the aborted and thwarted slave revolts in the islands. Historian Guillermo Baralt has identified those of Puerto Rico,[3] but the focus must be broadened to include Cuba and Spanish Santo Domingo, as well as the French and English islands.

Indeed as this author tried to show in an exploratory essay completed and published thirty years ago,[4] the nineteenth century was a period of increasing interest in political cooperation and integration within the Caribbean. More recently Carlos M. Ramos, drawing heavily on the original work, has added a few more details and rounded out the picture somewhat,[5] but there must be a wealth of untouched material now available to more demanding and ambitious young scholars to give a substantial analysis of the motivating forces behind the conferderation of the Caribbean.

Motivated as were the Americans on the southern continent, the Caribbeanists sought strength through unity in their struggle to free their islands from the bonds of Spanish imperialism. The story is scattered and multilingual, thus making its study much more difficult. There is a great deal of untouched and unidentified material available in the periodicals and journals of Paris and London, in the Spanish publications of New York and Key West, as well as the Caribbean depositories of St. Thomas and Curaçao. The role of the Dominicans in this struggle for Caribbean political unity is obviously large and yet, because of the problems of locating and utilizing archival material in that island republic, mostly untold.

1. See Lepkowski's essay, "The Haitian Revolution," pp. 278–83 in this volume.
2. Alejo Carpentier, *The Kingdom of This World* (New York, 1957), and *El Siglo de las Luces,* translated as *Explosion in a Cathedral* (Boston, 1962).
3. Guillermo A. Baralt, *Esclavos Rebeldes: Conspiraciones y sublevaciones de Esclavos en Puerto Rico, 1795–1873* (Río Piedras, Puerto Rico, 1981).
4. Thomas G. Mathews, "The Project for a Confederation of the Greater Antilles," *Caribbean Historical Review* (December 1954).
5. Carlos M. Ramos, *La idea de la Federación Antillana en los independentistas puertorriqueños del siglo XIX* (Río Piedras, Puerto Rico, 1971).

At more or less the same time a similar integrative movement of a different nature was occurring in the English-speaking Caribbean. Motivated mostly by the need for cutting the administrative costs of an unproductive empire, the islands were brought closer together often over their own protests. As has been shown by Bruce Hamilton, the usually tranquil and loyal island of Barbados erupted into riots as a result of the precipitous policy of the Colonial Office to bring about political integration.[6] As yet there is no study of the reaction and effects of the consolidation of governments in the Leeward and Windward Islands. Douglas Hall mentions the integration in passing in his study of the Leewards,[7] and C. S. Salmon offers contemporary observations,[8] but there is nothing to refer to in the former French colonies or the spice islands.

Thus when a similar move occurred three quarters of a century later, again motivated primarily from London, there was little to orient the student. Not that the human race is noteworthy for being able to profit from past mistakes, but the dearth of material on political integration in the Caribbean cannot be ignored.

Two world events occurring in the first third of the twentieth century had an integrating effect on the Caribbean, but there has been little effort made to compare and evaluate this effect on the region as a whole.

World War I saw the creation of the West Indian regiment, and, although a concerted study of the impact of such an experience on the West Indian is missing, sufficient evidence has been uncovered of the enlightening effect on some individuals, such as Cipriani in Trinidad, to justify further analysis on a regional basis. For example, there is no study whatsoever of the effect of the war mobilization in the United States on the newly acquired colony of Puerto Rico, even though it is very clear that the psychological impact of racial segregation in the armed services had a devastating effect on the ego of one Pedro Albizu Campos, the brilliant Puerto Rican nationalist. No study has been made from a regional point of view, or for that matter from a military point of view, of the growing German commercial influence in the Caribbean. The United States' commercial growth in the region has been the object of many studies, but the response from a regional point of view has been ignored.

The second event was the Great Depression, which obviously had a more direct and devastating effect on the Caribbean communities already living on the margin of poverty than did World War I. Riots, strikes, pro-

6. Bruce Hamilton, *Barbados and the Confederation Question, 1871–1885* (London, 1956).

7. Douglas Hall, *Five of the Leewards, 1834–1870* (Edinburgh, 1971), 177–79.

8. C. S. Salmon, *The Caribbean Confederation* (London, n.d. but probably 1887 or 1888).

tests, and violence were experienced on every island, but there is no comparative study of this phenomenon. The Moyne Commission and its important report on the situation in the English-speaking territories have not been the subject of any close analysis. The dictatorships of Cuba, the Dominican Republic, Venezuela, and Haiti of the early 1930s are seen as national phenomena and not as regional manifestations of protest toward Caribbean-wide economic conditions.

World War II brought into sharp focus the regional perspective with the creation of the Anglo-American Commission. Soon French and Dutch interests were added, and the commission came to be known as the Caribbean Commission. However, with the exception of one or two introductory efforts, there is very little analysis of the day-to-day operations of these integrating efforts by the imperial powers active in the area.

Even after the war when the Caribbean Commission was converted slowly into the Caribbean organization—one of the few unique regional experiments in international cooperation—only one serious effort has been made to study its problems and reasons for failure. Further research by a multilingual specialist is essential.

Surprisingly, even when the focus is exclusively on the English-speaking efforts toward Caribbean integration among the British colonies of the Caribbean, few studies have been forthcoming. The ill-starred West Indian Federation is widely referred to as a failure not to be seriously considered for possible revival in any foreseeable future, but still few scholars are concerned with dissecting the cadaver to reveal the causes of death.

The creation of the West Indian Federation was the effort of a mere handful of visionaries, and yet in-depth biographies of almost all of them are lacking. Sir Philip Sherlock's recent biography of Norman Manley is one of the exceptions.[9] However, even this important and pregnant study raises questions which future historians will have to answer. Specifically, why did Manley, one of the strong defenders of regionalism, refuse to accept a leadership position in the fledgling federation?

With the recent death of Dr. Eric Williams, the obvious challenge to young scholars to study his enigmatic role in regional movement needs no stress. Yet, more will be written about his successful role in Trinidad politics than the very powerful impact of his personality on regional affairs.

The slightly more successful effort among the English-speaking islands toward economic integration—now in its second decade of operation—still have to be studied by the economic historian. While it is plain that a

9. Philip Sherlock, *Norman Manley* (London, 1980).

critical and objective study of Caricom is long overdue, it is perhaps impossible to hope for a critical and certainly unheard of objective study of Cuba's economic integration into not only a regional organization but for that matter into the economic organization of the communist bloc.

Finally although material is being stored and is available in the Caribbean Regional Library, there will probably never be a scholar to study the most successful experiment in Caribbean integration and cooperation— that of the Association of Caribbean Universities and Research Institutes (1967) now in its fifteenth year of existence.

The history of Caribbean integration, whether it be of political, economic, or educational organizations, is extremely difficult to research adequately. The archives of Europe and North America are far removed from the region. The one regional library is woefully inadequate and impoverished, with little or no hope for any concerted effort to improve this deplorable state of affairs. Local or national facilities are not concerned about regional matters, and the material available locally has to be collected and preserved by those with specialized interests. The disintegration of the region is obvious in every direction. One example is sufficient to stress the sad state of interest in regional affairs. In a recent (1981) conference on Caribbean Integration held in Santo Domingo, several outstanding Dominican scholars not only rejected any efforts toward Caribbean integration as impractical and visionary but called for the closer integration of their independent nation within the economic and cultural orbit of the United States.

Integration as a concept in the Caribbean may survive into the twenty-first century, but, if one were to judge by the degree of interest expressed currently, Caribbean integration will go the way of the Puerto Rican parrot.

Bibliography

Corkran, Herbert, Jr., *Patterns of International Cooperation in the Caribbean* (Dallas, 1970).

Froude, James Anthony, *The English in the West Indies* (New York, 1900). See pages 162–64 for comments on the Leeward Islands Federation.

Lowenthal, David, *The West Indies Federation* (New York, 1961).

Mathews, Thomas G., "The Project for a Confederation of the Greater Antilles," *Caribbean Historical Review* (December 1954): 70–107.

Mordecai, John, *The West Indies, the Federal Negotiations* (London, 1968).

Moya Pons, Frank, "Caribbean Consciousness," *Caribbean Educational Bulletin*, 5, 3(1978): 40.

Thomas, J. J., *Froudacity: West Indian Fables Explained* (London, 1969; first pub. 1889), chap. entitled "The West Indian Federation," 146–59.

Williams, Eric, "The Historical Background of British West Indian Federation: Select Documents," *Caribbean Historical Review,* 3–4 (1954): 13–69.

University of the West Indies, Institute of International Relations, *Regionalism and the Commonwealth Caribbean* (St. Augustine, Trinidad, 1969).

University of the West Indies, Institute of Social and Economic Research, "Federation of the West Indies," a special issue of *Social and Economic Studies,* 6, 2(June 1957).

46   Class, Race, and Religion in Caribbean Research
Franklin W. Knight

Despite the growing interest in Caribbean studies and the increasing sophistication of research in the region, the historiography reveals some surprising lacunae.[1] Nowhere is this illustrated more than in the amorphous fields of class cleavages, the social implications of race, and the nature and impact of religious practices.[2]

Caribbean historiography defines itself along the general conventional chronological demarcations of American history: European discovery, colonization, independence, and modernization. Imperialism, slavery, and the plantation socioeconomy as well as the polyglot cultures and peoples brought to the Caribbean created wide discrepancies in both the pace as well as the nature of change. Uniformity, therefore, was not a characteristic of Caribbean development. Each island and each territory experienced a variation—sometimes slight, other times profound—in the general pattern of regional commonality. Within imperial divisions as well as

1. The expanding bibliography on the Caribbean may be followed in: Lambros Comitas, *The Complete Caribbean, 1900–1975: A Bibliographic Guide to the Scholarly Literature* (Millwood, New York, 1977); the relevant sections of the *Handbook of Latin American Studies,* ed. Dolores Moyano Martin and currently published in Austin; and the surprisingly thorough *Bibliography of the English-Speaking Caribbean,* ed. Robert J. Neymeyer (Parkersburgh, Iowa, 1980).

2. These topics have had some important pieces written, but in general they remain, by comparison with other topics, less rigorously examined.

across imperial boundaries, the Caribbean colonies manifested systadial parallels within the context of their chronological disparity.[3]

For example, all the colonies evolved from early colonialism through imperialism toward independence and nationhood—or more precisely, mininationhood. The Spanish colonies preceded the English, French, Dutch, and Danish colonial presence in the region by more than a century. But the Spanish participation in the intensified agricultural revolution of slavery and the plantation economy lagged behind its European peers by nearly a century. Haiti emerged as an independent state in 1804, wresting its political liberty as well as its early nationhood with revolution and bloodshed. Cuba, which gained its political independence from Spain and the United States in 1902, only began to establish national cohesion with the Revolution of Fidel Castro after 1959. Jamaica, Barbados, Guyana, Grenada, Dominica, Trinidad and Tobago, Suriname, and the Bahamas all began the process of modernization prior to their separate achievement of independence within the past two decades. As new states are being established, new political relationships are being created, such as the Puerto Rican Associated Free State, the French Antilles Departments, and the Associated States of the former English and Dutch Antilles.

If the overall political conditions have been fluid, the social conditions have been equally so. Emphasis on class structure in the patterns of evolution has taken a subordinate role to the general social-structural changes. Nevertheless, class divisions and class conflict emerge as an integral part of all the principal studies of the Caribbean from Lowell Ragatz, *Fall of the Planter Class in the British Caribbean, 1763–1833* (New York, 1928; reprint ed., 1971), through the works of Elsa V. Goveia, Philip D. Curtin, Orlando Patterson, Edward Brathwaite, C. L. R. James, Franklin W. Knight, Gwendolyn M. Hall, B. W. Higman, Michael Craton, Gaston Martin, and François Girod.[4] More explicit treatment of class relations

3. For further development of this theme, see Franklin W. Knight, *The Caribbean: The Genesis of a Fragmented Nationalism* (New York, 1978), especially pp. 50–66.

4. Elsa V. Goveia, *A Study of the Historiography of the British West Indies to the End of the Nineteenth Century* (México, 1956), and *Slave Society in the British Leeward Islands at the End of the Eighteenth Century* (New Haven, 1965); Philip D. Curtin, *Two Jamaicas: The Role of Ideas in a Tropical Colony, 1830–1865* (Cambridge, Massachusetts, 1955; 2d ed., New York, 1970); Orlando Patterson, *The Sociology of Slavery: An Analysis of the Origins, Development and Structure of Negro Slave Society in Jamaica* (London, 1967); Edward Brathwaite, *The Development of Creole Society in Jamaica, 1770–1820* (New York, 1971); C. L. R. James, *The Black Jacobins: Toussaint L'Ouverture and the San Domingo Revolution* (2d rev. ed., New York, 1963); Franklin W. Knight, *The Caribbean: The Genesis of a Fragmented Nationalism* (New York, 1978), and *Slave Society in Cuba During the Nineteenth Century* (Madison, 1970); Gwendolyn M. Hall, *Social Control in*

may also be found in Raul Cepero Bonilla, Ramiro Guerra y Sánchez, et al., Manuel Moreno Fraginals, Jerome S. Handler, Mavis C. Campbell, or D. W. Cohen and J. P. Greene.[5] For the twentieth-century Anglophone Antilles, Rex M. Nettleford has a provocative essay, *Identity, Race and Protest in Jamaica* (New York, 1972),[6] while David Lowenthal and Lambros Comitas have brought together a fine selection of relevant articles in *Consequences of Class and Color: West Indian Perspectives* (New York, 1973).[7] Across the Caribbean the contemporary scene is extremely complicated as the previously formal distinctions of sociopolitical caste have largely been dissolved, revealing the categories of social class, which, if anything, have become more pronounced.

Much research remains to be done, however, on the nature of class relations not only in the distant past but also in the changing present. With the increasing availability of local and estate records—used with such exemplary efficacy by Gabriel Debien, B. W. Higman, Michael Craton, Manuel Moreno Fraginals, and Francisco Scarano[8]—it should be possible to analyze more fully the underlying class significance of the threefold caste divisions of colonial plantation society. Within the past ten years the accessibility of estate records in local archives in Puerto Rico, Cuba, Jamaica, Barbados, as well as private and public metropolitan archives in

Slave Plantation Societies: A Comparison of St. Domingue and Cuba (Baltimore, 1971); B. W. Higman, *Slave Population and Economy in Jamaica, 1807–1834* (New York, 1976); Michael Craton, *Searching for the Invisible Man: Slaves and Plantation Life in Jamaica* (Cambridge, Massachusetts, 1978); Gaston Martin, *Histoire de l'esclavage dans les colonies françaises* (Paris, 1948); François Girod, *La vie quotidienne de la société creole (Saint-Domingue au 18 siècle)* (Paris, 1972).

5. Raul Cepero Bonilla, *Obras históricas* (La Habana, 1963); Ramiro Guerra y Sánchez, et al., *Historia de la nación cubana* (10 vols., La Habana, 1952); Manuel Moreno Fraginals, *El ingenio: el complejo económico social cubano del azúcar* (3 vols., La Habana, 1978; first pub. 1964; English translation of first two vols., *The Sugarmill* [New York, 1976]); Jerome S. Handler, *The Unappropriated People: Freedmen in the Slave Society of Barbados* (Baltimore, 1974); Mavis C. Campbell, *The Dynamics of Change in a Slave Society: A Sociopolitical History of the Free Coloreds of Jamaica, 1800–1865* (London, 1976); D. W. Cohen and J. P. Greene, eds., *Neither Slave nor Free: The Freedmen of African Descent in the Slave Societies of the New World* (Baltimore, 1972).

6. First published as *Mirror, Mirror* (Jamaica, 1970).

7. This is one of the four books edited by these two authors which deal with Caribbean history and social development.

8. Gabriel Debien, *Les esclaves aux Antilles Françaises (XVIIe–XVIIIe siecles)* (Basse-Terre, Guadelupe, 1974); Higman, *Slave Population and Economy;* Craton, *Invisible Man,* and with James Walvin, *A Jamaican Slave Plantation: The History of Worthy Park, 1670–1970* (Toronto, 1970); Moreno Fraginals, *The Sugarmill;* Francisco Scarano, "Labor and Free Labor in the Puerto Rican Sugar Economy, 1815–1873," in *Comparative Perspectives on Slavery in the New World Plantation Societies,* ed. Vera Rubin and Arthur Tuden, 553–63 (New York, 1977).

Great Britain, France, and Spain, promises a fresh era of model studies on the colonial societies of the seventeenth, eighteenth, and nineteenth centuries.[9]

New quantitative data, combined with the new computerized techniques of processing and retrieval, make possible ambitious studies whose time-consuming labor demands would have negated any attempts only a generation ago. It is hoped that one trend likely to continue and expand is that toward more regional studies which would treat the region as a whole, without necessarily neglecting or denying the individual variations. The basis for such studies already exists in a small coterie of fine essays and books such as Sidney Mintz and Richard Price, *An Anthropological Approach to the Afro-American Past: A Caribbean Perspective* (Philadelphia, 1976); Arturo Morales-Carrión, "El reflejo en Puerto Rico de la crisis Dominico-Haitiana" (revista *EME–EME estudios dominicanos,* 27 [noviembre–diciembre 1976]: 19–39), and also suggested in his *Albores históricos del capitalismo en Puerto Rico* (Río Piedras, Puerto Rico, 1972); Vera Rubin and Arthur Tuden, eds., *Comparative Perspectives on Slavery in New World Plantation Societies* (New York, 1977); Ciro Cardos, "Proprieté de la terre et technique de production dans les colonies esclavagistes de l'Amerique et des Caraibes an XVIIIe siècles (*Cahiers des Ameriques Latines* [Paris], 13/14 [1976]: 127–52); the selected essays of the Fourth Annual Conference of Caribbean Historians;[10] Franklin W. Knight, *The Caribbean;* and Margaret E. Crahan and Franklin W. Knight, eds., *Africa and the Caribbean: The Legacies of a Link* (Baltimore, 1979). These books, and others not listed here, form a good foundation for the further pursuit of narrower themes across disciplines and across time and locale.

Still pertaining to the topic of Caribbean class formation are two areas fully deserving of further scholarly research. The first is the development of the Caribbean peasantry.[11] The second is the evolution of the rising commercial bourgeoisie of the period from the later eighteenth century to the present time.

9. See, for example, the fine collection of original essays presented at the symposium entitled "Problems of Transition from Slavery to Free Labor in the Caribbean," jointly sponsored by the Fondo para el Avance de las Ciencias Sociales, Santo Domingo, and the Social Science Research Council, New York, and held in Santo Domingo, June 11–13, 1981. See also, Andres Ramos Mattei, *La hacienda azucarera: Su crecimiento y crisis en Puerto Rico (siglo XIX)* (San Juan, Puerto Rico, 1981).

10. *Social Groups and Institutions in the History of the Caribbean* (Mayaguez, Puerto Rico, 1975).

11. A beginning bibliography on peasants may be found in Sidney W. Mintz, "A Note on the Definition of Peasantries," *Journal of Peasant Studies,* 1, 1(October 1973): 91–106.

The subject of the peasantry is a highly controversial one, as the limited available literature amply illustrates. The problem, however, is partly semantic, and the definition of what constitutes a peasant within the context of the Caribbean would be a valuable contribution to the historiography. Beyond that loom numerous questions on the growth of the peasantry: factors of stimulation or inhibition within the colonial and postcolonial societies, relationship to land, the internal marketing system, and the entire scope of the secondary economy so prevalently overlooked in the treatment of export economies of the Caribbean.

Aspects of Caribbean peasantry, of course, have long attracted the attention of anthropologists, especially M. G. Smith and Sidney Mintz, and have been reported on for Haiti, Jamaica, and a few of the eastern Caribbean islands.[12] What is urgently needed is a series of major research efforts focused specifically on describing the structure of the Caribbean peasantry across the entire spectra of time and region, and relating that structure to the political and economic forces with which the peasants have had to contend.[13] A particularly valuable study would be the response of Cuban peasants to the various agrarian reform programs of the Instituto Nacional de Reforma Agraria (INRA) after 1959, a study which would ascertain the degree to which one may continue to speak of a peasantry within a socialist politicoeconomic system.

Commercial groups have not had as much attention as the peasants. The best group study for any of the Caribbean territories is Roland T. Ely, *Cuando reinaba su majestad el azúcar: Estudio histórico-sociológico de una tragedia latinoamericano* (Buenos Aires, 1963). Ely used the private papers of the Tomas Terry family of Matanzas, Cuba, as the basis of his study. Private papers abound in Cuba, Spain, Great Britain, and the United States on many of the leading merchants and planters of the "golden years" of the Cuban bourgeoisie, between 1776 and 1956. Complementary studies ought to be done on both the new wealthy families such as the Bacardí and Zulueta as well as on the older, more established families such as the Calvo, Penalver, O'Reilly, Zayas, Montalvo, and O'Farril. Hugh Thomas, *Cuba, the Pursuit of Freedom* (New York, 1971) provides some sketches of a number of the most powerful members of the large Cuban oligarchy, and both Moreno Fraginals, *The Sugarmill*, and Knight, "Origins of Wealth and the Sugar Revolution in Cuba, 1750–1850" (*Hispanic American Historical Review*, 57, 2[May 1977]), offer useful in-

12. See, for example, M. G. Smith, *The Plural Society in the British West Indies* (Berkeley, 1965); and James Leyburn, *The Haitian People*, with a new foreword by Sidney Mintz (New Haven, 1966; first pub. 1941).

13. Michael Louis, "An Equal Right to the Soil: The Rise of the Peasantry in Saint Lucia, 1838–1900," Ph.D. dissertation (The Johns Hopkins University, 1982).

sights into the political, economic, and philosophical views of the sugar oligarchy. None of these authors, however, focuses on the oligarchy as a class. Nevertheless, the material resources for a detailed study of the Cuban merchant class are abundant and, fortunately, relatively accessible.

For the other Caribbean territories, the lack of such detailed studies is equally evident. Since Richard Pares's two studies—*A West Indian Fortune* (London, 1959) and *Merchants and Planters* (London, 1960)—dealing with the Pinney family and the smaller eastern Caribbean islands, there really has been no major attempt to study the mercantile groups in Jamaica, Barbados, Trinidad, or British Guiana. All these larger territories had flourishing and important merchant communities, and the local archives probably contain considerable data of great importance to the general socioeconomic development of these local communities.

Studies of the merchant groups should not, however, be confined solely to the larger, more successful entrepreneurs. They are an easier and more attractive target because of the higher probability of locating relevant documents to facilitate such studies. But as a group, *petit* entrepreneurs were of invaluable importance to the entire local economies, and formed crucial links between the important urban factors and their world of an export-import-oriented economy and the basic, semibarter transfer of rural higglers and the small farmers. The extent to which individual Caribbean economies responded during the nineteenth and twentieth centuries to fluctuations in the world economy can be properly gauged only by the evidence derived from these small and middling participants.

Two areas of considerable recent scholarly interest have been the free colored groups (as a class within the colonial slave societies) and the rise of the labor movement during the present century. Even here, single-unit studies prevail, with little or no attempt to place the particular study within the broader regional context. By contrast, the fields of crime and the sociolegal structure or its expansion have received little attention. Also neglected is the study of women as a subclass of the occupational, economic, and cultural structure of Caribbean societies.

Despite its patent racial complexity, relatively few scholars have seriously studied the contemporary implications of race in the Caribbean. Of course, *race* like *peasant* contains complex semantic connotations, which tend to weaken or obscure its applicability. Notwithstanding, race remains an unavoidable aspect of any historical work on the Caribbean. Most studies of slavery treat the theme explicitly. Harmannus Hoetink in *Caribbean Race Relations: A Study of Two Variants* (New York, 1971), and *Slavery and Race Relations in the Americas: Comparative Notes on Their Nature and Nexus* (New York, 1973); M. G. Smith in *The Plural Society in the British West Indies;* and Philip Mason in *Prospero's Magic: Some*

Thoughts on Class and Race (London, 1962) have all made enormous theoretical contributions to this area. Rex Nettleford, *Identity, Race and Protest in Jamaica* and Walter Rodney, *The Groundings with My Brothers* (London, 1969) are *pensador* pieces which are difficult to categorize, but important essays in understanding the social complexity of a reality more easily captured by the creative writers and artists than the academic historian.

Race assumes importance both locally in terms of a Caribbean identity, and internationally in terms of the political repercussions of foreign involvement in Caribbean affairs, or vice versa. Cuban foreign policy, for example, has consistently stressed its African and "Latin" components and traces its legacy of international brotherhood to the writings of José Martí. The Black Power political slogan and philosophy native to the United States had to undergo considerable contortions in places like Trinidad or Guyana to find acceptable applicability. As far as scholarly research on race is concerned, the field is still relatively open for investigation into the local situations and into the role race plays in political state- and nation-building.

Some good studies have already been done on religion in the Caribbean. Alfred Caldecott, *The Church in the West Indies* (London, 1898; reprint ed., 1970) has never been superseded as a thorough general examination of the formal religious structure of the English Antilles. Caldecott's work, however, strongly requires updating and, in the process, some further examination of broader questions on the role of religion in the Caribbean and a dilution of much of the English Episcopalian ethnocentricity which permeates the original study. In a way, this has already begun on a limited scale as exemplified by Inez K. Sibley, *The Baptists of Jamaica, 1793– 1965* (Kingston, 1965). What has been done for the Jamaican Baptists must be extended to the other territories, not only for the Baptists but also for all the other denominations.

The nonformal religious structure—the basic religious practices of the masses outside the major denominations—has also been well served. Major studies have been done on Vodun in Haiti by Roger Bastide, Alfred Metraux, and Melville Herskovits.[14] Fernando Ortiz, Lydia Cabrera, and Migene González-Wippler have studied Lucumí adherents in Cuba.[15]

14. Roger Bastide, *African Civilizations in the New World,* trans. Peter Green (New York, 1971); Alfred Metraux, *Voodoo in Haiti,* trans. Hugo Charteris (New York, 1972; first pub. 1959); Melville J. Herskovits, *Life in a Haitian Valley* (New York, 1937; reprint ed., New York, 1964).

15. Fernando Ortiz, *Los negros brujos* (Miami, 1973; first pub. 1906); Lydia Cabrera, *Abakuá* (Miami, 1970), *Añago: Vocabulario Lucumí* (Miami, 1970), *El Monte* (Miami, 1969), *Otan Iyebiyé* (Miami, 1970), and *Refranes de Negros viejos* (Miami, 1969); Migene González-Wippler, *Santería African Magic in Latin America* (New York, 1973).

Leonard Barrett, George Simpson, Monica Schuler, and Edward Seaga have examined the Rastafarian and other popular Afro-Caribbean cults in Jamaica,[16] while Simpson and Maureen Warner-Lewis have done the same for Trinidad.[17]

Far more needs to be attempted with the theme of religions at the two levels—that of the formal, European- or North American-derived denominations—and the popular level of folk religions with their strongly eclectic African components. While more case studies of the denominations are always welcome, the most valuable contributions would be those which seek to analyze the ideological, political, and cultural activities of the religious groups at the local base of operations as well as at their international nexus. Some valuable steps in this direction have already been made in the series of essays in the *Journal of Inter-American Studies and World Affairs* (21, 1[February 1979]), or in the interesting, scattered essays of Margaret E. Crahan on religion in Cuba.[18] Crahan sees the various denominations, including the Roman Catholics, as agents of cultural transmission and facilities for the creation and perpetuation of cultural dependency. In this light, individual decisions to join any denomination reveal personal evaluations of local society and politics, as well as the persuasion of theological beliefs.

Folk religions, likewise, stand in need of more case studies, with less emphasis on their apparently exotic qualities and more considerations of their social and cultural roles. In this respect, the work already done by Monica Schuler on Akan-based religions in Jamaica (*"Alas, Alas, Kongo"*) represents an invaluable model. Schuler is convinced that African-derived religious movements respond to felt needs in certain communities and form important agents for group cohesion. She adamantly protests the misleading tendency to categorize syncretic African folk religions as millennial cults and by so doing obscure their primary symbolic value as vehicles of social commentary and political protest. This is the type of analysis which, added to the description of folk-religious practices, can immensely expand understanding of Caribbean societies. At the same time, such studies cannot be satisfactorily done in archives or from sec-

16. Leonard Barret, *The Rastafarians: A Study in Messianic Cultism in Jamaica* (Río Piedras, Puerto Rico, 1968); George Simpson, *Black Religions in the New World* (New York, 1978); Monica Schuler, *"Alas, Alas, Kongo": A Social History of Indentured African Immigration into Jamaica, 1841–1865* (Baltimore, 1980); Edward Seaga, "Revival Cults in Jamaica: Notes Toward a Sociology of Religion," *Jamaica Journal*, 3 (1970): 3–13.

17. Simpson, *Black Religions;* Maureen Warner-Lewis, "Trinidad Yoruba: Notes on Survivals," *Caribbean Quarterly*, 17 (1971): 40–49.

18. Margaret E. Crahan, "Salvation through Christ or Marx: Religion in Revolutionary Cuba," *Journal of Inter-American Studies and World Affairs*, 21 (February 1979): 156–84, and "Religious Penetration and Nationalism in Cuba: U.S. Methodist Activities, 1898–1958," *Revista/Review Interamericana*, 8 (1978): 204–24.

ondary reports, owing to the limited and often biased nature of the sources. Extensive fieldwork, utilizing much of the disciplinary tools of anthropology and sociology, is the only satisfactory method of capturing the value and the reality of popular religions. In the case of African-derived religious groups, however, the time may be running out for practical studies to be done, as the communities themselves face critical challenges, either from external political changes as in the case of Cuban Yoruba, or internal sociodemographic changes as in the case of Jamaican Myalism. Nevertheless, these studies must be done if social history is to be properly attempted throughout the Caribbean.

It is clear, then, that much remains to be done in the fields of class, race, and religion in the Caribbean. The resources are available, the tools and skills are available, and adequate models already exist in most cases. What is now required seems to be the formulation of some new approaches and the projection of more studies on a regional rather than an insular plane.

47   Pan-Africanism and Black Power in the Caribbean
Tony Martin

Despite the fact that West Indians have always played prominent roles in Pan-African struggles, the study of West Indian aspects of this movement still represents an underdeveloped field. In part, this is reflective of the Euro-centric bias that has dominated West Indian historical writing in the past. Happily, an assault on this bias is underway, and an increasing number of theses, articles, and books are surfacing which take the West Indies as their primary point of reference. The relatively underdeveloped nature of West Indian-related Pan-African studies is due also to the fact that so many of the major West Indian Pan-Africanists achieved prominence, not in the West Indies, but in Afro-America, Europe, or Africa.

The term *Pan-Africanism* has traditionally been used in at least two different but related ways. First, it connotes the recognition by peoples of African descent throughout the world of a common heritage and similar political struggles, especially in the period beginning with the trans-Atlantic slave trade. Those who have advanced this definition over the years have seen the need for Pan-African cooperation against the common foes of colonialism, neocolonialism, imperialism, and racism, and for economic and social development. The second definition is almost as old as the first and historically was advanced as a corollary to it. It speaks to the need for a strong and united African continent, which would take its rightful place in the forefront of the struggles of African peoples world-wide. West Indians have always been active in the field of Pan-Africanism, as understood by the first definition.

The dispersal of African peoples as a result of the trans-Atlantic slave trade provided the preconditions for the establishment of Pan-African sentiment. Africans, whether in North or South America, Europe, or the Caribbean, found themselves faced with a similar condition of servitude. In the West Indies, cooperation across political boundaries in dealing with this common problem sometimes took the form of flight by runaway slaves from one island to join Maroons on another.[1] In North America, Brazil, and the West Indies, proto-Pan-African activity often manifested itself in a desire to reunite with the African homeland, sometimes allied with a desire to help extirpate the slave trade in West Africa.

There were a number of slave revolts and attempted escapes in the West Indies, and several manifested the desire to lead a return to Africa. Most notably, West Indians were connected with the two English-speaking countries established in West Africa as havens for returning ex-slaves. The first of these, Sierra Leone, received its first repatriates from England in 1787. They were later followed by returnees from Nova Scotia and Jamaica, among other places.[2] Sierra Leone's neighbor on the West African coast, Liberia, had its beginnings as a refuge for Afro-American emigrants in 1820, under the auspices of the white American Colonization Society. This society helped finance the transportation of 346 Barbadian volunteers to Liberia in 1865, among them Arthur Barclay, a future president of Liberia. Much of the initiative for this move came from another West Indian, St. Thomas born Edward Wilmot Blyden, then Liberian secretary of state and for long a major advocate of emigration to that country.[3]

Postslavery West Indian interest in helping develop Africa also took the form of missionary activity. European missionary societies were bombarded with requests from black West Indians anxious to assist in the "redemption" and modernization of their motherland. Though sometimes reluctant to comply for a variety of selfish reasons, these missionary bod-

1. As early as the seventeenth century, slaves from neighboring islands were joining the Black Caribs in St. Vincent. See Sir William Young, *An Account of the Black Caribs in the Island of St. Vincent's* (reprint ed., London, 1971; first pub. 1795), 7.

2. The Sierra Leone story is well known. See, e.g., Edward Scobie, *Black Britannia: A History of Blacks in Britain* (Chicago, 1972), 56–76.

3. Hollis R. Lynch, *Edward Wilmot Blyden: Pan-Negro Patriot, 1832–1912* (London, 1967), 33–34.

ies could not totally resist this interest and some black West Indians served under their auspices. The West Indian Church Association for the Further-ance of the Gospel in western Africa, based at Codrington College in Barbados, was founded in 1851 and established missions at Río Pongo, in present day Guinea, in 1855.[4]

Yet other West Indian churchmen found expression for their Pan-African desires through participation in Afro-American churches. Among these might be mentioned Bishop John Bryan Small of the African Meth-odist Episcopal Zion church. Born in Barbados, Small traveled widely and lived in Africa before emigrating to the United States and joining the AMEZ church. He was in charge of the denomination's missionary activ-ity from the 1890s to his death in 1905 and paid his first visit to the West Indies in this capacity in 1899.[5] Another outstanding churchman in this category was Bishop George Alexander McGuire of Antigua. After many years of laboring in the Protestant Episcopal church in several areas of the United States, McGuire became chaplain general of Marcus Garvey's Uni-versal Negro Improvement Association (UNIA), the greatest Pan-African organization of its kind of all time. He soon afterwards founded, in 1921, the African Orthodox church, with headquarters in New York and branches in North America, the Caribbean, and Africa.[6]

Churchmen were by no means the only West Indians emigrating to the United States in the nineteenth century, and several of the others also dis-tinguished themselves in Pan-African activity. Among them may be men-tioned Jamaican-born John B. Russwurm, who cofounded Afro-America's first newspaper, *Freedom Journal,* in 1827 and migrated to Liberia in 1829. There he founded West Africa's first English-language newspaper, the *Liberia Herald,* and from 1836 to his death in 1851 served as governor of Maryland colony (now part of Liberia).[7] Blyden, too, perhaps the most celebrated of nineteenth-century Pan-Africanists, made the journey to West Africa via the United States.[8]

---

4. A. H. Barrow, *Fifty Years in Western Africa: Being a Record of the Work of the West Indian Church on the Banks of the Río Pongo* (London, 1900; reprint ed., New York, 1969), iii; C. P. Groves, *The Planting of Christianity in Africa, Vol. 2, 1840–1870* (London, 1964), 24 ff. Tony Martin, "Some Refections on Evangelical Pan-Africanism, or, Black Missionaries, White Missionaries and the Struggle for African Souls, 1890–1930," in *The Pan-African Connection* (Dover, Massachusetts, 1984), 35.

5. For more on Small and the AMEZ Church in general, see William J. Walls, *The African Methodist Episcopal Zion Church* (Charlotte, North Carolina, 1974).

6. Tony Martin, *Race First: The Ideological and Organizational Struggle of Marcus Garvey and the Universal Negro Improvement Association* (Westport, Connecticut, 1976), 71–73; *The Negro Churchman* (organ of the African Orthodox church), reprinted with an introduction by Richard Newman (2 vols., Millwood, New York 1977).

7. Lynch, *Edward Wilmot Blyden,* 9.

8. Ibid., 4.

Emigration to Africa was, however, but one aspect of a two-way traffic. Even after the end of slavery, Africans entered several of the West Indian territories as indentured laborers and West India Regiment recruits.[9] These postslavery arrivals must have had some influence on the fairly strong African retentions noted in some parts of the West Indies well into the twentieth century.[10] This surge of Africanness may in turn have augmented the predisposition toward Pan-African activity.

In the West Indies, as in the United States, the small, developing element of educated blacks in the later nineteenth century resorted widely to the weapons of racial pride and African-consciousness in their struggle against racial discrimination and political disfranchisement. This tendency gave rise to a vibrant Afro-West Indian press.[11] Several persons from this group in the late nineteenth and early twentieth centuries provided international leadership for the resurgent Pan-African movement. Prominent among these were Benito Sylvain of Haiti, who made Paris his base for several years, visited and befriended Emperor Menelik II of Ethiopia, and attended the first ever Pan-African Conference in London in 1900.[12] This historic conference was itself organized chiefly by Henry Sylvester Williams of Trinidad, who later emigrated briefly (1903–04) to South Africa.[13]

Major events in Africa (such as the Boer War of 1899–1902) could always be counted upon to generate interest among the Afro-West Indian public. With the exile of King Jaja of Opobo (in present-day Nigeria) to St. Vincent in 1888, the British government provided West Indians with an ideal rallying point for expressions of Pan-African solidarity. Manifestations of support for the exile took place on more than one island. After

9. On indentured laborers see, e.g., Monica Schuler, "African Immigration to French Guiana: The Cinq-Frères Group, 1854–1860," *African Studies Association of the West Indies (ASAWI) Bulletin No. 4* (December 1971): 62–78; and Donald Wood, *Trinidad in Transition* (London, 1968), chap. 4.

10. Maureen Warner, "African Feasts in Trinidad," *ASAWI Bulletin No. 4* (December 1971): 85–94, and "Africans in 19th Century Trinidad," Parts 1 and 2, in *ASAWI Bulletin No. 5* (December 1972): 27–59 and *ASAWI Bulletin No. 6* (December 1973): 13–37, respectively; Andrew Carr, "A Rada Community in Trinidad," *Caribbean Quarterly,* 9, 1 and 2(1963–64): 26–52.

11. Well documented in Rupert Lewis, "Robert Love: A Democrat in Colonia Jamaica," *Jamaica Journal,* 11, 1 and 2(August 1977): 58–63; and in Bridget Brereton, "The Negro Middle Class of Trinidad in the Later Nineteenth Century," in Association of Caribbean Historians, *Social Groups and Institutions in the History of the Caribbean* (Mayaguez, Puerto Rico, 1975), 50–65.

12. Tony Martin, "Benito Sylvain of Haiti on the Pan-African Conference of 1900," in *The Pan-African Connection,* 201–6.

13. There are two recent biographies of Sylvester Williams, namely, Owen C. Mathurin, *Henry Sylvester Williams and the Origins of the Pan-African Movement* (Westport, Connecticut, 1976); and James R. Hooker, *Sylvester Williams* (London, 1975).

his departure from the West Indies, King Jaja's name passed into the local folklore.[14]

The early twentieth century witnessed a proliferation of Pan-African organizations, which included West Indian participation. Henry Sylvester Williams' Pan-African Conference of 1900 resulted in the establishment of a Pan-African Association, which quickly set up a large number of branches in Jamaica, Trinidad, and elsewhere, as well as attracting the attention of Africans in Cuba.[15] The short-lived Hamitic League of the World, founded in Omaha, Nebraska, ca. 1919, was said to have had a branch in British Guiana.[16] The Afro-American scholar and civil rights leader, W. E. B. Du Bois, included persons from Haiti, the French West Indies, the British West Indies, and the Dominican Republic among the fifty-seven invited delegates to his first Pan-African Congress held in Paris in 1919.[17] The Society of Peoples of African Origin, founded in London in 1918, had as its general secretary F. E. M. Hercules of Trinidad.[18] Marcus Garvey's Universal Negro Improvement Association, which swept the world from its Harlem headquarters, was actually organized in Jamaica in 1914. Many of the international leaders of the UNIA were West Indians, and branches proliferated all over the greater Caribbean area. The organization played an important role in workers' struggles in Trinidad, British Honduras, and elsewhere, especially in 1919.[19]

The international Communist movement from the 1920s also provided some stimulus to Pan-African contacts, through the holding of international conferences, the publication of international journals, and other global activity, coordinated ultimately through Moscow. Black Communists in the United States provided the initial leadership for these activities, and many of them were immigrants from the West Indies. These included George Padmore of Trinidad, Cyril Briggs of Nevis, Otto Huis-

14. This author, as a child in Trinidad, heard frequent references to King Jaja and was surprised to discover in graduate school that the king had been a real person. On the esteem in which the black Vincentians and Barbadians held King Jaja, see Sylvanus Cookey, *King Jaja of the Niger Delta: His Life and Times, 1821–1891* (New York, 1974), 144, 159.

15. See: Lewis, "Robert Love"; Martin, "Benito Sylvain of Haiti"; and Brereton, "The Negro Middle Class of Trinidad."

16. W. F. Elkins, "'Unrest Among the Negroes': A British Document of 1919," *Science and Society*, 32, 1(Winter 1968): 72.

17. W. E. B. Du Bois, "The Pan-African Congress," *Crisis* (April 1919): 271–74; and Martin, *Race First*, 290–93, 307–8.

18. W. F. Elkins, "Hercules and the Society of Peoples of African Origin," *Caribbean Studies*, 11, 4(January 1972): 48.

19. Martin, *Race First*, 16, 369–73, and passim, "Marcus Garvey—A Caribbean, Not Jamaican Hero," *Caribbean Contact* (April 1978): 19, and "Revolutionary Upheaval in Trinidad, 1919," in *The Pan-African Connection*, 47–58.

woud of Suriname, and Richard B. Moore of Barbados.[20] From the 1930s, Trinidadian C. L. R. James played a similar leadership role in Pan-African activity for the Trotskyite wing of the Communist movement.[21]

Members and former members of Garvey's organization were active in two of the major expressions of Pan-African interest during the 1930s. The first of these was the Rastafarian movement, taking its name from Ras Tafari, who was crowned emperor of Ethiopia in 1930. The second, also involving Ethiopia, was the Ethiopian-Italian War of 1935–36. West Indians participated in demonstrations and protest meetings against the Italian fascist invasion of one of the two remaining independent countries in Africa. Dockers refused to handle Italian ships, and men volunteered for military service against the Italians to the dismay of the British colonialists, who rejected all such offers.[22] In Afro-America, pro-Ethiopia feeling was equally intense, and there many of the myriad pro-Ethiopia organizations were led by West Indian immigrants. Former Trinidadian Colonel Hubert Fauntleroy Julian (the "Black Eagle") journeyed to Ethiopia to help train Haile Selassie's air force.[23] And even before the war, from 1930, several former Garveyites, many of them West Indian-Americans, emigrated from the United States to Ethiopia, under the leadership of Rabbi Arnold J. Ford. Barbados-born Ford was a former musical director of the UNIA and composer of its anthem, the "Universal Ethiopian Anthem."[24]

There are ample sources available in the known depositories to enable detailed study of this phenomenon in the West Indies.

The Public Record Office in London has been mined so extensively that it hardly requires mention here. Yet, only recently has it been used significantly for studies on such West Indian Pan-Africanists as Edward Wilmot Blyden, Marcus Garvey, and Henry Sylvester Williams. There are monographs on Garvey and George Padmore, among others, published as late as the 1970s, which did not use this obvious and essential source.

The National Archives of the United States represent a major, easily accessible, and hitherto neglected source for historians of Pan-Africanism. The fact that so many major (and minor) West Indian-led Pan-African

20. See: James R. Hooker, *Black Revolutionary: George Padmore's Path From Communism to Pan-Africanism* (London, 1967); Martin, *Race First*, especially chap. 10; Harry Haywood, *Black Bolshevik: Autobiography of an Afro-American Communist* (Chicago, 1978); and Theodore Draper, *American Communism and Soviet Russia* (New York, 1960).

21. Tony Martin, "C. L. R. James and the Race/Class Question," in *The Pan-African Connection*, 165–78.

22. Robert G. Weisbord, *Ebony Kinship* (Westport, Connecticut, 1973), 102–10, and "British West Indian Reaction to the Italian-Ethiopian War: An Episode in Pan-Africanism," *Caribbean Studies*, 10, 1(April 1970): 34–41.

23. See Julian's autobiography, *Black Eagle* (London, 1964).

24. Martin, *Race First*, 42, 63 n.5, 138.

movements originated in, or impacted upon, the United States has usually brought them under the close scrutiny of the United States government. The National Archives of the United States will in time rival the Public Record Office as a major official source of West Indian history.

Nongovernmental archives are also a major source of information. Those of several European and United States missionary bodies have already been tapped. These include the Church Missionary Society (London), the Methodist Missionary Society (London), the Society for the Propagation of the Gospel (London), and the Presbyterian Board of Foreign Missions (New York). Less often used but very important are the records, where available, of Afro-American churches such as the African Methodist Episcopal church, the African Methodist Episcopal Zion church, the National Baptist Convention, U.S.A., and the African Orthodox church. All of these Afro-American churches were active in the West Indies and Africa, in addition to having West Indian bishops and the like in their Afro-American field. West Indian church archives, if available, will also be important. West Indian churchmen can be found, for example, in Guinea up to this day, a phenomenon dating back over a hundred years to the West Indian Church Association for the Furtherance of the Gospel in western Africa.

Students of Pan-Africanism share with students of many other aspects of West Indian history the problem of the relative scarcity of manuscript sources in the West Indies. Biographers of several major West Indian Pan-Africanists (among them George Padmore, Frantz Fanon, Henry Sylvester Williams, and Dr. J. Robert Love) have had to contend with the absence of a single, comprehensive source of their subject's papers, whether in the West Indies or elsewhere. In this situation painstaking searches of the local press assume added importance, supplemented where possible by interviews with spouses and children of important figures, as well as surviving members of organizations and movements. A beginning has already been made in the collection of oral traditions to document African cultural retentions. The potential for this type of research is greater than most historians realize. Not only in obviously "traditional" African-Caribbean communities, for example, among the Djukas of Suriname, but also in the urban areas is there a significant scope for this type of research. It is quite common to find Afro-West Indians today who can recite their family histories back to slavery and, sometimes, to Africa.

Much of the printed matter produced by Pan-African-oriented movements has been ephemeral in nature. Limited-edition pamphlets, mimeographed newsletters, irregular newspapers, occasional broadsides, short-lived small-circulation magazines—these have all too often been the principal means by which such movements have been able to put their own point of view on the record. In addition, in times of persecution and crisis, such as during the Black Power era of the 1960s and 1970s, these items have sometimes been published underground to protect their sponsors from prosecution. On occasion such publications have been published abroad and surreptitiously or otherwise introduced into the home territories. And even where Pan-African publications have had a very wide circulation, seditious publications' ordinances and similar laws have sometimes driven them underground. This was the case with Marcus Garvey's *Negro World* newspaper (published in Harlem) in the post–World War I years. In the absence of systematic and aggressive work on the part of librarians, many of these types of material could easily be lost to posterity.

Pan-Africanism is a major and persistent theme running through West Indian history, but remains largely frontier territory, however, as far as historical writing is concerned. Yet extensive research regarding this theme is possible with imaginative use of sources, and hence the study of this important dimension of Caribbean history promises to add significant insights regarding this area in the future.

48   An Appraisal of Caribbean Scholarship
Gordon K. Lewis

Traditionally, most scholarship on the Caribbean region has tended, so to speak, to follow the territorial imperative rather than the regional imperative. The linguistic fragmentation and the political balkanization of the region have been echoed in the tendency of scholars, both metropolitan and local, to write on a particular territory or particular group of territories. That insularity still remains much a part of continuing scholarship in the Commonwealth Caribbean. Thus, James Millette and Selwyn Ryan on Trinidad,[1] Trevor Munroe and Owen Jefferson on Jamaica,[2] and Harold Lutchman on former British Guiana[3] concentrate exclusively on the theme

1. James Millette, *The Genesis of Crown Colony Government: Trinidad, 1783–1810* (Port of Spain, Trinidad, 1970); Selwyn Ryan, *Race and Nationalism in Trinidad and Tobago: A Study of Decolonization in a Multiracial Society* (Toronto, 1972).

2. Trevor Munroe, *The Politics of Constitutional Decolonization: Jamaica, 1944–1962* (Mona, Jamaica, 1972); Owen Jefferson, *The Post-War Economic Development of Jamaica* (Mona, Jamaica, 1972).

3. Harold Lutchman, *From Colonialism to Cooperative Republic: Aspects of Political Development in Guyana*, Caribbean Monograph Series No. 9 (Río Piedras, Puerto Rico, 1974).

of national historical development; the selected readings put together by David Lowenthal and Labros Comitas cover, with a few exceptions, the English-speaking area only;[4] while of the five already-published chapters of the projected University of the West Indies work, *A History of the West Indies,* only two, those by Elsa Goveia and Richard Sheridan, manage to break through the exclusively West Indian orientation so characteristic, over the years, of University of the West Indies historical research.[5]

It is true that this temper of *insularismo* has begun to give way to a broader pan-Caribbean perspective. The works by Eric Williams and Juan Bosch, oddly enough with similar titles, attempt a general Caribbean history.[6] But the first is limited by its heavily economic emphasis, the second by its tendency, in an almost heroic-romantic fashion, to deal almost exclusively with the old imperialistic struggle for the Caribbean colonies. David Lowenthal bravely attempts a macroview of Caribbean societies, especially in the general area of race relations; but the work is marred by a sort of top-heavy erudition, based on massive quotation, to the degree that one quoted opinion will often openly contradict another on the same page.[7] The field of collected bibliographical material is also somewhat insularist; witness the various island bibliographies put together by Robert Nodal.[8] The single exception is the bibliography put together by Lambros Comitas, for its deliberate omission of Cuba, Haiti, Puerto Rico, and the Dominican Republic is justified by the fact, as the author notes, that extensive bibliographies already exist on those non-English-speaking societies.[9] Other works further demonstrate the continuing weakness of the

4. David Lowenthal and Lambros Comitas, *West Indian Perspectives,* 4 vols. (Garden City, New York, 1973). Individual titles include: *Slaves, Freemen, Citizens; Consequences of Class and Color; Work and Family Life;* and *The Aftermath of Sovereignty.*

5. The five chapters are: Richard Sheridan, "The Development of the Plantations to 1750," and "An Era of West Indian Prosperity"; Elsa Goveia, "The West Indian Slave Laws of the 18th Century"; C. J. Bartlett, "A New Balance of Power; the 19th Century"; and K. O. Laurence, "Immigration to the West Indies in the 19th Century." All are published by Caribbean University Press, 1970–71. I owe this reference to Dr. Thomas Mathews, "Caribbean Historical Research in the Last 25 Years" (Río Piedras, University of Puerto Rico, n.d.), mimeo.

6. Eric Williams, *From Columbus to Castro: The History of the Caribbean, 1492–1969* (London, 1970); Juan Bosch, *De Cristobal Colón a Fidel Castro: El Caribé frontera imperial* (Madrid, 1970).

7. David Lowenthal, *West Indian Societies* (London, 1972).

8. Robert Nodal, "A Preliminary Bibliography on African Cultures and Black Peoples of the Caribbean and Latin America" (1972), mimeo., "An Annotated Bibliography of Historical Materials on Jamaica," (1974) mimeo., *An Annotated Bibliography of Historical Material on Barbados, Guyana, and Trinidad-Tobago;* all issued from the Department of Afro-American Studies, University of Wisconsin–Milwaukee.

9. Labros Comitas, *The Complete Caribbean, 1900–1975: A Bibliographical Guide to the Scholarly Literature,* 4 vols. (Millwood, New York, 1977).

genre. Thus, Robert Crassweller attempts a full survey of the Caribbean community, but there is little of historical interest, and the emphasis is on Caribbean politics as they affect United States interests.[10] Likewise, the volume by Harold Mitchell suffers from its unexamined assumption that national development along the lines of the now-discredited "industrialization by invitation" strategy is still the path to follow.[11]

Clearly enough, the one large gap in ongoing historical research stems from all this: a competent general history of the Caribbean, covering both the colonial and national period, is still needed. The historian who will do for the Caribbean what Braudel has done for the Mediterranean and Darcy Ribeiro for Latin America has yet to appear. There is something of it in Sidney Mintz's collection of analytical essays.[12] Gordon Lewis in a recent work attempts a critical and descriptive analysis of the Caribbean thought-systems for the major period 1492–1898, concentrating on the general theme of Caribbean ideology, an element neglected, except marginally, by the main academic disciplines dealing with Caribbean studies.[13]

Beyond this, there are serious lacunae still in the field. The "plural society" debate of the 1950s and 1960s fell into sterile academic argumentation. But its central thesis—that West Indian society is divided both horizontally (by ethnic groups) and vertically (by social classes)—was appropriate and correct. What is needed now are systematic studies, either in historically linear form or in sociological structural form, of those divisions. The works of Frances Karner, Martha Dreyer Magruder, Edith Kovats-Beaudoux, and Isaac and Suzanne Emmanuel show what can be done in other Caribbean areas.[14] The studies of Stanley Reid and Anton Camejo on the strategic commercial elites of Jamaica and Trinidad, respectively, attempt a socioeconomic analysis, but neither has the solidity of, say, Edith Kovats-Beaudoux's study of the Martiniquan beké class.[15]

10. Robert Crassweller, *The Caribbean Community: Changing Societies and U.S. Policy* (New York, 1972).

11. Harold Mitchell, *Caribbean Patterns* (New York, 1972).

12. Sidney Mintz, *Caribbean Transformation* (Chicago, 1974).

13. Gordon K. Lewis, *Main Currents in Caribbean Thought: The Historical Evolution of Caribbean Society in its Ideological Aspects* (Baltimore, 1983).

14. Frances Karner, *The Sephardics of Curaçao: A Study in Socio-Cultural Patterns in Flux* (The Netherlands, 1969); Martha Dreyer Magruder, *Son of Bootstrap* (Santurce, Puerto Rico, 1976); Edith Kovats-Beaudoux, "Une Minorito dominante," Ph.D. dissertation (University of Paris, 1969); Isaac and Suzanne Emmanuel, *History of the Jews of the Netherlands Antilles* (2 vols., Cincinnati, 1970).

15. Stanley Reid, "An Introductory Approach to the Concentration of Power in the Jamaican Corporate Economy and Notes on its Origin," in *Essays on Power and Change in Jamaica,* ed. Carl Stone and Aggrey Brown (Kingston, 1977); Anton Camejo, "Racial Discrimination in Employment in the Private Sector in Trinidad and Tobago: A Study of the Business Elite and the Social Structure," *Social and Economic Studies,* Institute of Social and Economic Research (Mona, Jamaica), 30, 3(September 1971).

Hardly anything is known about the nature of the new ruling echelons of the new state sector of public capitalism and quasi socialism in Trinidad or Guyana or Jamaica; indeed, more is known, ironically, about the early family dynasties of the Columbus, Velázquez, and Ponce de León groups in the sixteenth-century Caribbean than is known about their twentieth-century successors.

That paucity of knowledge is, without doubt, due to two factors. In the first place, the academic disciplines, including history, have been too much tempted to look at the lower-class groups (they make more amenable subjects). The tradition continues in new studies such as those of Jill Sheppard on the Barbados "Redlegs" and the continuing rash of studies on the Jamaican Rastafarians.[16] The tradition, without doubt, produces rich documentary studies of the poor, like Oscar Lewis' *La Vida*. But it still leaves an imbalance: much more knowledge about the power-making echelons at the top, both in the political and economic spheres, is needed. Second, there is the factor that most West Indian leaders do not write memoirs, always a rich primary source for political history. What does exist in that field is eminently unsatisfactory. Cheddi Jagan's autobiography is more a spirited polemic;[17] Forbes Burham's piece is a carefully selected collection of set speeches, nothing more;[18] Dr. Eric Williams' book reflects the concern of the professional historian to write a justificatory self-portrait that future historians may look at with admiration;[19] A. N. R. Robinson's book reveals practically nothing about the internal life of his political party, of which he must know a great deal, but more about the author as an Eric Williams manqué;[20] while both F. A. Hoyos' life of Grantley Adams[21] and Rex Nettleford's life of Norman Manley[22] read like official family histories, sounding like, say, Sir Sidney Lee on Edward VII, or, to cite a more recent example, James Schlesinger on Robert Kennedy. Only Albert Gomes's autobiography manages to become a frank discussion of life and labor in the Byzantine politics of the Trinidadian *picaroon* society over the last forty years or so.[23]

16. Jill Sheppard, *The Redlegs of Barbados* (Millwood, New York, 1978); and continuing work on the Rastafarian cult-religion, noted in Comitas, *Complete Caribbeana*.

17. Cheddi Jagan, *The West on Trial: My Fight for Guyana's Freedom* (London, 1966).

18. Forbes Burnham, *A Destiny to Mould* (London, 1970).

19. Eric Williams, *Inward Hunger: Autobiography of a Prime Minister* (London, 1970).

20. A. N. R. Robinson, *The Mechanics of Independence: Patterns of Political and Economic Transformation in Trinidad and Tobago* (Port of Spain, Trinidad, 1971).

21. F. A. Hoyos, *The Rise of West Indian Democracy: The Life and Times of Sir Grantley Adams* (Bridgetown, Barbados, 1963).

22. Rex Nettleford, *Norman Washington Manley and the New Jamaica: Selected Speeches and Writings, 1938–1968* (London, 1971).

23. Albert Gomes, *Through a Maze of Colour* (Port of Spain, Trinidad, 1974).

What is needed in this field of political history is the work of a historian–political scientist team which would produce a reliable and sound analysis of the rise of the typical anticolonial nationalist parties in the twentieth century: the Peoples National Movement in Trinidad, the two major Jamaican parties, the two leading Guyanese parties, the two Barbadian labor parties, and the trade union–political party groupings of the smaller islands. Such work should be founded, ideally, on a healthy mixture of the history and political science disciplines—both of which have suffered, in the West Indies as elsewhere, from the modern specialization and departmentalization process of the social sciences—and summed up in Seeley's nineteenth-century couplet: "Political science without History has no roots, and History without Political Science has no fruits."

Speaking more generally, the twentieth-century Caribbean, including the Anglophone Caribbean, has witnessed three seminal socioeconomic-cultural processes: (1) the transformation of the old rural poor into the new urban poor, resulting from industrialization and rural depopulation, (2) the transformation of the old middle class of doctor and lawyer into the new urbanized middle class, and (3) the transformation of old aristocratic elements, based on land ownership, into the new oligarchies of financial and industrial elites, based on fluid capital resources. West Indian scholarship has only just begun to come to grips with these massive transformatory processes. They all require systematic examination. It may be answered that all this is the province of the sociologist or the political scientist rather than of the historian. But since it is now the ninth decade of the century, it hardly seems plausible to argue that history ends, say, in 1898 in the area; it is more plausible to argue—if a cut-off date must be set—that it ends as late as the World War II period. There is still a marked tendency for West Indian historians to settle for 1898, as may be inferred from the fact that the articles contained in the recently announced rebirth of the *Journal of Caribbean History,* out of the Department of History of the University of the West Indies, all relate to nineteenth-century historical subjects.[24] There is always the danger that historical inquiry will become merely antiquarian inquiry; it is the occupational disease of the historical science.

What is being noted here is the wide sweep of culture history and the grand manner of the older culture-history tradition. That tradition, as Edward K. Brathwaite has noted, is very weak in the West Indian field. "But it is in the area of cultural life and expression," he writes, "that the scholarship of the Caribbean has so far been most wanting. This deficiency is a

24. Printed advertisement for the *Journal of Caribbean History* for Vols. 10 and 11, 1978. See also the *Jamaican Historical Review,* 11 (1978).

product and result of our outer plantation emphasis, the concern with our constitutional and economic relationship with the metropoles, and our reaction for or against the norms of the former masters. We have, therefore, most of us, been involved with little more than 'creole' versions of the imposed plantation."[25]

There is a need to organize new pathways, concludes Brathwaite, in particular, new work on the "inner plantation" aspects of the sociocultural-historical process, and on the creolization process of persons, families, and institutions. "All the ethnic groups which make up Caribbean society could be studied in this manner, moving through the period of settlement, through slavery and the post-emancipation period and the arrival of new ethnic immigrants, into the more recent phenomenon of vicarious culture contact through tourist, book, magazine, film, television: a process which is particularly interesting since here we find an increasing reaction to external stimulus from the segmented orders as a whole."[26]

Implicit in this challenging argument are a number of points worth elaborating. It requires a history of social dynamics, not of social statics, with new work that looks at acculturation and creolization as ongoing processes, not as photographic stills. It notes the absence of moral imagination in West Indian history writing: to date, observes Brathwaite, there is no one of the vision of, say, Gilberto Freyre in the Caribbean. It wants history scholarship to include the creative arts; in that sense Brathwaite might have asked why it is that English-speaking Caribbean scholarship has so far not been able to match the monumental work of the Fernando Ortiz school in Cuba and the Jean Price-Mars school in Haiti in the rich relationship between history on the one hand, and the popular cultures of the Caribbean masses in religion, cults, dance, music, and folklore on the other. The answer is, of course, that the English-speaking scholarship has been trained in the British and North American history-writing tradition, so profoundly different from the Gallic and Hispanic schools. The Anglo-Saxon tradition is stolid, even dull, tremendously industrious but lacking the imaginative dimension; the Continental tradition is lively, even romantic, concerned with the totality of human experience. It is the difference— if the total Caribbean historiography is looked at in terms of the complete Caribbean historical time span—between Hakluyt and Las Casas, between Clarkson and Raynal, between Aime Cesaire and Eric Williams. It is, perhaps, only because Brathwaite himself is at once a poet, like Cesaire, and deeply conscious, again like Cesaire, of his rich African roots that he can perceive this fundamental lack in Anglo-Saxon West Indian

25. Edward K. Brathwaite, "Caribbean Man in Space and Time," *Savecou* (Jamaica) (September 1975).

26. Ibid.

historical scholarship. It follows from all this that any serious discussion of new pathways in future Commonwealth Caribbean history writing and research is meaningless unless some serious attention is given to the background training of the history profession.

Finally, Brathwaite's argument emphasizes the need to add to the history of institutions the history of people. As he phrases it in a separate essay, historians must begin to search for the face within the archives. The implied indictment is surely justified. For there is a type of Caribbean scholarship that sees slavery but not the slave; imperialism but not the imperialist; emancipation but not the emancipated slave-person; immigration and emigration but not the immigrant or the emigrant. The reports of the experience of the victims themselves need to be heard; and that, again, despite its shortcomings, is the virtue of Oscar Lewis' *La Vida*. This requires a whole new reinvigorating effort in the field of oral history, still very deficient in Commonwealth Caribbean history writing. It is at least heartening to note that something along these lines is beginning to be done: Michael Craton, for example, has used the device in seeking to trace generational changes in the latter chapters of his book *Searching for the Invisible Man: Slaves and Plantation Life in Jamaica* (Cambridge, Massachusetts, 1978) in Jamaican plantation history, although the unwitting reader, on coming to that rather melodramatic title, might be forgiven for believing that he is about to read a Caribbean version of a famous novel by H. G. Wells. It is also worth noting that Jerome Handler and Frederick Lange, in their new book on Barbados plantation slavery, have begun to explore novel archaeological and ethnographical methodologies in seeking to reconstruct the culture of a social group that, because of the very nature of slavery, left few records of orthodox historical-literacy character behind it.[27] Scientific archaeological excavation, indeed, is already a matured art in Jamaica and Puerto Rico, because of the work of pioneers like Frank Cundall (Jamaica) and Ricardo Alegria (Puerto Rico). But it is still in its infancy in Trinidad, the Guianas, and the Leeward and Windward islands.

Every age, wrote Emerson, must write its own books. That injunction points to another emerging note in Caribbean historiography: the growth of a new genre of work, written usually by the more radical professional historians and social scientists, on the general theme of anticolonial and anti-imperial struggle. There is a new concern with rectifying what is perceived as the bias of the older schools, as in Richard Jacobs on the figure of Uriah Butler in Trinidad;[28] in E. David Cronon on Garvey;[29] and in

27. Jerome S. Handler and Frederick W. Lange, *Plantation Slavery in Barbados: An Archaeological and Historical Investigation* (Cambridge, Massachusetts, 1978).

28. Richard Jacobs, *Butler Versus the King* (Port of Spain, Trinidad, 1976).

29. Edmund David Cronon, *Black Moses: The Story of Marcus Garvey and the Universal Negro Improvement Association* (Madison, 1968).

Trevor Munroe on the left-wing Marxist minority group in the Jamaican Peoples National party of the 1950s.[30] But this is only a beginning. There are still no authoritative works on the life and times of Bustamante in Jamaica, of Payne in Barbados, of Critchlow in British Guiana, not to mention neglected figures like Rienzi in Trinidad and Moore in Barbados. With the exception of the Virgin Islands,[31] there are no studies on the development of anticolonial movements and their leaders in the smaller eastern Caribbean islands. O. Nigel Bolland and C. H. Grant have provided this in their separate books for Belize/British Honduras.[32] The brain drain of talent to the larger islands, the absence of local collegial centers, the intolerance of dissent so easy to exercise in small island societies—all of these factors help to explain the continuing neglect of these smaller societies by scholarship. Like oral history, it is a gap that still remains to be filled.

There remains the final point of the relationship between the Commonwealth Caribbean and the United Kingdom. It is related, of course, to the fact that the history of the Caribbean folk-peoples has been throughout a history of massive uprooted emigratory processes. The old metropole-colony relationship has thus received a new chapter in the form of a substantial post-1945 emigration to Canada, the United Kingdom, and, to a lesser degree, the United States. But, curiously enough, that phenomenon has not yet excited the interest of the local West Indian social scientist and historian. Indeed, it is a rare scholar, like Nancy Foner, for example, who deals with aspects of West Indian migration to Britain on the basis of an earlier scholastic interest in West Indian society itself;[33] this explains why so much of the new "race relations" academic subindustry in the British universities has produced a literature based on an extremely inadequate knowledge of the colonial background of the immigrants. It is, curiously enough, the West Indian novelist—Lamming, Naipaul, Selvon, Carew, Salkey, Dathorne, and others—who has richly documented this experience. But so far the West Indian social scientist and historian have not followed suit. It is equally curious that, by comparison, the Puerto Rican academic intelligentsia have shown a lively interest in the comparative emigration of Puerto Ricans to the United States, seeing it as yet further evidence of how North American colonialism has generated a divided nation, those of the homeland and those of the diaspora. Only scholars like

30. Trevor Munroe, "The Marxist Left-wing Group of the Peoples National Party Jamaica," *Social and Economic Studies* (Kingston) (September 1976).

31. Gordon K. Lewis, *The Virgin Islands: A Caribbean Lilliput* (Evanston, 1972).

32. O. Nigel Bolland, *The Formation of a Colonial Society: Belize, from Conquest to Crown Colony* (Baltimore, 1977); C. H. Grant, *The Making of Modern Belize* (Cambridge, England, 1976).

33. Nancy Foner, *Jamaica Farewell: Jamaican Migrants in London* (Berkeley, 1978).

Archie Singham—whose earlier work on Gairyism in Grenada is well known—have attempted analytical work that sees West Indian emigration as part of a new, emergent global system of transnational capitalism based on a new class of exploited Third World lumpen proletariat and serving global imperialist needs.[34] This, clearly enough, is a rich field of inquiry that begs aloud for the attention of the Caribbean scholarly class. It would, indeed, be interesting to see a West Indian scholar like Gordon Rohlehr, who has excavated deeply into the mine of rich verse, poetry, essay, and pamphlet that emerged out of the Trinidadian black underworld in the early 1970s, with all of its populist and millenarian ideological content, turn his attention to the not dissimilar upsurge of underground black literature on the part of the exiled groups in Britain itself.[35] It is not too much to say that West Indian scholarship in the postindependence period has almost a moral obligation to undertake that task. It is, to say the least, necessary that when that task is undertaken it will have to go beyond analysis of what is commonly called the Caribbean Community idea, if only because too much of that discussion on the community theme has concentrated exclusively on the home Caribbean region, along with its internal and regional problems, to the almost total neglect of the relationships with the overseas emigrant communities.[36]

There is one final footnote to all this. There now exists a large body of creole West Indian writing special to the twentieth century, with most of its practitioners having essentially reached the end of their work. This includes (1) the regional historians like Eric Williams and C. L. R. James, as well as outsiders like Paul Blanshard, and (2) the island-national historians that include, to cite examples only, Frank Cundall, H. P. Jacobs, and Philip Sherlock in Jamaica, Ottley and Andrew Pearse in Trinidad, P. H. Daly, Norman Cameron, and the two Roths in British Guiana, Frank Collymore in Barbados, and many others, some of whose work lies forgotten in the local historical and literary journals of the time. There is clearly room for historiographical work on this rich material, history writing on history. Elsa Goveia did that for the period before 1898 in her early seminal work of 1956.[37] The field is obviously open for bringing her magisterial treatment up to date, say, for the period 1900–60. Such work,

34. A. W. and N. L. Singham, "Cultural Domination and Political Subordination—Notes Towards a Theory of the Caribbean Political System," (May 1972), mimeo.

35. Gordon Rohlehr, Articles published in *Tapia* (Port of Spain, Trinidad) for the period 1975–78. For the latest in this series, see "Poetry, Politics, and the February Revolution," *Trinidad and Tobago Review* (Port of Spain), 2, 10(June 1978).

36. For an example of this type of analysis, see Vaughn A. Lewis, *The Idea of a Caribbean Community,* pamphlet No. 9 published by New World (April 1974).

37. Elsa Goveia, *A Study of the Historiography of the British West Indies to the Nineteenth Century* (México, 1956).

whether single or multiple, would obviously deal with the history of ideology, since all of the figures mentioned were concerned in one way or another with the general ideology of "national building" in the period preceding independence. It is true that there is already occasional critical literature on some of them, most notably on the better-known figures like Eric Williams and C. L. R. James. What is needed now is a more general and systematic treatment of the material as a whole. Such a work will have to be a labor of love. Far too much of the criticism of, say, Eric Williams by the younger West Indian historians of the Marxist-Leninist persuasion too readily condemns him as an agent of continuing colonialism; these critics lack the spirit of historical broadmindedness, which enabled Elsa Goveia, by contrast, to see even in the eighteenth-century planter-historians like Edward Long and Bryan Edwards intimations of a burgeoning creole nationalism, albeit from the viewpoint of a proslavery sentiment. In any case, this is a direction of history writing that badly needs to be taken. For it is not too much to say, as a generalization, that Commonwealth Caribbean historians have tended too much to write on the slavery and postslavery emancipation periods and to neglect, by contrast, the earlier sixteenth and seventeenth centuries and the later twentieth century. It is time to rectify these serious omissions.

49 Authoritarianism, Democracy, and Dependency in the Dominican Republic
Unexamined Research Frontiers of the Trujillo and Balaguer Eras
Michael J. Kryzanek
and Howard J. Wiarda

A bias exists in Latin American studies in favor of the larger countries, which receive greater attention and are often assumed to represent the leading cutting edge or the model patterns of Latin American development. The smaller Central American and Caribbean countries are often viewed as lacking significance and fated merely to imitate the bigger nations' patterns. The authors wish to challenge that view and suggest that

Central American and Caribbean city-states[1] may be as worthy of study, as important, typical, and representative as those with larger territories.

This essay focuses on the research possibilities in one such nation, the Dominican Republic, specifically the authoritarian regimes of Rafael Trujillo (1930–61) and Joaquín Balaguer (1966–78). Until now still woefully understudied, this nation offers both excellent research facilities and a long list of existing topics. The Dominican Republic has had virtually everything a researcher could want: a long history of caudilloism, "order-and-progress" dictators, populist leaders and modernizing oligarchies, rapacious multinationals, repeated American interventions, a revolution (albeit frustrated), corporatist regimes (both inclusionary and exclusionary), breakdowns of authoritarian regimes, periods of middle-sector dominance and of mass challenges, and dependency and efforts to break out of same. All the main analytical themes of Latin American development and underdevelopment are present.

The regime of Rafael Trujillo was one of the bloodiest and longest-lived tyrannies ever in Latin America. Most of the early studies of Trujillo—by Jiménez-Grullón, Galíndez, Ornes, and Wiarda—focused on the political aspects of his dictatorship: the initial seizure of power, his methods of control, the dictatorial apparatus.[2] Other considerations were largely ignored: the class bases of his rule,[3] the new social forces of which Trujillo himself was both product and stimulator, the economic transformations of "the era," changing dependency relations.[4]

While the early books on Trujillo were overwhelmingly condemnatory, more recent studies and approaches may force some reassessment: (1) the work of Juan Linz on authoritarianism obliges a look at the Trujillo system not just as a bloody dictatorship but in comparison with other authoritarian regimes ruling during periods of societal transition and in contexts of weakly institutionalized polities;[5] (2) the development literature suggests

1. See Roland Ebel, "Governing the City-State: Notes on the Politics of the Small Latin American Countries," *Journal of Inter-American Studies and World Affairs,* 14 (August 1972): 325–46, for some provocative ideas.

2. J. I. Jiménez-Grullón, *Una gestapo de América* (La Habana, 1946); Jesús de Galíndez, *La era de Trujillo* (Santiago, 1956), now available in an English language ed. (Tucson, 1973); Gérman Ornes, *Trujillo* (New York, 1958); Howard J. Wiarda, *Dictatorship and Development: The Methods of Control in Trujillo's Dominican Republic* (Gainesville, 1970).

3. But see Juan Bosch, *Trujillo* (Caracas, 1958).

4. Howard J. Wiarda and Michael J. Kryzanek, "Dominican Dictatorship Revisited: The Caudillo Tradition and the Regimes of Trujillo and Balaguer," *Revista/Review Interamericana,* 7 (Fall 1977): 417–35.

5. Juan Linz, "An Authoritarian Regime: Spain" in *Cleavages, Ideologies, and Party Systems,* ed. E. Allardt and Y. Littunen, 291–342 (Helsingfors, 1964).

an examination not just of the regime's repression but of its modernizing, nation-building aspects;[6] (3) the superb Crassweller biography, which examines Trujillo sympathetically in the light of Dominican history and culture;[7] and (4) recent survey and opinion data which reveal widespread public admiration for Trujillo.[8]

In the fields of comparative politics and development studies, a number of general models have also been put forth recently, which may spur further reexaminations of the Trujillo regime: (1) The *Corporatist Approach and Model*. In Wiarda's earlier book on Trujillo a chapter on the regime's ideology was included;[9] this plus its corporatist institutional structures merit closer examination, as also does how the regime corresponds to the general "corporatist mode."[10] (2) The *State and State-Society Relations*. The Trujillo regime saw an enormous increase in state power; changing state-society relations need to be studied.[11] (3) *Inclusionary Populism vs. Bureaucratic Authoritarianism*. At the beginning Trujillo's caudilloism was semipopulist and brought in some new (middle-class) actors; later it turned to suppression of the newer social forces. (4) *Economic Transformations*. The Dominican Republic in the 1930s was poor and underdeveloped; by the 1950s its economy and economic infrastructure had grown enormously. A study of the economic instruments employed and the "state-capitalist" model used is needed.[12] (5) *Class Changes*. By the end of Trujillo's rule the trade unions were a force to reckon with, the middle class had grown, a new-rich bourgeoisie had emerged. There is still no complete study of these class changes or the class bases of the regime.[13] (6) *Dependency and Interdependence*. The Dominican Republic has been a dependency of the United States for nearly a century; Trujillo both cemented these ties and pursued more nationalistic strategies.[14] (7) *Compar-*

6. E.g., Samuel P. Huntington, *Political Order in Changing Societies* (New Haven, 1968); Howard J. Wiarda, "Dictatorship and Development: The Trujillo Regime and Its Implications," *Social Science Quarterly,* 48 (March 1968): 548–57.

7. Robert Crassweller, *Trujillo* (New York, 1966).

8. Howard J. Wiarda and Michael J. Kryzanek, *The Dominican Republic: Profile of a Caribbean Crucible* (Boulder, 1981), chap. 7.

9. Wiarda, *Dictatorship and Development,* chap. 6.

10. Howard J. Wiarda, "Toward a Framework for the Study of Political Change in the Iberic-Latin Tradition: The Corporative Model," *World Politics,* 25 (January 1973): 206–35, and *Corporatism and National Development in Latin America* (Boulder, 1981).

11. See Alfred Stepan, *The State and Society* (Princeton, 1978) for some orienting concepts.

12. Julio C. Estrella, *La moneda, la banca y las finanzas en la República Dominicana* (2 vols., Santiago, 1971).

13. Andre Corten and Andreé Corten, *Cambio social en Santo Domingo* (Río Piedras, Puerto Rico, 1968); Franklin J. Franco, *Trujillo: Genesis y rehabilitación* (Santo Domingo, 1971).

14. See Crassweller, *Trujillo.*

ative Development Analysis. The 1930s to the 1950s was a period of considerable change in Latin America, often under authoritarian auspices; fascinating comparisons could be made between Trujillo, Perón, Vargas, Somoza, Rojas Pinilla, Ubico, Carías, Batista, Odría, and other "authoritarian modernizers" of this period. (8) In terms of the *Breakdowns of Authoritarian Regimes and of Democratic Ones*,[15] the Dominican Republic offers both fascinating cases and special features not treated in the general literature.

The Trujillo regime provides a fertile terrain for future research. Since Trujillo was so important in shaping Dominican development and since much of national politics still revolve around attitudes toward his regime, such research would be especially significant. The documentation is abundant; interviewing could also be usefully employed. Not only are there entire areas and subject matters never explored before, but topics already studied merit reexamination in the light of the newer concepts and approaches.

After Trujillo had been assassinated, the Dominican Republic entered a period in which there was an explosion of political participation, a brief experiment with democracy, democracy's overthrow and a return to conservative rule, and then a revolution in 1965 frustrated by United States military intervention. These events attracted worldwide attention. The Dominican Republic was seen, variously, as a microcosm of the struggle between democracy and dictatorship, a showcase for the Alliance for Progress, an alternative to Castroism in the Caribbean, a case study of foolhardy American interventionism and heavy-handedness, and a prologue to the even greater United States intervention in Vietnam. A considerable number of serious scholarly books have been written analyzing these events in detail.[16]

Less attention was paid to the succeeding Balaguer regime. Once the civil war had ended and the United States occupational forces were withdrawn, attention was directed elsewhere. As the Dominican revolution and events faded from the headlines and as the larger conflict in Southeast Asia came to dominate the news, scholars also turned their attention to

15. Juan Linz and Alfred Stepan, *The Breakdown of Democratic Regimes* (Baltimore, 1979). On the fall of Trujillo, see Bernard Diederich, *Trujillo: Death of the Goat* (Boston, 1978); and Howard J. Wiarda, "The United States and the Dominican Republic: Intervention, Dependency, and Tyrannicide," *Journal of Inter-American Studies and World Affairs*, 22 (May 1980): 247–60.

16. Eugenio Chang-Rodríguez, ed., *The Lingering Crisis: A Case Study of the Dominican Republic* (New York, 1969); Abraham Lowenthal, *The Dominican Intervention* (Cambridge, Massachusetts 1968); Jerome Slater, *Intervention and Negotiation* (New York, 1970); Howard J. Wiarda, *Dictatorship, Development, and Disintegration: Politics and Social Change in the Dominican Republic* (Ann Arbor, Xerox University Microfilms Monograph Series, 1975).

other nations and subject areas. The Dominican Republic returned to its earlier anonymity and was largely ignored in the scholarly literature.

Hence the studies available on the Balaguer regime remain exceedingly sketchy. That is unfortunate, since, as with the Trujillo era, a host of important and interesting subject areas remain almost wholly unexamined. The twelve-year Balaguer period was crucially important in shaping the direction of Dominican development, yet his regime has not been studied in depth, and the economic policies and accomplishments of the regime have been stressed at the cost of attention to political and sociological factors. As a result of the regime's extensive public relations and the accomplishment of the nation's economic "miracle," the Dominican Republic was widely viewed abroad as a peaceful and progressive nation. That perception requires considerable qualification.

The extensive repression of political oppositionists, the grim and *worsening* conditions of the urban poor, and eventually the perception that Balaguer was in trouble politically slowly redirected media and scholarly attention back to the Dominican Republic. The efforts of private research organizations and human rights groups were especially important in challenging the regime's public image. The Balaguer administration came eventually to be seen as a newer and more sophisticated form of authoritarianism that exhibited many parallels with the old Trujillo system and that at best could be viewed as a regime of "relative democracy."[17] On most of these issues, however, scholarly analysis still remains noticeably lacking, and a number of research areas remain entirely unstudied. Only some of these research gaps are noted here.

(1) The *Aftermath of the Intervention*. A host of topics remains to be examined in this area: the withdrawal of the United States forces, Dominican perceptions of these events, the gradual substitution between 1966 and 1968 of the military occupational forces by civilians, the effects of the massive commitments of U.S. money and personnel during this period, the gradual replacement of U.S. public assistance by direct private investment. One of the most fascinating issues that could be explored is the widespread, and still current, perception in Washington that the Dominican intervention was a case of "successful" intervention—the United States moved in quickly, accomplished its major purposes, and left fairly quickly and cleanly—in contrast to the unsuccessful imbroglio of Vietnam.[18] Surely that thesis requires close examination.

17. Carlos Gutiérrez, *The Dominican Republic: Rebellion and Repression* (New York, 1972); North American Congress on Latin America, *Smoldering Conflict: The Dominican Republic, 1965–1975* (NACLA, 1975); Michael J. Kryzanek, "Political Party Decline and the Failure of Liberal Democracy: The PRD in Dominican Politics," *Journal of Latin American Studies*, 19 (May 1977).

18. Samuel P. Huntington has advanced this proposition.

(2) The *Nature of the Balaguer Regime*. Was it Trujilloist, democratic, or some crazy-quilt Dominican combination of both? As illustrated by the Balaguer regime, is the sharp distinction drawn by the United States analysis between democracy and dictatorship in Latin America a useful and realistic one, or are new categories required to encompass regimes that combine features of both?[19]

(3) The *Role of the Armed Forces*. The relationship between Balaguer and the military is a critical area of study. Balaguer was a strong leader, but he could not always control the so-called uncontrollable forces in his own military. Power was thus exercised on at least two distinct levels, with Balaguer largely dominating politics and administration but the armed forces often operating as an almost separate fourth branch of government. Balaguer was masterful at manipulating the armed forces, but he also realistically recognized there were bounds beyond which he could not go before his own regime's survival would be at stake. The internal politics of the armed forces, the changes in it following the revolution, its relation with the government and with other social groups all constitute areas of rich research potential.[20]

(4) *Who Governed?* Although Balaguer served as president, it has been variously asserted that it was really the military, the economic elite, or the United States Embassy that ran the country. In fact, the relations between these four were very complex and varied over time and issues. So far, there have been almost no studies of these relations or of the processes of decision making.[21]

(5) The *Economy*. The bulk of the available literature on the Dominican Republic in the Balaguer years concerns the vaunted economic accomplishments of the regime. The so-called Dominican miracle of 7–12 percent growth rates in the early to mid-1970s, massive public-works projects, skyrocketing sugar prices, and heavy foreign investment are well documented. Lacking are studies of the impact of the boom on the society, an examination of who benefited and how much during this period, the costs of high inflation and unemployment imposed on the poor, the political advantages from the boom reaped by Balaguer, as well as the disastrous political consequences for him once the boom ended and there was no longer so much economic pie to be parceled out.[22]

19. See Howard J. Wiarda, ed., *The Continuing Struggle for Democracy in Latin America* (Boulder, 1980) for the concepts.

20. G. Pope Atkins, *Arms and Politics in the Dominican Republic* (Boulder, 1981).

21. See Howard J. Wiarda, "The Politics of Population Policy in the Dominican Republic: Public Policy and the Political Process" in *The Dynamics of Population Policy in Latin America*, ed. T. McCoy, 293–322 (Cambridge, Massachusetts, 1974) for one study of these interrelations.

22. See James Whalen, "The Dominican Republic: Achievements of the Balaguer Ad-

(6) The *Society*. Under Balaguer vast sociological changes occurred. Urbanization accelerated, the countryside grew more impoverished, a huge urban lumpen proletariat came into existence, the middle class increased in size and influence, a variety of new economic elites emerged, and vast fortunes were made. Some have argued the new middle class will be a bastion of future stability and moderation, others have strong doubts; the thesis has not been tested, and in any case a stable middle class may be offset by the equally profound changes occurring at the level of the masses. There is considerable evidence that once the economic "miracle" years ended, the middle class turned away from supporting Balaguer, and he never gained the support of the urban masses, who bore the brunt of the regime's austerity measures. There are partial sociological studies of some of these phenomena,[23] but no complete study has been done of the transformations under way.

(7) *Relations with the United States; Changing Dependency Relations*. Although the troops have left, the United States remains strongly involved in Dominican affairs. But the "special relationship" is changing. The emphasis has shifted from military and political concerns to aid, trade, and investment. As U.S. public assistance decreased, private investment increased. What is missing so far is an analysis of the impact of the U.S. presence since 1966, the implications of the shifts in priorities over time, the way massive amounts of U.S. assistance in the 1966–68 period were used to effect some basic changes, and the repercussions of this as well as of the later period when aid was greatly reduced. The argument has been put forth, for instance, that Dominican nationalism and anti-Americanism became strongest not when the U.S. presence was greatest but as it decreased.[24]

There is no detailed study of the overall role of the United States in the Dominican Republic since the revolution. The gaps in knowledge include the impact of the U.S. aid programs, the activities of large United States companies operating in the country, their relations with the Dominican government and the United States Embassy, the political pressures to nationalize these concerns, the continued dependence of the Dominican economy on U.S. markets, as well as the Dominican efforts to change these dependency relations. Although U.S. assistance for social, educa-

---

ministration," *Bank of London and South America Review* (November 1974) for a glossy view. A good survey is Ian Bell, *The Dominican Republic* (Boulder, 1981).

23. See Kenneth Sharpe, *Peasant Politics: Struggle in a Dominican Village* (Baltimore, 1977); Malcolm Walker, *Politics and the Power Structure: A Rural Community in the Dominican Republic* (New York, 1972); and Nancie González' various articles on society, emigration, urbanization, and class.

24. Based on studies conducted by the authors in the 1960s and 1970s.

tional, agricultural, and public health projects has declined substantially since 1966, military assistance remains large. This implies a continuing U.S. commitment to maintaining stability in the country, to bolstering the armed forces as an anti-Communist bastion, to continuing a strong strategic presence in the boiling Caribbean cauldron.

(8) The *International Environment*. The Dominican Republic is caught up in the shifting international currents of recent times. While still obviously dependent on the United States, it has sought to change the terms of its dependency. It has tried to diversify its trade, involved itself more in the politics of the Caribbean (Cuba, Jamaica, Puerto Rico, the smaller islands), and increased its ties and trade with Europe. It has diversified its economy, sought to reduce its dependency on sugar, increased its involvement in several international bodies, and, through tourism as well as emigration, broken down some of its barriers of isolation. None of these trends have yet received the attention they deserve.

(9) Finally there remains the *Enigma of Balaguer Himself*. Seemingly meek and unassuming, Balaguer as president proved forceful, clever, strong-willed. He was a master manipulator of domestic political forces including the U.S. Embassy. He cleverly played off the complex Dominican political factions, accepting advice from all sources but making decisions himself. Hardly cast in the mold of other Latin American strong, macho, men-on-horseback, he nonetheless dominated his country for twelve years—no mean feat in the shifting quicksands of Dominican politics. Yet in many respects he remains a mystery, unknown both to the outside world and even to his own people. His rule and its anomolies provide abundant materials for a fascinating study of political leadership.[25]

In 1978 Balaguer was defeated by Antonio Guzmán in an election. In this transition from an authoritarian regime to a more liberal-democratic one, there are numerous other possibilities for research: the decline of Balaguer's popularity and the reasons for it; the resurgence of the Dominican Revolutionary party (PRD); the interventionist role of the United States during the election count; the transfer of power from a rightist regime, whose base had been the economic and military elites, to a social-democratic one, whose backing came from the lower and middle classes; the changed possibilities for democracy in the Dominican Republic in 1978 as compared with the last experiment in 1963 under Juan Bosch. It would be interesting also to trace the changing public policies of Guzmán

25. Michael J. Kryzanek, "Diversion, Subversion, Repression, Anti-Opposition Strategies in Balaguer's Dominican Republic," *Caribbean Studies*, 17, 1–2(April–July 1977): 83–103.

as compared with Balaguer, the new economic circumstances, the changed priorities, the altered international context in the Caribbean, the new ties to international socialist and social-democratic movements, the changed relations with the United States, the shifting configurations of domestic Dominican politics.[26] But these topics, although fascinating and worthy of much further and continuing study, lie outside the scope of this chapter.

The Dominican Republic offers numerous advantages to scholars and students of Latin America. Travel and living expenses are not exorbitant, and it is a relatively virgin, unspoiled research terrain. There is now a growing body of Dominican social scientists and agencies established to help facilitate research.[27] There are excellent archival materials for the periods here covered (Trujillo insisted that all newspapers, pamphlets, and books published during "the era" be sent to the National Archives and, as with most Trujillo orders, this one was unquestioningly carried out; for the Balaguer period, the new Biblioteca Municipal became a major depository) and a host of exciting subject areas and research terrains that have either never been explored or deserve reexamination in various new lights. With the revived interest in the Caribbean and Central America, the immigration of large numbers of Dominicans into the United States, and the preoccupation with this southern "soft underbelly" of the U.S., the foundations and research-assistance agencies have also elevated the Dominican Republic to a priority area.

The Dominican Republic's chief drawback as a prime research area seems to be its relatively small size, its perceived relative lack of significance, and what has here been termed the myth of exceptionality. However, small size can be a major advantage in terms of the manageability of a research project dealing with a national sociopolitical system, "importance" is often in the mind of the observer, and the "exceptionality" thesis requires far closer examination. The case could be argued that the Dominican Republic is no more exceptional and is as much typical of the general Latin American development patterns as any other country of the area. The Dominican Republic has had virtually everything the student of Latin America could wish for in a research sense, and all the main themes of both the older and newer interpretations of the region are present there. It is hoped that this statement of existing research gaps and areas where

26. Wiarda and Kryzanek, *The Dominican Republic*. See also by same authors, "Caribbean Crucible: Development Strategies and Prospects in the Dominican Republic," paper presented at the conference on the "Dynamics of Development and Change in the Caribbean," University of Pittsburgh (March 11–12, 1981).

27. For a survey of the work being done, see Fondo para el Avance de las Ciencias Sociales, *Las ciencias políticas en la República Dominicana* (Santo Domingo, 1977).

older themes might be reexamined in the light of newer research perspectives will help stimulate the investigations that are surely needed.

50   La Guerra Libertadora Cubana de los Treinta Años, 1868–1898
Research Prospects
Louis A. Pérez, Jr.

The climax obscured the antecedents. El Cancy, Daiquirí, Siboney, and San Juan Hill eclipsed Mal Tiempo, Mantua, Cacarajícara, and Guáimaro. Cuba's Thirty Years War became the United States' "splendid little war; begun with the highest motives, carried on with magnificent intelligence and spirit, favored by that fortune that loves the brave."[1]

When the smoke cleared in August 1898, the Americans arrived at a startling conclusion: the Cubans had played no part in the defeat of Spain. "While the freedom of Cuba was being decided under their very eyes," one American correspondent wrote, "they stood by inefficient, inactive. The rewards were theirs, but the Americans made the sacrifice. By the blood of Americans the victories were won." Theodore Roosevelt agreed: "They accomplished literally nothing, while they were a source of trouble and embarrassment."

This conclusion had far-reaching policy implications and in part served to justify three decades of tutelage under the regimen of the Platt Amendment. Two generations of historians subsequently agreed and conferred upon policy constructs of 1898 an enduring historiographical legitimacy. The literature of the Spanish-American War, as the conflict became known, corroborated the official version of the war. Indeed, the very name of the war lent credence to the proposition that Cubans had played no part in the defeat of Spain.

The policy considerations that gave decisive form to the literature soon provoked historiographical reaction in Cuba. By the late 1930s and early 1940s, the first republican generation of Cuban historians, organized in the Sociedad Cubana de Estudios Históricos e Internationales, had challenged the central assumptions of traditional historiography. Herminio Portella Vilá, Emilio Roig de Leuchsenring, and Enrique Gay-Calbó, most notable among others, disputed prevailing historiographical ortho-

---

1. John Hay, as quoted in Frank Friedel, *The Splendid Little War* (New York, 1962), 9.

doxy and insisted that Cubans had all but formally defeated Spain by the time of the American intervention. After World War II, the dispute assumed formidable political proportions and ultimately led in 1946 to the Cuban congress officially changing the name of the war to the Spanish-Cuban-American War. By the early 1960s, the debate reached full circle as the historiographical pendulum swung to the opposite extreme with the generation of the Cuban Revolution dismantling the monuments to the *Maine* in Havana, implying in more than symbolic terms that the United States had played no part in the defeat of Spain.

Whatever may have happened in 1898, and however the events of 1898 are interpreted, it has become increasingly apparent that Cuba's struggle for independence is virtually incomprehensible without a broader historical context. Indeed, as historians on both sides of the Straits of Florida search for a fuller understanding of 1898, a growing consensus has acknowledged the inadequacy of the preoccupation with the year 1898 and the insufficiency of a periodization that confines the independence struggle to the years 1895 and 1898. In fact, the Cuban struggle for independence was a process, a continuum that extended through two generations and over three decades.

The redefinition of the periodization associated with Cuba's struggle for independence offers a fresh if not vital vantage point through which to approach Cuban separatism. To be sure, the period punctuated by the Ten Years War (1868–78), "La Guerra Chiquita" (1879–80), and the war of 1895–98, and dominated by such towering personalities as Carlos Manuel de Céspedes, Antonio Maceo, Máximo Gómez, Calixto García, and José Martí, is not without its historians. The existing literature, however, tends to be disjointed, without the conceptual unity necessary to set these events and personalities in the context of a process—a sweep stretching in time and space from Yara to Barguá to Biare and from Ibarra to Santiago.

A thirty-year framework for Cuban separatism serves immediately to set in relief new areas of historical investigation. After 1868 and in the course of the next three decades, some 100,000 Cubans sought refuge abroad, emigrating to Europe, Latin America, and the United States. The Cuban diaspora, a crucial aspect of the separatist struggle with enormous implications for the twentieth-century republic, has not received adequate attention. To be sure, much has been written about the Cuban cigar workers' communities in Key West and Tampa. Indeed, that this expatriate proletariat was the first to embrace José Martí's vision of Cuba Libre and continued thereafter to support the war with weekly contributions of nickels and dimes makes for a charming if not inspiring national hagiography and is not totally without foundation. Little, however, is known about the community of Cuban *hacendados* and planters in Paris and middle-class expatriates in Boston, New York, and Philadelphia. Cuban planters in exile thought nothing of periodically contributing tens of thousands of dollars to support the cause of separatist arms. The middle-class emigrés in the United States provided the organizational leadership to the political organizations of exiles and served as the primary conduit through which American attitudes toward Cuba were shaped. Many of the perceptions held in government and the press in the United States were primarily promoted by the expatriate middle class. This latter group is particularly important, for it was representative of the exiled creole middle class, educating its children in the United States and preparing the way for the close collaboration between Cuba's twentieth-century leaders and the United States. Four Cuban presidents between 1902 and 1934 emerged from this group and held American citizenship. It is necessary to examine the emigration phenomenon as a distinctive historical entity, with a diverse and heterogeneous composition, forming over a period of thirty years.

Nor is much known about the secondary stratum of insurgent separatist leaders in Cuba. Biographical studies of middle-echelon separatist chieftains, such as the types that have in recent years been completed about Mexican revolutionary leaders, are necessary to flesh out the insurrectionary struggle. Such men as Quintín Banderas, Pedro Betancourt, Agustín Cebreco, José Luis Robau, Pedro "Mayía" Rodríguez, Flor Crombet, and Pedro A. Pérez, to name only a handful, all served as senior commanders, yet remain virtually unknown. Such studies would shed much light on the social origins of Cuban separatism, regional differentiation, generational differences, and political tendencies within the separatist polity.

If little is known about the men occupying positions of secondary leadership, there is even less information about the women at any level of the revolutionary polity. Only Ana Betancourt, a passionate feminist separatist during the Ten Years War, and Marta Abreu, a wealthy planter who donated generously to separatist coffers after 1895, have received serious attention. Yet in fact, women occupied key positions in separatist ranks. In exile, women organized patriotic juntas and established revolutionary clubs to support the war effort on the island. Paulina Pedrosa, María Teresa de la Torriente, Graciella Cuervo, and Laura Carvajal, to mention only the most conspicuous expatriate leaders, worked indefatigably in behalf of Cuba Libre. Throughout Latin America, Europe, and the United States, wherever a Cuban expatriate community emerged, there also emerged women's revolutionary clubs. In Cuba, women enrolled in the ranks of the Liberation Army and participated directly in the armed conflict. Women distinguished themselves in all the conflicts of the Thirty Years War as both officers and enlisted personnel. Captain Isabel Rubio, Captain Adela Azcuy Labrador, and Comandante Rosalía Hernández, among the most notable, have only recently attracted the attention of historians.

Much more, too, needs to be known about the socioeconomic conditions that drove men and women to arms between 1868 and 1898. Traditional historiography, both Cuban and American, with its emphasis on the political grievances of the colony, is inadequate. Indeed, there is sufficient evidence to suggest that the Iberian metropolis was well on its way toward resolving many of the outstanding colonial complaints by the early 1890s. Too often the Cuban revolutionary experience has been loosely set against the earlier South American experience. There are, to be sure, many striking similarities, including creole-peninsular dichotomy, Spanish mercantile exclusivism, and incipient Cuban nationalism. But the Cuban experience presents the historian with profoundly distinctive features, the implications of which remain imperfectly understood if not perhaps altogether unknown. The relationship between the socioeconomic dislocation of the 1870s and 1890s, culminating in the crisis of 1894, and Cuban separatism remains unclear. At various times, slave owners and slaves, cigar manufacturers and cigar workers, police officers and bandits, and Spaniards and Cubans joined together in behalf of Cuba Libre.

All by way of suggesting that at the most fundamental level, we are not quite certain what Cuba Libre means. The assumption that Cuba Libre suggests complete independence for the island is not always borne out by the documents of the period. In fact, many Cubans (and Spaniards) understood the ultimate objective of Cuba's drive for independence to be annexation to the United States—at the time, a fate perfectly natural for an island politically tied to Spain with a growing economic dependence on the United States. In short, much more needs to be known about the structure of Cuban separatism. Is Cuban separatism *anexionista* or *independentista*—or both? If the evidence currently available is correct, it would appear that the war of 1868–78 was anexionista and the conflict of 1895–98 was independentista. This construct, too, raises a series of questions that can be answered only through further investigation.

And what of Cuban nationalism—*cubanidad*, to be more precise? Unfortunately, here too there is little to be learned from the extant literature. Is Cuban nationalism a function of Cuban regionalism? This is a recurring theme, always present but muted. There is evidence to suggest that cubanidad is an extension of the Orient world view. Cubanidad, to be sure, with its emphasis on egalitarianism, individualism, and antistatism, received some ideological coherence at the hands of José Martí. The question remains, however: Could the world view of the impoverished provincial eastern interior be compatible with the world view of the wealthy cosmopolitan west? In many ways, the recurring island conflicts between 1868 and 1898 were civil wars. That Cuban separatists repeatedly spoke of "the invasion"—the eastern provinces invading the western provinces—offers palpable conceptual corroboration to the depth of Cuban regionalism.

Cuban separatism was a house divided. Until the conflicts and contradictions contained within the separatist polity are explored further, understanding of the independence process will remain incomplete. That Cuban separatism failed to complete the final hurdle of independence in 1898 may be in no small measure due to the weight of these contradictions. This has far-reaching implications for the Plattist republic.

New research, if not new approaches, are required on United States policy toward Cuba during the Thirty Years War, particularly during the period between 1895 and 1898. Preoccupation with the *Maine*, the de Lome letter, and "yellow journalism" has effectively obscured some of the more compelling forces culminating in the war resolution of April 1898. Briefly stated, by early 1898, Spain was presiding helplessly over the collapse of the social system in Cuba, as insurgent columns prepared to lay siege to Havana itself. Further research may very well indicate that the intervention of 1898 represented the first of a twentieth-century genre of American intervention in Latin America: a counterrevolutionary intervention to rescue a dependent socioeconomic system threatened by indigenous revolutionary forces.

More research on Spanish national history, particularly between the years 1895 and 1898, is also essential, as understanding of the Cuban conflict will remain one dimensional without a corollary understanding of Spanish developments. Indeed, research in this area would shed considerable light on the state of the Cuban insurrectionary war. Only an examination of Spanish history will yield some understanding about the climax of 1898. Spain was straining under the war. Colonial insurrections in Cuba, the Philippine Islands, and Africa, and the threat of an uprising in Puerto Rico required Spain to maintain some 300,000 troops distributed over three continents. Political intrigue in Spain paralyzed the foreign queen regent, who sought only to preserve the throne for the nine-year-old monarch. Carlists and army generals on the Right and republicans, syndicalists, and anarchists on the Left conspired to overthrow the monarchy. Catalan and Basque separatists were at war with Madrid. The treasury was exhausted. Recurring currency and exchange crises foretold of economic collapse. Food riots, draft riots, peasant riots, and labor riots converted Spain into an armed camp. By 1897, resounding antiwar protests reverberated across the peninsula. In January 1898, Spain was coming apart.

Historians approaching Cuban separatism must, in the end, first review the prevailing conceptual framework and include the process of the thirty-year struggle. This approach will answer some old persistent questions and, more important, point the way to new research for the period between 1868 and 1898.

51   Research Perspectives on the Cuban Revolution

A Twenty-Five Year Assessment
Louis A. Pérez, Jr.

The Cuban Revolution erupted in something of a historiographical vacuum. Quite suddenly the deficiencies of American scholarship on Cuba were set in sharp relief. In no other Latin American country had the United States been so thorough a presence—nowhere else had the United States so totally penetrated the economy, so completely dominated the political process, so fully influenced cultural forms. But despite the ubiquity of this presence, perhaps because of it, Cuba remained largely unknown to all but a small and dedicated group of aficionados of things Cuban. Fifty years of intimate political and economic relations had generated nothing more than casual scholarly interest in Cuba, producing for the most part a rather meager and singularly inauspicious corpus of scholarship. There were many exceptions, of course. But it is entirely probable that Americans knew less about Cuba in 1958 than their grandparents did in 1898. Rarely have modern historiographical antecedents been so ill-prepared to receive and render comprehensible an event of such transcendental magnitude as the Cuban Revolution.

That was twenty-five years ago, and much has happened since then. That a successful popular rebellion ousted an unpopular dictator was itself not an especially newsworthy item—not from Latin America. But the revolutionary processes deepened, and ultimately the revolution embraced Marxism-Leninism and aligned itself totally with the socialist block—all this occurring ninety miles from the United States, in a region traditionally secure as an American sphere of influence in a country historically secure as an American client-state.

These were rather dramatic developments and served to give decisive shape to the structure and substance of Cuban historiography. The revolution immediately brought to life the prospects of Cuba as a subject of historical inquiry, and, for the first time in a generation, research on Cuba became a flourishing enterprise.

In the more than two decades that have passed, the corpus of the scholarship has acquired truly prodigious proportions. Almost from the outset, postrevolutionary research assumed several notable characteristics. In a very real sense, this research was not without an agenda, for it was an

272

effort inspired largely by a search for the antecedents of the revolution, resting on the unstated assumption that somewhere in the unrevealed Cuban past was to be found the cause of the Cuban conversion to the socialist faith. The past became a means through which to understand the nature of revolutionary change in Cuba, to determine more concretely, in the words of one anthology title, "What happened in Cuba?"

At the same time, the very developments that stimulated research interest in Cuban history served also to close off the island to foreign scholars. With the suspension of diplomatic relations in 1961, access to Cuban archival and manuscript holdings and library collections was all but completely denied to American researchers. These developments, in turn, had far-reaching consequences, for they effectively served to limit the nature of research materials available to scholars. This, in turn, influenced decisively the direction of the historical inquiry. The most accessible records were those located in the document collections in United States depositories, including presidential libraries, the official records of such government agencies as the Departments of State, War, and Commerce, and the vast collections of personal papers of diplomats, soldiers, administrators, and businessmen, all of whom at one time or another had something to do with Cuba.

In many important ways, these records, rich and diverse as they were, served to skew the direction of historical research. Inevitably, and of necessity, the vast body of American scholarship came to reflect the sources available for research. The preponderance of articles, monographs, and dissertations were attracted to those aspects of Cuban history for which there existed sufficient research resources in the United States. Emphasis fell on political and diplomatic history within a periodization schema spanning the late nineteenth and the mid-twentieth centuries. The principal areas of this scholarship included studies of the Spanish-Cuban-American War and the subsequent military occupation (1898–1902), the second intervention (1906–09), and the revolutionary upheavals of 1933. In addition, a number of works examined various aspects of Cuban-American relations for part or all of the period between 1895 and 1959/61.

A second and related development involved the use of Spanish archival sources as a means to get at the Cuban past. This research examined the late colonial period during the nineteenth century, with particular emphasis on social and economic history. Research based on Spanish archival sources has produced several landmark studies treating slavery and race relations in nineteenth-century Cuba.

In the course of the past twenty-five years, often under difficult circumstances and frequently over formidable obstacles, historiographical advances have been made, and they have been constant and noteworthy. The accumulated scholarship is generally impressive, often inspired. But even as the gaps of the prerevolutionary past were being closed, a lacuna of another sort opened: specificially, the postrevolutionary past. For in addition to everything else, the corpus of the Cuba scholarship shared one other feature in common: the scope of the historical inquiry did not advance much beyond 1959. With several notable exceptions, historians have been conspicuous in their absence from the vast literature dealing with the Cuban Revolution. The scholarship has been the work largely of political scientists, sociologists, economists, and anthropologists. Certainly there were compelling reasons to justify the initial reticence with which the historian contemplated research on the revolution. Information was incomplete. Sources were scarce. So complex were the problems posed by the revolution, so complete was the state of flux, so close were historians to these developments that it was enormously difficult to work out appropriate questions, much less derive adequate "answers." Cuban authorities controlled access to research materials, and preference was extended to scholars perceived sympathetic to—or at least not hostile toward—the revolution. Scholarly interchange, lastly, was itself always a function of diplomatic relations between Cuba and the United States, and periods of relative tranquility created wider research opportunities.

The passing of twenty-five years has allowed some perspective and has resulted in the accumulation of an impressive body of research materials. Access to Cuban archival sources and library collections, to be sure, remains subject to the vagaries of Cuban-American relations. But the records are becoming increasingly available to researchers as scholarly contact between both countries increases. In short, research prospects are now excellent. Twenty-five years of the Cuban revolutionary experience are before the historian, and the opportunities are as vast as they are varied.

The extensive body of research materials that has accumulated over the past two decades offers extensive opportunity for the study of key aspects of the revolution. Memoirs, oral histories, and lengthy published interviews of past and present participants provide rich sources of information. Important data are available from voluminous statistical abstracts published by the Cuban government. Indeed, almost all government agencies, including the Comité Estatal de Trabajo y Seguridad Social, the Ministerio de Comercio Exterior, the Ministerio de la Industria Azucarera, and the Ministerio de Educación, more or less regularly publish statistical series containing vital data relative to population and demography, production and manufacturing, commerce and trade, transportation and communication, industry and agriculture. In addition, the office of Dirección Central de Estadística periodically publishes statistical abstracts that deal with specific trends, including mortality, divorce, and health.

Newspaper collections fully spanning the last twenty-five years of socialist Cuba are available in complete holdings. The now-defunct newspapers of the early years, including *Diario de la Marina, El Mundo, Hoy,* and *Revolución,* as well as newspapers still current, including *Granma, Juventud Rebelde,* and *Trabajadores,* are available in complete microfilm collections. The principal foreign and domestic policy speeches and addresses by the revolutionary leadership appear in *Cuba Socialista* and *Obra Revolucionaria.*

Perhaps one of the richest sources of research materials is found in the form of Cuban periodicals and journals. As the longest running news magazine, the weekly *Bohemia* is indispensible for all research of the revolutionary period. It deals with a host of topics, including politics, economy, foreign relations, medicine, art, and literature. *Carteles* was a similar publication during the early years, but did not continue long into the revolutionary period. In addition, other periodicals and journals deal with specific interests and serve as the cornerstone of all research on these subjects. These include: *Verde Olivo* (military), *Mujeres* (women), *Trabajo* (workers), *ANAP* (peasants), *Con la Guardia en Alto* (Committees for the Defense of the Revolution), *UPEC* (journalism), *Economía y Desarrollo* (economy), *Vida Universitaria* (University of Havana), *Cuba Tabaco* (tobacco), *Cuba Azúcar* (sugar), *Mar y Pesca* (fishing), *Unión* (artists and writers), *Etnología y Folklore* (ethnology), *Pensamiento Crítico* and *Casa de las Américas* (literature and politics), and *Revolución y Cultura* and *Cuba* (culture). In addition, a number of specialized journals deal with developments in public health, medicine, and health care delivery systems.

Also of great importance to the historian is the body of the scholarship that has originated in Europe, Latin America, and the United States these past twenty-five years. A literature of truly vast proportions has emerged, much of which was based on fieldwork in Cuba. So prodigious has this scholarship been that it has in turn summoned into existence an equally vast body of bibliographical compilations. The publication of bibliographical guides to the literature has itself become an enterprise of no small proportions, without which research on the Cuban Revolution would be a daunting prospect indeed. One of the most useful guides available on a continual basis is provided by *Cuban Studies/Estudios Cubanos.*

In addition to published materials, there are several important archival and manuscript collections of considerable use in research dealing with key aspects of the revolution. Among the records housed at the Archivo Nacional in Havana is the Fondo Banco Nacional de Cuba. This collection of reports, correspondence, and memoranda spanning the early 1960s deals with finance, trade, foreign commerce, and credit. Also important are the records of the Instituto Cubano de Estabilización del Azúcar (ICEA), materials treating virtually every aspect of sugar production through the early 1960s. A smaller collection but essential to the study of the early years of the revolution is the material of the Instituto Nacional de Reforma Agraria (INRA). Perhaps the single most important agency during the early years of the revolution, the INRA records contain materials dealing with agrarian reform, agricultural policy, rural education, credit transactions, and agricultural stabilization programs. The INRA records go through 1966. Scattered through the various archival collections, lastly, are records containing materials that deal with the period of the revolutionary struggle against the Batista government during the 1950s, including the Fondo Especial, the Tribunal de Urgencia de La Habana, Presidencia, and the Archivo Jorge Quintana.

The research opportunities for the historian interested in the Cuban Revolution are as open as they are obvious—in short, they include virtually everything. While some important advances have been made for the years of the armed struggle (1953–58), understanding of these crucial years remains in large part uneven and incomplete. Perhaps no other period of the revolution is possessed of both such abundance of research materials and availability of sources as are the years of the insurgency. In addition to the aforementioned archival collections, the revolutionary war has produced a vast corpus of memoirs and reminiscences that have appeared variously in books, journals, and newspapers on both sides of the Straits of Florida. For no other period, moreover, is the potential for the use of oral history as promising, for many key participants of these events—both members of the Batista government and representatives of various revolutionary organizations, including the 26 of July Movement, the Organización Auténtica, the Directorio Revolucionario, and the II Front of Escambray—are in exile in the United States.

The 1950s were more than years of political conflict, however. The drama of the revolutionary struggle has served to bias the research in favor of the political and military developments of the decade. Just as important, but not as clearly recognized and essential to an understanding of the course of the revolution in the following decade, were the shifts occurring in Cuban society. Cuba during the 1950s was a society in transition and flux. The economy had stalled and unemployment/underemployment soared. The cost of living was increasing, making Havana the fourth most expensive city in the world. Living standards were in decline. Cuban culture was in crisis, and everywhere uncertainty cast a distant pall over the island. It was against this backdrop that the politicomilitary drama unfolded. These developments are in need of further examination and must serve as the essential coefficients to an understanding of the revolutionary process.

The first decade of the revolution presents the historian with four distinct periods, each embodying a distinctive theme in the Cuban transition to socialism: the years of the 26 of July ascendency (1959–61), the period of the Organizaciones Revolucionarias Integradas (1961–63), the Partido Unido de la Revolución Socialista Cubana (1963–65), and the emergence of the Partido Comunista de Cuba (1965–69). The subsequent decade commenced with the debacle of the ten-million-ton sugar crop of 1970. This failure, which was nothing less than catastrophic, caused profound disruption and dislocation of the economy, which in turn had far-reaching and long-lasting repercussions on virtually every aspect of domestic and foreign policy.

No understanding of the revolution would be complete without a study of the development of the principal institutional structures of socialist Cuba, foremost of which include the PCC and the armed forces. Equally important are the organizations summoned into existence as vehicles of political mobilization, including the Committees for the Defense of the Revolution, the Federation of Cuban Women, the Cuban Labor Confederation, and several Cuban youth organizations.

Even greater research opportunities are available in the investigation of such interrelated themes as the literacy campaign, education, and the public health system. The study of the impact of the revolution on the lives of women and blacks, the young and old are themes of particular importance by which to evaluate Cuban achievements. The revolution affected everyone and everything, presenting the historian with a research agenda of almost limitless possibilities, chief of which includes the family, race relations, the workplace, religion, crime, and art.

Foreign policy, too, is a subject that invites inquiry. Cuban relations with the United States and the Soviet Union serve as the essential points of departure, against which all other foreign policy considerations must be set. Cuban relations with Latin America, particularly during the period of Havana's support of armed struggle during the 1960s, and Cuban involvement in Africa in the 1970s and 1980s are subjects of necessary research.

The Cuban Revolution stands out as an event of enormous historical significance. The policies and the personalities of the revolution have had an impact of truly global proportions. The time is propitious to inaugurate investigation of this impact, both in and out of Cuba.

While the opportunities for research in Cuba have improved, it is still necessary to stress that access to Cuban archival materials and library holdings is limited and possible only by prior authorization from Cuban authorities. In the end, however, the research potential offered by the revolution is restricted only by the limits of historical imagination.

52   The Haitian Revolution
Tadeusz Lepkowski

The historiography of the Haitian Revolution obviously transcends the present importance of Haiti within the framework of the Caribbean, Latin America, and the world. As a matter of fact historiography rarely does justice to the small and weak. Although it is normal or at least comprehensible that the interest in French history, as reflected in the number of works on the subject, is greater than that in Albanian history (a similar comparison could be made between United States history and Honduran history), it does not alter the marked difference between the attention extended to the great powers in contrast to the lesser powers or between the rich and the "wretched of the earth." Despite this tendency, the historiography of the Haitian Revolution is extensive, perhaps because researching the subject turns out to be so exciting. Indeed, the blacks and mulattos of St.-Domingue produced a revolution which was larger than themselves, a revolution which had a powerful impact on not only the destiny of their small country but also on other communities of this region, and a revolution which has given and continues to give rise to very different interpretations.

Thousands of books and articles of disparate value have analyzed the history of the revolution.[1] Interest in the problems of the Haitian Revolution has had its ups and downs. There has been a revival of interest in the present and previous decades. This is perhaps due to the obvious rise of interest in current political events connected with the lively history of the emancipation of the Third World countries.

In addition to Haiti, where it would be natural to find ongoing studies of the revolution, studies are being written in France, the Dominican Republic, and other countries of the Caribbean as well as the United States. At the same time a certain increase in interest can be seen in Great Britain,

1. Max Bissainthe, ed., *Le Dictionnaire de la bibliographie haitienne* (Washington, D.C., 1951); C. Pressoir, E. Trouillot, and H. Trouillot, *Historiographie d'Haiti* (México, 1953); and see also *La Revue de la Société d'Histoire, de Geographie et de Géologie, Optique;* and the bibliography in T. Ott, *The Haitian Revolution, 1789–1804* (Knoxville, Tennessee, 1973).

Spain, Germany, the Soviet Union, and Poland. One must not overlook the fictionalized accounts, novels,[2] and dramatic plays which the revolution has inspired. For many years political, military, and biographical works dominated the historical works. In the last quarter of a century interest has grown in economic, ethnic, and social history, but religious, psychological, cultural, and ideological studies have not drawn much serious attention.

Historians have not been able to agree upon the parameters of the problem known as the Haitian Revolution (this term must be explained: the Revolution of St.-Domingue sounds too neutral; the Haitian Revolution emphasizes independence; the Revolution Against Slavery emphasizes the social aspects). The majority of the French historians have considered the revolution on the island of Santo Domingo as an integral part of the French Revolution, but Haitian historians, without denying the importance of this indisputable fact, have preferred to take a more autonomist point of view, more Afro-Antillean than European and colonial. Other questions have remained. Was the Haitian Revolution primarily a social insurrection (antislavery, antiracist, and problack emancipation)? Or was it a national liberation movement (a revolution for independence)? One might ask if it was not a social movement of the masses in its first phase and a mass political movement controlled by the elite in its second phase. Was the revolution anticolonial in a formal sense, or "secessionist" (like that of the Latin American countries from the years 1810–25), or was it more profound (a break-away from dependence)? According to the criteria used, one adopts in historiography different periodization of the Haitian Revolution. The most commonly utilized period runs from 1789 to 1804. However, it seems better to take a broader period embracing the whole revolutionary process from 1789/91 to 1825 and even 1838.

Whatever the periodization one adopts, be it short, medium, or long, the establishment of the independent Haitian state is considered to be, implicitly or explicitly, a major problem. In classic and contemporary works of Haitian historiography,[3] two issues arise: the insurrection of the slaves (1791) and the formation of the Haitian state (1800/1804–25); the problem of independence is always the main one in the French, American, and Dominican monographs.

All the principal facts and even the secondary ones are well known. This assertion is true, of course, within the framework of the history of events *(histoire événementielle)*. One could, it is true, find more documen-

2. For example, Alejo Carpentier, *El reino de este mundo* (La Habana, 1943).
3. See the works by T. Madiou, B. Ardouin, J. Saint Rémy, D. Bellegarde, F. Dalencourt, J. Price-Mars, J. C. Dorsainvil, E. Charlier, T. Brutus, L. F. Manigat, J. Fouchard.

tation in the archives to clarify the "Haitian question" or, to be more exact, the diplomatic game of the great powers (France, Great Britain, the United States, Spain) with Haiti, but such research will not revolutionize the historiography of the revolution. In the French archives in Paris more or less everything has been read, but the provincial archives and the private collections can enrich the documentation with new details. On the other hand it seems that not all the material has been gleaned from the British archives, especially for the period from 1792 to 1805. A similar observation holds true for the Spanish archives, which still have not received much attention.

As far as the problem concerning the establishment of the Haitian state, the question frequently arises as to whether the birth of Haiti was the result of exceptional chance, of an international situation highly favorable to the Haitians (i.e., Anglo-French rivalry), or whether it was brought about through the purpose and design of the black rebels and by the social conditions of St.-Domingue itself within the international framework, including the struggle between the great powers.

The evolution of the idea of independence and the structure of the new state have not been analyzed enough. Topics which deserve further study include: (1) the indigenous roots, African or Congo, including the reconstruction of African life on the island and parallels with independence movements, and (2) coexistence of European and Afro-Antillean influences (Toussaint L'Ouverture), isolated independence (Dessalines), limited and delegated sovereignty (Pétion, Boyer), and complete sovereignty after the European model (Christophe). There is a great deal to analyze in the structure of the state and the classist base in this structure: plebian and revolutionary armed democracy evolving into a type of premature democratic cesarism (Moise, Dessalines), enlightened absolutism (Christophe), an oligarchic state with parliamentary and democratic aspects evolving toward a "liberal dictatorship" (Rigaud, Pétion, Borgella, Boyer).[4]

The problems of independence, the creation of the state, and the military aspects are studied in the rich biographical histories of the movement's leading figures, which have been written and rewritten many times without contributing any new information. Almost everything about Toussaint and Christophe and just about everything concerning Dessalines and Pétion is known. On the other hand detailed biographies of the middle-level leaders—men like Jean-François, Biassou, Ogé, Chavannes, Rigaud, Pinchinat, Moise, Boisrond-Tonnerre, Clervaux, Goman, Inginac, Gérin, Cangé, Capoix, Yayou, whose biographies it is very important to

4. For some observations on this issue, see T. Lepkowski, *Haiti* (2 vols., La Habana, 1968–69).

have in order to understand the political history of the revolution—are
lacking. In the field of traditional political and biographical history, it
would appear that one should reread and reinterpret the already-known
sources, most of which have been published.

The chronological and tactical history of the war (1802–03) is fairly
well known.[5] As far as the details are concerned, there are some gaps in
the period of the Haitian War of Independence and above all the periods
preceding it (1790–1801) and following it (1805–09). The reconstruction
of the facts, for example, of the resistance against the British (1792–98)
and the War of the South (1799–1800), is still to be completed. Little is
known about the war economy, military equipment, guerrilla tactics, and
logistics. No one has seriously tried to assess the human and material
losses of the revolutionary wars by utilizing the modern methods of quantitative analysis and a meticulous analysis of the archives of France, Great
Britain, Haiti, the Dominican Republic, Spain, and Poland. It is obvious
that a new military history, correcting and filling in the gaps in the old
standard-but-obsolete works, should now be written. The enormous documentation of the military maps found in the Cabinet des Estampes of the
national library of France has not been touched by historians. Certain gaps
have been filled by J. Pachoński, *Polacy na Antylach i Morzu Karaibskim*
(The Poles in the Antilles and the Caribbean Sea) (Warszawa, 1979),
which goes beyond being a mere study of the Poles in the military operations in St.-Domingue.

All the general works on the history of Haiti and above all the monographs on the Haitian Revolution emphasize the primary importance of
the breakdown of the slave system. The abolition of slavery "from the
bottom up," by the slaves themselves, is the heart of the revolution. Without this rupture with the old socioeconomic system, the revolution would
not have achieved its political and national purposes. The work by
C. L. R. James is the best known of the general works.[6]

There remains a major problem to study and restudy. When one says
that a socioeconomic institutional system has been destroyed (the destruction of the slave system), one must be able to describe the new system
which has come to replace the old. But this is very difficult. The thesis
put forth by G. Pierre-Charles[7] is much too schematic: After the slave

5. See A. Metral; H. de Poyen; and above all A. Nemours, *Histoire militaire de la
guerre d'indépendance de Saint-Domingue* (3 vols., Paris, 1925–29).

6. C. L. R. James, *The Black Jacobins: Toussaint L'Ouverture and the San Domingo
Revolution* (2d ed., New York, 1963), a classic, dogmatically Marxist book of political
struggle, but always read and up to date, even though based on a limited number of sources
and containing many errors.

7. Gerard Pierre-Charles, *La economia haitiana y su via de desarrollo* (México, 1965).

society comes feudalism and, specifically in the Haitian case, its military variation.[8] Our hypothesis is the following: The new social structure is capitalism tinged with feudal elements. But what kind of capitalism—that which was dependent, as was the slave system, upon a framework of world capitalism, or an autonomous kind? Does the revolution seek to establish an independent and egalitarian capitalism, like that set up by Dr. Francia in Paraguay, or does it seek to remain in the orbit of dependent capitalism? There are many contradictory currents. Toussaint and Christophe reject a break with the world system and wish to preserve the prerevolutionary regime without slavery and colonialism. It is impossible because the former slaves do not want a fictitious and superficial change. Dessalines seems willing to break firmly with a state of dependency employing the model of state capitalism with socialistic and antibourgeois tendencies, while Pétion wants a halfway dependency through mostly resignation. It is under Boyer that the trial and experience of economic independence fails completely. Haiti, a country of two faces (peasantry and large estates), remains a country of marginal and dependent capitalism.

The major problem to resolve before arriving at valid conclusions concerns the agrarian reforms of Toussaint, Dessalines, and Pétion, and the National Domain. Not much is known about these problems, and the studies of L. F. Manigat, P. Moral, T. Lepkowski, F. Moya Pons, and F. Franco, just to cite a few, only skim the surface of the problem because of the lack of a wider documentary base. Will it be possible to view this problem with new eyes after further research? It would not be possible on the basis of Haitian archival material from the revolutionary period (ca. 1802–25). An attempt at a new interpretation of the problem of rural land use eventually may succeed through the use of material relative to the post-Boyer period.

Concerning the tribal and ethnic origin of the African slave population living in St.-Domingue on the eve of the revolution, the works of G. Debien are fundamental and seem for the most part to be definitive.[9]

The formation of the Haitian national community has caught the attention of many researchers (among those who have studied this very complex problem are J. G. Leybourn, E. Charlier, J. L. Franco, T. Lepkowski). In addition there are studies concerning the Dominican-Haitian relationship, in which the racial factor is more important than the political aspect.[10]

8. Paul Moral, *Le Paysan haitien* (Paris, 1961).
9. See especially Gabriel Debien, *Les Esclaves aux Antilles Françaises (XVIIᵉ–XVIIIᵉ)* (Basse-Terre and Fort-de-France, 1974).
10. J. Price-Mars, *La Republique d'Haiti et la Republique Dominicaine* (Port-au-Prince, 1953); E. Cordero Michel, *La Revolution haitiana y Santo Domingo* (Santo Domingo,

The racial and national integration carried out in Haiti under the influence of the state—and in the face of the ever-present threat of slave-colonial reconquest—through language (Haiti continues to be a bilingual country) and culture was difficult and sometimes has had negative repercussions. The reinterpretation of already-known material is possible and useful in light of the methods of socio- and ethnohistory. The problem of interracial breeding has been researched by S. Mintz and H. Hoetink especially in the postrevolutionary period. To understand the influence of the revolutionary tradition, oral history techniques could be of some benefit. It is probable that a new look at the French consular correspondence (up to the end of the presidency of Boyer) could enrich knowledge of this matter.

All of the studies about the Haitian Revolution emphasize the color prejudice and rivalry between Negroes and mulattos.[11] This is virtually an obsession in Haiti, but class division based on skin coloring also characterizes French, American, and other studies. It seems that the juxtaposition of two structures (social and racial "classes") in the history of the Haitian Revolution is the only valid perspective of the interpretation of Haitian social history. It is not a question of researching unknown documents but rather a reevaluation based on a new focus: an analysis of the economic and social position of the Negroes and mulattos in the so-called elite (the land owners, the military, and the government bureaucracy).

While rejecting the nationalistic emotions of the Haitian researchers and writers who are inclined to believe that their revolution shook the whole world, the influence of the revolution upon the emancipation process of slaves and of blacks in general, as well as the influence on the independence movement of Latin America, has already been accorded its just recognition.[12] But the fear of the Haitian Revolution in the Americas from about 1791 to 1825 has not been sufficiently studied. Only examination of this major issue will enable assessment of the true importance of this exceptional revolution. The Cuban, Dominican, French, British, Dutch, Brazilian, Spanish, Mexican, Venezuelan, and many more archives will offer abundant material, indicating the reaction of the terrified slave owners but not of the masses, especially if used in conjunction with the edited

---

1968); G. Pierre-Charles, "Genesis de las naciones haitiana y dominicana," in *Política y sociología en Haiti y la República Dominicana,* ed. Gerard Pierre-Charles (México, 1974).

11. Lorimer Denis and François Duvalier, *Problems des classes atravers l'histoire d'Haiti* (Port-au-Prince, 1948).

12. J. L. Franco, *La conspiración de Aponte* (La Habana, 1963); R. W. Logan, *The Diplomatic Relations of the United States with Haiti, 1776–1891* (Chapel Hill, 1941); I. Marion, *Expédition de Bolívar* (2d ed., Port-au-Prince, 1929); J. L. Salcedo Bastardo, *Visión y revisión de Bolívar* (Caracas, 1957).

documents (correspondence, memoirs, parliamentary records, etc.) and the press of many countries. The effort should be carried out by an international team of researchers.

53   The French West Indies
René V. Achéen

The history of the French West Indies is still to be written. The historical background of the French Caribbean territories is totally unknown, because they lack any academic institution and hold last place in French historical research. In the last decade a number of historical studies have been published by researchers living in the area, but on the whole these efforts are still limited.

From a chronological viewpoint, many periods remain unexplored or hardly touched. The seventeenth-century history of Martinique is comparatively well known, but little is known about what happened in the eighteenth century and the first part of the nineteenth. Of course, a few significant works have been written about the revolutionary period, the slave economy in French Guiana, the commercial policy, and generally speaking the commercial relations between the colonies and the metropole, as well as life on some of the plantations, which Professor Gabriel Debien has studied. Nevertheless, the political, economic, and, above all, the social histories of the slave period remain to be written. The periods involving the empire (1804–15), the restoration, and the July Monarchy are practically uninvestigated, except for the period from 1815 to 1848.

The end of the nineteenth century and the beginning of the twentieth are probably the best-known periods. In the late 1960s historical research was directed toward social and economic history, political history, the history of the press, and the history of labor and political movements. This might indicate a broad coverage, but, all things considered, some areas were only partially touched upon and many of these themes are dealt with briefly in publications which are very partial, are concerned with short periods only, or which consider only a single French territory. What happened between World War I and World War II remains mostly unknown, except for some research which has just been undertaken about the "Vichy period" in Martinique.

The reasons for the underdevelopment of the historical research in the French West Indies are many. First, Martinique, Guadeloupe, and French Guiana have no academic research department. Although there is a history department at the university in Martinique, the students cannot earn a graduate degree before they have studied for two more years in a metropolitan university. If it were possible for students to prepare a thesis for the M.A. degree and later on a dissertation for the Ph.D. degree, historical research would increase considerably, but no plans exist to change the present situation.

Equally important, there are no centers within the French universities that specialize in the history of the West Indies. Now and then some eminent university professor worked on this subject or directed research carried out by West Indian students, but those efforts are scattered, geographically speaking, and cannot be considered the result of research centers for the history of the West Indies. There is nothing comparable to the famous Center of Tropical Geography, whose director is Professor Guy Lasserre. The geographical dispersion is also an obstacle to a favorable research environment. One finds it difficult to consult the work that has been done in this or that university or mentioned in different bibliographies. Besides, in France, only the doctorate dissertations are systematically indexed, and consequently there are no extensive card indices for existing M.A. theses. Apart from the above-mentioned obstacles, other problems exist. There is difficulty of access to the sources and in using them, again reflecting the absence of a single depository and the difficulties of working in the territories themselves. An essential part of the documentation can be found in Paris and in a number of metropolitan seaports that used to have commercial relations with the West Indies, such as Nantes, Bordeaux, Marseille, and Le Havre.

No doubt it is possible to find an enormous variety of documents at the departmental record offices of Martinique, Guadeloupe, and French Guiana, but there has not been a systematic examination of the documents for lack of money, and therefore there are no card indices for the sources. Also, many of the documents have deteriorated because of the climate and therefore are not available. The recent reorganization of the Record Office has also made it difficult to locate material. Except for Martinique, where new buildings have recently been built, the other centers have neither air conditioning nor any other means of protecting the documents from humidity, so many documents are in very bad condition.

In France, the situation of the archives regarding the West Indies is not much better. One can most certainly locate a great number of documents in the National Library, in the Overseas Department of the National Record Office, and in the library of the National Archives. But the prospective researcher still confronts an incomplete inventory of the records and very incomplete card indices. A few years ago the National Library was unable to provide a list of its holdings of the Martinican and Guadeloupean newspapers of the nineteenth and twentieth centuries. It was suggested that a searcher be paid to do this classification, but no such measures have been taken. The documents and West Indian newspapers and magazines are stored far from the reading rooms in the National Library in Paris. The documents must be requested beforehand and are not all immediately available. The same problems crop up again in the Overseas Department of the National Record Office. The reading rooms of these two centers cannot handle many researchers. At the Overseas Department of the National Record Office, only a few dozen people can sit, while at the National Library, there are only 320 seats. Moreover the hours of service are very limited and inconvenient. One last obstacle, but not the least, is that of the high cost of the photocopies and microfilms at the record offices and libraries in the West Indies as well as in France. The price of the microfilms is prohibitive, often costing several times comparable services at depositories in the United States. In the provincial record offices and libraries, the working conditions are far better than in Paris, but the sources are incomplete and less abundant.

Lastly, some libraries of universities in the United States, particularly the University of Florida at Gainesville, have excellent collections of documents on the French West Indies. Many of the documents were microfilmed by Mrs. Ada S. Corbeau during 1958–62 with funds provided primarily by the Rockefeller Foundation. At the University of Florida, one can obtain copies of these microfilms for about ten dollars a roll. Efforts should be made at the University of Florida, or some other American university specializing in the history of Latin America, to continue this microfilming started twenty years ago. This project should also include microfilming and gathering of documents on the French West Indies located in West Indian record offices as well as the record offices and libraries in Paris.

The beginning of French colonization and the transition to the slave system, a period which is essential in understanding the origin of the West Indian society, has been little studied from the economic and demographic point of view. A study of the transition from the first settlers' food-producing economy to the origin of the plantation economy has yet to be made, particularly regarding such vital themes as the process and causes of the gradual decrease of food-producing activities, the growth of the large sugar plantations, and the land concentration. Was there a decrease of the white population? No definite statistics regarding the evolution of the population, its characteristics, or the growth of sugar production exist. Can the "Barbadian pattern," which Ramiro Guerra y Sánchez describes in *Azúcar y población en las Antillas,* be applied to Martinique's case? What accounts for the slower development of Guadeloupe?

The social, economic, and political history of the islands is still to be written. While studies of the relation between the metropole and the West Indian colonies exist, hardly anything is known about the internal history of the islands. What are the stages of economic evolution? In which areas were there mostly food crops and which produced products for export? What about the other activities such as fishing and handicrafts, which are usually considered to have been very limited or nonexistent but about which no systematic study is available? The study of social groups is lacking too. Although it resembles in some ways a caste, does the group of white creoles actually form a homogeneous class? What are the differences between the large plantation owners, the medium-sized land owners, and the class of tradesmen, "the commissionaries"? Are the actions of the white creoles of Guadeloupe and those of Martinique comparable? There is no complete study about the economic and social situation of the mulatto middle class in the slave society. Existing studies of slavery mainly refer to Santo Domingo, but very little attention is paid to the lesser French West Indies. No surveys comparable to those which can be found in Brazil, in the United States, or in Jamaica are available for the slave society in Martinique or Guadeloupe. There is no study on the origins and historical development of the creole language. Documents concerning the plantations have not yet been systematically investigated; they can be found especially in the National Record Office in Paris.

The abolition of slavery is a many-sided question, which has long caused controversy. Some insist on the primacy of internal political factors, such as the slave rebellions of May 22 and 23, 1848, in Martinique, while others give preference to the external political factors such as the Revolution of 1848, the abolitionist movement, and the role played by Victor Schoelcher. Others insist on economic factors such as the crisis of the sugar economy, France's position in the New World at the time of the industrial revolution, and England's rule over the world.

The economic evolution of the island after 1900 is little known. There is a focus on the sugar crisis and the replacement, up to a point, of sugar by rum then by the banana, but few precise details about this change are known. What about the state of the economy during World War II? The social history, that of the labor movement, and the workmen's conditions remain terra incognita. Extensive research, particularly in the numerous records of the sugar mills, is necessary, but sources are unfortunately private and kept by bekés families.

Generally speaking, a study is needed of the history of the different social groups in the postslavery society, particularly the evolution of the white creole group, the bekés, and the "creolization" of the metropolitan groups that settled in the West Indies in the second half of the nineteenth century and made important investments in the sugar industry. The cause and effect of the different evolution of Martinique and Guadeloupe, such as the bekés' retention of control over the lands and the factories in Martinique compared with the sale of property, the lands, and factories to metropolitan societies in Guadeloupe, could then be studied comparatively. Another important problem is the situation and the evolution of the mulatto group after the abolition of slavery. This intermediate class, owing to its education, played an important role in politics. Relations between the mulattos and both the former slaves and the bekés await examination. A study of the agreements concluded between those groups in 1913, 1919, and 1931 is badly needed. One of the least-known and most-debated issues is that concerning the struggle for assimilation and the role played by the mulattos in the movement for political integration with the metropolis, which they saw as the best means to obtain equality with the white creoles. Analysis of the West Indies political future, the alternative routes of self-government, assimilation, or complete integration, and the reason why the sense of independence has been less strong in Guadeloupe and in Martinique than in the other islands of the Caribbean also await investigation. Another issue relating to the postslavery period is the study of St.-Pierre (Martinique) society. It was, as everyone knows, a very brilliant one, until destroyed by the 1902 volcanic eruption.

Historical demography, quantitative history of the economy, and oral history remain practically untouched. Among the possible themes are a systematic study of parish and registry offices, quantification and the drawing up of statistical data relating to the economy, and the history of business concerns and of the plantations. One must not forget that these countries have oral traditions, and inquiry by interviews is sometimes the only way to study the customs of the former slaves, who, for reasons easily understood, have not left many written traces.

54   The Netherlands Antilles and Suriname
Jaap van Soest

On the history of the (former) Dutch West Indies—with their rather modest size of territories and populations—there exists a relatively large number of publications, if one includes the hundreds of smaller articles with mainly *petite histoire;* but there are few book-length monographs or theses of academic depth. Much research for the latter type of work has been done by amateurs, who by their serious approach have lent a new and highly respectable status to the word *amateur;* but professionally trained historians have up to now paid little attention to the history of Suriname and the Netherlands Antilles.

The Dutch Caribbean is no exception to a more general regional pattern, in that the majority of the earlier historians were of European origin. In the last few decades, however, some discrepancy emerged. The Dutch overseas territories in the Caribbean came to face political independence only recently. They went through the process of awareness that gave birth to a historiography of, for, and especially by the native-born citizens of the respective countries much later and to a much lesser degree than most other territories of the region. Almost no historical works have been published in the popular creole vernaculars of Suriname (Sranangtongo) or of the main islands of the Netherlands Antilles (Papiamentu). The major part of the relevant literature is in Dutch, although some studies have been published in English and Spanish during the last few decades.

No monograph covers both Suriname and the Netherlands Antilles during the whole period of history. Such a joint approach might be expected if their colonization by the Dutch—being almost the only common denominator—is taken as point of departure. Several studies do indeed exist on Dutch colonial policy in general, but they mostly discuss the West Indies as a variant of the East Indies, without appreciating the specific developments in this hemisphere. A comparative study of Dutch colonial policies for the East and West Indies has still to be made.

Just as the West Indies is rarely discussed in one breath with the East Indies, the same is true for Suriname and the Netherlands Antilles. The commercial centers on the islands of Curaçao and St. Eustatius had little to do with the plantation society on the Wild Coast. One of the few common traits has been described by Schiltkamp in his history of the notarial office in the territories under the charter of the West India Company. With the independence of Suriname in 1975, it is hoped that there will be further comparative thematic studies among the (former) Dutch West Indies. A more comprehensive historical analysis of the political, social, economic, and cultural relations between Suriname and the Netherlands Antilles during three centuries is also needed.

Few works include all the Dutch West Indies over specific periods of their colonial history. Goslinga's study on the activities of the Dutch in the Caribbean and on the Wild Coast between 1580 and 1680 is an outstanding exception;[1] it also includes Brazil and Tobago, where the Dutch interference was of a temporary character. Bachman has directed attention to

---

1. Cornelis Ch. Goslinga, *The Dutch in the Caribbean and the Wild Coast* (Gainesville, 1971).

the economic policies of the Dutch West India Company in Holland in the early seventeenth century. De Laet's thirteen volumes with contemporary reports on the company's activities between 1624 and 1636 constitute an important source book.[2] But there are no other such publications or monographs that cover the Caribbean during the late seventeenth and the whole of the eighteenth century from a Dutch point of view. A comparative analysis of the ups and downs of the Dutch Caribbean colonies during the Napoleonic era is also conspicuously absent. Between 1828 and 1845 all Dutch West Indian possessions were united administratively under one governor-general, but no studies exist on their joint experiences. The abolition movement is another topic for a comparative study of Suriname and Antillean histories. Jumping almost a century, the effects of World War II on bauxite-producing Suriname and oil-refining Curaçao and Aruba, as well as the political developments immediately after the war, lend themselves to comparative studies.

A few interesting articles have been recently published on certain aspects of the prehistory of the Netherlands Antilles, such as rock drawings, artifacts, and physical anthropology. The data have since been supplemented and corrected where necessary, but no general survey of the prehistory has as yet been published. The results of the fieldwork of the last decade have not been made available as yet.

The Spanish period (1544–1634) has been described fairly well by the Venezuelan historian Felipe Cardot, although his is a rather biased view. Undoubtedly there is more to be found in Seville's vaults than has been incorporated in the monograph of Cardot or in the indispensable collection of documents published by Irene Wright and Cornelis F. A. van Dam.[3] Especially Curaçao's position as a stepping stone between Hispañola and continental Latin America might be subjected to further research.

Little has been published on the era of the first Dutch West India Company (1621–74) and not much more on that of the second company (1675–1791). The publications mentioned above deal with the seventeenth century. Hamelberg and Hartog have collected data on the eighteenth century as well, but their presentation of the material sometimes leaves much to be desired.[4] A thematic approach has been used by Van Grol in his study

2. Johannes de Laet, *Historie ofte laerlijck Verhael van de verrichtinghen der Geoctroyeerde West-Indische Compagnie*, ed. Samule P. L'Honore Naber (13 vols. in 4 vols., 's-Gravenhage, 1931–37).

3. Irene A. Wright and Cornelis F. A. van Dam, eds., *Nederlandsche zeevaarders op de eilanden in de Caribische Zee en aan de kust van Colombia en Venezuela gedurende de jaren 1621–1648* (2 vols., Utrecht, 1934–35).

4. J. H. J. Hamelberg, *De Nederlanders op de West-Indische eilanden* (Amsterdam, 1901–3); Johannes Hartog, *Geschiedenis van de Nederlandse Antillen* (5 vols., Oranjestad, 1956–64).

on the companies' land policy,[5] and also by the Emmanuels in their already-classical work on the Jews of the Netherlands Antilles.[6] The latter stretches from the seventeenth well into the twentieth century and discusses not only the religious and ethnic, but also the social, economic, and political aspects of this group. A major study by Knappert focuses on the Dutch Windward Islands in the eighteenth century.[7] Here, St. Eustatius' role in the American War of Independence has led to more detailed studies.

The archives of the West India Companies, the main source for material on the history of the seventeenth and eighteenth centuries, have hardly been explored. Their sorry state presented a reasonable excuse until now, but this alibi will soon no longer be valid, as most archival material relating to the Netherlands Antilles will become available on microfiche. All colonial laws of the seventeenth and eighteenth centuries that could be found have been published. Other useful source material should follow.

Curaçao and St. Eustatius, for a short span of time, were important as international commercial centers. Remarkably, their economic history of the seventeenth and eighteenth centuries has never been studied in detail. Very little is known about their roles in the slave trade; the purely quantitative questions are still completely unanswered and the qualitative aspects are—after Unger and Postma—also for a major part still open for research.

The staple trade and the other economic relations of the Dutch West Indian islands with their Caribbean and continental neighbors have hardly been dealt with by historians. The quantitative problems of such research cannot be solved easily, but the field promises to be most rewarding to a versed practitioner of cliometrics. In the most descriptive and analytical parts, Dutch commercial activities may be compared with Spanish, British, French, and Danish centers of trade and smuggling in the region.

The internal economy of the individual islands has been described only in a generalized way. Some material on the Curaçao plantations in the seventeenth and eighteenth centuries has been collected but not published. The plantations of the later eighteenth and complete nineteenth century have recently been analyzed by Renkema. Because the pillars of insular economics were trade and agriculture, it seems as if other economic-historical studies on specific sectors, such as mining or ship building, are not justified for the time being. They rightly may find their place in a

---

5. G. J. van Grol, *De grandpolitiek in het Westinisch domein der generaliteit* (3 vols., 's-Gravenhage, 1934–37).

6. Isaac S. Emmanuel and Suzanne E. Emmanuel, *History of the Jews of the Netherlands Antilles* (2 vols., Cincinnati, 1970).

7. L. Knappert, *Geschiednis van de Nederlandsche Bovenwindsche eilanden en de 18de eeuw* (1932–33).

more general economic history of the islands under the companies' rule. For the latter, financial (including monetary) history will also be an indispensable component. The origin, volume, destination, and other qualifications of the capital-flows involved with trade, public administration, and defense are an attractive subject for research and will contribute to economic as well as political and social history.

The social structure of Curaçao's society in the seventeenth and eighteenth centuries has been examined by Hoetink[8] and the Emmanuels. Until a detailed inventory has been made of the companies' archives, it is an open question whether they contain sufficient data for further social research. However, it should be stressed that even Curaçao, the largest and most cosmopolitan island of the Antilles, had a population of scarcely fifteen thousand at the end of the eighteenth century.

There is little on the history of the administrative and legal system, in spite of available material in this field, and many subjects are waiting for researchers. During the last few years, the Law Department of the University of the Netherlands Antilles has initiated studies of the local application of old Dutch and Roman law, offering a fine training ground for Antillean students.

For the history of the nineteenth and twentieth centuries, the historian is not so dependent upon a single type of source. There are available government archives, both colonial and metropolitan, and private collections, including company archives. More printed material is available in newspapers, half a dozen travelers' books (Hering, Bosch, Teenstra, Simons, Brusse, Martin, Van Kol), government documents, and the customary numerous pamphlets of the nineteenth century. There is also the option of oral history. Although more has been published on the last two centuries than on the previous ones, the general collections of articles that exist do not present an integrated history of these last two centuries. The lacunae relate, not only to specialized areas, but often to the whole period.

The political history of the Netherlands Antilles, both internally and in relation to the mother country, has hardly been studied. Kasteel[9] and Van Helsdingen concentrate on the years between 1940 and 1955, without looking very much at the age that preceded the renovation of the political system. Bordewijk has been the only one to pay attention to the constitutional changes in the nineteenth century. Among the many topics that still have to be studied are Dutch colonial policy vis-à-vis the islands; the re-

---

8. Harmannus Hoetink, *Het patroon van de oude Curacaose Samenleving* (Assen, 1958).

9. Annemarie C. T. Kasteel, *De staatkundige ontwikkeling der Nederlandse Antillen* ('s-Gravenhage, 1956).

lations among the islands of the Netherlands Antilles (a very relevant subject, as the islands threaten to split on their way to independence); the history of the political parties and pressure groups; and the peoples' influence upon their own government.

In the administrative and legal fields, there are dozens of articles by lawyers with historical interests and a good analysis of the political system in Curaçao after 1954 by Verton. Some research in this field is being done within the University of the Netherlands Antilles.

In the field of international politics, the relations between Curaçao and Venezuela have been subjected to a certain degree of investigation. However, Corporaal and Goslinga had a special interest in the nineteenth century and left the twentieth century for others. Much might also still be said on the relations with Colombia, Suriname, and the various Caribbean islands (especially Cuba, Santo Domingo, and Jamaica), but these—as well as the Venezuelan connection—cannot be studied from a purely political point of view and have to be put in the context of international economic relations.

On the modern economic history of the Netherlands Antilles until quite recently, De Jong's study on Dutch economic policy vis-à-vis the Caribbean in the first decades of the nineteenth century and two laudatory company histories by Hartog stood alone. Lately, van Soest has published a detailed factual survey of the Curaçao economy between 1900 and 1955, and a more general outline of the economic history of the Netherlands Antilles in the nineteenth and twentieth centuries, interwoven with a history of money and banking.[10] Moreover, nineteenth-century agriculture has been studied by Renkema. Many other aspects of the economic history might be subjected to further investigations, such as international economic relations, transport and communications, the government's role in the promotion of economic development, Aruba in the era of the oil refineries, various company histories, and the development of tourism in relation to trade and shipping. In the preparation of many research projects, the complete absence of historical-demographic studies will be felt as a vacuum that has to be filled.

Social history is reflected in the published documents on the slave revolt of 1795, in monographs by Hoetink on the nineteenth-century Curaçao society in general, by Goslinga on the slave emancipation, and by Römer on social developments after that event.[11] After a serious gap, the line is then resumed by contemporary sociologists and anthropologists. Among

---

10. Jaap van Soest, *Trustee of the Netherlands Antilles* (Curaçao, 1978).

11. Rene A. Römer, "Sociale Stratificatie en Sociale Mobiliteit in de Curacaose Samenleving," in *Lustrum van een Ideaal* (Curaçao, 1977).

the missing links are the histories of the labor movement in general and labor unions in particular, which have been discussed only in a few minor articles.

In the sociocultural field, finally, much is yet to be done. The numerous publications on Church history, mainly by Catholic priests, present many facts but fewer insights and should be deepened and integrated into a book-length general survey. The history of educational organizations and institutions also needs attention. Boskaljon published fragments from Curaçao's musical history, but many additional data have been collected—albeit not published—since his days. The history of Antillean literature has not yet been described, again with the exception of a few fragments. Historical architecture received attention for the first time with the precious book of Ozinga, but has certainly not yet been dealt with exhaustively. On the history of health care there is one source publication and one reader, but here also ample opportunities for further research are left.

The Netherlands Antilles are of historical interest because they are a special case in the Caribbean: they have never known the classic type of plantation society. At the same time they have a good deal of characteristics in common with other territories in the region. The three Leeward Islands of the Netherlands Antilles are probably more Hispanicized than any other part of the non-Spanish Caribbean. Their close connections with continental Latin America have put them in an intermediate position. As such they constitute a special category that cannot be left out of studies that cover both the Caribbean and Latin America.

Although Suriname's history cannot be regarded as a variant of Antillean history, a comparison of the historiography of both countries is inevitable. Striking the eye immediately is the fact that for the last five or six decades Suriname's past has been studied to a much lesser degree than that of the Antilles, reflecting at least in part the relatively high standard of living attained on the islands since the turn of the century. Yet, in previous centuries it was Suriname which drew more attention than Curaçao, especially in travelers' reports including historical surveys. Indicative of the lack of a recent historiography on Suriname is the frequency with which Wolbers' work of 1861 is still being quoted or referred to. For over a hundred years the period before 1861 has not been described again in the form of a general survey, and Wolbers' work has been complemented only summarily for the years up to 1940 by Van Traa.

For much of Suriname, prehistory did not end with the pre-Columbian era but was closed at a much later date. Geijskes devoted a few articles to the subject, stressing in particular the need for further research. However, important activities have not yet been developed in this field.

For the Wild Coast, including Suriname, Cayenne to 1676, Demerara,

Essequibo, and Berbice, the period until 1667 was a time of confusion. Goslinga has been the first to map it out clearly from a Dutch point of view, and Williamson had previously tried to do the same from a British point of view. These two general publications, the partial study of Oppenheim on an early Jewish colony in Guiana, and that of Warnsinck on the capture of the colony by the Dutch in 1667, leave much yet to be done. Research is hampered by the scantiness and poor condition of the sources and by the fact that they lay scattered in Dutch, British, French, and Spanish archives.

During the era of the West India Companies (1667–1792), Suriname enjoyed a flourishing period. From an almost uncontrolled preserve for private adventurers, the territory became a highly valued possession, which received much attention from the mother country. Herlein, Pistorius, Fermin, Hartsinck, De Leon, Nassy, Stedman, and others, after a stay of a more-or-less long duration in the colony, gave their impressions of the land and the people, and often also some history of Suriname. Those works provide important material for historians. However, less has been published on Suriname's seventeenth and eighteenth centuries ex post than by these centuries' contemporaries.

Both the numerous contemporary travel reports and the few more recent scholarly studies reflect how predominant agriculture was in Suriname. Quintus Bosz did a study on the land policy in the colony over the course of three centuries; Panday published a general survey of its agriculture between 1650 and 1950; and Van de Voort looked into the financial aspects of the plantations and the marketing of their products. But on other aspects of eighteenth-century economic life, such as trade, shipping, the monetary system, or the crafts sector, no detailed studies have been made. One exception here is Unger, who took a first step with regard to the slave trade, but his work is not comprehensive. Until quantitative data are supplied, more comprehensive studies on the slave trade in the Dutch Caribbean will not be possible. The lack of quantitative data hampered some of the studies on agriculture, as well as those on trade and shipping in the eighteenth century.

From a sociohistorical point of view, the eighteenth century has been dealt with even more scantily. Van Lier in his classical work describes social relations within Suriname's plantation society, but his main focus is on the nineteenth century. Neither he nor others can reach back into the eighteenth century with more thoroughness as long as the archival material is not more easily accessible. It may even be stated that, with the exception of Van Lier's work, hardly anything has been added to the contemporary accounts of social relations and conditions in the eighteenth century.

On administrative and legal affairs, almost nothing has been published for the company period. This may partially be ascribed to the system of patronships, which limited the role of the company in Suriname in comparison with its role in Curaçao. The relations between the patrons and the company would be an absorbing subject for research, and specialists in the field of legal history would have no problem in enumerating a dozen similar important topics. The recent publication of the colonial laws is a sign of fresh interest and has eliminated a few obstacles.

Among the travelers of the nineteenth century—such as Quandt, Von Sack, Vos, Benoit, Van Sypesteyn, and Kappler—Wolbers has a special place with his very detailed general history of Suriname. The list of publications by contemporaries stretches into the twentieth century, but by then both the quantity and quality of the travelers' reports reflect the decreasing interest in Suriname.

In social history, Van Lier's is the most comprehensive survey, although his book might benefit from a supplement that encompasses more than the few additions that have been made to later editions. Lamur covers part of the field with his study on the demographic evolution between 1920 and 1970, and in another respect De Bruijne does so with a sociogeographic study of Paramaribo between 1850 and 1970. Apart from these three, all sociohistorical research into the last two centuries has been limited to one or another racial segment of the Suriname society. Class-oriented studies (e.g., on the labor movement) are nonexistent.

Aside from Emmer's study on the abolition of the slave trade, the social and economic consequences of the abolition are unstudied. On the emancipation there are many polemic essays from the middle of the nineteenth century; serious studies have since been published by Van Winter on the role of public opinion, by Waaldijk on the function of the press, by Altens on the attitudes of parliament, and by Siwpersad on the role of the Dutch government. These same publications should be analyzed also from the local point of view.

Some attention has been given to the legal position of the emancipated slaves, but sufficient research has not been done on their social and economic position after 1863. Gemminck alone has made an effort in the form of a sociodemographic study on a certain slave and her descendants. The indentured labor from the Netherlands East Indies is given attention in a general study by Ismael and in a commemorative reader; specific studies on the Javanese or Hindustani are sociological rather than historical. Here, many research possibilities are still open for historians; nearby Guiana and Trinidad offer many examples of studies of indentured labor.

On the runaway slaves, or Maroons, and their descendants, also more sociological research has been done than historical, as Price has demonstrated in his detailed bibliographic account. De Groot is one of the very few historians in the region who has made use of oral sources, covering both the nineteenth and twentieth centuries and various of the bush Negro communities; but there are considerable intervals of time and space left for further research.

The same should be said for the Amerindians, who—as is quite natural—have also been drawing more attention from anthropologists than from historians. There are numerous articles on folktales, ornamentation, etc., but no answer has been given to questions such as how the Indians were perceived by their various fellow countrymen in different periods of time.

Among the Europeans the well-to-do Jews were an important subgroup. Meyer's publication on the Suriname Jews in the nineteenth century is very thin compared with Emmanuel's monument to the Jews of the Netherlands Antilles. The rest have so far succeeded in escaping the critical attention of any historian.

The economic history of Suriname in the nineteenth and twentieth centuries is limited to the two works already mentioned on land and agriculture (by Quintus Bosz and Panday). Nothing has been done on trade or shipping, on inland transportation such as the impact of the railroad, electrification, and further infrastructure for modernization. There are only a few summary articles on the very important gold mining and bauxite industries. Lacking such previous studies, Adhin could hardly expect to succeed in his effort to put Suriname's development planning in a historical perspective. It remains a question how long Suriname can proceed in looking to its future economic development without being aware of the economic experiences of the past.

The same goes for political history, where equally few historical studies are available. The era between the British interim government of the early nineteenth century—covered by Einaar—and the constitutional developments of the mid-twentieth century is completely terra incognita. The last decades, moreover, have been viewed mainly from the legal point of view by Mitrasing, Van Helsdingen, and Ooft. In studies on the previous history of recent political and constitutional events, attention might be given to Dutch colonial policy; to the relations with the Caribbean (especially a history of the border conflicts with the Guianas and Venezuela); to the internal political and administrative machinery and the role of certain interest groups in this machinery; to the history of democracy, of political parties, and of the proportional representative system as related to race, party, and economic occupation.

A similar amount of work awaits historians with an interest in cultural affairs. As in the Netherlands Antilles, so in Suriname are there many publications on Church history, containing many facts but not yet presenting an insight into the function of the ecclesiastical organizations and the evangelical inspiration in Suriname's past. No monographs are available on the history of education, music, or literature. Interesting studies have been published on Suriname's historical architecture by Temminck Grol, Tjin A. Djie, Quintus Bosz, and Fontaine, but all sorts of constructions outside the urban agglomeration have not yet been investigated. No historical studies have been done on public health or institutional health care.

Suriname provides a special attraction for historians. It was the only real Caribbean-type plantation society that for a long period was operated under the Dutch flag. As such, Suriname provides material for comparative studies with British and French plantation societies (especially the nearby Guianas, and also Jamaica with its Maroons). Secondly, Suriname was the main destination of government-sponsored migration of indentured labor from the Netherlands East Indies. As such it provides a rare variant upon the migration of the British East Indian to the Caribbean. There must be interesting possibilities for comparative research on both types of migration, and on the migrants and their descendants coming from India or Indonesia. Thirdly, whereas the economy and society of Curaçao were open to all, Suriname had a rather closed system, directed almost exclusively toward the metropole. This must have had its impact upon local attitudes. It might be interesting to see if and how this historical orientation has marked Suriname's way to independence and influenced the heavy migration toward the Netherlands.

55   Puerto Rico
Blanca G. Silvestrini and
Maria de los Angeles Castro

In the last decade research on Puerto Rican history has changed toward a more efficient use of the sources available in Puerto Rico to complement those in Spain and in the United States. This change perhaps is a result of a reorganization of the Archivo General de Puerto Rico to be the depository of the municipal archives. Although by law since 1955 the Archivo General is the official depository of all public documents in Puerto Rico, the scarcity of resources prevented the incorporation of the vast amount of materials pertaining to the municipal archives until 1972.

The records of the municipal archives today at the Archivo General in

San Juan may be divided into three broad categories, depending on the state of classification and availability of the materials to the public: (1) those that are fully organized with an inventory, index, or catalogue, (2) those that are not yet classified but which have a general description and are available to researchers only under special circumstances, and (3) those that due to disorganization or deterioration are not open to the public. In some cases, as in the case of San Juan, part of the documents are indexed while others have been placed in boxes without any chronological or thematic order.

The following is a list of the materials by organizational categories (with cubic feet in parentheses):

Organized with a thematic list
   Aguadilla (13.62)
   Aibonito (16.92)
   Cabo Rojo (2.35)
   Carolina (107.16)
   Cayey (17.39)
   Ceiba (1.88)
   Ciales (94.97)
   Cidra (.92)
   Corozal (5.64)
   Dorado (7.99)
   Gurabo (10.34)
   Hormigueros (47.94)—detailed inventory
   Isabela (124.93)
   Juana Díaz (66.27)—preliminary inventory
   Lares (166)—preliminary inventory
   Loíza (1.88)
   Manatí (143.35)—inventory
   Maunabo (1.88)
   Moca (3.76)
   Naguabo (15.4)
   Naranjito (4.23)
   Orocovis (12.69)
   Patillas (4.23)
   Peñuelas (14.57)—preliminary inventory
   Quebradillas (.47)
   Rincón (1.88)
   San Juan (15.41)—catalogue for one-third of the materials
   Utuado (88.78)
   Vieques (4.70)

Yauco (188)—preliminary inventory; general description by decades
Yabucoa (12.22)—preliminary inventory
Organized with a general description
Culebra (2.35)
Fajardo (252.39)
Río Grande (39.48)
Sabana Grande (31.96)
Toa Alta (1.13)
Toa Baja (6.11)
Disorganized, not open to the public
Arecibo (779.87)
Arroyo (55.46)
Barceloneta (57.90)
Barranquitas (40.38)
Bayamón (28.67)
Camuy (111.86)
Coamo (31.02)
Comerío (44.71)
Guayama (207.27)
Guayanilla (174.42)
Hatillo (121.75)
Trujillo Alto (29.61)
Vega Alta (21.9)

There are five exceptions in which the municipal archives are still in their places of origin: Ponce (with inventory), Mayaguez, San Germán, Caguas, and Vega Baja (with inventory). In these cases, the records are relatively well organized, well preserved, and open to researchers. Materials for Río Piedras are part of the records of San Juan.

The materials found in the municipal archives are very valuable for reconstructing aspects of Puerto Rican history yet to be studied, especially in the areas of social and economic history. Besides the Libros de Actas, which recorded the decisions, problems brought to the assembly, and the opinions of some citizens on major issues, the municipal archives contain documents such as demographic registers, general correspondence, appointments, budgets, *padrones* (registers of property and wealth), reports on the conditions of the town, plans and projects for public works, population censuses, rules and regulations, permits, licenses and patents, *ordenanzas municipales,* and others. These records are very useful for the study of how the Puerto Rican people lived at a certain moment and how the local government faced the problems that emerged. They complement the more official view provided by the documents of the government branches.

Although not part of the municipal archives, the *protocolos notariales* (notarial registries) are of much value in understanding the local history of Puerto Rico and the socioeconomic processes affecting the island. They complement the municipal archives, since they contain civil transactions among citizens, such as contracts of sale and exchange, mortgages, wills, articles of marriage, powers of attorney, and others. The series of protocolos notariales in general has a chronological index up to 1850, a toponymic index, an inventory by notary, and a summative inventory that includes the notarial index, towns or cities included in the district, and years and number of volumes. The following is a summary of the records available:

	Number of volumes
San Juan (4 towns), 1751–1911	754
Bayamón (10 towns), 1768–1906	224
Humacao (15 towns), 1772–1915	520
Aguadilla (7 towns), 1790–1905	439
Mayaguez (3 towns), 1855–1923	80
Arecibo (8 towns), 1800–1908	411
	2,428 vols.

Ponce (13 towns), 1763–1926, has a separate guide, which is organized by notary with specific information on each volume.

Guayama's records are still at the Archivo de Protocolos Notariales in Guayama.

The University of Puerto Rico is the second largest depository of materials for the study of Puerto Rico. The Puerto Rican Collection of the José M. Lázaro Library comprises perhaps the most complete book collection available in Puerto Rico. Its newspaper section is very valuable because it contains newspapers published since the last third of the nineteenth century. At present, the library is microfilming those that are not available to the public because of their poor condition. The newspaper section has thematic catalogues for *El Mundo* and for the magazines, reviews and other periodical publications. Although some of the newspaper series are not complete, they are still useful, since they are unavailable anywhere else.

The Puerto Rican Collection also has some documentary series of interest:

The papers of Miguel Guerra Mondragón, basically consisting of official correspondence of the legislature and documents related to the Liberal party and the Unión Puertorriqueña (in process of cataloguing).

The papers of Ana Roqué de Duprey (without catalogue).

The papers of Emilio Pasarell, containing newspaper clippings related to

the history of theater in Puerto Rico, including photographs (without catalogue).

The papers of Félix Franco Oppenheimer, useful for the history of literature.

The papers of Eugenio Rentas Luccas—about one hundred documents of
general correspondence and literary critiques of his work (with catalogue).
The papers of the Committee of Transition of Government, 1972 and
1976—donated by Mr. Ramón García Santiago—which includes the special reports of each government division (with catalogue).

A collection of documents of the nineteenth century, consisting of typed
transcriptions of documents related to the captain generals of Puerto Rico
in the nineteenth century. There are some original documents particularly
related to military matters (in process of cataloguing).

The Sellés Collection, consisting of documents (mostly copies) pertaining
to the history of public education from 1770 to 1943. Among the original
papers, the registers with statistics for various public schools in Puerto
Rico in the nineteenth and twentieth centuries are very valuable. The collection also contains some published materials, for example, the *Consti-
tución y reglamento de la Asociación General de Maestros* (1910) and
several *Informes de la Asociación de Padres y Maestros* (1922).

The papers of the Department of Consumer Affairs, mainly consisting of
newspaper clippings organized by topics.

The documents of the parish archives, which is a special project of the
Puerto Rican Collection to microfilm the parish books of the eighteenth
and nineteenth centuries. To the present the project contains Hormigueros,
Añasco, and some documents of the town of San Germán, of the Hospital
de la Concepción, and of the Orden Tercera de San Francisco.

The Papers of the Real Sociedad de Amigos del País (29 volumes).

A series of bound manuscripts including:
   a. pupils' work (1900–03), organized by school districts
   b. Diario de las Cortes (April 15 to May 6, 1885)
   c. Reales Ordenes (1833–84)
   d. manuscripts from Vieques (nineteenth century)

A collection of photographs by A. Moscioni, early twentieth century.

The papers of Ruby Black (not open to the public).

The Center for Historical Research of the Department of History is also
a depository dedicated exclusively to materials for Puerto Rican history.
Its main objective is the location and acquisition of copies of the historical
documents on Puerto Rico in foreign archives (to date from Spain, the
United States, Cuba, France, England, Denmark, Sweden, and Mexico).
At present, the center is collecting materials pertaining especially to the

fifteenth through the eighteenth centuries, though it is also interested in completing the records of the consular agents in Puerto Rico. Among the materials at the center, the researcher may find the *consultas* of the civil and military government to the Consejo de Indias, accounts of the Real Hacienda, *bandos* (or rules) of government, papers related to El Situado (financial help from Mexico), rules and regulations for Puerto Rico, documents pertaining to the foundation of towns and visits of bishops, materials of the Real Compañía Barcelonesa and of the Real Factoría Mercantil, population censuses, slave registers, correspondence of governors, and other general documents on the political, social, and economic life of Puerto Rico.

In the long run, all these materials may open new topics of historical research, because they provide a different picture of Puerto Rico, not so dependent on government official records but more closely related to the people. It must be remembered that up to 1898 the municipalities had more autonomy, and they dealt with matters which were later left to the responsibility of the general government—matters such as education, police, health, public works, collection of taxes, etc. Also, many of these testimonies, for example, the notarial records and the demographic registers, are not typically thought of as having a historical purpose, but in fact are very important in interpersonal relations, therefore providing a more neutral view of the situation. The records collected from foreign archives, used in conjunction with the municipal archives and the papers of the general government, are an excellent source for the study of trade and industry and other economic matters as well as for the reconstruction of the external relations of Puerto Rico. In general the quality and quantity of these records are really a challenge to imaginative research.

56 The National Archives of the Dominican Republic
Frank Moya Pons

The General Archives of the Nation

Most of the historical material of the Dominican Republic has been deposited in the Archivo General de la Nación, an institution created by Law 912, passed on May 22, 1935, with the purpose of collecting in one centralized place all of the documents and material found in the old National

Archives and in the various and diverse ministries and departments of the government.

The documents contained in the General Archives of the Nation include these major categories:

Documents of the Spanish colonial period, which covers the years from 1492 to July 22, 1795.

Documents of the French colonial period, which covers the years from July 22, 1795, to July 11, 1809.

Documents of the second Spanish period, running from July 11, 1809, to December 1, 1821.

Documents during the brief period of de facto independence, covering the few months from December 1, 1821, to February 9, 1822.

Documents relating to the period of Haitian domination from February 9, 1822, to February 27, 1844.

Documents of the first republic, which covers the years between February 28, 1844, and March 18, 1861.

Documents during the Spanish annexation and the War of Restoration from March 19, 1861, to July 12, 1865.

Documents of the second republic from July 13, 1865, to November 29, 1916.

Documents during the military occupation by the United States from November 30, 1916, to October 21, 1922.

Documents covering the contemporary period from October 21, 1922, until the present.

Most of the documents of the colonial period are divided among the following collections and groups: the notary and protocol papers; the Lugo Collection; the Coiscou Collection; the municipal archives of Bayaguana, Higuey, El Seybo, and Monte Plata; ecclesiastical books, and diverse papers donated by researchers or papers obtained from the Spanish archives, particularly the National Historical Archives of Madrid and the General Archives of the Indies in Seville; and a few items from family collections and the Real Audiencia de Santo Domingo.

The paucity of documentation from the colonial period in the General Archives of the Nation is explained by the political and economic calamities suffered by the island during the time of Spanish domination. Practically all local documents were destroyed by Francis Drake and his soldiers, who invaded the island in 1586. In the subsequent centuries earthquakes and hurricanes destroyed most of the official and private collections, and in 1795 the remaining official archives of the Real Audiencia were sent to Cuba in fifty-nine large crates by way of Maracaibo, and now can be found in the General Archives of Cuba.

Most of the Dominican colonial documentation can be found in the General Archives of the Indies and other Spanish archives. For this reason the Dominican Republic government has sent various missions to copy these collections, thus creating on the island several important documentary collections, the most important ones being the Lugo Collection, in the General Archives of the Nation; the Coiscou Collection, in the General Archives of the Nation; the Herrera Collection, located in the home of the historian Cesar Herrera and a small part in the General Archives of the Nation; the Utrera Collection, located in the Rodríguez Demorizi Foundation; the Emilio Rodríguez Demorizi Collection, found in the Rodríguez Demorizi Foundation; the Inchaustegui Collection, deposited in the Catholic university Madre y Maestra.

All these collections include the Spanish and French colonial periods through February 9, 1822. Most of the material available in the Dominican Republic on the period of Haitian domination is located in the notarial and protocol archives in the General Archives of the Nation.

Most of the documents related to the Haitian domination were taken to Port-au-Prince at the end of the domination and the beginning of the independence of the republic in 1844. However, this material seems to have been lost, since all efforts to locate it in the National Archives of Haiti in Port-au-Prince have failed. In the Saint Louis Gonsague Library of the Christian Brothers in Port-au-Prince, some printed material is preserved from this period, particularly memoirs of some of the military generals and a few other Haitian government officials.

The republican period provides documentary material collected from each one of the ministry offices and governmental departments; this includes the first and second republics, the annexation, the restoration, and the period of United States military occupation. The General Archives of the Nation contain almost all of the official documentation of the Dominican Republic up to 1924 and a good part of that documentation produced by the many governmental departments up to 1955. From this date on there was a general laxness on the part of the directors of many of the governmental departments, and documentation was not sent to the General Archives, thus failing in effect to comply with the legal requirements, which establish the obligation to forward to the archives all those papers and records which deal with matters that have been inactive for more than five years. Thus to write contemporary history it is necessary to search for the material in the diverse governmental departments and agencies.

Documents accessioned prior to 1961 are well organized, classified, and catalogued. Because this work has not continued, many private collections which would naturally have gone into the General Archives of the Nation have been retained by their owners and their families, making it now essential for any researcher to seek out these private collections in order to do any serious historical research. The most important of these private collections are: the Rodríguez Demorizi Foundation, belonging to the historian Emilio Rodríguez Demorizi; the Collection of don Vetilio Alfau Duran; the Collection of don Julio Ortega Frier, part of which may be found in the National Library; and the Collection of Cesar Herrera. Former presidents in recent years, including Rafael Bonnelly, Donald Reid Cabral, Juan Bosch, and Joaquín Balaguer, all retain valuable collections of documents, which some day will be made available to the public.

Municipal Archives

The history of the municipal archives has followed the same disastrous pattern as that of the national archives, since the lack of funds, neglect, pillage, wars, revolutions, invasions, and natural disasters have practically wiped out all of the municipal documentation relating to the colonial period and to much of the national period. Only the archives of the municipalities of Higuey, El Seybo, Bayaguana, and Monte Plata conserve some material from the colonial period, the latter two retaining material from the beginning of the seventeenth century. These municipal archives are kept in the General Archives of the Nation.

The more recent municipal archives are still in the hands of the local governments and are in a deplorable state of neglect in most cases. Some, such as the municipal archives of Santiago and of La Vega, like those of San Francisco de Macoris, Azua, and San José de las Matas, contain interesting material in spite of the lack of organization and the practically chaotic state in which they are now found.

In the towns of the interior there are some notary archives of great importance. Their collections fill in the void when local municipal archives are missing, because through the litigations between neighbors over property often an extensive amount of documentary material was produced concerning the living conditions of the people in the countryside, all of which is of great interest to the historian. There still is no inventory of these collections to provide a list of the communities which have available material.

57   The Church Archives of the Dominican Republic

Hugo Polanco Brito

The archives of the Catholic church in the Dominican Republic contain considerable material useful to historians, despite the damage caused by climate and natural disasters, along with political turmoil resulting in the loss of some materials. There is no central location within the nation; rather the materials are distributed throughout the country's various dioceses, with each maintaining its own records.

The most important collection is that of the archdiocese of Santo Domingo, reflecting both its status as the oldest diocese in the nation and its location in the capital city. The holdings include volumes of baptismal and marriage records beginning in 1590 and death records beginning in 1666. Separate records containing the same information are available for each of the parishes within the diocese. The years vary in accordance with the functioning of the parish. Records during the era of French domination are, of course, in French rather than Spanish.

The diocesan archives of the capital also include the Libros de Capellanias, covering the years 1732–1816. The volumes recording the action of the Cabildo Eclesiastico cover the years 1768 through 1858. Records of the ordination of priests cover the years 1820 through 1977, while marital dispensation records are available for the years 1827 through 1977. The records include the correspondence of the diocese with the nation's government and its clergy for the years 1859 through 1977. Also available are records of the creation of various parishes, confirmation records covering the years 1862 through 1977, and of the ecclesiastical government for the years 1858 through 1977. The Libros de Cuentas cover the years 1871 through 1977. There are also some records of the national cemetery and individual convents, though they are quite spotty and cover a narrow span of years. Correspondence with the apostolic delegates and nuncios are available for the years 1870 through 1883 and 1931 through 1977.

Among the archives' important holdings are the papers of the various bishops of the diocese. Of particular importance are those of Adolfo Alejandro Nouel and Fernando Arturo de Meriño, both of whom served as president of the republic. The papers in the ecclesiastical archives include their service as the head of the government. The archives also include the orders of the day of the French army in Santo Domingo for the years 1807–08.

307

Extensive records for each of the various parishes in the archdiocese are also available and many have never been utilized by researchers. They cover both the colonial and the modern era.

Extensive records also exist for the nation's second most important diocese, that of Santiago de los Caballeros. They can, of course, be found in the city of Santiago. As in the case of the archdiocese, they include the records of the diocese itself as well as those of its various parishes, filed by parish.

Similar collections are also available in the dioceses of La Vega, Higuey, San Juan de la Maguana, and Barahona. Again the dates reflect the functioning of the parishes and the dioceses.

Of special value is the library of the archdiocesan archivist, the author of this study, which can also be found at the archdiocesan archives. It includes a card file covering clerics who served in the nation for the years 1494 through 1977. This extensive card file is still being compiled and offers the most complete record available of clergy serving within the country. The collection also includes seventeen volumes of correspondence of General Francisco Gregorio Billini, five volumes of correspondence of a well-known diplomat, Licenciado Federico Llaverías, letters and documents of Monsignor Fernando Arturo de Meriño, and manuscripts dealing with the well-known poet Melinda Delgado Viuda de Panteleon.

58   The Archivo Nacional de Cuba
Louis A. Pérez, Jr.

The Archivo Nacional de Cuba is an imposing public building in an otherwise modest residential neighborhood in La Habana Vieja—a juxtaposition that confers on the archivo something of sovereignty over this section of the capital. The depository of the nation is located at Compostela and San Isidro, only blocks from the docks on the Ensenada de Atares in Havana Bay and the Central Railroad Station, and virtually around the corner from the birth place of José Martí. Monday through Friday and on every other Saturday during the hours of 8:30 A.M. to 12:30 P.M. and 1:30 P.M. to 6:00 P.M. the archive's main reading room fills with investigators, largely Cubans from the Academy of Sciences and the university, and writers and researchers from various government agencies. On any given day, the scene in the main reading room is one of scholarly serenity, with

a courteous and competent staff working in close collaboration with researchers.

But it was not always so. Indeed, the Archivo Nacional has had a rather
infelicitous history. During the early years of the republic, archival administration remained under Joaquín Llaverías. For years, Llaverías was an
indefatigable director, making up with zeal and commitment what he
could not obtain through government funds and public support. And while
these were not good times for the archivo, the worst was still to come. By
the 1940s and through the 1950s, the Archivo Nacional fell victim to the
wholesale political graft and administrative corruption that had come to
characterize Cuban public life. During these decades, the archivo lan-
guished somewhere between disregard and desuetude, important only as
a source of political appointments and partisan sinecures *(botellas)*. After
the revolution, the archivo passed through several reorganizations, and by
the late 1970s, it had found a new home under the authority of the Academy of Sciences, a relationship that has served to promote the professionalization of the archivo's staff and services.

The Archivo Nacional possesses an extensive and enormously diverse
collection of records. Consisting of some seventy-five different record
groups *(fondos)*, the document collections fully span the period between
the Spanish conquest and the Cuban Revolution. It is an uneven span, to
be sure, but one that nonetheless offers the investigator a rich assortment
of research materials. All records are loose and must be identified at the
time of request by citing the fondo, *legajo,* and document number. There
are few published guides to individual record collections;[1] the finding aids
to most fondos consist of card catalogues and typescript inventories, arranged either chronologically or by name and frequently cross-listed by
subject. The guides and inventories, located in the main reading room,
vary in quality and are often found waiting and incomplete.

Records are principally of official and semiofficial character, drawn
largely from government agencies and administrative offices. There are
some personal and family collections, including the papers of Máximo
Gómez, Calixto García, Francisco V. Aguilera, Jorge Quintana, and the
Valle Iznaga family. In the main, however, the large portion of the record
collections are governmental in nature. For the colonial period, these in-

1. The guides that are available are complete and enormously useful. See, for example,
Cuba, Archivo Nacional, *Catálogo de los fondos de Las Floridas* (La Habana, 1944);
Cuba, Archivo Nacional, *Catálogo de los fondos del Real Consulado de Agricultura, Industria y Comercio y de la Junta de Fomento* (La Habana, 1943); and Cuba, Archivo Nacional, *Inventorio general del archivo de la Delegación del Partido Revolucionaria Cubano
en Nueva York* (2 vols., La Habana, 1955–56).

clude such collections as the *audiencia* records, the Gobierno Superior Civil, the Real Consulado y Junta de Fomento, the Gobierno Autonómico (1898), and the Consejo de Administración. For the republican period, representative collections include Secretaria de Agricultura, Ministerio de Estado, the cabinet office of Presidencia, and records of the constitutional conventions of 1928 and 1940. The principal body of materials on deposit in the archivo for the period after 1959 consists of the early records of the Instituto Nacional de Reforma Agraria (INRA).

The principal strength of the archivo collections consists in the nineteenth-century materials, especially the years between 1868 and 1898, the decades of the Cuban struggle for independence. Almost all the fondos tend to be miscellaneous collections. There is, further, a considerable overlap of subjects, so that materials relevant to the subject of slavery, for instance, might well be located in any number of different record collections.

It is, lastly, important to stress that access to the Archivo Nacional is limited and possible only by prior authorization from the Academy of Sciences. Once permission has been extended, however, the archivo has no further control or limitation over the use of its collections other than the requirement that researchers complete a request form *(cargo)* identifying the document and giving the investigator's name, local address, and affiliation.

Researchers should be prepared to take notes by hand, although typewriters are permitted. Photocopying facilities are almost nonexistent, and use is severely limited. A snack bar in the basement is open to nonstaff researchers from 1:00 to 1:30 P.M. and from 3:15 to 3:30 P.M.

59   The Biblioteca Nacional de Cuba
Thomas Mathews

In December 1977 the distinguished Cuban historian Dr. Julio Le Riverand was appointed director of the Biblioteca Nacional, José Martí, in Havana, Cuba. At that point in time the library contained 610,000 volumes, somewhat less than three times the number of volumes (250,000) it contained at the time of the Castro Revolution, eighteen years before.

The largest source of the increase came from the private libraries taken over by the state from persons and families leaving Cuba. Approximately 400,000 volumes were acquired in this way, of which only 130,000 were incorporated into the collections and thus made available to the public as of 1978. Other private collections such as those of Antonio María Eligio de la Puente and don Fernando Ortiz have also been acquired by the National Library.

Of interest to the historians would of course be the vast Cuban Collection which, in addition to books, contains pamphlets, manuscripts, extensive and valuable collections of photographs, recordings, newspaper clippings, journals, and maps. Of the last category the famous Ponce de León Collection, which formerly had been stored in the Castillo de la Fuerza, is worthy of mention.

The Cuban Collection contains material covering the five centuries since the discovery of Cuba, but the bulk of the material comes from the nineteenth and twentieth centuries. In 1965 the library published a *Catálogo de publicaciones periódicos cubanos de los siglos XVIII y XIX*. More recently a second revised and extended edition has been prepared. Several important indices of Cuban periodicals have been published, covering the period from 1837 to 1878. The department of the Cuban Collection has also undertaken to compile the annual bibliography of works published in Cuba from 1959 to the present, as well as preparing a compilation of works appearing from 1911 (when Carlos M. Trelles ceased to publish his compilation) to 1937 (when Fermín Peraza initiated his *Anuario bibliográfico*).

60   Haiti
Henock Trouillot

The principal sources for Haitian history can be found in the national archives of Haiti. The Civil Affairs Section contains birth and death certificates, records regarding divorce decrees, and legal papers relating to adoption and the recognition of parentage. The official government records can be found in the Historical Archives Section, including the records of the local government and diplomatic correspondence. This section encompasses the official publications of the government, customs papers, documentation relating to budget matters, and the records of the various government institutions and ministries. It also contains a collection of newspapers, books, and journals.

Additional materials can be found in the national museum, which, in addition to collections of artifacts, contains a collection of books and journals dealing with Haiti. The ethnological museum contains the Andre Bistouri Library, which consists of rare publications concerning general ethnology and general social sciences. Many refer to the people and society of Haiti.

Data regarding the census of 1948 can be found in the Haitian Statistical Institute, which contains all information compiled in connection with the census. It also contains a great deal of material relating to commercial and industrial enterprises within the nation.

The Library of the Brothers of Christian Teaching is the most important private library in Haiti. It is open to the public and contains an extensive section of brochures, pamphlets, and books relating to all aspects of Haiti—its government, society, geography, and literature—as well as a collection of newspapers, journals, historical maps, and geological maps. This library also contains the Edmond Mangonés Collection, consisting of letters, papers, and historical documents relating to all aspects of Haitian life. The library is open to researchers during the morning, Monday through Thursday.

61   Guadeloupe
Jean-Paul Hervieu

The Archives of the Department of Guadeloupe were officially created by the prefectorial decree of August 23, 1951, implementing the ministerial decree of June 28, 1947, which extended to the French overseas departments, the metropolitan legislation in matters of archives.

For the previous period, only two accomplishments are worth noticing in the area of the protection of the public archives in Guadeloupe: the creation by the governors of a small service of archives (connected to their cabinet) designed to keep only the papers of the "government" offices and especially to bind the official gazettes, the government decrees, and the ministerial dispatches; and, secondly, the organization, following the decree of November 30, 1920, of a depository of public papers to preserve, starting only from 1912, the copies of the notarial records, the mortgage registers, and the decrees and judgments of the court and tribunals. For the previous period, these documents are preserved, in Paris, at the depository of overseas public papers connected to the Overseas Section of the National Archives.

Approximately from 1951 to 1960, the departmental archives strived particularly to gather together the papers of the different offices of the prefecture. Since 1960, their sphere of action has extended to all the public services and even to the notarial services, as the French regulation of the archives anticipates.

The archives are located in the former Orleans Barracks in Basse-Terre, and are open to researchers Monday through Friday from 7:30 A.M. to 12:45 P.M. and from 2:45 P.M. to 6:00 P.M., though closing Wednesday afternoons. Photocopy facilities and microfilm equipment are available at the archives. The mailing address is P.O. Box 74, 97102 Basse-Terre Cedex, Guadalupe.

The principal source material actually kept and accessible to researchers is divided into the following groups:

Ministerial dispatches, containing the correspondence addressed by the minister of the navy (later of the colonies) to governors of Guadeloupe. The letters were bound in registers (one to four per year) and date from 1826 to 1947. There also exists a register composed of copies of ministerial dispatches concerning the customs (1817–38).

Decrees and decisions of the governors and prefects, also bound in registers (one to twelve per year), beginning in 1894 and extending to 1963.

Source material of the Private Council of Guadeloupe and of the Council of Administrative Contentious Matters. These two organizations, which were suppressed in 1947, played, next to the governor, (1) the role of a consultative organ in the administration of the island, and (2) the part of an administrative jurisdiction. Their registers of deliberations and decisions date from 1826 to 1947.

Swedish source material of Saint-Barthélomew, containing the public archives of the island of St. Barthélemy during the Swedish period (1784–1878). These archives, very complete for the entire Swedish period, actually form several groups, including the papers of the governor, archives of the tribunal, of the customs (manifestos), and material records, etc. These archives were transferred to Basse-Terre for the most part in 1932 and the remainder in 1962, and in the same year received a summary classification. Temporarily this collection has been transferred to Aix-en-Provence for microfilming at the request of the Swedish Royal Archives. Upon completion the documents will be returned to Guadeloupe.

Mortgage (real estate transfer) registers, constitute a source of utmost importance for economic and social history. The registers start in 1811 for the district of Basse-Terre, in 1830 for those of Pointe-à-Pitre and St.-Martin, in 1857 for those of Marie-Galante, and in 1878 for St. Barthélemy.

Civil status registers, including baptisms, births, marriages, deaths, and burials for all the parishes in the department. These documents date back to 1714 for the parish of Trois-Rivières, 1726 for the island of St. Barthé-

lemy, and various dates for the other parish. The Archives of Guadeloupe have also a complete set (to 1871) of microfilm and photocopies of the registers of civil statistics of the parishes of Guadeloupe.
Notarial records starting in 1759 and extending to 1900. These archives are very important also for social and economic history.

After this enumeration of the principal *fonds* of the departmental archives of Guadeloupe, it is advisable not to neglect the "printed archives"—administrative publications of great importance for the history of the nineteenth and twentieth centuries: minutes of the deliberations of the colonial council, then of the General Council (from 1834 to the present), official bulletins, and gazettes and newspapers of Guadeloupe (from 1828 to the present).

The archives also have a very important set of microfilms reproducing papers relating to Guadeloupe, which are kept overseas mainly in Paris but also in London, Rome (the Vatican), Washington, D.C., and Stockholm, etc.

The archives preserve the manuscripts of the local historian Jules Ballet (1825–1904): nineteen volumes and ten files concerning the political, economic, and social history of the nineteenth century. For the seventeenth and eighteenth centuries, the works of Jules Ballet were published, in five volumes from 1890 to 1899, under the title *La Guadeloupe, Information on the History*.

An important historical reference library mainly on the West Indies is annexed to the archives. It includes books acquired since 1960, the works on the history of Guadeloupe, and local newspapers of the nineteenth and twentieth centuries. It constitutes at the present time the most complete historical library existing in Guadeloupe.

This general view of the documentary resources of the archival depositories of Guadeloupe will no doubt leave the reader perplexed: there are very few documents over one hundred years old and none before 1714. The explanation is simple: in addition to the destructive tropical climate, Guadeloupe has suffered wars, earthquakes, and cyclones, but the most important damages are due to the multiple fires, which, until recently, have destroyed the administrative services including, in the city of Basse-Terre alone, fires at the town hall (1905), the registry of the lower court (1918), the directories of the domains (1922), the registry of the higher court (1929), the office of the local assembly (1931), and even the archives (1955).

Since 1956, the warehouse of the archives has been protected from fire and is air conditioned. A new building will soon be constructed to preserve more effectively the historical patrimony of Guadeloupe.

62   Martinique
Liliane Chauleau

Constructed on the site of an ancient fort overlooking the roadstead of
Fort-de-France, the archives of Martinique are located at Tartenson: Road
of the Clairiere B.P. 649–97262 Fort-de-France. The archives are open
from 7:30 A.M. to 1:00 P.M., Monday through Friday, as well as from 3:00
P.M. to 6:30 P.M. on Tuesday, Wednesday, and Thursday. French readers
are admitted by presenting their identification card, while foreign readers
are admitted with proper identification. The archives contain about 4.0
linear kilometers of documents. Created in 1949, the service has salvaged
all that the tropical climate has spared. The principal holdings are from
the nineteenth and twentieth centuries. For the seventeenth and eighteenth
centuries the majority of the holdings consists of copies of documents kept
elsewhere, primarily in the National Archives of Paris.

A system of classification has been adopted fairly recently, which is
logically the same as that which exists in the whole of the French departmental archives. That is, the holdings (in French, *fonds*) are divided into
series, which are designated by the letters *A* through *Z*, with the series
from *A* through *H* representing the documents prior to the period of the
French Revolution (exactly 1790); the series *L* representing the documents
of the Revolution and the empire; the series *M* through *Z* representing the
documents for the nineteenth century (starting with 1814) and the twentieth century. Documents, arranged in chronological order within the alphabetical order of the series, include the records of the Sovereign Council—in series *B* from 1712 to 1790, in series *L* from 1790 to 1814, and in
series *U* starting from 1814. All are available to researchers. Created in
1645, the Sovereign Council had jurisdiction in matters of administration,
policy, finances, justice (as the court of last resort), and was the equivalent
of the parlement in France. The Sovereign Council registered the acts of
the king of France (concerning the Antilles) and those of the local administrators (the governor and the intendant). It also registered titles of nobility. In certain exceptional cases it exercised its right of remonstrance. It is
a source that has supplied much information about the history of the seventeenth century and particularly of the eighteenth century. An analytical
inventory for series *B*, covering the period until 1790, is available. During
the English occupation from 1794 to 1802 and from 1809 to 1814, the
Sovereign Council continued to sit. In the interval under the First French
Empire it received the name of Tribunal of Appeal then Court of Appeal,

and its jurisdiction was purely judiciary. The Sovereign Council was suppressed on November 22, 1819, and replaced by the Royal Court. The expression "Superior Council" persists, nevertheless, until 1820 in the registers of deliberations.

Series *E*, civil state, communal collection, and collection of Greffe, extends from the last quarter of the seventeenth century (1669 from the parish of Marin) to the second half of the nineteenth century, and is particularly valuable for the eighteenth century and the first half of the nineteenth century. Tables exist up until 1923 (1933 for Fort-de-France). For a given parish, the certificates of baptisms, marriages, and burials for the free population are generally regrouped in a single register. Some registers for the nineteenth century concern the slaves. The nineteenth-century holdings, particularly the date of the abolition of slavery in 1848, contain registers (called *dits*) of individuality, which conferred a civil state on the newly liberated slaves. These registers permit studies of demography and social history.

Records for the period prior to the end of the First Empire of Napoleon I include the general correspondence of the administrators of Martinique to the Ministry of the Marine; the seventeenth-century series *J*, a photocopy of series C^8A, is kept at the National Archives in Paris. For an indication of its holdings, consult Etienne Taillemite, *Inventory of the Series Colonies C^8A Martinique* . . . (2 vols., Paris, 1967–71).

The archives contain a complete set of microfilm of the *Official Journal of Martinique* for the period 1834–1947 (microfilms on side 2 Mi 1 to 109). This journal contains information on the economy, administrative and cultural life, as well as information on the foreign Antilles (Jamaica, Barbados, etc.).

The *Official Bulletin of Martinique* (1828–1940), which records the ordinances, decrees, and official decisions, is also available. The Private Council records (subseries 5 *K*) are available up to 1940. Created first in 1825 on the island of Bourbon (the actual Reunion), the Private Council was established in Martinique by the royal ordinances of August 21, 1825, and January 2, 1826. It included members of the administration (the governor, the director of the interior, the general procurator, and the inspector of the administrative and financial services) as well as two inhabitants. It considered reports of the local accountants, along with the adjunction of two magistrates and the Council of Contentious Administrative Matters, and is now called the Council of Disputed Claims. Its records, the fonds (approximately 173 articles, i.e., bound volumes or packets of documents) (1826–1943), include the deliberations (1827–1943) with tables (1826–1900). The archives of the Council of Contentious Administrative Matters, the register of decrees and appeals to the Council of State, are also available for the years 1854–1918. These contain records of the administration of the patrimony of Martinique, its works and equipment.

The General Council, created in 1827, became the Colonial Council from 1833 to 1847, and then again the General Council in 1847. Suppressed in 1848, it was reestablished in 1854. It had as its mission to deliberate and to give its advice on local affairs. It benefited also from financial powers, which were reduced in 1841 but extended again in 1866. The minutes of the meetings of this council from 1835 to 1961 can be found in subseries 1 *N*. Records of the General Council (1858–1961) (approximately two hundred volumes) include miscellaneous reports and booklets up to 1887. The Registry of Mortgages (subseries 3 *Q*) is available for public consultation at the end of one hundred years. The preservation of mortgages was established in Martinique by a decree in 1805, was organized by the royal ordinance of 1829, and modified on July 7, 1856, for the transcription of mortgages. The fonds comprise approximately one thousand registers, dating from 1806. They are especially important for the history of houses and real estate.

The judicial organization records are available to the public after one hundred years. The records of the following departments are available: Council of Appeals (subseries 2 *U*)—sentences, hearings, appeals for reversals of judgment (starting from 1829, with a few items from 1814); Assize Court (also subseries 2 *U*)—sentences (1829–80); country court (subseries 3 *U*)—Fort-de-France, civil and commercial judgments (starting from 1822), hearings, diverse affairs (nineteenth century), correctional role (twentieth century), etc., Saint-Pierre; judgments (1875–94). Justice of the peace (subseries 4 *U*) (starting from 1923); Tribunal of Commerce (subseries 6 *U*)—some documents (1835–1936); provost court (subseries 7 *U*)—one register (1822–27).

Liliane Chauleau, *Guide to the Archives of Martinique*, prepared by the director, describes the collection of preserved fonds.

63   The Netherlands Antilles Archive
Jaap van Soest

Most of the governmental documents on the history of Curaçao during the period from approximately 1848 to 1938 can be found in the Central Historical Archive (CHA) on Curaçao. Despite the absence of an archive statute, the documents are found in a fair-sized storage area and are under the management of responsible people. The documents are open to the public. Among other things, one finds here the governor's annual report to the minister of colonies in the Netherlands, where it was also printed (1848–1953). The report was accompanied by a number of statistical records. Until 1930 the reports and statistics were recorded in the supplement to the *Handelingen der Staaten-General* (Proceedings of the States General). Since 1932 they have been published separately. The quality of the reports is inconsistent; in some reports it is noticeable that the governor or a number of top officials were not present during a specific period. The reliability of the statistical records is also uncertain. Since 1951 the series of reports was succeeded by the *Verslag von het Eilandgebied Curaçao* (Report of the Island Administration of Curaçao) (1951–52, 1953–73).

The series of printed documents from the Colonial Council, later the State of Curaçao, and even later the States of the Netherlands Antilles, all form an important collection. They contain projects for land regulation and inspection, their written proceedings by the governor and Council/States, and their oral discussions (minutes of the Colonial Council/States). The laws were published in the *Publicatie Blad* (Official Record), which also contained some of the hundreds of government decisions (called original government decisions) which were adopted yearly. The *Publicatie Blad* is accessible through Noordenbos' systematical description of its content. Unfortunately, there is (still) no similar inventory of the bundles wherein all the governmental decisions were annually combined.

A third important arsenal of data is found in hundreds of folders at the CHA where only the principal documents that relate to certain subjects are filed. In all, it forms an artificial archive that might seem strange to professional archivists but facilitates the researcher's first stages of investigation. An index makes this collection of documents easily accessible.

Two collections that were just recently transferred to the CHA are the archives from the Curaçao Mortgage Bank N.V. and the Savings and Loan Bank of Curaçao N.V. One finds further in the CHA a small collection of documents from the Curaçao Association of Hatmakers, Arbeit Adelt. Numerous printed works that one seldom or never comes across in libraries are available here.

At the Central Bureau for the Registration of Archives (Centraal Bureau voor Registratuur en Archifzaken) (CBRA) are records which, on the whole, date back from the present to 1940, although a relatively large number of files extend further into the past. Divided between static and dynamic archives, the documents are grouped into subject files, which are based on a decimal system. Both archives, which are not easily available to outsiders, can be consulted only with the special permission of the prime minister of the Netherlands Antilles. There is further a secret archive which, quantitatively speaking, is not very extensive. Subjects which one frequently comes across in the files of the static archives are, among others, agriculture, water supply, housing, trade, prices, harbors, tourism, aviation, and West Indian cooperation.

Generally speaking, departments, services, and businesses of both the national and island governments do not have archives for the period preceding 1955. The Department of Real Estate Management on Curaçao is an exception. It has at its disposal the title deeds from plantations and other properties, which are sometimes more than two centuries old. They are well kept but should be considered for preservation. At the Department of Public Works mountains of files and documents, many from the last quarter of the nineteenth century, are rotting away without anyone paying attention. The national government's Office of Land Registry owns a good collection of old maps.

In contrast to Curaçao, a fair amount of material about the nineteenth and early twentieth centuries is still present in an island government office on Aruba; presently an inventory is being made of this collection. The principal records from Bonaire, St.-Martin, Saba, and St. Eustatius were immediately brought over to the Central Historical Archive of the Netherlands Antilles on Curaçao, although incidentally, parts of the documents are still found in an extremely neglected condition on the said islands.

The General Audit Office for the Netherlands Antilles has been established only since 1953. Before then, control was exercised from the Netherlands. The archives concerned are not found on Curaçao. Also the General Military Command Archive, an important source for the history of the Netherlands Antilles during World War II, is located at the Department of Defense in the Netherlands.

All the original sources from the Chamber of Commerce and Industry were destroyed by a fire. A typescript summary exists for the period 1884–1922 ("Jaarverslag van de Kamer can Koophandel, 1884–1922"). The reports from 1906 until 1918 were published in the *Curaçao Courant*. Thereafter, they were printed separately. First of all, they contain an almost exclusive view of the economic life, often in literally the same words as one finds in the Colonial Reports; later on copies of correspondence, minutes of meetings, and texts of speeches were included.

Between the public sector and the business archives, some private collections such as the Curaçao Museum and the S. A. L. Maduro Foundation are worth mentioning.

The search for business records from Curaçao enterprises, especially in the commercial sector, is a time-consuming occupation which offers little satisfaction. Almost every businessman begins by denying that he has more than one piece of paper which is older than ten years. After repeated conversations he will admit that he had searched the night before but could not find anything. The manner in which he makes the statement leaves no doubt as to the sincerity of businessmen. In the absence of evidence to the contrary, our preliminary conclusion is that virtually no records for Curaçao enterprises exist.

The big exception to the above is S. A. L. Maduro & Sons, the oldest of the still-existing Curaçao trade houses. A small number of documents, called the *Grootboeken* (Great Books), is well preserved and has been kept in a safe since 1837. The annual balances of profit-and-loss reckonings, both in the books and the accountant reports, contain interesting data. A curious volume is the one entitled and containing hundreds of Important Letters of Praise, 1900–1938. The greater part of the documents, which is housed elsewhere, shows signs of fire damage. Although a lot appears to have been lost, it would be well worth making an inventory of the remains.

Among the business archives under Dutch supervision, the Shell Curaçao N. V. (SCNV), which includes the records from the legal predecessors of CPM and CPIM and the daughter company CSM, should be mentioned first. It is without a doubt the most extensive and well-organized business archive on Curaçao. In 1973 the board of directors for the first time granted access to the documents to an outsider, with the exception of the rather extensive secret archive, which is said to contain hardly any older materials.

The Shell archive has relatively little data on the period prior to 1930. These data are found primarily in the Netherlands at the head office of Shell International Oil Company in the department General Archive. The most important source on Curaçao about this period is the monthly refinery reports, where all personnel, financial, technical, commercial, etc., aspects are described in detail. They were begun in July 1918. Moreover, since 1930 a mimeographed summary has been published as an annual report, just like the monthly reports, though intended for internal use and factually just as trustworthy.

Other businesses of Dutch origin or with main offices in the Netherlands have less to offer than Shell. Some of them no longer control relevant archives, while others are not interested in research. Among them are the NIGM/OGEM (which provided Curaçao with electricity from 1927 to 1977), the KNSM Group (which constitutes the principal shipping connection between the Netherlands and the Antilles since the nineteenth century), the Curaçao Trading Company (which has operated between Amsterdam and Curaçao since 1890), and the Curaçao Mining Company (which under peculiar circumstances let its Curaçao archives burn some years ago).

The Lago Oil and Transport Company on Aruba is the principal non-Dutch industry. It is a branch of the Exxon Group, which refuses anyone access to its records, so nothing can be said about the quantity or the quality of this collection.

The Bank of the Netherlands Antilles, formerly the Curaçao Bank, is the oldest of the banks. The archive is fairly complete; several series go back to 1828. Until 1906 the bank published only a few yearly statistics in the Colonial Report or in a supplement to it. Since 1926 the yearly report was published separately.

The Savings and Loan Bank of Curaçao N.V. has a fairly complete series of books since its establishment in 1850, but the remaining papers are in a chaotic state. A provisional inventory has recently been made.

Just like the Savings and Loan Bank, the Curaçao Mortgage Bank N.V. (of 1875) has put its old archive roughly in order and transferred it to the CHA. In general, the documents have been well preserved.

Maduro & Curiels Bank, the oldest commercial bank, cannot open its archives for research or give access to the archives of its predecessors, the Maduro Bank and the Curiel Bank. The same applies to the older commercial banks.

Literature about the Netherlands Antilles can be found, first of all, in ordinary hand libraries such as the public libraries of Curaçao and Aruba (where publications sometimes seem to disappear) and the Library of the Academy of the Netherlands Antilles (which was founded recently). The most important private collection is from the late S. A. L. (Shon Mongui) Maduro; whoever seeks rare printed works has the best chance of succeeding here. A second good source is the library of the friar on Pietermaai, which is not easy to consult because it lacks an inventory.

64   The Netherlands
Harmannus Hoetink

The principal depository for Dutch history is also the location of the most important material regarding the Dutch rule of the Netherlands Antilles. Any researcher will find it necessary to start in the General State Archives (Algemeen Rijksarchief), located at Prins Willem Alexanderhof 20 in The Hague.

The principle files relating to the Netherlands Antilles and Suriname include the archives of the States General (1576–1796); the archives of the Admiralty boards (1586–1795); the archives of the office of the secretary to the stadholder, especially a special collection, West Indian Affairs (1747–95); the archives of the first West India Company (1621–74); the archives of the second West India Company (1674–1795); the archives of the Direction *ad interim* of the West Indian Colonies and of the Council of the Colonies in the West Indies; the archives of the Society of Suriname (1683–1795); the archives of the Direction of Berbice (1720–95); a collection of miscellaneous West Indian documents; and the archives of Suriname (1669–1828) (comprising the archives of the Government Secretariat of the Colony of Suriname [1684–1824]). Inventories for all of the above are available at the General State Archives.

The same depository also contains the archives of the Policy Council (1669–80); the Council of Policy and Justice (1680–83); and the Court of Policy and Criminal Justice (1684–1828); as well as the Military Court Martial in Suriname and the archives of the Petty Council of Suriname (1778–1828); the archives of the Council of Justice (1669–89); the archives of the Court of Civil Justice (1689–1828); the archives of the Netherlands-Portuguese Israelitic Community in Suriname (1662–1909); the archives of the governor general of the Netherlands West Indian possessions (1828–45) (during which period Suriname and the present Netherlands Antilles were united under one governor general); the governmental archives of Curaçao, including the dependent islands of Aruba, Bonaire, St.-Martin, Saba, and St. Eustatius, divided into the period prior to 1828 and the period 1828–45; and a large number of family archives and sundry collections.

Additional files of use to the historian include the archives of the Ministry of Colonies (1796–1813); the archives of the general state secretariat and of the king's cabinet (1813–97) (inventory in manuscript); the archives of the Ministry of Foreign Affairs (1813–70) (inventory in manuscript); the archives of the Ministry of the Colonies (1814–70); and the archives of the States of Holland and West Friesland and of their delegate councils (1572–1795) (inventory in manuscript).

Material pertaining to the period of British intervention (1802–16) in Suriname is to be found in the Public Record Office, London. Similarly, materials pertaining to the French annexation of the Netherlands Antilles (1810–13) are to be found in the National Archives, Paris.

The Archives of the Ministry of Foreign Affairs, 10 Casuariestraat, The Hague, cover the period 1870–1918. They are open for the years prior to 1918, but material relating to the post-1918 era may be used for research purposes only after permission of the secretary of foreign affairs has been granted.

The State Archives of Zeeland, 38 St. Pietersstraat, Middelburg, contain the archives of the States of Zeeland and their preceding and succeeding bodies (1574–1799) (printed inventory) and the archives of the Middelburg Commercial Company (1720–1889) (printed inventory). The State Archives of North Holland, 12 Caeciliasteeg, Haarlem, contain notarial archives of great importance to the trade on the West Indian islands in the first half of the seventeenth century (inventory in manuscript). The Municipal Archives of Amsterdam, 67 Amsteldijk, Amsterdam, contain the Resolutions of the Municipal Council (1536–1795) (notarial archives, 1578–1842); the archives of the Dutch Reformed church, Amsterdam (1572–1816); and the archives of the Portuguese-Israelitic Community, Amsterdam (1614–1870). The State Archives of Utrecht, 27 Drift, Utrecht, contain the archives of the Moravian Brethren (Hernhutter Church), of great importance to Suriname after 1750, and correspondence to the Moravian Brethren. The Archives of the Netherlands Missionary Corporation (Protestant), 11 Leidsestraatweg, Oegstgeest, contains some material pertaining to the Dutch West Indies (1797–1927).

Published bibliographies providing information regarding the archival sources dealing with this area can be found in M. P. H. Roessingh, *Guide to the Sources in the Netherlands for the History of Latin America* ('s-Gravenhage, 1968); and M. A. P. Meilink-Roelofsz, "A Survey of Archives in the Netherlands Pertaining to the History of the Netherlands Antilles," *De West Indische Gids*, 35 (1955): 1–38; as well as J. Felhoen Kraal, "Libraries and Archives for Research in West Indian History," *De West Indische Gids*, 37 (1957): 71–92.

65   The Danish and Swedish Archives
Ove Hornby

Both Denmark and Sweden have on a modest scale appeared as colonial powers in the Caribbean region, and archival sources in Scandinavia focus on these colonial possessions. The Danes established themselves on the island of St. Thomas in 1671, assumed control of St. John in 1718, and purchased St. Croix from the French in 1733, holding them until their sale to the United States in 1917. From the Swedes there came a number of unsuccessful colonization projects throughout the eighteenth century, centered around the Barima region in British Guiana and the island of Tobago. However, in 1784 the island of St. Barthélemy was acquired from France, and, for a brief period during the Napoleonic Wars (1813–14), Guadeloupe was also in Swedish hands. In 1877–78 France regained St. Barthélemy by purchase.

Excellent presentations of the history of the Danish West Indian posses-
sions are readily available. The extant source groups contain good and in
many respects still-unexplored possibilities for following the Danish and
Swedish colonies' economic, social, and internal political development.
Obvious fields for future research would particularly be the function of St.
Thomas and St. Barthélemy as entrepôt centers for a large part of the
Caribbean trade at the end of the eighteenth century and beginning of the
nineteenth, while the cycle of the plantation system can be closely ob-
served on St. Croix. A large amount of material is available, too, for
illuminating the course and final abolition of slave trade and slavery in the
Danish possessions.

The Danish State Archives, Rigsarkivet (Rigsdagsgården, DK-1218
København K), contain the collections from the central administration,
and a large part of the source groups are specified in the registration guides
that the archives constantly prepare and publish. Until 1754 the islands
were administered by the Danish West India and Guinea Company under
the sovereignty of the Crown. Both the Copenhagen records and those
sent to Denmark by company officials are fully registered in *Asiatiske,
vestindiske og guineiske handelskompagnier* (Archive register guide XIV)
(København, 1969), which also has an index of the surviving source material from the Royal Danish Chartered West Indies Trading Company
(1778–1816). In 1754 the Danish state assumed control of the West Indian
possessions which were administered first through the West India and
Guinea Department of the Exchequer (1754–60)—see *Rentekammeret I*
(Archive register guide XII) (København, 1964)—and later by the West
India and Guinea General Custom House and Department of the Exchequer (1760–1816) and the General Custom House and Board of Trade
(1816–48). Unfortunately, so far only a summary and out-of-date register
exist of the extensive source material from this period in *Rentekammeret,
Generaltoldkammeret og Kommercekollegiet, 1660–1848* (Archive register guide II) (København, 1892). From 1848 to 1917 West Indian matters
were dealt with by a central colonial committee, which came within the
sphere of the Ministry of Finance; see *Koloniernes Centralbestyrelse* (Archive register guide XX) (København, 1975), which also contains an instructive survey of the history of the West Indian central administration.
In addition to the above-mentioned main, responsible authorities, other
central authorities also handled particular economic, military, religious,
and external political aspects in connection with the Danish possession of
the islands (see, for example, G. F. Tyson, Jr., *The Historical Records of
the U.S. Virgin Islands: A Report and Program Plan* [St. Thomas, 1977]).
The Danish State Archives also contain the primary material of the West
Indian censuses from 1841 onwards and the local administration's exten-

sive records, which were brought to Denmark after the sale of the islands. The latter are exceedingly difficult to use for research purposes, because of an almost complete absence of restoration and registration.

The Provincial Archives of Zealand (Landsarkivet for Sjaelland) (Jagtvej 10, DK-2200 København N), contain the parish-register material from the West Indian Lutheran-Evangelical congregations from 1740 onwards and from the Dutch Reformed congregation on St. Croix (1776–1814). The Danish National Business Archives (Erhvervsarkivet) (Vester Allé 12, DK-8000 Arhus C) contain records from a number of Danish trading houses that during the nineteenth century and at the beginning of the twentieth were trading with the Caribbean area and the Danish West Indies in particular. In the Danish National Library (Det Kongelige Bibliotek) (Christians Brygge 8, DK-1219 København K), a great amount of West Indian material is to be found in the map and picture collections.

The Swedish sources on the history of the Caribbean (and the whole of Latin America) are extensively registered in the indispensable aid to the interested researcher, M. Mörner, *Fuentes para la historia de Ibero-América* (Stockholm, 1968), which, in spite of the title, predominantly deals with those materials extant in Sweden, although the work concludes with a brief survey, "Sources for the history of Latin America in the Danish National Archives." Virtually all surviving material from the colonial administration is to be found in the Swedish National Archives (Riksarkivet) (Fack, S-100 26 Stockholm), which include the archive of the Swedish West Indian Trading Company, the administrator of St. Barthélemy from 1786 to 1805, as well as the special Barthélemy and Guadeloupe collections. However, some material, including that from the so-called Colonial Ministry (1816–45), has entered other collections; the same is true of the records from the local Swedish administration on St. Barthélemy, which were only rediscovered in 1961 and are now stored in Guadeloupe (see Jean-Paul Hervieu's essay, chapter 61). Sources for Sweden's West Indian colonial projects are to be found in Uppsala University Library (Box 510, S-751 20 Uppsala) and in the manuscript collection at the Swedish National Library (Kungliga Biblioteket) (Box 5039, S-102 41 Stockholm), which also possesses a large map and picture collection.

In addition to the above-mentioned collections from the colonial period, the Danish and Swedish consular reports from the Caribbean area are of particular interest for research. Additional information about these groups of materials is most readily obtained by application to the above-mentioned institutions or to the Institute of Latin American Studies (Latinamerika-institutet) (Odéngatan 61, Fack, S-102 30 Stockholm), which functions as the secretariat for the Nordic Joint Committee on Latin American Research (NOSALF).

The English-Speaking Caribbean

East Indians in the West Indies
Research Possibilities
Brinsley Samaroo

In recent years there has been considerable interest in the movement of peoples into and within the Caribbean area. This interest has found expression, particularly in relation to the African experience, in a number of useful studies.[1] Over this period too, much interest has been shown in the life of the East Indians who were brought to the region as part of the planters' attempt to solve the labor problem created in the immediate aftermath of slave emancipation. However, this interest has manifested itself primarily at the popular level. Published scholarly work in the field is limited.

This is not to say, however, that the field is devoid of important ongoing research. Significant work has been done on the East Indians of Guadeloupe[2] and Suriname.[3] Dwarka Nath's book on East Indians in Guyana is a mine of statistical information, although it lacks analysis.[4] More useful from the analytical point of view is Professor Jayawardena's study compiled after much fieldwork.[5] This general interest in Caribbean East Indians has stimulated some other interesting writing. Vidia Naipaul in his novels has attempted to re-create the East Indian experience in Trinidad from the late nineteenth and early twentieth centuries;[6] he has also looked at the acculturation of the East Indian into a Western environment in his *Mimic Men* (London, 1967) and in "A Christmas Story" (in *Flag on an Island* [London, 1969]). He has proceeded to look at India and its cultural influence on the Caribbean East Indian.[7] Similarly Sam Selvon, another East Indian–West Indian writer, has taken a contemporary look at East

1. See, for example, Philip D. Curtin, *The Atlantic Slave Trade* (Madison, 1969); Laura Foner and Eugene D. Genovese, eds., *Slavery in the New World: A Comparative Reader* (Englewood Cliffs, New Jersey, 1969); and Vera Rubin and Arthur Tudin, eds., *Comparative Perspectives on Slavery in New World Plantation Societies* (New York, 1977).

2. Singaravelou, *Les Indiens de Guadelupe* (Pointe-à-Pitre, Guadeloupe, 1975). See also Singaravelou, "Indian Religion in Guadeloupe," *Caribbean Issues*, 2, 3(1976).

3. J. D. Speckmann, *Marriage and Kinship among the Indians in Surinam* (Assen, 1965).

4. Dwarka Nath, *A History of Indians in Guyana* (London, 1970).

5. C. Jayawardena, *Conflict and Solidarity in a Guyanese Plantation* (London, 1963).

6. See, for example, V. S. Naipaul, *The Suffrage of Elvira* (London, 1958); also, *A House for Mr. Biswas* (London, 1961).

7. V. S. Naipaul, *An Area of Darkness* (London, 1964).

Indian life in central Trinidad.[8] Trinidad East Indians have been the subject of specialized treatment by a number of United States scholars.[9] More recently, local researchers have been writing on the same topic.[10] East Indian adaptation to the ecosystem in Jamaica, as well as their integration into the larger society, has engaged the attention of at least one serious scholar;[11] and cultural survivals among these people are being studied, aptly, by two academics who derive from the major nineteenth-century labor-recruitment area of Uttar Pradesh in northeastern India.[12] Similarly, some exploratory work is being pursued in relation to East Indians in Grenada.[13] There has been considerable publishing on the general theme of East Indians in the Caribbean,[14] with some interesting theses in areas which relate to their activities in the region.[15]

The need for additional research and publication is now underlined by a number of interesting developments in the Caribbean region. First, as Caribbean states with substantial numbers of East Indians have moved toward independence, the problems of pluralistic societies have become increasingly complex. For this reason carefully researched studies of East

8. Sam Selvon, *The Plains of Caroni* (London, 1970).

9. Morton Klass, *East Indians in Trinidad, a Study of Cultural Persistence* (New York, 1961); Judith Weller, *The East Indian Indenture in Trinidad* (Río Piedras, Puerto Rico, 1968); Y. Malik, *East Indians in Trinidad: A Study of Minority Politics* (London, 1971); also, Arthur and Juanita Niehoff, *East Indians in the West Indies* (Milwaukee, 1960).

10. K. Bahadursingh, *Trinidad Electoral Politics: The Persistence of the Race Factor* (London, 1968); also, John La Guerre, ed., *Calcutta to Caroni: The East Indians of Trinidad* (Port of Spain, Trinidad, 1974).

11. Allen Ehrlich, "History, Ecology and Demography in the British Caribbean: An Analysis of East Indian Ethnicity," *South Western Journal of Anthropology,* 27 (1971): 164–75, and "East Indian Integration in Rural Jamaica," *Actes du XLIIe Congrès Internationale des Américanistes* (Paris, 1977). Also by the same author, "East Indian Cane Workers in Jamaica," Ph.D. dissertation (University of Michigan, 1969).

12. L. Mansingh and A. Mansingh, "Indian Heritage in Jamaica," *Jamaica Journal,* 10, 2,3,4(1976). This article is illustrated by useful photographs depicting East Indian life in Jamaica.

13. See B. Steele, "East Indian Indenture and the Work of the Presbyterian Church among the Indians in Grenada," *Caribbean Quarterly,* 22, 1(March 1976).

14. For example, *Caribbean Quarterly,* 22, 1(March 1976) is almost wholly devoted to this theme, as is *Caribbean Issues,* 2, 3(December 1976). See also B. Brereton and W. Dookeran, eds., *East Indians in the Caribbean* (Millwood, New York, 1982).

15. For example, S. Basdeo, "Labour Organisation and Labour Reform in Trinidad, 1919–1937," Ph.D. dissertation (Dalhousie University, 1975); G. Tikasingh, "The Establishment of the East Indians in Trinidad, 1870–1900," Ph.D. dissertation (University of the West Indies, St. Augustine, Trinidad, 1976); T. Ramnarine, "The Growth of the East Indian Community in British Guiana," Ph.D. dissertation (Sussex University, 1977); D. Bisnauth, "The East Indian Immigrant Society in British Guiana, 1891–1930," Ph.D. dissertation (University of the West Indies, Mona, Jamaica, 1977).

Indian attitudes toward politics, the interrelationship between secular and ecclesiastical matters in Hinduism and Islam, and the "host/guest" relationship in some Caribbean societies can do much to ease tension in Guyana, Trinidad, or Suriname.[16] In addition, the search for roots has become a quest of major concern for Caribbean peoples, and in this quest young East Indians are second to none. This has certainly led to a revival of cultural traditions among East Indians in the region. Even among as small a community as the East Indians in Jamaica (3.5 percent of the total population), the revival can be seen in such activities as a reversion to Hindu and Moslem names, an Indian cultural program on radio, which lasted for ten years prior to 1976, an increase in Jamaican East Indians studying in India, and the formation of an Indo-Jamaican Cultural Society in 1978, one of whose aims is to "preserve and promote the essentials of Indian culture and philosophy."[17] Surely it ought to be one of the purposes of Caribbean scholarship to provide guidelines to those who seek to understand themselves by knowing their past. There is, finally, a genuine demand from the non–East Indian sector of Caribbean society to learn more about East Indians; the subject now finds itself in secondary school and university courses and in increasing media coverage. Researchers should be concerned to satisfy this demand.

What, then, are some of the areas still in need of research? First, historians must bring sociological, political, and anthropological insights to bear on the life of East Indians in the Caribbean. Secondly, because far more work has been done in relation to the smaller Christian East Indian communities than to the larger Hindu and Moslem groups,[18] historians must examine the latter. This focus reflects the fact that the Christian churches which came to work among East Indians had government support and active encouragement from the time of their arrival, whereas non-Christian groups did not enjoy support until the mid-twentieth century. Consequently, the Christians were able to organize their records efficiently and could expand their activities, while the non-Christians were handicapped. Nevertheless, there existed a powerful movement of cultural ac-

16. Two useful initial works in this area are Paul Singh, *Guyana: Socialism in a Plural Society* (London, 1972); and Selwyn Ryan, *Race and Nationalism in Trinidad and Tobago* (Toronto, 1972).

17. See "Indo-Jamaican Cultural Society" (Kingston, 1978), leaflet.

18. For example, J. B. Harricharan, "History of the Catholic Church in Trinidad to 1852," M.A. thesis (University of the West Indies, St. Augustine, Trinidad, 1976) offers a discussion of the work of Roman Catholics among East Indians. For the work of the Canadian missionaries, see Graeme S. Mount, *Presbyterian Missions to Trinidad and Puerto Rico, 1868–1914* (Hantsport, Nova Scotia, 1983); and also C. Alexander Dunn, "The Canadian Mission in British Guiana: The Pioneer Years, 1885–1927," M.A. thesis (Queen's University, Kingston, Ontario, 1971).

tivity accompanied by the establishment of Hindu and Moslem schools, places of worship, and welfare organizations.

Researching such activities involves interviewing scores of older people and laboriously collecting scattered data from pamphlets, religious tracts, and newspapers, many of which are held in peoples' homes. This search often leads to "adoption" of the researcher by East Indian families over extended periods, so that information can be obtained in a situational setting; and, for those prepared to work in this manner, the rewards have been significant. Robert Jack Smith was "adopted" by a Moslem family in the Charlieville district of the Caroni plains, and from this vantage point was able to trace the life cycle of a Moslem in Trinidad.[19] His work is also useful as a study in the development of Moslem organizations in Trinidad. Angrosino, during his research, lived with a family near Princes Town in central Trinidad—a major sugar cane area—and his insights into East Indian family organization reflect an understanding of and real sympathy for the problems of the people with whom he worked.[20]

An understanding of the development of the East Indian community in the Caribbean will certainly be enhanced by research into India, from which the indentured immigrants came, particularly the economic and cultural milieu in which they operated. From such a study it should be possible to appreciate the East Indian attachment to the land, which the Indians have elevated into their pantheon of deities (calling it Dharti Mata). A better understanding of the plants and the skills which they introduced to the region and of the inability of the traditional Indian to see any separation between the religious and the political spheres of life is also needed. In addition, there is no satisfactory account of the experience of the East Indian immigrants on board ship, particularly as this changed social relations, a process which continued long after the *jahajis* (shipmates) had completed the crossing. There is no study of resistance to the indenture system or indeed of the larger movement for the abolition of indentureship.

For historians who are interested in more recent events, there is considerable scope. A full-length study of the role of the East Indians in Guyanese politics is clearly needed. So too is a study of the activities of East Indians at the level of local government both in Trinidad and in Guyana. East Indian participation in the region's trade union movement offers another significant potential, particularly in view of the close connection between trade unionism and politics in the life of Caribbean peoples. To

19. Robert J. Smith, "Muslim East Indians in Trinidad: Retention of Ethnic Identity under Acculturative Conditions," Ph.D. dissertation (University of Pennsylvania, 1963).

20. Michael Angrosino, "Outside Is Death: Alcoholism, Ideology and Community Organization among East Indians in Trinidad," Ph.D. dissertation (University of North Carolina, 1972).

what extent have East Indians seen their trade union activities in terms of race rather than of class? And how have East Indian leaders in the trade union movement been regarded by the non–East Indian sector of the population? Given the dynamic state of regional politics, is there the emergence of new East Indian leadership, and if so, how do these new leaders differ from the traditional ones? There has been a considerable amount of pamphleteering on this subject and some basic analysis,[21] but generally the field is wide open.

There is also the question of the economic organization of the East Indian in the new environment. What was the input of the indentured East Indians in terms of semi-industrial skills, such as pottery, weaving, irrigation, jewelry, and banking? What new modes of production and attitudes to work and to profit did they bring from the ancestral land? From this survey the researcher must turn to look at the ways in which the free East Indians transformed themselves from virtual slavery to wage earners and later to manufacturers and entrepreneurs. In this connection, studies must be continued particularly in relation to sugar and rice—those areas of production in which the East Indian contribution has been most pronounced.[22] These studies should deal not only with the economics of production and ownership but equally with workers' organizations, conditions of life on the estates, and the educational and cultural activities in these sugar belts and rice belts. There is much debate at present among Caribbean academics, politicians, and government planners, focusing on the question of a shift from sugar cultivation to other forms of land use, using customary sugar lands.

The East Indian family demands attention. The indenture system played a major role in the breakdown of the extended family, which existed in the ancestral villages, since indentureship placed a premium on men, not on women. Indeed, at best there were never more than forty women to every hundred men, and this resulted not only in family breakdown but also in extreme pressure upon the few available women, often culminating in infidelity and wife murders. By the end of the nineteenth century, as the proportion of women increased through natural growth, East Indians attempted to re-create the extended family, but without much success. Faced by such socializing tendencies as Western/Christian values, the extended family slowly disintegrated and was replaced by the nuclear family. As a facet of East Indian life in the Caribbean, this needs to be examined.

Birth, initiation, and death rites—all important features of family life

21. For example, "Indian Leadership in the Indenture Period," *Caribbean Issues*, 2, 3(1976).
22. D. Maharaj, "Canefarming in the Trinidad Sugar Industry," Ph.D. dissertation (University of Edinburgh, 1969).

among the East Indians—urgently demand investigation. In this connection too is the crucial role played by East Indian women in the development of East Indian society in the region. Like the African woman who preceded her, the East Indian woman was far more than mother to her children and wife to her husband. She was a laborer in the field, a refuge to which the slave or indentured Indian would go for support, and often a participant in the movement of resistance against the brutalities of the plantation. In a male-oriented society, historians have tended to neglect the revolutionary role played by East Indian women.

Other worthwhile subjects of investigation are East Indian pressure groups and religious organizations as they have been functioning since the late nineteenth century. Generally neglected by the larger society except when their labor was required, non-Christian East Indians had to fend for themselves to a large degree. This they did by banding together in organizations such as the East Indian National Association, or the East Indian National Congress in Trinidad, or the British Guiana East Indian Association. There is evidence of correspondence and of mutual visits between these groups in Trinidad and Guyana and the formulation of common programs of activity. These associations tended to include Hindus, Moslems, and even Christian Indians, and they campaigned for the abolition of indentureship, recognition of Hindu and Moslem marriages, government assistance for non-Christian educational establishments, and other matters affecting the general welfare of East Indians. At the same time the Hindu and Moslem communities in both colonies formed their own religious organizations to propagate their faiths and to look after the religious welfare of their particular groups. The activities of such organizations and their influence on their own group and on the larger society constitute a rich area for exploration.[23]

Thus, whether one's primary interest is the nineteenth or twentieth century, male or female, political, economic, or social, there are many opportunities for the enterprising researcher.

23. In this regard, useful exploratory work has been done regarding Trinidad. See J. C. Jha, "East Indian Pressure Groups in Trinidad, 1897–1921," in *Political Protest and Political Organisation in the Caribbean from the Late 19th Century*, ed. Brinsley Samaroo, Vol. 1, 75–174 (St. Augustine, Trinidad, 1976); also, Tikasingh, "East Indians in Trinidad."

67   The West Indies Federation
Elisabeth Wallace

Of the several books and articles written on the West Indies Federation, the ablest full-length study is *The West Indies, the Federal Negotiations* (London, 1968) by Sir John Mordecai. Among the federation's most distinguished public servants and for a time its governor general, Sir John was closely involved with every stage of the federation's history. A more recent analysis is Sir Fred Phillips, *Freedom in the Caribbean: A Study in Constitutional Change* (Bridgetown, Barbados, 1977). The author is a well-known West Indian lawyer, a former administrator, and a sometime-secretary to the federal cabinet. As the title suggests, his book concentrates on constitutional aspects of the federation. Briefer, but thoughtful and illuminating, is a pamphlet by Hugh Springer, *Reflections on the Failure of the First West Indian Federation,* Occasional Papers on International Affairs, No. 4 (Cambridge, Massachusetts, 1962).

A more general study, not primarily concerned with the federation, is David Lowenthal, *West Indian Societies* (London, 1972), published for the London Institute of Race Relations in collaboration with the American Geographical Society in New York. Intelligent political analysis of any country and especially of the Commonwealth Caribbean requires knowledge of its history, economics, and social conditions. From Dr. Lowenthal's perceptive and immensely informative book every student of the area may learn much.

The able West Indian authors of the first three of these four studies all had first-hand experience with the events they discuss and personal knowledge of the federation's leading statesmen and civil servants. All utilized both Caribbean and British documents. Future students of the federation will, however, find gaps in the materials used by these pioneer writers. They were naturally compelled to leave unexplored the sources that were inaccessible at the time they wrote, sources such as personal papers of West Indian politicians. Although few of these are yet available, more may be in the future. Among the existing biographies and autobiographies of leading regional statesmen are F. A. Hoyos, *The Rise of West Indian Democracy: The Life and Times of Sir Grantley Adams* (Bridgetown, Barbados, 1963); Eric Williams, *Inward Hunger: The Education of a Prime Minister* (London, 1969); and Cheddi Jagan, *Forbidden Freedom: The Story of British Guiana* (New York, 1954). Other useful studies are Rex Nettleford, ed., *Norman Washington Manley and the New Jamaica: Selected Speeches and Writings, 1938–68* (London, 1971); and Michael

Manley, *The Politics of Change: A Jamaican Testament* (London, 1974). These are, however, exceptions to the general absence of biographies and collected papers of West Indian political leaders, especially of those in the smaller islands.

Scholars in the Commonwealth Caribbean are rapidly filling gaps in the history, politics, economics, and sociology of this area. As graduate studies at the University of the West Indies expand, the number of such studies will increase. Politicians willing to allow interviews and access to their personal papers may understandably give a preference to West Indian over foreign scholars.

Intelligent examination of the rise and fall of the federation depends on knowledge of the personalities and goals of its leading supporters and opponents, both federal and insular. Almost equally important is knowledge of the roles played by outstanding federal public servants, such as Sir John Mordecai and Sir Shridath S. Ramphal, now secretary general of the Commonwealth. The need for biographies of outstanding West Indians is obvious.

In every Commonwealth Caribbean territory except Trinidad and Tobago, political parties and trade unions have long been closely linked. Party leaders often head supporting trade unions, while senior officials in one frequently also hold responsible posts in the other. Although parties and unions are seminal institutions in West Indian societies, there has been little detailed examination of either.

Among the few studies of parties are C. L. R. James, *Party Politics in the West Indies* (San Juan, Trinidad, 1962); two articles on Jamaican politics by O. W. Phelps and C. Paul Bradley in *Social and Economic Studies,* 9 (December 1960); Eric Williams, *History of the People of Trinidad and Tobago* (Port of Spain, 1962); and Selwyn D. Ryan, *Race and Nationalism in Trinidad and Tobago* (Toronto, 1972). There are also some useful books on Guyana, although their discussion of political parties is often peripheral.

Little more has been written about Commonwealth Caribbean labor movements. Among the most useful are W. Arthur Lewis, *Labour in the West Indies: The Birth of a Workers' Movement,* Fabian Society Research Series No. 44 (London, 1939); Cedric O. J. Matthews, *Labour Policies in the West Indies* (Genève, 1952); Walter Bowen, *Colonial Trade Unions,* Fabian Research Series No. 167 (London, 1954); F. W. Dalley, *General Industrial Conditions and Labour Relations in Trinidad* (Port of Spain, 1954); William H. Knowles, *Trade Union Development and Industrial Relations in the British West Indies* (Berkeley, 1959); B. C. Roberts, *Labour in the Tropical Territories of the Commonwealth* (Durham, North

Carolina, 1964); and Ashton Chase, *A History of Trade Unionism in Guyana* (Ruimveldt, Guyana, 1964).

Despite the usefulness of these general studies, the position and influence of individual West Indian unions deserve a much more detailed analysis. Here, again, an important gap remains to be filled, but to do so will not be easy. Few unions are likely to maintain comprehensive files and even fewer to be willing to make available such records as they have. Future students of Caribbean labor movements will need to seek information from union leaders, their friends, and their papers. To such sources, as to those for parties and political leaders, foreign students may find access difficult.

These considerations do not, however, apply to one rich and still largely unexplored source of material on the federation, as on other aspects of the West Indian scene: namely, newspapers and periodicals. Open to all, because they are in the public domain, the regional press offers a promising quarry for research.

Some West Indian papers, like the Jamaican *Gleaner,* have been published for more than a century. Editorials, feature articles, and letters to the editor give an illuminating picture of local concerns and opinions. For style, wit, and good sense, few columnists in any country can rival Morris Cargill of Jamaica, who, under the pseudonym of Thomas Wright, has long brightened the pages of the *Gleaner*. The best British weeklies boast no abler commentator.

Among the foremost leaders of the movement for self-government in the British Caribbean was T. Albert Marryshow of Grenada, who in 1915 founded a newspaper significantly named the *West Indian*. This journal is still published. It long supported the closer union among British Caribbean territories, which Mr. Marryshow himself passionately espoused. Yet he and his paper eventually opposed the West Indies Federation, mainly because this was not, from the outset, autonomous. No biography of Mr. Marryshow or any book on his influential *West Indian* has been written.

The only serious study of Commonwealth Caribbean newspapers is a doctoral dissertation by Hector Massey for the University of Toronto on the attitude of the Jamaican press toward the federation. Much more work might well be done in this field.

Many West Indian territories, unlike Jamaica and Guyana, have only one newspaper. Some like the *Gleaner*—which, although not the sole paper on the island, has long dominated the Jamaican scene—have shown a marked sense of responsibility in trying to give their readers various points of view on controversial issues such as federation. Others on the smaller islands, with little or no competition, have often served mainly as government spokesmen and, without fear of contradiction, have largely confined themselves to expounding the opinions of those in office.

Among the few avowedly federalist journals during the life of the federation was the *West Indian Economist,* published in Jamaica. This was the only nongovernmental organ dedicated to discussing issues of concern to the whole Commonwealth Caribbean. Careful study of its files would undoubtedly be rewarding.

Histories of individual islands, which examine social and economic as well as political problems, are conspicuous by their absence. There are no comprehensive modern histories of Jamaica, Barbados, or the Leewards and Windwards. Here is an open field for further research.

The reasons why the federation failed have been inadequately explored. Any real enthusiasm for nationhood must rest on a lively sense of community or fellow-feeling among those involved. Such a sentiment was difficult to develop among the scattered peoples of the West Indies Federation, who had had few opportunities for contacts with and knowledge of each other. For this there were obvious geographical, historical, and economic causes. During the lifetime of the federation, insular attachments remained strong and nascent regionalism weak. Poverty was endemic and economic problems acute. The absence of close ties among the units of the federation bred distrust and made understanding difficult. While these issues have been discussed by various writers, all deserve further study.

The role of the United Kingdom in the establishment of the federation is examined in a thoughtful article by Jesse H. Proctor, Jr., "Britain's Pro-Federation Policy in the Caribbean: An Inquiry into Motivation," *Canadian Journal of Economics and Political Science,* 22 (1956). This topic also would repay more detailed examination, as would the United Kingdom's relationship to the federation throughout its four troubled years. On this theme there is much material available in the *Hansard Parliamentary Debates* of the West Indies and of the British House of Commons and House of Lords. Scholars have as yet made little use of these potentially very valuable debates or of those in individual Commonwealth Caribbean territories.

A major reason for the formation of the West Indies Federation was anticolonial sentiment. After the attainment in the 1960s and 1970s of independence or quasi autonomy by its former territories, attacks on neocolonialism were often adroitly substituted for earlier attacks on the sins of imperialism. There has, however, been no attempt at objective analysis of what the colonial heritage involved in the Commonwealth Caribbean, or an assessment of its assets and liabilities. Such an appraisal is overdue.

Few comparative studies of federal states have included the West Indies, although its experience is instructive. During its lifetime various able West

Indians argued that in the Commonwealth Caribbean the best chance for preserving the civil and political liberties vital to democratic government lay in an effective federal state. It remains for future scholars to assess the validity of this contention and the prospects for democracy under independence.

Clearly, much remains to be learned about the experience and tribulations of the West Indies Federation. This includes the history, politics, economics, and social problems of its ten units; the lives and policies of its political and labor leaders; and the development and influence of regional parties, unions, and journals. Other fruitful topics for study are the federation's relationship with the United Kingdom, local attitudes toward civil and political liberties, and the broad theme of what West Indians conceived federalism to involve. The federation had barely collapsed when its former member territories began to explore various types of continued collaboration. It is time to appraise the success of these endeavors. The reasons for the rise and fall of the federation pose to students of the Commonwealth Caribbean many important but as yet unanswered questions.

68   The Emancipation Era, 1820–1870
William A. Green

Caribbean history has entered the creole stage. The Euro-centered imperial orientation of scores of traditional scholars has been questioned in the last few years by a new generation of West Indian writers who deplore the implication that Britain's nineteenth-century Caribbean colonies were mere cogs in the machinery of empire and curiously distorted social and institutional reflections of the metropolitan community. In a recent book on Jamaica before the abolition of slavery, Edward Brathwaite asserts that Britain's preeminent sugar colony was a "viable, creative entity" developing its own set of social and political institutions that were neither British nor African.[1] The island, he contends, was much more than a unit of empire, and it deserves study on its own terms as a distinct, developing human community. A similar view has been expressed by anthropologists who deplore the use of metropolitan yardsticks in assessing the cultural merits of Caribbean societies. They insist that West Indians must develop

1. Edward Brathwaite, *The Development of Creole Society in Jamaica, 1770–1820* (Oxford, 1971), xiii.

a new sense of regional and national awareness, acknowledging those qualities of their collective heritage which are unmistakably creole. In effect, historians of the region, whether West Indians or not, are being invited to contribute to the evolution of a distinct Caribbean identity. This viewpoint, commonly expressed by social scientists and clearly prevalent among the academic elite of the islands, is likely in time to influence historians in their choice of research topics as well as in their critical evaluation of published work.

Historians have always been responsive to political stimuli, and the creolization of West Indian history should help to fill voids in understanding the past without jeopardizing adherence to strict canons of historical scholarship. It is a question of changing perspectives, not a matter of new methods or techniques, although the creolization of Caribbean history will demand a more extensive use of nontraditional research methods. Old controversies will not die—historical controversies rarely do—they will simply take on new dimensions. Even historians of empire whose sole reason for venturing into the Carribean may be the elucidation of particular imperial theses will probably risk criticism if they do not exhibit adequate appreciation for the special conditions that shaped the consciousness and values of the island people. At the same time, there is considerable danger that West Indian history written from a decidedly Caribbean perspective will generate distortions as grave as anything heretofore produced by writers with a metropolitan orientation. Whatever special qualities evolved within the British Caribbean colonies, those communities were profoundly linked to the mother country and to the whole developing nexus of the Atlantic world. What is needed in West Indian history is a balanced approach to the past, not the flip side of the coin.

The emancipation of slaves is a topic which could benefit from broader trans-Atlantic treatment. Although D. J. Murray's excellent book, *The West Indies and the Development of Colonial Government, 1801–1834* (Oxford, 1965), offers detailed assessment of the interaction between colonial governments and Downing Street on the slavery issue, the struggle of the abolitionists against the West India interest has drawn the lion's share of historical attention. Even Murray minimizes the vital role played by black West Indians in achieving their own freedom.

Two books appeared in 1978, focusing on slavery in Barbados and Jamaica.[2] In each case, the authors drew the bulk of their evidence from a

2. Jerome S. Handler and Frederick W. Lange, *Plantation Slavery in Barbados: An Archeological and Historical Investigation* (Cambridge, Massachusetts, 1978); Michael Craton, *Searching for the Invisible Man: Slaves and Plantation Life in Jamaica* (Cambridge, Massachusetts, 1978).

single plantation, and both studies used imaginative techniques in collecting and assessing data. Together they serve as models for forthcoming projects, though a word of caution is in order. The profession may not have reached the point of surfeit for studies on Caribbean slavery, but the literature already available renders it unlikely that further research on estate slavery in the sugar industry will produce a wealth of fresh insights. Work on urban slavery, life in the jobbing gangs, and slavery in secondary crops and livestock pens offers greater promise. Regretably, sources in these areas are limited.

Recent literature on the profitability of West Indian slavery will require verification by further work covering a wide range of colonies. It would be valuable if scholars with quantitative skills would draw comparisons between the profitability of plantation agriculture in Barbados, Trinidad, and British Guiana at appropriate periods before *and after* emancipation. For most of the British West Indies, emancipation (followed shortly by the abolition of the sugar duties) proved catastrophic to plantation agriculture. Barbados, for reasons of its dense population, and Trinidad and British Guiana, by virtue of Indian immigration, remained important sugar colonies throughout the nineteenth century. It would be interesting to know whether the profitability of plantation agriculture increased, sagged, or remained stable in those colonies during the decades of the "great experiment."

Another aspect of plantation agriculture that demands fresh treatment is the institution of absentee proprietorship. The standard denunciation of absenteeism written by Ragatz in 1931 and widely accepted by two generations of historians has been called into question.[3] Whatever its economic liabilities, absenteeism may have provided important yeast in creating distinct colonial societies. Where resident proprietorship was heaviest, namely Barbados, the intensity of the color bar and the rigidity of the white agrarian aristocracy were greatest. To what extent was absenteeism—conversely expressed as the management of plantations by locally resident agents—a factor in the generation of a distinct creole society?

Emancipation produced a fundamental conflict between those forces seeking the perpetuation of plantation agriculture and those desiring the widespread establishment of peasant farming. The planters and their allies sought the former, demanding disciplined wage labor from the freedmen.

3. Lowell Joseph Ragatz, "Absentee Landlordism in the British Caribbean, 1750–1833," *Agriculture History,* 5 (1931): 7–26. For a challenge to some long-standing attitudes, see Douglas Hall, "Absentee Proprietorship in the British West Indies, to about 1850," *Jamaican Historical Review,* 10 (1964): 15–35.

The freedmen wanted independence from the plantations; they did not try deliberately to destroy the estates, but they were, by and large, unwilling to provide the regular, disciplined labor necessary to keep them afloat. This conflict between peasant and plantation agriculture constitutes the fundamental drama of the postemancipation period. Because West Indian intercourse with the rest of the world was largely dependent on the export of plantation staples, the outcome of the conflict had enormous implications for Caribbean society. Civic as well as individual prosperity was linked directly to the export trade, and schools, churches, roads, and all public amenities were financed directly or indirectly by the proceeds of trade. Detailed study has been done on the desperate plight of the plantations between 1830 and 1865. The social and economic history of the West Indian peasantries during this era is much more vaguely known. We have gross figures on the growth of British Caribbean peasantries after 1838, but there is no penetrating, intimate, and analytical work of quality on the peasantry.

Research on the peasantry presents thorny problems. In Jamaica, for example, the vast majority of literary sources for the postemancipation period have been written by people who favored the preservation, if not the domination, of the plantations. This includes most European clergymen, magistrates, colonial bureaucrats, foreign travelers, newspaper editors, and assemblymen (black, white, and colored), as well as the planters and their merchant allies. Sources of this type cannot be ignored simply because their orientation to the peasantry might be hostile. Rather they must be mined with subtlety and discretion. The work of anthropologists is very instructive in this regard.[4]

There is no detailed work on religion in the British West Indies in the aftermath of emancipation, though education, a correlated topic, has received attention. It was the hope of antislavery enthusiasts that freedmen would warmly embrace Christianity. To facilitate their conversion, missionary societies stepped up their activities on the islands and in British Guiana in the years after emancipation. The sensational early successes of European clergymen melted away in the grim depression years following the withdrawal of tariff protection for colonial sugar (1846). Even the Jamaican Baptists, whose efforts in behalf of the slaves had endeared them to a large portion of the black population, suffered a massive deterioration in numbers. Scores of black preachers, slightly educated by European missionaries, launched careers in the ministry, pirating congregations

---

4. Sidney Mintz and Richard Price, *An Anthropological Approach to the Afro-American Past: A Caribbean Perspective* (Philadelphia, 1976). This is a brief but insightful piece produced for the Institute for the Study of Human Issues.

from their hapless tutors. Obeah was revived—or at least it asserted itself more openly—and the spiritual lives of white and black West Indians grew increasingly separate. How can this be explained? What prompted and sustained the separation of the freedmen from the orthodox Christian churches? These are questions that deserve further exploration, and the rich archives of the mission societies in London—particularly that of the London Missionary Society—provide excellent starting points. As in the case of the peasantry, researchers will require careful discretion in their use of missionary correspondence, for no one could express outrage more outrageously than a missionary whose flock had abandoned him in favor of a poorly educated and self-appointed black preacher.

Political history in the mid-century British West Indies is fairly uninviting, and political writing has probably suffered some distortion from the imposition of metropolitan values. Only scholars who have worked through the political record can appreciate the labyrinthian character of colonial politics. Even in Jamaica, where the breadth of the island and the size of its population lent formality and structure to the political process, the absence of orthodox parties and the shifting of personal alliances have created confusion for researchers. Despite the common use of terms such as King's House party, Country party, Popular party, or Town party, there was no clear pattern of political action in Jamaica. The colony's politicians prided themselves on their independence. Attachments were fleeting and fragile, and personal feelings, powerfully influenced by race, seemed to govern behavior as much as substantive issues. To a greater or lesser extent this was the case in other colonies as well. It would be useful if a few diligent scholars would sort out the political tangles of the mid-century British West Indian colonies, offering a clearer conceptual framework for our understanding of colonial politics. At the same time, this author would be reluctant to commend the task to anyone. Although the work can be accomplished by research in British and island records, including West Indian newspapers held in London, the Institute of Jamaica, and the American Antiquarian Society, there seems to be little current interest in the political infighting that persisted through the postemancipation years. Much of that infighting seems personal and purposeless; even many serious issues that aroused intense local interest have lost their cogency. Colonial political history tends to be a dull and tedious business; it makes for dull and tedious writing. There is work to be done, but the performers of that work may have difficulty attracting an audience.

Social history is more easily undertaken for the period before emancipation than after. During slavery the population was compartmentalized by estates and castes; records of the population were kept on estates, and the imperial government collected massive slave registration and compensation records. The postemancipation collapse of the plantations and the concurrent geographical dispersal of the population impaired the accumulation of reliable demographic records. It would be very difficult to produce a book like B. W. Higman's *Slave Population and Economy in Jamaica, 1807–1834* (Cambridge, England, 1976) for the mid-century years; yet that work raises a number of issues which demand further attention.

Higman contends that most slaves on the plantations he surveyed resided in simple family households, nuclear in character. On the basis of his findings, he challenges the traditional view of the slave family as matrifocal and promiscuous. Can it be determined, however, whether there was a significant stability among mates living in the nuclear households identified by Higman? Stability is crucial. If mating alliances shifted frequently, the appearance of stable nuclear families could have been afforded through the impersonal process of record taking when, in fact, a matrifocal rather than nuclear pattern of family living actually existed. Higman admits that a resolution of the problem of stability may not be possible.

The West Indian family has long been a subject of academic concern. Believing it to be matrifocal, Herskovits considered the West Indian family an African cultural survival. E. Franklin Frazier rejected this view and argued that matrifocality was a pragmatic adaptation to harsh conditions; Patterson urged that slavery virtually precluded the development of nuclear families.[5] Some studies of the modern Caribbean family ignore historical considerations and argue that current practice of matrifocality represents a reaction to contemporary socioeconomic conditions.[6] If Higman's conclusions can be widely confirmed and if matrifocality is a standard modern pattern, the next step will be to determine why the nuclear family degenerated after emancipation and at what pace that degeneration occurred.

The role of freedmen in slave society has been assessed in some detail, and additional studies are expected. The role of the colored segment (i.e., people of mixed Afro-European heritage) in the free period is particularly interesting. Further studies in this area along with penetrating work on the peasantry will constitute necessary preliminaries to our undertaking comprehensive social histories of the British West Indies.

5. Melville J. Herskovits, *The Myth of the Negro Past* (New York, 1941), 167–84; E. Franklin Frazier, *The Negro Family in the United States* (Chicago, 1939), 125–45; Orlando Patterson, *The Sociology of Slavery* (Cranbury, New Jersey, 1967), 167.
6. See, for example, Raymond T. Smith, *The Negro Family in British Guiana* (London, 1956); or Hyman Rodman, *Lower Class Families: The Culture of Poverty in Negro Trinidad* (London, 1971).

The emancipation era, though well trodden by scholars, continues to offer interesting avenues for new research. Work on the West Indies should attempt to be as geographically encompassing as possible. Studies which focus exclusively on one colony, even so large a colony as Jamaica, frequently leave readers wondering whether the conditions observed in that island were reproduced elsewhere. There has been a tendency among writers of West Indian history to focus their studies upon Jamaica and to draw general conclusions about the whole British Caribbean from the particular experience of that island. Officials at the Colonial Office, members of Parliament, and spokesmen for the Anti-Slavery Society were guilty of that practice. In many respects, Jamaica was the extraordinary, not the ordinary, West Indian colony, often constituting a caricature, not a likeness, of the others. Research on the West Indies tends to be more time consuming than that for many areas of the British Empire, because each of the islands had its own executive, its own courts, its own legislature, and, consequently, its own official records. Scholars who examine those records are confronted with the task of perusing a much larger number of documentary sources than would be the case if they were studying colonial history in a large continental land area. It is a problem that cannot be circumvented. Where appropriate, researchers should reconcile themselves to a weighty investment of time in the archives. The alternatives are undesirable—either a narrowing of the focus of one's work, limiting the overall perspective and value of it, or relying on the dubious practice of drawing general conclusions about the Caribbean colonies from the experience of one or two islands.

Consideration should also be given to alternative perspectives. Life in the West Indies during the mid-nineteenth century often involved enormous human hardship. Historians who pore over the record of that hardship are prone to condemn, often hastily, colonial governments, the Colonial Office, the planter class, or whatever other group exercised political or economic power, asserting that influential elements either neglected "the people" or exploited them to satisfy their own greed. Value judgments are necessary to good history, and those who deserve condemnation should receive it. But scholars must be earnest in exploring what alternative courses of action were available to the colonies, where those alternatives might have led, and whether, in the end, those alternatives were likely to be more promising for the population at large than the routes actually taken. There have been too many unexamined and cavalier assertions about this or that missed opportunity in the mid-century Caribbean, particularly in economic matters. If opportunities were missed, then historians must show that those opportunities were viable. Historical sympathy is a worthy sentiment, but in the West Indies, as in all areas, it is

important to temper one's natural sympathy with a stubborn sense of reality.

69   Research on the Loyalist Exodus
Primarily to the Bahamas,
Jamaica, and Dominica
Wallace Brown

About one in five (over 500,000) white Americans alive during the revolutionary era opposed the war and the creation of the United States of
America. This stance was shared by many black Americans and most
Indians. Perhaps eighty thousand white Loyalist refugees plus an undeter-
mined number of blacks and Indians were driven permanently abroad by
the Revolution. Despite the peace treaty of 1783, there were lingering,
frustrated hopes that Maine, the old North West, the Floridas, and Louisiana would become continental havens. Even Puerto Rico and Australia
were considered. Actually, the refugees ranged forth widely to the future
Canada (Prince Edward Island, Nova Scotia, Quebec, New Brunswick,
and Ontario, of which the latter two provinces they virtually created),
Bermuda, the Bahamas, the West Indies, Central America, Sierra Leone,
Great Britain, and Europe. Many of these areas have received serious
attention from scholars, but the Caribbean, including the Bahamas, is by
far the most neglected.[1]

Outside the United States, some Loyalists remained in the Spanish Floridas; many more moved to several of the islands and the Mosquito Shore.
The most important locations were the Bahamas (2,000 Loyalists and
6,000 slaves), Jamaica (3,000 Loyalists and 9,000 slaves), and Dominica
(about 465 Loyalists and perhaps an equal number of slaves). They had
important effects on politics, the economy (especially agriculture), and
social institutions, especially in the Bahamas where the white population
doubled and the black quadrupled.

The interaction of old and new inhabitants illuminates each group. For
Jamaica, Edward Brathwaite has described what he calls a creole response—local, conservative, and unimaginative—and similar attitudes

---

1. For a general, somewhat-dated discussion of Loyalist historiography, see Wallace
Brown, "The View of Two Hundred Years: The Loyalists of the American Revolution,"
Proceedings of the American Antiquarian Society, 80 (April 1970): 25–47.

are found among the Conchs, as the old inhabitants of the Bahamas were derisively known.[2] Generally, there is great scope for comparative history, which is perhaps the chief attraction for studying the Loyalist refugees across the globe.

The Loyalist diaspora must not be viewed as simply a white phenomenon. In addition to important numbers of slaves, there were some free blacks. Also, the pro-British mainland Indians and Indians from the Mosquito Shore remained a factor. A few Creeks actually left the United States and settled in Nassau. Nor must Loyalism among whites be thought of as confined to the well-to-do. On the islands, as elsewhere, a recurring theme is the split between patricians and plebians.

There is a shortage of material on Loyalists throughout the islands.[3] Siebert's two volumes on the Loyalists of East Florida contain pertinent information;[4] but although Siebert was the great pioneer of Loyalist history, he included scattered material not satisfactorily pulled together, interesting beginnings not followed through.

Turning to the areas under discussion today,[5] the Bahamas have been best studied. In 1960 Thelma Peters wrote a Ph.D. dissertation entitled, "The American Loyalists and the Plantation Period in the Bahama Islands" (University of Florida, 1960), a valuable, at times impressionistic, work that by no means exhausts the topic. Two general histories of the Bahamas—one by a professional historian, Michael Craton, the other by an able dentist, Paul Albury—have good, but necessarily limited sections on the Loyalists.[6] This vein of Bahamian history has certainly not been exhaustively drilled. Histories of Jamaica contain at most a fleeting reference to the Loyalists. The best account consists of short but suggestive bits of Edward Brathwaite's excellent *The Development of Creole Society in Jamaica, 1770–1820* (Oxford, 1971). Joseph Borome has pioneered the history of Dominica, but the period beginning with the arrival of the Loy-

2. Edward Brathwaite, *The Development of Creole Society in Jamaica, 1770–1820* (Oxford, 1971), 84.

3. Authors who have studied the Loyalists throughout the islands include Wallace Brown; North Callahan, *Flight from the Republic* (Indianapolis, 1967); Wilbur H. Siebert, *The Legacy of the American Revolution to the British West Indies and the Bahamas: A Chapter out of the History of the American Loyalists* (Columbus, Ohio, 1913; reprint ed., Boston, 1972).

4. Wilbur H. Siebert, *Loyalists in East Florida* . . . (2 vols., Deland, Florida, 1929; reprint ed., Boston, 1972).

5. Wallace Brown is currently writing a book that will deal with Loyalist refugees everywhere, partly in a comparative way. It will be a sequel to his early work, *The Good Americans: The Loyalists in the American Revolution* (New York, 1969).

6. Michael Craton, *A History of the Bahamas* (London, 1968); Paul Albury, *The Story of the Bahamas* (London, 1975).

alists is virtually terra incognita, apart from the relevant sections of Lenox Honychurch's *The Dominica Story: A History of the Island* (Bridgetown, Barbados, 1975).[7]

There is room for geographical expansion. British Honduras and the Mosquito Shore will repay further study during this period. The white settlers there considered themselves Loyalists and were joined by some East Florida refugees who fled to the Mosquito Shore. After the Shore was ceded to Spain in 1786, some settled on Andros Island in the Bahamas, others went to Jamaica, and many more to Belize (an area which also sent a number of settlers to Jamaica). This whole group seems to have been people of very modest means. Another "low-yield" area worth study is St. Lucia.

Conversely, it might be instructive to explain why some islands failed to attract Loyalists in any numbers. This is particularly the case with St. Vincent, for which John Graham, the lieutenant governor of Georgia, drafted a plan for the settlement of two thousand Loyalists and five thousand slaves.[8]

Some source material has been neglected, including contemporary newspapers in the Floridas, the United States, Great Britain, and the islands. Loyalists themselves were significant journalists. Alexander Aikman founded two newspapers in Jamaica and served as printer to the king and the House of Assembly; on the same island his brother joined with David Douglass in a printing business that included another paper. John Wells began the first newspaper in the Bahamas, and his other publications included the *Bahama Almanack*. In the Bahamas Alexander Cameron, a Virginia Loyalist, founded a second, so far largely lost, newspaper, and Joseph Eve, architect and inventor, printed items for the Assembly. In Dominica during the time of the Loyalists, there were three English newspapers, all largely lost, one of which was possibly printed by a Loyalist.[9] The history of printing at this time deserves to be written, as does the whole Loyalist cultural contribution.

The cultural front includes the theater to which many Loyalists were devoted. Inactivity stimulated amateur, professional, and combined shows in the occupied American towns, and exile brought theatrical endeavor to Bermuda, East Florida, Jamaica, and Nassau. Judith Layng has recently published an account of David Douglass, the printer mentioned above,

7. See also *Aspects of Dominican History*, a book published by the government of Dominica in 1972.

8. "Sketch of a plan . . . ," C.O. 260/7.

9. Wallace Brown, "The Loyalists in the West Indies," in *Red, White and True Blue: The Loyalists in the Revolution*, ed. Esmond Wright, 90–92 (New York, 1976).

and the American Company of Comedians in Jamaica.[10] The contributions of William Augustus Bowles, who fled from New York City to Nassau with a company of actors, has yet to be written.

To return to sources, there are some good, familiar travelers' and other contemporary accounts for the Bahamas, but little for elsewhere.[11] The little-utilized MacKay-Stiles and Cowper papers, lodged at the University of North Carolina, provide in the letters of the daughters of the Georgian Basil Cowper a rare glimpse of the life of one Loyalist family on the north coast of Jamaica in the 1790s. These Cowper letters and the Telfair Family Papers in the Georgia State Historical Society, which contain letters from William Telfair of Great Exuma to Georgia, suggest there may be much more in American depositories. Similarly, the letters (in the Bedford County Record Office) of the South Carolinian Henry Rugeley suggest further possibilities in the U.K.

In Nassau the Records of Lands and Sales and the registry have not been fully exploited. In Spanish Town the Parish Vestry Records will re-pay attention. In London the archives of the United Society for the Prop-agation of the Gospel throw light on the Bahamas and possibly elsewhere, and the records of the Loyalist Claims Commission require more atten-tion.[12]

At least in the Bahamas some local studies seem possible. The Loyal-ists, their slaves, and some free blacks were the first to settle many of the out islands. An interesting start is the recent establishment of the Wyannie Malone Historical Museum (named after a South Carolina Loyalist) at Hope Town, Abaco. The museum has located Carleton, an ephemeral, squabbling settlement of New York Loyalists that included some free

10. Judith Layng, "The American Company of Comedians and the Disruption of the Empire," *Revista/Review Interamericana*, 5, 4(Winter 1975/76): 665–75. See also Wallace Brown, "The American Loyalists in Bermuda," *Bermuda Historical Quarterly*, 33 (Winter 1976): 80–92, and *Authentic Memoirs of William Augustus Bowles* (London, 1791), 46.

11. William Wylly, *A Short History of the Bahama Islands, Their Climate, Production &c, 1788*, Add. mss 6058, the British Library, London (London, 1789); J. D. Schoepf, *Travels in the Confederation, 1783–1784* (Philadelphia, 1911); Daniel McKinnon, *A Tour through the British West Indies in the Years 1802 and 1803* (London, 1804); Crosbie Gar-stin, ed., *Samuel Kelly: An Eighteenth Century Seaman* (London, 1925); Report of Lieu-tenant John Wilson (1783), manuscript in Boston Public Library; Barbara G. Teller, "The Case of *Some* Inhabitants of East Florida, 1767–1785," *Florida Historical Quarterly*, 33 (October 1954): 97–110 (letters from Mary Stout in Nassau to her brother in England).

12. See Wallace Brown, *The King's Friends: The Composition and Motives of the Amer-ican Loyalist Claimants* (Providence, Rhode Island, 1965); Eugene Fingerhut, "Uses and Abuses of the American Loyalist Claims: A Critique of Quantitative Analysis," *William and Mary Quarterly*, 25 (April 1968): 245–58.

blacks.[13] Here and elsewhere there are archaeological possibilities. Only one Loyalist manor (on the Exumas) remains occupied, but there are still many ruins and tombs that should be recorded one way or another.[14]

The general list of biographies (single or group) has recently been growing. There is a good life of William Augustus Bowles by J. Leitch Wright, Jr.,[15] but more opportunities exist for Loyalists involved with the islands. Bowles was associated with Miller, Bonnamy and Company, the great rival of another Nassau, partly Loyalist trading concern, Panton, Leslie and Company. Their history is still not fully written. Still needed is a life of Bowles' patron, Lord Dunmore, governor of Virginia and later the Bahamas.

Other possibilities include the whole fascinating Wells-Aikman families of South Carolina, East Florida, Nassau, Kingston, and Britain; Henry Hamilton, governor of Detroit, Quebec, Bermuda, and Dominica; and many others mentioned in this essay.

Many Loyalists who do not merit biographies should be better known: Roger Kelsall, who introduced long staple cotton to Georgia from the Bahamas; Adam Dolmage, a New Yorker who became an important officeholder in Jamaica; Samuel Quincy, a Boston lawyer who practiced in Antigua, St. Kitts, Tortola, and St. Croix; Colonel Thomas Browne of Georgia, Nassau, and eventually St. Vincent; James Robertson, from the same state, who became chief justice of the Virgin Islands.

The mass of white Loyalists is susceptible to some analysis via the Loyalist claims, land grants, and certificates of loyalty issued in Jamaica, the eighty biographies of Bahamians collected by Lydia Parrish, and, at least in the Bahamas, through wills.[16]

If the history of the whites is not always easy to unravel, that of blacks is even more difficult, although by no means hopeless. Three groups are

13. Steve Dodge, *The First Loyalist Settlements in Abaco: Carleton and Marsh's Harbor* (Hopetown, Bahamas, 1979).

14. See the pictures in Albury, *Story of the Bahamas,* 118–19; and in Callahan, *Flight from the Republic,* 12ff.

15. J. Leitch Wright, Jr., *William Augustus Bowles* (Athens, Georgia, 1967). Two more books by this author (including the bibliographies) repay consultation: *Florida in the American Revolution* (Gainesville, 1975), and *Britain and the American Frontier, 1783–1815* (Athens, Georgia, 1975). Another Loyalist biography is Grace A. Cockcroft, *The Public Life of George Chalmers* (New York, 1939). Chalmers was the colonial agent for the Bahamas.

16. The Jamaican certificates are found in George F. Judah, "Loyalists," manuscript in the Institute of Jamaica, and the Wilbur H. Siebert Papers, Box 35, available on microfilm from the Ohio Historical Society, Columbus, Ohio. Lydia Parrish, "Records of Some Southern Loyalists," manuscript in the Houghton Library, Harvard University.

involved: bona fide black Loyalists, the slaves of Loyalists, and a few contingents of black soldiers.

The islands attracted southern white Loyalists, partly because of climate and nearness but primarily to employ the slaves, upon "whose labour," as one group frankly states, "the future subsistence of our families depends."[17] Some whites who never came themselves sent slaves to work in Jamaica because of employment opportunities.[18]

The blacks were a sizable and more permanent addition to the labor force than the whites, particularly in the Bahamas where they were the mainstay of the cotton boom that lasted almost until 1800. American slaves contributed to many activities including indigo production in Dominica and shipbuilding in Jamaica and the Bahamas. Paul Albury argues that when the cotton boom ended in the Bahamas the idle ships, manned largely by slaves, very successfully took up *the* great *Bahamian* enterprise—wrecking. He also says that after emancipation, in contrast to freed blacks off slave ships, "the plantation Negroes made a success of their little villages . . . because of the skills and discipline taught them by the Loyalists."[19]

This leads to the differences between American blacks and others, which in some ways paralleled the differences between whites. According to the early nineteenth-century historian of Jamaica, the Reverend George W. Bridges, the Loyalists' "faithful slaves . . . , much further advanced on the scale of civilized society than the . . . negroes, amongst whom they were . . . dispersed," brought a "beneficial influence," that is, an acceptance of the benefits of slavery![20]

On the other hand there is evidence of much less "beneficial" American influence. The important Baptist movement in Jamaica was started by a group of Loyalists' slaves spearheaded by George Liele and Moses Baker. Liele was pacifist, accepted slavery, and was supported by some whites, but Baptist leadership, organization, discipline, and teaching were inherently subversive. The Baptists faced and survived persecution. They were accused of being, and may well in fact have been, connected with insurrection. The slave revolt of 1831–32 was known as the Baptist War, the Morant Bay rebellion of 1865 possibly had Baptist influence, and there are links with Revivalism, Pocomania, and Rastifarianism. This clear example of Loyalist influence persists to this day in Jamaica. The quite

17. Historical Manuscript Commission, *Report on American Manuscripts in the Royal Institution* (4 vols., London, 1904–9), Vol. 3, 45.

18. Brown, *The Good Americans,* 214.

19. Albury, *Story of the Bahamas,* 120, 134–35.

20. George W. Bridges, *The Annals of Jamaica* (2 vols., London, 1828), Vol. 1, 507.

astounding story of Liele and company, including their relationship with British Baptists, has still not been completely told.[21]

Just as the Baptists were seen as a threat to slavery, so was the example of free black soldiers, which, despite an excellent, recent article by George Tyson, requires more study.[22]

George Liele had already set up what was probably "the first Negro church gathered in America" before he arrived in Kingston.[23] Thus as Edward Brathwaite remarked, he "helped form a black cultural bridge (more than ever evident today) between the two areas."[24] This cultural bridge is intriguing if elusive. A man called Baker, a member of the Carolina Black Corps, preached Methodism in the Prince Rupert's Bay area of Dominica.[25] In her pioneering book, *Slave Songs of the Georgia Sea Islands* (first pub. 1942; reprint ed., Hatboro, Pennsylvania, 1965), Lydia Parrish pointed out that Afro-American slave songs were carried to the Bahamas by the Loyalists' slaves (and indeed were probably taken to Liberia by later-transplanted American slaves). Parrish found that the pre–Civil War term *anthem* rather than *spiritual* persisted in the Bahamas. Just as the back country of the southern United States is held to have preserved seventeenth-century English, so the out islands of the Bahamas preserved eighteenth-century American slave songs. Parrish also witnessed the custom of "settin'-up" with the dying, which she believed was brought to the Bahamas by the slaves from South Carolina and Georgia.[26]

It is not too late to expand Parrish's pioneering oral history, though the islands will never equal the United States' oral slave-record collections. In view of the Baptist element in American slave songs, one wonders if similar influences can be found in Jamaica. Parrish herself speculated that Liele may have brought the practice of "trooping," a sort of speaking in tongues, to that island.[27]

The Jamaican Baptists were linked with the black Loyalists who went from Nova Scotia and New Brunswick to Sierra Leone, which, incidentally, offers another example of the interaction between American blacks

21. Brathwaite, *Creole Society*, 66, 162–64, 210–11, 219, 253–55, 260; Beverley Brown, "George Liele: Black Baptist and Pan Americanist, 1750–1826," *Savacou*, 11/12 (September 1975): 58–72; Philip D. Curtin, *Two Jamaicas: The Role of Ideas in a Tropical Colony, 1830–1865* (Cambridge, Massachusetts, 1955), 32–35.

22. George F. Tyson, Jr., "The Carolina Black Corps: Legacy of Revolution (1783–1798)," *Revista/Review Interamericana*, 5, 4(Winter 1975/1976): 648–64.

23. Brown, "George Liele," 58.

24. Brathwaite, *Creole Society*, 66.

25. Tyson, "Carolina Black Corps," 657.

26. Parrish, *Slave Songs*, 3–5, 175. See also Charles L. Edwards, *Bahama Songs and Stories* (Boston, 1895).

27. Parrish, *Slave Songs*, 35.

and another society. Liele was a childhood friend of David George, who took the Baptist denomination to Sierra Leone. Their continuing relationship after 1783 caused one writer to hail Liele as not only the precursor of Martin Luther King, Jr., but also of Marcus Garvey![28] Another African link was what Brathwaite described as "strong, syncretized African elements" in Jamaican Baptism.[29]

It is far from clear whether black Loyalists were in any way connected with the Maroons. In the Bahamas by the end of 1787, Governor Dunmore was complaining of "outrages," which sound Maroon-like, committed by runaways, who included some free black Loyalists illegally enslaved by white Loyalists—a not uncommon occurrence. Dunmore defused the situation with a pardon.[30] In Jamaica during the Maroon War, Moses Baker was arrested for quoting a Baptist hymn: "We will be slaves no more, / Since Christ has made us free."[31] On the other hand black American troops may have been used against the Maroons in Jamaica and Dominica, and in Grenada they definitely were used.

An interesting footnote is that there seems to have been a Loyalist strand, persisting well into the nineteenth century, in the composition of the little-known Maroons of Virginia and the Carolinas.[32]

Black and white Americans affected the institution of slavery. In the Bahamas the whites became outnumbered for the first time; the result was a much stricter slave code and control. Despite the antislavery stance of William Wylly, the attorney general of the Bahamas, most Loyalists probably agreed with the Jamaican who questioned the sanity of a British government that first tried to enslave its free American colonists and then in "a similar frenzy . . . wanted to make slaves free."[33]

Finally, the very appropriate sentiments of George Tyson indicate more about blacks:

> The story of the Carolina Corps, like those of Henry Christophe,
> Denmark Vesey and George Liele, underscores a further salient fact:
> that in the age of revolution which commenced in 1775 the fabrics of

28. Brown, "George Liele," 66–67. See also James W. St. G. Walker, *The Black Loyalists: The Search for a Promised Land in Nova Scotia and Sierra Leone, 1783–1870* (New York, 1976).

29. Brathwaite, *Creole Society,* 254.

30. November 1, 1787, C.O. 23/27.

31. Brathwaite, *Creole Society,* 255.

32. Personal communication between the author and Hugo P. Learning, University of Illinois at Chicago Circle, April 2, 1976. Mr. Learning was completing a doctoral dissertation on the Maroons of Virginia and the Carolinas.

33. William Dwarris to Lilley Smith, April 22, 1788, in the William Dwarris Letters, West India Committee, London.

Afro-Westindian and Afro-American history were closely inter-
meshed, and more generally, that the black experience in the New
World deserves to be treated from a hemispheric as well as a nationalistic perspective.[34]

Today in the islands, both scholars and the general public neglect the
Loyalists. One reason is that although the bicentennial of the Revolution
stimulated the United States' academic powerhouse regarding the Loyalists, Americans still tend to ignore them after they left the colonies/states.
Another reason is that the Loyalists' influence was or at least seems
ephemeral. Those who stayed were absorbed. Many moved away. Even in
the Bahamas emigration or conversion to Conch ways has dulled their
memory. There is dispute as to how far Bay Street dominance is a Loyalist
inheritance. Lydia Parrish reported a lack of white Bahamian interest,
because the Loyalists were too poor and left too many mulatto descendants![35] Generally, the black Loyalist inheritance is dogged by the problems
of discovering "the invisible man." Yet, Loyalist studies are worthwhile
for the late eighteenth and early nineteenth centuries. The Baptist movement shows that in Jamaica the Loyalist heritage is relevant to the present.
And in 1973, at the time of Bahamian independence, a secessionist threat
appeared on the island Abaco, where the whites, many of whom were
descended from Loyalists, needed "a little while" to "overcome their res-
ervations about leaving the protection of Britain"![36]

70   Jamaica
B. W. Higman

Jamaica possesses a rich collection of archives capable of supplying
source materials for major historical studies. Access is easy. A thirty-year
rule applies to official documents, but this may be relaxed on special application. Conditions for research are good, with most materials stored in
modern, air-conditioned buildings and in a fair state of preservation. Documents are delivered to readers rapidly and efficiently. In addition to the
four major depositories described below, smaller archives are to be found
in the hands of government ministries, churches, firms, and private individuals, access to these being a matter of private negotiation. There is no

34. Tyson, "Carolina Black Corps," 664.
35. Parrish, "Records of Some Southern Loyalists," 49.
36. Reported in the *Royal Gazette* (Hamilton, Bermuda), July 9, 1973.

central catalogue of all archives in Jamaica, but Ingram covers the period 1655–1838 very thoroughly.[1]

The Jamaica Archives, Spanish Town, are the principal depository for the island's official documents. Open weekday mornings and afternoons, access requires a letter of introduction from one's home institution to the archivist. Responsible for preserving materials produced by government ministries and other institutions, the archives also house a large collection of private manuscripts for the period since 1655. All these archives, classified according to origin, have been catalogued in fair detail. Catalogues are available in the search room. Black has published an abbreviated listing.[2]

Notable among series originating in the seventeenth century are the Plat Books (1661–1710) and Patents (1661–1905), providing materials for the study of land settlement following the British conquest. More important sources for social and economic history are the Inventories (1674–1881) of personal property drafted for the execution of wills, many with detailed descriptions.[3] Original parish registers of baptisms, marriages, and burials (Church of England) cover the years 1666–1925. Other valuable series for social and economic history are the Accounts Produce (1740–1927), or annual returns of produce sold by plantations belonging to nonresident proprietors, and the Accounts Current (1807–1919), which provide additional information on expenditure.[4] The last two series are fairly comprehensive for the period before 1870, but more limited for later years. Court records cover the period 1680–1882, with gaps for particular courts. Series relating to briefer periods include Manumission Registers (1740–1838), registrations of slaves (1817–32), Records of the Protector of Immigrants (1872–1959), Proceedings of the Commissioners for Forts (1769–72), and the Jamaica Schools Commission Minutes (1888–1949).

For the political history of Jamaica, valuable material is available in the Minutes of Council (1661–1745), Journals of Council (1711–1854), and the Legislative Council Minutes (1869–). Governors' Dispatches to England (1726–1898) are duplicates, lacking the valuable enclosures attached to the originals (to be found at the Public Record Office, London). Dis-

1. K. E. Ingram, *Sources of Jamaican History, 1655–1838: A Bibliographical Survey with Particular Reference to Manuscript Sources* (2 vols., Zug, Schweiz, 1976).

2. C. V. Black, "A List of the Records in the Jamaica Archives . . . as well as . . . Island Record Office and Registrar General's Department," *Report of the Caribbean Archives Conference, 1965* (Kingston, 1965), 371–78.

3. See R. B. Sheridan, "The Wealth of Jamaica in the Eighteenth Century," *Economic History Review,* 18 (1965): 292–311.

4. See B. W. Higman, *Slave Population and Economy in Jamaica, 1807–1834* (Cambridge, England, 1976).

patches to and from British Honduras and the Turks Islands are preserved
for the periods in which those territories were under the jurisdiction of the
government of Jamaica. Records of local government, chiefly parish vestry minutes, date from 1735 but are very spotty.

The Jamaica Archives also hold private material relating to various
schools, churches, plantations, and manufacturing plants.[5] They also contain some private papers of individuals, notably those of Norman Manley.

The Island Record Office and Registrar General's Department, Spanish
Town, are specialized depositories under the Ministry of Health and Environmental Control. Search fees are charged but may be waived on application to the ministry; this is best done after a visit to the archives.
Operating hours are identical to those of the Jamaica Archives. Letters of
introduction from one's home institution are necessary and should be addressed to the permanent secretary of the ministry.

The Island Record Office is important for its long series of Deeds
(1661–), Wills (1663–1871), Powers of Attorney (1671–), and Laws
(1681–). The Registrar General's Department holds copies of the Church
of England parish registers (1664–1880), and birth and death registration
certificates for all denominations from 1880 forward.

The National Library of Jamaica, East Street, Kingston, has a wide
range of archival materials and an extensive collection of printed works.
Open weekday mornings and afternoons, it also requires a letter of introduction from one's home institution to the librarian, usually presented
twenty-four hours ahead of use, from anyone intending to read manuscripts. A full catalogue of manuscripts is available at the library. There
are several important collections of governors' correspondence, including
those of Henry Morgan, Roger Hope Elletson, George Nugent, and the
Marquis of Sligo. Numerous journals and descriptive accounts from the
hands of travelers, settlers, and missionaries are also available, as are
plantation journals and accounts; army, court, and medical records; and
items relating to natural history and ethnography. For the twentieth century there is an extensive collection of literary and dramatic manuscripts.
The library also possesses a major collection of original maps of estates
and settlements, most of them from the nineteenth century and largely
uncatalogued. Prints and other pictorial evidence are both available and
well catalogued. The library has the largest collection of West Indian
newspapers, but many are in bad condition.

The University of the West Indies Library, Mona, has a small collection
of manuscripts, particularly strong in twentieth-century literature and eth-

5. See M. Craton and J. Walvin, *A Jamaican Plantation: A History of Worthy Park,
1670–1970* (London, 1970).

nography. It also has a valuable collection of printed works and some newspapers. Microfilm of manuscripts relating to all parts of the Commonwealth Caribbean are concentrated here, and some lists have been published.[6] The library is open weekdays as well as Saturday mornings during the academic year (October to June, except for a four-week break from mid-December to mid-January and a three-week break from late March to mid-April), with somewhat shorter hours during vacation. It too requires a letter of introduction from one's home institution to the librarian.

71   Trinidad and Tobago
Bridget Brereton

The institutions containing materials on the Commonwealth Caribbean in Trinidad and Tobago are located in four major centers.[1] St. Augustine, about eight miles to the east of Port of Spain, is the site of the Trinidad campus of the University of the West Indies. Most of the libraries and the National Archives are in downtown Port of Spain, the nation's capital. San Fernando, the second major town, is situated forty miles to the south of Port of Spain. Scarborough is the capital of Tobago, the smaller sister island of Trinidad.

The West Indian section of the University of the West Indies Library in St. Augustine contains some very valuable material on the Commonwealth Caribbean, and Trinidad and Tobago in particular. There are many government publications of the English-speaking islands, generally dating from the early twentieth century: Blue Books, the official *Gazette, Parliamentary Debates* of the Federation of the West Indies (1958–62), the West Indian Law Reports (legal cases, 1959–71). On Trinidad and Tobago the library has: the *Royal Gazette* (1951–present); Government Notices (1947–present); Acts, Ordinances, Bills (1940–present); Council Papers and Minutes of the Legislative Council (1920–59); Blue Books (1902–38); *Hansard* (1962–present); Laws, volumes 1–10 (1950).

The library has the holdings of the former Imperial College of Tropical

6. See E. C. Baker, *A Guide to Records in the Leeward Islands* (London, 1965), and *A Guide to Records in the Windward Islands* (London, 1968); M. J. Chandler, *A Guide to Records in Barbados* (London, 1965).

1. For a more detailed survey, see G. S. Mount and J. E. Mount, "Historical Resources in Trinidad," paper presented to the Conference of Latin American Historians, Washington, D.C. (December 1976).

Agriculture, founded in 1922, now the Faculty of Agriculture of the regional university. These include complete runs of regional agricultural journals, periodicals, and pamphlets, dating from the 1890s and covering the whole Commonwealth Caribbean. It also contains numerous theses relating to West Indian agriculture and natural history, and some old and rare books on the same subjects.

Of more general interest, the library holds many published books on the Caribbean, including some old eighteenth- and nineteenth-century titles. The holdings include several Royal Commission Reports on the region, nineteenth and twentieth centuries, and some old journals, for example, *Timehri* (1882–99, 1911–44); the *West India Committee Circular* (1898–1962); the *Trinidad Almanack* (1875–99); the *Trinidad Reviewer* (1899–1901). The library holds the great majority of University of the West Indies graduate theses, and many foreign universities' theses on Caribbean subjects.

The library has a small but growing microfilm collection. Among the most important items are: the *Port of Spain Gazette* (1825–1956); the *Trinidad Guardian* (1917–50); the *San Fernando Gazette* (1850–96, incomplete); the *Tobago Chronicle and Gazette* (1871–99); Annual Reports on Emigration from Calcutta to British and Foreign Colonies (1891–1922); Public Record Office, C.O. 295/1–103 (many missing) and C.O. 296/ 1–11.

The West Indian Section is open weekdays from 8:30 A.M. to 4:30 P.M. and on Saturday mornings. The staff is professional and helpful.

The National Archives at 105 St. Vincent Street, Port of Spain contain much that is important and unique; but unfortunately, the materials are badly housed, are often in poor physical condition, and are inadequately organized and catalogued. The archives are open on weekdays between 8:00 A.M. and 4:00 P.M.; the staff do their best under the circumstances. Among the major holdings is a large collection of Trinidad newspapers, dating from 1820 to recent times, with a concentration on the period 1860–1940. Many are unique copies. There is a mass of material on the indentured immigration system: estate registers, registers of returning immigrants, ship records on arrivals, Immigration Department letter books. These valuable materials do not appear to be catalogued or listed.

The archives hold runs (all incomplete) of Council Papers (1893–1939); Blue Books (1875–1935); and the Trinidad *Royal Gazette* (1838–1905). The Trinidad Duplicate Despatches—copies of outgoing correspondence between the governors and secretaries of state—cover the years 1800–28 and 1898–1920, with many items missing, and also contain limited items for the 1829–98 period. However, the archives hold a microfilm set of the Public Record Office, C.O. 295 and 296 for the nineteenth century. These series contain original correspondence between governors and secretaries of state. There are also some microfilmed items of correspondence, official papers, the *Port of Spain Gazette* (1825–1956), and the *Trinidad Guardian* (1917–50).

The Parliamentary Library, the Law Library, and the Attorney General's Library are all situated in the Red House, the main government building opposite the Woodford Square, and are open on weekdays, 8:00 A.M. to 4:00 P.M., although the Parliamentary Library is usually closed when Parliament is in session. Their major holdings are: Minutes of the Legislative Council and Council Papers (ca. 1890 onward); *Hansard* (printed) (1900–50); Legislative Council Debates (1950–present); the Trinidad *Royal Gazette* (1880 onward); annual reports of government departments (1902 onward, incomplete); Laws of Trinidad and Tobago (1832 onward); Ordinances, Proclamations, Orders in Council (1880–1952); West Indian Law Reports; and some Royal Commission Reports.

The Registrar General's Vault at the Red House in Port of Spain has incomplete runs of the *Royal Gazette,* Blue Books, Council Papers, and some books and papers recently published in the country. The vault contains records of births, deaths, and marriages, and a large collection of legal records of all kinds, some dating to the late eighteenth century, in very poor condition and completely unorganized. Working conditions here are very bad, although the staff try to help.

The main branch of the Trinidad Public Library on Knox Street opposite Woodford Square in Port of Spain is open weekdays, 8:30 A.M. to 4:30 P.M., and some Saturday mornings. It contains incomplete runs of the *Royal Gazette,* Blue Books, Council Papers, and miscellaneous published works on the region.

The Trinidad Public Library, West India Reference Collection, 10 Belmont Circular Road, Port of Spain, open weekdays, 8:30 A.M. to 12:00 noon and 1:30 to 5:00 P.M., and Saturday mornings, holds many published works on Trinidad and the region, including nineteenth-century items. There are runs of the *Trinidad Register* and *Almanack* (1850–1916); *Hansard* (1900–26); and Blue Books (1900–37). The branch holds several Royal Commission Reports and the valuable series of publications of the Trinidad and Tobago Historical Society. It has a good collection of newspapers, including the *Port of Spain Gazette* (1828–69, 1887–1914), the *Catholic News* (1892–1917), the *Mirror* (1898–1914), the *Trinidad Guardian* (1917–present). Various other nineteenth- and twentieth-century Trinidad newspapers are represented for short periods.

The Central Library, 81 Belmont Circular Road, Port of Spain, is open weekdays, 8:30 A.M. to 4:30 P.M. The Reference West India Collection contains various papers and periodicals on Trinidad and the region, mostly after 1940, and a fairly good collection of books on the region, including the publications of the Trinidad and Tobago Historical Society.

The Port of Spain Town Hall on Knox Street opposite Woodford Square has a vault which is open weekdays, 8:30 A.M. to 4:30 P.M. It holds the minutes of the *cabildo* and its successor, the city council, complete from 1813 to the present. It also holds rate books and records, plans, and maps of the city, dating from early in the nineteenth century, though most date from this century.

The town hall on Harris Promenade, San Fernando, contains the City Council Minutes of San Fernando from 1874 (incomplete); and letter books, rate books, and account ledgers from the late nineteenth century, all very irregular and unorganized.

The Tobago branch of the public library in Scarborough, Tobago, has a small noncirculating West Indian collection of books on the region. More important, an air-conditioned room holds archival materials on Tobago in the nineteenth century (before its union with Trinidad in 1889). Access to these materials can be gained by permission of the librarian. The library is open weekdays, 8:30 A.M. to 6:00 P.M., and Saturday mornings. The most important holdings are: Minutes of the Tobago House of Assembly (1794–1874, with some years missing); Minutes of the Legislative Council (1811–70); governors' and lieutenant governors' Letter Books (1807–56, with some missing); Privy Council Minutes (1803–75); Executive Committee Minutes (1855–76, with some missing); Poll and Vote Books (1842–45, 1862–70); Blue Books (1836–89, with some missing); Slave Registers (1820–22); and Orders in Council (Tobago) (1857–80). There are other miscellaneous holdings.[2] One should note that the Trinidad National Archives have a few items relating to nineteenth-century Tobago.

72   Guyana
Mary Noel Menezes

Most of the major records for Guyana before the early eighteenth century are located either in the Netherlands or in Great Britain. The University of Guyana Library has started a program to obtain microfilm copies of the

2. Monica Regisford, postgraduate student of the Department of History, University of the West Indies, Trinidad, provided information on Tobago.

major foreign records, but the task is not likely to be completed before the late 1980s.

In general, the archival depositories in Guyana have suffered from serious neglect, and it is regretably the case that many of the materials need repair or duplication before anyone can safely use them for research purposes.

Although the following inventory does not include the many small private collections and archives in Guyana, in particular the Church depositories, the University of Guyana (through the collaboration of the History Department and the Caribbean Research Library) is presently compiling a detailed inventory of these holdings.

The Berbice Legal Registry in New Amsterdam contains Minutes of the Court of Civil Justice (1745–1951); Minutes of the Court of Policy and Criminal Justice (from the eighteenth century to 1825); miscellaneous records of various Berbice courts (nineteenth and twentieth centuries); petitions, execution sales; conditions of sales (1764–1935); letter books; registers and journals; inventories and letters of decree (1781–1804); protests; contracts; publications; wills; laws; transports; surveys; case registers; copies of the *Official Gazette* (since 1841); and miscellaneous books and manuscripts. Anyone seeking admission should be able to indicate sponsorship by a reputable institution or proof of research needs. In 1975 these archives, severely damaged by a flood, transferred some of the holdings to the National Archives Annex at Company Path in Georgetown. These records are not in good condition.

Holdings of the Caribbean Research Library, a special section of the main library of the University of Guyana at Turkeyen, include books, pamphlets, manuscripts, newspapers, maps, microfilm, and visual materials. Normally this section caters to the research needs of the university, although visiting researchers can usually gain access. This collection is very strong in the area of secondary historical material on Guyana. The policy is to acquire either originals or copies of all the important early works. In 1976 the acquisition of part of the now-defunct Guyana Society Library and the gift of the valuable Union of Cultural Clubs Library augmented its resources. It has a fast-growing microfilm collection of theses and archival materials on Guyana deposited abroad; in particular, it has been systematically acquiring microfilm sequences of the major records in the Public Record Office. This collection possesses a substantial number of photocopies of significant archives of the nineteenth century. The map collection contains rare seventeenth- and eighteenth-century items on Guyana. Plans include a microfilm program for early Guyanese newspaper sequences. This library provides a comprehensive bibliographic service for all researchers.

The Deeds Registry, Supreme Court, on the Avenue of the Republic in Georgetown, has registers (1786–present) of transports, deed polls, wills, land encumbrances, property, probates, administrative letters of decree, acts of substitution, business names, transfers, patent applications, revocations and renunciations, bills of sale, trademarks, bonds and mortgages, maps, and surveys. The only condition of access is sponsorship by a reputable institution.

The Department of Lands and Surveys at Lodge Backlands, Georgetown, has a depository with permissions, leases, grants and transports (1820–present); surveys (ca. 1790–present); and miscellaneous printed maps (ca. 1798–present). Again, access depends upon sponsorship by a reputable institution. Early records and surveys are often badly damaged, and many items are missing.

The General Registrar Office in the General Post Office Building, Georgetown, has records of births, deaths, and marriages since the mid-nineteenth century, as well as Indian immigration records. The condition of access is sponsorship by a reputable institution, and again, the oldest records need repair and sorting.

The Georgetown Town Council, Regent Street, Georgetown, has Minutes of the Town Council (1838–1920); Minutes of the Board of Police (1815–36); general apportionments (1880–1950); reports of medical officers (1920–30); papers and reports about water, lighting, sewerage, and fire (1950 onward); Minutes of the Georgetown Sewerage and Water Commission (1936–50); cash books (1890–1975); Blue Books (1881–1931); local guides; ordinances (1856–1953); Laws of British Guiana; Guyana Year Books; newspapers, including the *Colonist* (1880–90) and the *Royal Gazette* (1870–80); and the *Official Gazette* (1861–1965). A researcher should be able to provide evidence of his needs.

Guyana House on Main Street, Georgetown, offers official correspondence, government files, and other materials. Normally admission is restricted, but bona fide researchers may gain access.

The National Archives on Main Street, Georgetown, contain correspondence (dating since 1784); Orders of the West India Company (1747–91); Orders of the States General (1747–94); Minutes of the Courts of Policy for Essequibo/Demerara, Berbice and British Guiana (1744–1928); Minutes of the Court of Policy and Criminal Justice of Berbice (1735–1820); Minutes of the Berbice Council (for much of the nineteenth century); Minutes of the Combined Court (1831–1928); Debates of the Combined Court (1896–1928); Ordinances; Publications and Proclamations (since 1773); Minutes of the Court of Justice of Essequibo (1735–79); emigration certificates (1865–1917); petitions (1813–30); official dispatches to and from the secretary of state; files of government departments; government orders (since 1881); the *Official Gazette;* Blue Books; sessional papers; newspapers; miscellaneous books; pamphlets; and maps. The researcher ought to be able, if asked, to offer evidence of his research needs. No modern indices or guides to these archives exist, although a *Guide to the Archives,* published in Georgetown in the 1940s, gives a rough indication as to some of the important contents. There still are many bundles of letters and printed materials which have not been examined, and although the archives have the largest collection of early newspapers on Guyana, many are in poor condition.

The National Library on Main Street, Georgetown, has some books and pamphlets. Recipient of a gift of rare historical books from the National Commission for Research Materials, this library has benefited from the acquisition of the major part of the collection of the now-defunct Guyana Society Library. It is open to the public.

The Supreme Court Registry on the Avenue of the Republic in Georgetown holds Minutes of Summary Execution; Admiralty actions; Minutes of Inferior Court; books of suits; documents from the Supreme Court of Civil Jurisdiction; depositions and indictments of Supreme Court criminal matters; judges' minute books; petitions; execution sales; inquest proceedings; adoption proceedings; matrimonial cases; original civil jurisdiction documents from the Court of Appeal; civil actions from the Full Court of Appeal; summonses and applications; case registers; and many unsorted items. The material in this depository has not been properly organized, and plans call for the earliest materials to be placed, at least temporarily, in the custody of the library of the University of Guyana. Sponsorship of a reputable institution or proof of research needs is a condition of access.

73   Barbados
Woodville K. Marshall

There are at least seven depositories of relevance to the researcher of Barbadian history.

The Barbados Department of Archives, Black Rock, St. Michael (operating hours: 9:00 A.M. to 4:15 P.M.) is the main depository of basic source materials on Barbados. Among its more important contents are: Minutes of Council (called the Senate since 1964) and Minutes of Assembly (1650–present); verbatim *Parliamentary Debates* (1867–present); minutes of parochial bodies beginning in 1649 and more complete from 1875; censuses, for 1680, 1715, 1844, 1861, and every ten years thereafter; land tax and militia tax rolls, some from the eighteenth century and regularly after 1875; parochial registers of baptism, marriage, and burial (1640–1884); Deeds (1640–1901); Wills (1647–1884); inventories of property of deceased persons; and case papers of various law courts; plantation and business-house account books; and newspapers (1783–1900), both in the original form and on microfilm.

The Registration Department on Coleridge Street in Bridgetown (operating hours: 8:30 A.M. to 4:00 P.M., Monday through Friday) contains deeds, wills, records of births, baptisms, marriages, and burials, as well as court judgments for debt and case papers—all these from 1885 to the present.

The library of the University of the West Indies at Cave Hill (operating hours: during term, 9:00 A.M. to 10:00 P.M., Monday through Friday, and 9:00 A.M. to 5:00 P.M. on Saturdays; the rest of the year, 9:00 A.M. to 5:00 P.M., Monday through Friday) is mainly a depository of secondary source material. These materials pertain to all the Commonwealth Caribbean territories. There are also a few items of primary source material relating to Barbados: government *Gazettes,* the Register of Slaves (1817–34) (on microfilm), and a selection of the Colonial Office Correspondence (also on microfilm).

The Barbados Public Library on Coleridge Street, Bridgetown, operates Mondays through Fridays from 9:00 A.M. to 5:00 P.M. It contains secondary source material on Barbados and, to a lesser extent, on the other Commonwealth Caribbean territories. It has an extensive collection of twentieth-century newspapers and holds microfilm copies of a wide range of documents which have been deposited in the archives. It also holds the Lucas Manuscripts, a miscellany of historical jottings (1627–1828) compiled by Nathan Lucas (1770–1828).

The Library of Parliament in Bridgetown, available to researchers by arrangement with the librarian, contains parliamentary records and secondary source material on Barbados.

The Barbados Museum and Historical Society, The Garrison, St. Michael, has a library open for research by arrangement with the director of the museum. Valuable mainly for secondary source material on Barbados, it also contains plantation accounts, the largely genealogical Shilstone Papers (not yet indexed), and a fairly large collection of the *Barbados Almanack* from the nineteenth century.

The Richard B. Moore Library at Cave Hill, also accessible to researchers by arrangement with the university librarian, is a substantial collection of secondary source material dealing with African history and culture. The collection includes several rare books.

74   The Bahamas
Ruth Bowe and Gail Saunders

The Public Records Office (P.R.O.), Nassau, is the main depository for the permanent records and archives of the Bahamas government and also acts as a home for other deposited Bahamian archival materials.

The main depository on Mackey Street is known as the Archives. The depository area is properly air conditioned and pest controlled, and the necessary security systems have been installed against fire and theft. It contains approximately 1,134 linear feet of records, while the Mosko Building stores 248 linear feet of records, making a total of 1,382 linear feet. Already all the storage areas have reached full capacity, but it is hoped that a custom-built archives building will be erected in the not-too-distant future.

In addition to the main depository, the Archives offer research facilities and finding aids. In most cases there are detailed lists of records deposited, as well as a *Guide to the Records of the Bahamas*, published by the Archives in 1973. Duplication and photographic facilities are also available at a moderate charge. Thirty-five- and sixteen-millimeter microfilm readers are maintained in the general research area, while microfilming is done in the rear offices. General inquiries and written requests are dealt with by the research-room staff, which numbers five.

The conditions of access to the public records are set out in Section 8 of the Public Records Act 1971. Public records held at the Public Records Office are not available for public inspection until they have been in existence for thirty years. Regulations for researchers have also been set out under the Public Records Act, and each researcher is bound by them. Restrictions are set regarding the proper use of archival materials and facilities, copyrights, conditions of access, and the responsibility of the researcher to deposit his or her completed works with the Archives.

The largest deposit held by the Archives is from official government sources. To date most of these materials have been sorted, boxed, and listed. Many still remain in their original physical state, such as the Governors' Despatches (1817–1923), which are in bound volumes. The bulk of the records held predates 1964, when the Bahamas gained full internal self-government.

The official records consist primarily of those of the executive branch of the government, namely the governor's office and its precursors. These include Executive Council Correspondence (thirty-six bound volumes in manuscript form) (1726–1950, with gaps), Correspondence of the Secretaries of State (1800–1912), and Governors' Correspondence and Despatches (1817–1923). The legislative sector consists of the records of the Senate (formerly the Legislative Council) and of the House of Assembly. The proceedings of the Senate are contained in journals, "votes," minutes, and annual reports, and the sector also includes the Bahamas Laws, spanning 1718–1972, with some gaps. The deposit entitled House of Assembly, 1718–1966, includes all the relevant documents pertaining to the proceedings of that body, the main part being journals, minutes, laws, bills, and acts. They are mostly in bound printed volumes, but the journals (sixteen volumes) are in manuscript form. The judicial section consists of records (minutes, registers, action books, and wills) from the Supreme Court (1722–1963) and the magistrate's court (1872–1971).

Records have also been deposited from various government departments, some of which originated with the board system of colonial days. Most of these records are derived from the daily transactions of the departments: minute books, financial ledgers, registers, policy files, statistical reports, annual reports, and general correspondence. However, of the forty-four government departments, only twenty-one have made a substantial deposit in the Archives; the other departments maintain their own records in their respective offices.

Besides official public records, records have also been deposited from the family islands (formerly called the out islands), schools, the Anglican and Roman Catholic churches, public corporations and private associations, businesses, and individuals. Private individuals have made outstanding contributions; among them are the Mary Moseley Collection of rare books, magazines, photographs, and miscellanea (including an unpublished history of the Bahamas), the Royal Victoria Lodge's and J. E. Williamson's collections, and the original manuscript of Farquharson's journal (1831–32).

Microfilm copies of Bahamian newspapers, church records, wills, documents as well as other original documents held in foreign depositories, can also be found at the Public Records Office. In total, there are over six hundred rolls of microfilm. Items relating to the oral history of the Bahamas have been collected and stored on casette tapes (116), and some transcripts are available. There are approximately fifty miscellaneous volumes of photographs on varied Bahamian topics. The map collection is comparatively small but valuable, with its earliest print dated 1571. In addition, there is a reference library, which has over two hundred volumes on Bahamian history, art, folklore, geography, natural science, education, music, cookery, politics, and religion, and other selected books on the West Indies in general.

In keeping with modern archival trends, the Public Records Office has implemented a records management program, whereby noncurrent government records can be stored and properly preserved. A training program for clerical staff involved in this work was inaugurated in the autumn of 1978. The Public Records Office exists primarily to serve government agencies by preserving and making available records that are important for efficient and effective administration of the government and, secondly, to serve the public. The office is open to researchers for inspection of documents on Mondays through Fridays (except on public holidays), from 10:00 A.M. to 4:45 P.M.

Many of the private archival holdings listed by Arthur E. Gropp in 1941 have since been deposited with the Archives. There are, though, a few that remain outside. In 1978, an appeal was made to private individuals, societies, and associations possessing valuable archival materials to list and catalogue their holdings, because most private holdings were found to be unlisted and uncatalogued.

The Nassau Public Library, a historic site in downtown Nassau, houses a large number of documents and other government records of importance. The Harcourt Malcolm Collection, which was bequeathed in trust to the library, includes copies of various historical documents relating to the history of the Bahamas, maps, manuscripts, stamps, coins, and books of Bahamiana. The library also holds printed and microfilm copies of Bahamian newspapers (1784–present), as well as other printed government publications, for example, the Votes of the House of Assembly (1804–66) and Blue Books (1871–1938).

Notable among smaller archival holdings are those of Sir Alvin Braynen, former Speaker of the House of Parliament, whose large collection is particularly strong in nineteenth-century books but also includes Bahamian antiques. Another Bahamian, Mrs. Sally Woodruff, has inherited a similar collection of books and Bahamian records from her father. Lastly, Father Irwin McSweeney has collected a treasury of books, papers, and other manuscripts (including some church records) on the history of the Anglican church in the Bahamas.

75   Bermuda
Graeme S. Mount

While museums and forts, of service to social and military/naval historians, dot Bermuda's islands, the Bermuda Library on Queen Street and the Bermuda Archives on Parliament Street in Hamilton must be the center of any researcher's operations. Bermudian historian Cyril Outerbridge Packwood has commented:

> Bermuda is one of the few countries in the world to have preserved intact, the written records, from its birth. Never having suffered the ravages of war, or devastations by fire and flood, Bermuda's written records . . . , located in the Bermuda Archives . . . , are unique.[1]

Happily too, the library and archives operate at an optimum standard of comfort and efficiency.

The library and archives are air conditioned. The archives do not open Saturdays, and weekdays they close at 5:00 P.M.—an hour earlier than the library.

The historian's best friend for the period up to 1687 is unquestionably Major General J. H. Lefroy, governor of Bermuda from 1871 to 1877. He gathered the decaying papers of the early period and pasted them into thirteen volumes entitled the Colonial Records. These are all available at the Bermuda Archives, albeit difficult to read. Centuries of subtropical weather had taken their toll before Governor Lefroy rescued the papers, and the reading of handwritten documents is no mean feat under the best of circumstances. Fortunately, Governor Lefroy then edited two volumes entitled *Memorials of the Discovery and Early Settlement of the Bermudas or Somers Islands, 1515–1685*, extracting what he considered the most significant of the handwritten documents.

There are other handwritten items from the seventeenth century, most continuing into the twentieth century: wills (1640–1812), judicial records and books of bonds, bills, grants, and deeds (from 1693). Journals of the House of Assembly are available from 1691, Minutes of the Executive Council from 1698. There are compilations of Bermudian laws from the seventeenth century to the present, as well as unbound manuscripts of laws from 1672.

Students of the late eighteenth century can also appreciate Books of Protest—sworn statements of sea captains—which begin in 1781, as well

---

1. Cyril Outerbridge Packwood, *Chained on the Rock* (New York; Bermuda, 1975), xi.

368

as shipping (inbound and outbound) and customs information at Hamilton and St. George's, documented from 1788.

By the nineteenth century, sources widen. Two linear feet of documents relate to slavery and the slave trade. Correspondence from officials at the Colonial Office dates from 1809, the letters from the governor in Bermuda from 1814. A student of legal history can appreciate the daily logs from prisons in Hamilton and St. George's, which catalogue new arrivals and other important happenings (from 1851). Legislative Council Records date from 1831, Legislative Council Sessional Papers from 1866, and the registry of births, deaths, and marriages also from 1866.

The library owns an almost-complete run of the *Royal Gazette,* a newspaper which has appeared under different names since its inception in 1784. Social and economic historians will find value in the advertisements and news stories, while diplomatic historians will find foreign news coverage—particularly in matters of immediate relevance to Bermuda—more than adequate. Other newspapers and magazines provide a useful supplement, particularly for the most recent years.

A thirty-year rule prevails for most twentieth-century documents. If the documents are not physically present in the archives, the researcher must negotiate retrieval of materials from the appropriate department or ministry. Police records are available from 1925, and logs of criminal charges heard before Hamilton magistrates from 1927. The library owns a wide assortment of Bermudiana books—fiction, travel, science, history—and all issues of the *Bermuda Historical Quarterly,* founded in 1944. The *Quarterly* reprints a wide range of primary sources. In recent years, cultural, philanthropic, and businessmen's organizations, and certain businesses, have begun to donate records. Some rare, out-of-print books stay in a special area, and it is wise to ask about them.

The Anglican church has given material, handwritten and printed, to the Bermuda Library and Archives. Documentation dates from 1619 but is not complete; some sources remain in individual parishes. For the records of any other denomination, one would be wise to write in advance and ask what is available. The Methodist church has also contributed its records.

The Bermuda Archives also has:

a useful map collection, including two particularly interesting maps which may be originals—Sir George Somers' map of Bermuda of 1609–10, and Richard Norwood's survey of Bermuda of 1616–17;
a collection of private records, family and commercial; and
an extensive card index system.

Data on islands outside Bermuda are sparse.

Scholars are advised to write in advance, giving dates of any pending visit and requesting specific information about the project at hand. A useful reference work is Helen Rowe, ed., *A Guide to the Records of Bermuda* (Hamilton, 1980), a volume prepared by the archivist of Bermuda.

Bermuda College has little to interest the researcher, but plans called for a substantial library in the future.[2]

76   St. Vincent
John J. Hourihan

Aside from private holdings, the archival materials for St. Vincent basically are limited to three locations. These are the National Library, the Government Printing Office, and the registrar's office, all three of which are located in the capital city, Kingstown. Unfortunately, the holdings are in varying states of disarray, primarily resulting from inadequate storage space, poor data-retrieval systems, and/or poorly trained, though often well-meaning, public servants.

Of the three depositories, the best materials can be obtained from the National Library, which has set aside a West Indies Collection in a small, locked room. Access to this room is afforded to researchers, students, and the interested public through the on-duty librarian. Documents available in the library include: incomplete sets of the local newspapers; reports of various development projects (for example, on health and agriculture); copies of a variety of journals and magazines produced by local activist groups (for example, *Flambeau,* issued by a pro-decolonization group in the 1960s; *Youth,* issued by a youth organization stressing community self-help programs; *Forum,* a publication of an emerging political organization); a variety of documents stressing the economic growth and development of the state; and a few political and historical documents that, aside from two brief histories of the island, deal primarily with federation and decolonization. As an archival source, there are two basic problems with the holdings in the National Library. First, almost all the documents are concerned with events of the last twenty-five years; and, second, no documents may be removed from the West Indies Collection, even for purposes of photocopying.

2. Interview with Dr. Archie Hallett, Bermuda College, August 25, 1978.

The Government Printing Office is supposed to be the depository for all government-issued reports (for example, the *Hansard's* and annual ministry reports), but the lack of storage space and the lack of knowledgeable personnel impose limitations.

The registrar's office contains records of births, deaths, marriages, land holdings, tax rates, and other data on the general populace. However, this office is understaffed, and gaining access to this data is extremely time consuming.

Since all three of these archival holdings are housed in government buildings and staffed by civil servants, access to these resources is technically available Monday through Saturday, during the regular government hours.

77   The British Virgin Islands
John J. Hourihan

The archival materials for the British Virgin Islands are located in three separate areas, excluding the British Commonwealth Office. In the capital, Roadtown, Tortola, such records are available in the National Library, and in virtually all of the government ministries. The library, with very well-trained and cooperative personnel, houses a diversity of documents, including copies of the local newspapers, many government reports, and the few historical works, such as *The British Virgin Islands: A Chronology,* by N. Harrigan and P. Varlack, and *Tortola,* by C. F. Jenkins.

The government ministries, and particularly the chief minister's office, maintain very good files of annual and special reports. These cover such topics as demographic changes, agricultural and livestock development, tourism, and health care. Many of these documents may be purchased for nominal fees. Access to any of these archival sources is available Monday through Saturday, during the regular government hours. The greatest problem with the archival materials located in the British Virgin Islands is that the vast majority are concentrated on the last two decades.

Two additional sources are located on the neighboring island of St. Thomas, in the United States Virgin Islands (USVI). These include the public library and the Library of the College of the Virgin Islands (CVI), both of which are located in the capital of the USVI, Charlotte Amalia. Combined, these two libraries offer a good deal of historical documentation on early Danish and English colonization and plantation life (including land allocations and ownership, plantation locations and production, the slave trade, and so forth), and on the various historical conflicts between the European colonial powers. These documents include a variety of articles and books from the eighteenth and nineteenth centuries, including such useful historical texts as B. Edwards, *The History, Civil and Commercial, of the British Colonies of the West Indies* (1793); A. M. Belisario, *The Trial of Arthur Hodge* (1811); anonymous, *Letters From the Virgin Islands* (1843); and G. Suckling, *An Historical Account of the Virgin Islands in the West Indies* (1840).

In the public library, the archival material can be found in a special room devoted to the West Indies, with an emphasis on the Virgin Islands. The materials are well catalogued, and access to the material is through permission from the room's special librarian. The library is open Monday through Saturday. The CVI library is open during the days of the academic year, but researchers are advised to obtain permission through contact with one of the teachers at the college.

78 The Rest of the Western Caribbean
Eileen Goltz

The most useful center for historians on the Turks and Caicos islands is at Grand Turk, the capital city. Most locations are within easy walking distance of one another.

The government archives are located in the basement of the post office, adjacent to the government administrative offices. This facility, secured by a padlocked door, is not open to the public. Conditions within the archives are not conducive to either the preservation or the study of documents. Dampness, overcrowding, and the obvious presence of insects, spiders, and rodents all take their toll; while inadequate lighting and the absence of tables and chairs preclude easy utilization of the data. Government officials deplore these conditions and hope to remedy them in the near future. Little sorting of the documents, which date from mid-nineteenth century to the present, is evident. Much of the earlier material is on shelves lining the room, while newer material is stored in piles on the floor and in large canvas bags. Access to much of the shelved material is blocked by piles of these bags and a hodgepodge of loose documents. There are approximately 390 linear feet of documents on shelves and on the floor, plus the contents of approximately seventy-five canvas bags, each of which is about four feet high. Documents relative to all phases of governmental business are available in abundance. Specific items include government *Gazettes;* unsorted account books; handwritten correspondence relative to the presidential office (1852–68); Relief Committee Correspondence (1868); *Journals of the Salt Industry Board* (1940–62); and a Letter Book (1884–95) containing copies of government correspondence.

Some archival material is stored in the governor's office at Waterloo, Grand Turk. An incomplete collection of handwritten Minute Books of the Legislative Board (1852–1901) is in good repair.

The diligent staff of the judicial department has organized and saved from the worst ravages of climate and insects a valuable collection of documents. Included are the Public Records, from 1811 to the present. These large, handwritten volumes (eleven linear feet) contain data relating to bonding, conveyance, land transfer, mortgage, dower renunciation, etc. There are also 3½ linear feet of volumes in which are recorded marriages, births, baptisms, deaths, and burials from 1864 to the present. Land grant information is indexed from 1840, and material pertinent to the administration of property is available and indexed. Information relative to the administration of justice is retained by this department, as are the *Laws of the Turks and Caicos Islands* (three volumes to 1971, plus updatings).

All land has been surveyed and registered since 1968, and documents relative to that subject are kept at the Land Registration Office. A name index and parcel file are available for the twelve linear feet of documents.

The Victoria Library and Free Reading Room holds approximately fifteen fragile, handwritten documents relative to its construction in 1887. Some island newspapers have been preserved in the library, but the collection is incomplete and in a poor state of repair. Included are the *Turks Island Gazette and Commercial Reporter* (1849–54) and the *Royal Standard and Gazette of the Turks and Caicos Islands* (1890–1902). Other historical data include a *Report on the Hurricanes of 1926 and 1928* by William Richardson Tatem, hurricane relief officer for the Turks and Caicos islands (London, 1929), and J. Henry Pusey's second edition of *The Handbook of the Turks and Caicos Islands* (Kingston, 1906). Secondary sources include C. D. Hutching, *The Story of the Turks and Caicos Islands* (1977); H. E. Sadler, *Turks's Islands Landfall* (7 vols., 1976); and Hosay Smith, *A History of the Turks and Caicos Islands* (Hamilton, 1970). All of these have been privately published.

Records belonging to the parish of St. Thomas (Anglican) are in the charge of Father William N. Austin of Grand Turk. Included are marriage, birth, baptism, confirmation, death, and burial records dating from 1799 to 1929, with some gaps.

Persons wishing to research historical data in the Turks and Caicos should secure prior permission from government officials, such as the permanent secretary in the Ministry of Health, Education, Welfare and Local Government.

The historian of the Cayman Islands operates at a disadvantage. Records which might have assisted him were destroyed when the Government Administration Building burned in 1972. In the absence of a central archive, records are stored in several locations in George Town, the capital.

The office of the registrar general is located in the new Government Administrative Building on Elgin Street. Here are located handwritten records of births, marriages, and deaths from 1885 to the present.

The library within the Legislative Assembly, Fort Street, retains copies of all legislative documents, including *Minutes of the Legislative Assembly* and the *Cayman Islands Legislative Assembly Hansard Official Report*. The *Gazette* (government), although incomplete, goes back to 1927. A plethora of *Laws* and *Amendments* (thirty linear feet) and scrapbooks from 1937 on, containing news clippings relative to the Cayman Islands, gleaned from the world press, are also available.

Public Records are stored in a walk-in, fire-proof vault in the post office on Edward Street. These handwritten records, dating from 1810 to the present, are contained in sixty-two indexed volumes. The two earliest volumes have been damaged, but the balance of the collection has escaped the depredations of both climate and insects. The volumes contain records relevant to judicial matters and property transactions. Property transactions occurring after 1972 are recorded in the Lands Registry Office.

Since 1972, all land in the Cayman Islands has been surveyed and registered. The pertinent documents rest in the Lands Registry Office. The deputy registrar is the person to whom the researcher should apply for assistance. There are approximately twenty linear feet of indexed Land Registers, which are the final authorities regarding land tenure. Originals of land transactions recorded in the Public Records are held here as well.

The public library, on Edward Street, has copies of island newspapers and some government publications. Newspapers include: the *Caymanian Weekly* (from volume 1, 1965); the *Cayman Compass* (from volume 1, 1972); the *Caymanian Compass,* a combination of the two newspapers noted above (from 1973); and some copies of the *Tradewinds,* which published in the 1960s. The *Northwester,* a monthly news magazine is available from volume 1, 1971. The government *Gazette* (from 1975) and the *Cayman Island Laws* (also dating from 1975) are among the government publications kept in the library. There are also government studies, such as the *Cayman Islands Natural Resource Study* (1976), a six-volume publication of the Ministry of Overseas Development. Interesting secondary sources include George S. S. Hirst, *Notes on the History of the Cayman Islands*, first published in three volumes in 1909 and republished (1970?) in one volume, using unretouched negatives of the 1909 publication. A more modern work, published by the government of the Cayman Islands in 1970, is Neville Williams, *A History of the Cayman Islands*.

79   The Rest of the Eastern Caribbean
Joan E. Mount

Archival resources in the Windward and Leeward islands have been recorded in E. C. Baker, *Guide to Records in the Windward Islands* (Oxford, 1968) and *Guide to Records in the Leeward Islands* (Oxford, 1965). Since Baker reported, there has been a certain fluidity of location and a certain attrition, but few significant gains other than those afforded by the ongoing publication flow. Very recent reports are generally available in the office of the issuing ministry, and, in some cases, duplicate copies are located in the public library.

Church archives are frequently a good source for birth, marriage, and death records and, upon occasion, for other material. In Antigua, for example, the Anglican bishops have been keeping a diary since 1843. Denominational archives have often received better care than those in secular hands.

Early material in all contexts tends to be brittle and unable to withstand much handling. Climate, insect damage, and neglect have added to normal deterioration. Fortunately, some earlier material has been wrapped and also in some cases microfilmed and placed in the library of the University of the West Indies at Mona, Jamaica.

Access to depositories is generally available upon application to the appropriate authority, and one is very often accompanied by a junior employee during one's visits. Normal working hours are 8:00 A.M. to 4:00 P.M., Monday through Friday, the exception being the public libraries, which often remain open until 5:00 P.M. on weekdays and noon on Saturdays.

Most documentary resources on St. Kitts are in the archives in government headquarters, Basseterre. Among the items present in these clean, well-ventilated premises are a number of eighteenth- and nineteenth-century St. Christopher Council Minute Books, the earliest dating from the 1730s, and St. Christopher Legislative Assembly Minute Books, the earliest from 1744. St. Kitts–Nevis Legislative Council Minute Books and Executive Council Minute Books for the late nineteenth and early twentieth centuries are also available. There are correspondence records dating from the early nineteenth century and continuing to 1940. These include records of exchanges between the local administrators and the secretary of state, the colonial secretary (Antigua), or the governor of the Leeward Islands, as well as local and intercolonial letter books. Also present are the *Leeward Islands Gazette* (1872–1956); the *Official Gazette of St. Christopher–Nevis* (1904–present, with some recent volumes lacking); assorted issues of the St. Christopher Blue Book (1830–82); and a largely complete run of the Leeward Islands Blue Book (1889–1945). There are Deed Record Books dating back to the early years of the eighteenth century as well as miscellaneous other legal documents of the same vintage. Estimates for either St. Christopher–Nevis and Anguilla or the Leeward Islands are present for random years, mostly in the twentieth century. Also found are various compendia of *St. Christopher and Anguilla Acts*, or alternatively the *St. Kitts–Nevis Acts*, covering more than two centuries from 1711; *Leeward Islands Acts* (1871–1930); and *St. Christopher–Nevis–Anguilla Ordinances, Statutory Rules and Orders* for most years from 1958 to 1976.

In the archives, too, are a number of documents which relate solely to Nevis or to Anguilla. The *Nevis Acts of Assembly, 1664–1739* are bound with the *Acts of Assembly of the Charibee Islands, 1690–1730*. Also present are very early compendia of the laws of Nevis (e.g., 1681–1861); a number of eighteenth- and nineteenth-century Nevis Privy Council Minute Books and Nevis Council Minute Books; plus Nevis Blue Books (1862–82, with some gaps). There are, as well, Anguilla Council Minute Books and various Anguilla legal records of the late eighteenth and early nineteenth centuries.

Newspapers from the late nineteenth and the twentieth centuries occupy about forty linear feet in the archives.

At the Supreme Court in Basseterre one finds about seven linear feet of *St. Kitts–Nevis–Anguilla Acts and Ordinances* (1928–62, with many gaps); *Leeward Islands Acts and Ordinances* (1927–56, with many gaps); and *Leeward Islands Statutory Rules and Orders* (1927–60, with many gaps). In the registry of the Supreme Court are deed records from 1861 onward and registers of births, marriages, and deaths from 1880 onward.

The public library has about seventy-five feet of Caribbeana. There are approximately eight linear feet of primary material from St. Kitts, mostly from *Gazettes* and miscellaneous annual and special reports from the 1950s onward, plus approximately six linear feet of recent St. Kitts newspapers.

A sizable collection of documents pertaining to Antigua is stored in the "archives" in the Old Administration Building on High Street in St. John's, Antigua. To gain access, formal credentials must be presented to the permanent secretary for external affairs. The state of these archives is such that verification of holdings is very difficult.

The archives consist of two storage areas. On the second floor, there are approximately five linear feet of Estimates from 1888 to 1964. As of the mid-1950s, Estimates relate to Antigua alone, whereas those of earlier vintage cover the Leeward Islands. Present too are the Leeward Islands Blue Book (1889–1945, with very few gaps); the *Leeward Islands Gazette* (1873–1956, with very few gaps); and an assortment of *Antigua Acts, Leeward Islands Acts,* and *Leeward Islands Statutory Rules and Orders* (various compendia, 1668–1889; random volumes thereafter). Other items of interest include the Secretary of State and Crown Agents' Dispatches (1888–97), as well as assorted annual and special reports from various government departments.

The third floor of the archives houses about thirteen linear feet of records of exchanges between the secretary of state and the governor of the Leeward Islands or administrators of particular islands, and also dispatches from individual administrators to the governor of the Leeward Islands. Most are from the decade of the 1860s. In the remaining miscellanea are the very fragile House of Assembly Minute Books (1725–28); one dilapidated volume of the Board of Legislative Council Minutes Books (1801–03); some volumes of the Antigua Legislative Council Minutes Books (1875–1939); various Estate Record Books (1896–1943); and a few nineteenth-century Deed Record Books. Other Deed Record Books are at the courthouse.

In the Law Library in the courthouse on High Street, St. John's, are the *Leeward Islands Gazette* (1880–1953, with many gaps); the *Leeward Islands Acts* (1893–1953; with many gaps); a few issues of the *Leeward Islands Statutory Rules and Orders* (from 1926); and some relatively recent newspapers.

The registry at the courthouse has registers of births and deaths for the various parishes, usually from 1856 to the present, and of marriages from 1886. It also has two very early land registers from the late seventeenth through the early eighteenth century.

Excluding newspapers, the public library on Market Street, St. John's, has about eight linear feet of primary material relating to Antigua, including an almost complete collection of the *Leeward Islands Acts* (1877–1939); most of the Antigua Ordinances (1881–1939); a substantial run of the Leeward Islands Blue Book (1887–1942); and the Antigua Legislative Council Minutes (1878–91, with gaps).

Newspapers are accessible only with difficulty. While the public library has assorted newspapers for the period 1814–82, these are not available until they can be microfilmed. Otherwise, only very recent newspapers (from 1975) are available there. Newspapers predating 1975 are in disarray in the former library building on High Street, abandoned since a 1974 earthquake. Substantial backfiles of the *Worker's Voice* are available at its office on North Street.

At date of writing, documentary resources pertaining to Montserrat are limited. There is a storage area in Government House, Plymouth, but access is denied pending transferral of holdings to a more formal archive. Plans are indefinite. According to the governor, the contents of this storage area have been verified against Baker's *Guide,* with no major discrepancies found.[1]

In the registry at the courthouse on Parliament Street, Plymouth, are about twelve linear feet of early deed records in unbound bundles. These include random years from the eighteenth century and a substantial number from the nineteenth. Also present are registers of births, marriages, and deaths for the several parishes back to the early 1860s.

In the Law Library, also located in the courthouse, are about fourteen linear feet of assorted documents, all broken runs and somewhat smoke and water damaged. These include miscellaneous issues of the *Leeward Islands Gazette* from 1906 onward; a sizable run of *Leeward Islands Acts* (1872–1954); a number of *Leeward Islands Statutory Rules and Orders* (1927–54); and the *Revised Statutes of Montserrat* (1921).

Stored in the Administration Building on Church Street, Plymouth, are approximately three linear feet of documents labeled Montserrat Commissioner's Office. These are primarily Schedules of Mail dispatched to the secretary of state (1958–70, with gaps) and received from the secretary of state (1956–60), plus the Guard File of Telegrams from the administrator's office (July 1966–December 1970). There are about five linear feet of assorted issues of the *Leeward Islands Gazette* (1889–1958), plus a few miscellaneous items such as the Statement of Policy on Colonial Development and Welfare (1940). Access to this material is through the permanent secretary for administration.

Another source of material is the public library, attached to the Administration Building. Of the approximately 12½ linear feet of Caribbeana about Montserrat, many items are either annual or special government reports of recent issue. Also present are bundles of the *Montserrat Gazette* from 1960 onward, although a more comprehensive collection is on file in the clerk of council's office above the courthouse. The library has some

1. Conversation with His Excellency, Mr. Jones, Government House, August 26, 1978.

newspapers, including the *Montserrat Mirror,* from 1960, and the *Montserrat Observer* (1951–53, 1957–59). Back files of the *Mirror* are also available from the General Printing Office on Parliament Street.

The papers of the Sturge family, which played a prominent part in the history of Montserrat, are no longer on the island.

An attempt to retain past records in Dominica has led to the storing of documents and newspapers in a basement archive on High Street in Roseau under the direction of the head of the Carnegie Free Library (public library) and under the general purview of the permanent secretary for education, youth affairs, and co-operatives, to whom application for access must be made. There is no climate or insect control in this room and very little ventilation. Because of the basement location many of the documents have been damaged periodically by hurricane-related flooding, particularly in 1979, and consequently the condition and availability of the holdings described must be considered uncertain. Because there are no reader facilities, current practice is to retrieve resource materials from the archive for perusal in the library. Documents themselves have not been sorted or indexed, but some effort has been made to package and label. Baker's *Guide* is used as a holding list, although there have been additions and losses since its completion. At present there are about three hundred linear feet of documents, plus an additional twenty-six linear feet of newspapers.

Among the earliest holdings noted were House of Assembly Minute Books from 1787 to the mid-nineteenth century and Board of Legislative Council Minute Books for approximately the same period. Also present are case papers of the Vice-Court of Admiralty (1792–1872), unfortunately badly disintegrated. A substantial run of Deed Record Books begins in 1765 and of *Laws of Dominica* in 1763—i.e., various compendia such as the *Laws of Dominica, 1763–1849* (volume in very poor condition).

Present as well are a half-century collection of the Dominica Blue Book from 1838 onward (with gaps) and an equally long run of the Leeward Islands Blue Book from 1889 (with gaps). The author noted the *Dominica Official Gazette* (1865–1965) and Slave Registers (1817–1934) (with gaps). There are some issues of the *Leeward Islands Gazette* and fragmented records of official correspondence spanning more than a century to 1939. Coverage of Dominica's change of status from one of the Leewards to one of the Windward Islands is preserved among the correspondence records in the Government House Strong Room in Grenada. Other items of note relating to the second half of the nineteenth century and/or first half of the twentieth are Legislative Assembly Minute Books, Executive Council Minute Books, Legislative Council Minute Books, regular Minute Papers, and some confidential Minute Papers on such topics as

"Dominica Political Situation Reports" (1932–57). The archive also contains a substantial newspaper collection dating from the nineteenth century.

The courthouse on Victoria Street in Roseau and the office of the attorney general at government headquarters on Kennedy Street, also in Roseau, are good sources for legal materials from 1871 to the present. Located in the courthouse is a collection of the *Dominica Official Gazette* (1870–1967, with a few gaps) and the *Leeward Islands Gazette* (1874–1939, with very few gaps).

The Carnegie Free Library on Victoria Street has some retrospective material from the nineteenth and twentieth centuries, as well as current Caribbeana, although the policy is to transfer earlier documents to the archives. It also retains some backfiles of current Dominican newspapers, mostly from the 1970s.

Most of St. Lucia's documentary resources are in the care of the St. Lucia Archaeological and Historical Society, which currently is establishing an archival center in Vigie under government auspices. Into this center will go the records of official correspondence from 1845 to the turn of the century: exchanges between the island administration and both the secretary of state in London and the governor of Barbados, as well as intercolonial correspondence. These records are in the personal custody of the center's director. Also destined for the archives is a complete run of the St. Lucia Blue Book from 1879 to 1938; the *St. Lucia Gazette,* with a few gaps from 1893 to the present;[2] various nineteenth- and twentieth-century newspapers; plus the Roman Catholic church records, the oldest collection in St. Lucia and dating from 1750. The expectation is that scattered materials will find their way to the center, and already a substantial quantity of records, as yet unsorted, has come from police headquarters in Castries. The Department of Lands and Forests has also donated its early documents. Unfortunately, a fire, which destroyed much of Castries in 1948, has eliminated a number of St. Lucia's records.

Records of births and deaths since 1869 (organized by district) and registers of baptisms, marriages, and burials from earlier years (organized by denomination and parish) are available in the chief registrar's record room on Peynier Street in Castries. Also present at the registry are an extensive collection of deed records; eleven volumes of the *Registre de Depôt ou Remise d'Actes Futures à Enregistrer tenu en execution de l'Article sept. de l'Ordinance de son Excellence le Major General David Steward Gouverneur en commandant chief en cette Ile Ste. Lucie en date de trois juillet, 1829* and spanning three decades thereafter; Records of Sales (land)

---

2. The director, Robert Devaux, has a complete run of the *Gazette* from 1892 in his personal collection and will consider requests for its use.

(1852–53); Register of Grants of Crown Lands (1892–98); annual Estimates (with gaps, 1914–48; complete, 1949–70); about twenty-four
linear feet of bound annual volumes of twentieth-century St. Lucian newspapers.

Located in the office of the clerk of assembly close to the registry are
scattered years of the Legislative Council Minutes (1944–66) with a complete bound run from 1967. Present at Government House, Morne Fortune, are bound copies of the *St. Lucia Gazette* (1891–1960, with a few
gaps).

The *St. Lucia Gazette,* from 1938 (with gaps), is also in storage at the
public library on Laborie Street in Castries, as are annual volumes of the
Laws of St. Lucia, from 1949 onward. The library does not attempt to
keep back issues of local newspapers. The author was informed that a
complete run of the *Voice* is available upon application to the manager,
Voice Printing Plant, Darling Road, Castries.

Most early documents found in Grenada are in either the Supreme Court
registry on Church Street or the Strong Room in Government House on
Lucas Street, St. George's. In the registry are an almost complete collection of the *Grenada Gazette,* from 1883 onward; House of Assembly Minutes and Board of Legislative Council Minutes from the 1770s to the
1870s (with some gaps); plus a very fragmented run of Legislative Council Minutes, from 1864 to the mid-twentieth century. A number of Acts
and Ordinances of earlier date precede the *Laws of Grenada* (1897) and
Revised Laws of Grenada (1935). Also present are approximately three
linear feet of Slave Registers for the period 1818–33. Deed records go
back to the 1760s, with the text in French for the appropriate years, as do
assorted legal records. Records of births, marriages, and deaths are confined largely to the twentieth century.

The Grenada Blue Book (1828–1936, with some gaps) is in the Government House Strong Room. Correspondence records pertaining to Grenada
(about eighteen linear feet), to St. Vincent (about thirteen linear feet), and
to the Windwards in general (about eighteen linear feet) span the period
1833–1940. Included are records of exchanges between the island administrators and the secretary of state or the governor in Barbados, as well as
intercolonial correspondence. Of particular interest are records of Dominica's change of status from one of the Leewards to one of the Windward Islands. Also in the Strong Room are *Grenada Ordinances* (1875–
1950, with many gaps), *Grenada Laws* (1952–61), and assorted annual
and special reports, e.g., Administrative Reports (1893–1930) and Board
of Education Reports (1883 to the mid-twentieth century, with many
gaps). There is also a significant run of Executive Council Minutes from
1915, with early decades to 1950 shelved outside the Strong Room.

At the public library one finds some primary material mostly of recent vintage but including the Grenada Handbook, Directory, and Almanac (1897–1918, with a few gaps) and the Grenada Blue Book (1900–1934). Also present are Legislative Council Minutes (1891–1966, with gaps), and Legislative Council Papers (1931–63, with gaps). Some of these gaps are covered by backfiles, also incomplete, in the Legislative Council Chamber near the Supreme Court and in the registry. In the public library as well is Grenada's largest collection of newspapers, the earliest being the *St. George's Chronicle and Grenada Gazette* (1815–1902, with many gaps). The researcher may use all but about 10 percent of these newspapers, the remainder having become too fragile. In addition to those found in the library, batches of newspapers—mainly from the 1960s and 1970s—are found in the registry. The registry's run of the *Torchlight* from 1959 covers a gap in the public library holdings. Unfortunately, these newspapers showed considerable evidence of climate and insect erosion. Earlier newspapers had been sent to the University of the West Indies, Mona, Jamaica.

80   The Maritime Provinces of Canada
Harold H. Robertson

Historic connections between the Commonwealth Caribbean and the Maritime Provinces of Canada have tended to be centered around trade, particularly between Nova Scotia and the Caribbean. These links reach back to the mid-eighteenth century and have determined both the nature and the location of the resources pertaining to the Caribbean region which are available in these provinces. The majority of these resources are located in Nova Scotia.

The Killam Library is the main library at Dalhousie University in Halifax. During the academic year it is open between 9:00 A.M. and midnight and its holdings are accessible to all interested researchers. The main library itself contains only a small number of standard, general printed works and an assorted set of items dealing with some of the individual islands.

The archival division of the library, however, does contain some valuable information regarding trading connections between Nova Scotia and the Commonwealth Caribbean, particularly for the period after 1750. Among its holdings are Shipping Lists for Antigua, Montserrat, the Bahamas, Barbados, Bermuda, Dominica, Grenada, Jamaica, Trinidad, Tobago, St. Vincent, and the Virgin Islands. These are all microfilms of the Colonial Office series held originally at the Public Record Office in London. In addition the Killam Archives possess an assortment of business records and correspondence from many Nova Scotian business and merchant houses which have been involved in the West Indian trade since the late eighteenth century. In cases where these records extend to modern times, the thirty-year rule applies.[1]

The Public Archives of Nova Scotia are also situated on the Dalhousie Campus. While this institution does not contain any material specifically dealing with the Commonwealth Caribbean, it does possess the entire C.O. 217 series of Nova Scotian letters and original correspondence during the province's colonial era. Scattered among these files are references to the West Indian trade and to conditions in the islands affecting the trade, which the diligent researcher may find useful. These archives also possess additional business records and early Nova Scotian newspapers which contain frequent references to and information about the Caribbean. This institution is open to all interested persons between 8:30 A.M. and 10:00 P.M. on weekdays, 9:00 A.M. and 6:00 P.M. on Saturdays, and 1:00 P.M. and 10:00 P.M. on Sundays.

Another type of information is available from the United Church Archives housed at the Pine Hill School of Divinity in Halifax. These sources deal with the establishment of a Presbyterian mission among the East Indian population of Trinidad. The holdings cover from the formulation of plans to send the first missionary to the island in 1868 to the post-independence era, by which time some 6 percent of the island's population adhered to the Presbyterian faith. In addition to educational reports, financial accounts, correspondence, and copies of the church magazine, the *Trinidad Presbyterian,* the archives also contain newspaper clippings, mounted photographs, and manuscripts of the personal reminiscences of the early missionaries. Most important among the latter are the records of the Reverend K. J. Grant, whose sons were to found the firm T. Geddes Grant and Co. in Trinidad, which today is one of the largest import/export dealers in the Caribbean.

The archives also possess manuscripts of two scholarly articles based upon usage of the materials contained therein.[2] Operating hours are from

1. Some of these sources have been extensively used by the author during preparation of an M.A. thesis. See H. H. Robertson, "The Commercial Relationship Between Nova Scotia and the British West Indies, 1788–1822: The Twilight of Mercantilism in the British Empire," M.A. thesis (Dalhousie University, 1975).

2. The papers are G. S. Mount, "Reasons for the Success of the Canadian Presbyterian Mission to Trinidad, 1868–1912," (1976); and B. Samaroo, "Missionary Methods and Local Response: The Canadian Presbyterians and the East Indians in the Caribbean," (1975). More comprehensive use of these records has been made by A. Martell in "The Canadian Presbyterian Mission to Trinidad's East Indian Population, 1868–1912," M.A. thesis (Dalhousie University, 1974).

9:00 A.M. to 12:00 noon Mondays, Wednesdays, and Fridays, and all researchers are welcome.

The Vaughan Library at Acadia University, Wolfville, Nova Scotia, is another location where some material relevant to the region may be found. Holdings here are mostly printed, but the library contains some journals not available elsewhere in the Maritimes, especially *Social and Economic Studies* and the *Caribbean Quarterly,* copies of newspapers from all the major islands, and several yearbooks. The library also holds the entire series of Cass reprints of classic books on West Indian history. Also available for consultation here are a number of government reports, gazettes, and miscellaneous unsorted official documents relating to Jamaica, St. Vincent, and Barbados.

Professor Duncan Fraser of the university has some personal documents, which he is prepared to make available to researchers; among these are slides of the early operation of the bauxite industry in Jamaica, several articles on the region, and copies of his M.A. thesis.[3] The library also contains several works both modern and contemporary, dealing with the region in general as well as with individual islands. Operating hours are 8:30 A.M. to 11:00 P.M. on weekdays and 2:00 P.M. to 11:00 P.M. on Saturdays.

Outside of Nova Scotia the only institution of note as far as the study of the Commonwealth Caribbean in the Maritimes is concerned is the University of New Brunswick at Fredericton. Here the Harriet Irving Library contains over 180 volumes of printed matter dealing with the region. Titles range from bibliographies to ancient histories penned by travelers. These works are both general and specific and include material dealing with Guyana and Belize as well as the islands. These resources are also available to any researcher during operating hours, which extend from 8:30 A.M. to 11:00 P.M. on weekdays and 1:00 P.M. to 5:30 P.M. on Saturdays. Shorter hours are operated during the summer session.

In all the institutions mentioned, with the exception of the Public Archives of Nova Scotia, the researcher will also find such standard works of reference as the Sessional Papers and *Parliamentary Debates* of Britain, which contain several references to and reports and information about the Caribbean. Staffs are generally very accommodating and knowledgeable, and the researcher should encounter little problem while using the resources contained in these institutions.

3. D. G. L. Fraser, "Great Britain's West Indian Policy, 1600–1945," M.A. thesis (Acadia University, 1949).

81   Central Canada
David R. Murray

The Public Archives of Canada, located in Ottawa, are the major Canadian depository for Commonwealth Caribbean holdings. Most manuscripts relating to the Commonwealth Caribbean date from 1867, and the largest proportion is in the Public Records Division. The archives of the governor general's office (Record Group 7), and those from the Department of External Affairs (Record Group 25) and the Department of Trade and Commerce (Record Group 20) each contain papers on Canadian trade and diplomatic relations with the Caribbean. Another important archival source in the Public Archives is the Prime Ministers' Papers (Manuscript Group 26). Specific manuscripts connected with the Commonwealth Caribbean, predating confederation in 1867 and held by the Public Archives, have been documented in K. E. Ingram's published inventory.[1]

The Public Archives of Canada have useful finding aids and indices for all their major collections. The archives are open during regular office hours, Monday through Friday, and accredited researchers may consult records in the search rooms twenty-four hours a day.

A separate institution in Ottawa, the National Library of Canada holds official documents relating to the Caribbean islands, including collections of official journals, Blue Books, laws, and statutes. This collection is not complete for any period but is most extensive for the years 1900–39. The National Library's reading room is open around the clock seven days a week, with reference and circulation services limited to Monday through Friday, 8:00 A.M. to 8:00 P.M..

University libraries across the country have some holdings on the Commonwealth Caribbean. Douglas Library of Queen's University, Kingston, Ontario, has a diary and two letters of the Honorable William Morris (1786–1858), a Canadian merchant and member of the Legislative Council of the Province of Canada, relating to a visit he made to Jamaica from 1849 to 1850.[2] The library possesses photocopies of Public Record Office (London, England) papers on St. Vincent for the years 1790–1873. It also

---

1. K. E. Ingram, *Manuscripts Relating to Commonwealth Caribbean Countries in United States and Canadian Repositories* (St. Lawrence, Barbados, 1975), 311–15, entries #1001–1028.

2. Ingram, *Manuscripts,* 311, #999; "Twilight in Jamaica," *Douglas Library Notes* (Spring 1965).

houses a collection of British Colonial Office and Parliamentary Papers, which include the Commonwealth Caribbean. Library hours vary during the year, but the Douglas Library is open throughout the week—except for Sunday morning—during the fall and winter terms.

The Robarts Library at the University of Toronto has a varied book collection on the Commonwealth Caribbean, but no relevant manuscripts. It is strongest in histories and travel literature of the nineteenth century and modern Canadian government publications on Canadian-Caribbean relations. The library publishes a brochure outlining its service for external users, which researchers are advised to procure in advance.

The Metropolitan Toronto Library is another major center. It has a small book collection on the Commonwealth Caribbean, containing a selection of early and current travel accounts. It also possesses current topographical maps of all the islands and the Thomas Jeffery maps dating from the 1790s. Ingram discovered one manuscript holding related to the Commonwealth Caribbean in the Metropolitan Toronto Library, the military papers of Sir George Prevost for the years 1811–15.[3] Prevost was governor general of British North America in 1811–12 and previously had served as governor of St. Lucia and Dominica. These papers contain references to military matters connected with the British West Indies. Material cannot be borrowed but can be used in the library from 10:00 A.M. to 9:00 P.M. Monday through Thursday and from 10:00 A.M. to 6:00 P.M. Fridays and Saturdays.

In addition to its book collection, McGill University Library in Montreal has some manuscript letters of interest to Caribbean researchers. These are individual letters, petitions, and commissions, dating from the seventeenth to the early nineteenth century, referring mainly to military matters. Ingram has catalogued them.[4] The library itself normally is open seven days a week, but visitors should check in advance.

Canadian church archives retain manuscript collections on Canadian missionary involvement in the Commonwealth Caribbean. The largest of these, the United Church of Canada Archives, located at Victoria College, University of Toronto, possesses manuscripts on missionary activity in Trinidad (1868–1975) and Guyana (1885–1927). The archives are open Monday through Friday, 9:00 A.M. to 5:00 P.M. The Anglican church of Canada began direct work in the Caribbean only in the 1960s, and its records, accordingly, date from then—apart from a few early nineteenth-century documents pertaining to Bermuda, when that island was part of the diocese of Nova Scotia (1825–39). Anglican records are available at

3. Ingram, *Manuscripts,* 315–16, #1029–1030.
4. Ingram, *Manuscripts,* 317, #1031–1036.

the Archives of the Anglican Church of Canada, 600 Jarvis Street, Toronto; the hours are 9:00 A.M. to 4:30 P.M., Monday through Friday. The Presbyterian church in Canada houses its missionary records at Knox College on the St. George Street campus of the University of Toronto.

Of the Canadian businesses surveyed, only four currently permit limited access to their records. The Royal Bank of Canada is in the process of constructing an archives and museum at its Place Ville Marie headquarters in Montreal. The bank's files of Caribbean correspondence are restricted, and the archives will be open to researchers by appointment only. The Sun Life Assurance Company of Canada, with its Montreal headquarters in the process of moving to Toronto, has an extensive Caribbean collection, but it does not allow unlimited access. Anyone wishing to consult Sun Life records should correspond with the librarian of the company. The Bank of Nova Scotia's Toronto headquarters has a large collection relating to the Caribbean since the nineteenth century. Branch and department records, along with executive correspondence and financial records, are restricted, and the minutes of the board of directors are closed. All other records are open. The archives are open to scholars by special arrangement, Monday through Friday, from 9:00 A.M. to 4:30 P.M. The Aluminum Company of Canada (Alcan) also offers limited access to the holdings at its headquarters on Sherbrooke Street West in Montreal.

82   Great Britain
Brinsley Samaroo

Britain continues to be the best center of source material relating to the Commonwealth Caribbean. Unlike a number of Caribbean governments, the British government is keenly aware of the value of historical records and of the proper maintenance of depositories. In archives such as the Public Record Office (P.R.O.), modern computerized facilities have been recently added, and this has gone a long way toward easing the lengthy waiting period for the delivery of books. Yet in places such as the Foreign and Commonwealth Office Library and the British Library, the security system is unnecessarily cumbrous, almost ritualistic, and hardly as effective as it was surely meant to be. Of the resource areas to be discussed in this article, the author found the Rhodes House Library and that of the United Society for the Propagation of the Gospel (USPG) the easiest in which to work.

The primary center for Commonwealth Caribbean resources remains the Public Record Office. The P.R.O. archives are housed in two major centers: the original P.R.O. on Chancery Lane in Central London and the new office in the pleasant suburb of Kew. The records housed in the reading rooms at Chancery Lane do not contain much that is directly relevant to the Commonwealth Caribbean, save for particular British noncolonial records which relate to particular areas of study. For example, West Indian cases which came under the jurisdiction of the High Courts of Admiralty or of the judicial committee of the Privy Council may be found at Chancery Lane. Similarly, papers of secretaries of state from the sixteenth to the late eighteenth century or census reports for Britain during the nineteenth century are located at Chancery Lane.

Of greater value is the new office at Kew. Built on an expansive location with ample parking facilities, the reading rooms at Kew are well organized, and the days when readers had to be early in order to find a seat are now things of the past. The computerized ordering service ensures delivery of documents in about half an hour, often ten to fifteen minutes, and a copy service situated next to the reading rooms allows for immediate ordering of copies in xerox, microfilm, or microfiche. It must be pointed out, however, that copying costs at the P.R.O. are higher than in most other archives, so the researcher ought to use these facilities only when the documents are unavailable anywhere else.

The Kew office houses the extremely valuable documents of the former Colonial Office as well as the records of the British Cabinet, the Treasury, the Admiralty, the Foreign Office, and the War Office. The files contain outgoing and incoming correspondence, minutes by office administrators, and relevant cuttings from the British or colonial press. On one's first visit to the P.R.O. it would be advisable to ask for the *Guide to the Contents of the Public Record Office* (volumes 1 and 2 together with the supplements thereto). These contain detailed information relating to the archives of the P.R.O. Another useful document is a list of records on microfilm, which can be borrowed from the reading room attendants.

Located in central London is the world-famous British Library housed in the British Museum on Great Russell Street. As a source of secondary printed material, the British Library is second to none. The Caribbean pamphlet collection at the British Library is not particularly strong, but the holdings in books related to the area are extensive. Equally important is the fact that documents relating to other areas (e.g., Africa and India) are held at the same location, so that cross-referencing is easy. In addition to the main reading room where books of a general nature are available, the library's Map Room has a fine collection of historic maps of Caribbean territories and the State Paper Room contains most of the Royal Commission Reports, *Parliamentary Debates,* and Acts which concern the British

Caribbean. Because of the diverse nature of the holdings in the British Library, there is very heavy demand on its services. Readers are therefore advised to apply for documents a day in advance, so that there is minimum waiting. It is also possible to order books in the morning and have them available by the early afternoon.

The British Library also possesses a useful collection of West Indian newspapers at its Colindale Library. Most West Indian newspapers can be found there, quite often better preserved than in West Indian archives. The Colindale Library is seldom crowded and newspapers are delivered in about fifteen minutes.

Within easy walking distance of the British Library on Great Russell Street are a number of other useful collections relating to the West Indies. The London University Library has a fine collection of theses on Caribbean subjects and an open collection of parliamentary papers, similar to that in the State Paper Room of the British Library. The books on the Caribbean are limited. A major advantage of this library is that materials can be taken to the basement of the building to be photocopied on self-service machines at a very reasonable cost. Situated in the same building is the library of the Institute of Historical Research. This library contains little for the Caribbean researcher that is not available in the British or the London University libraries. However, its periodical collection is very extensive and up-to-date, and there is much of value for the Caribbean scholar who is interested in reading material relating to general questions about imperialism and British or American history. More than anything else the Institute of Historical Research is a base for historians. It offers useful services for visiting historians such as letters of introduction to various libraries (essential for admission), a place to collect mail or to leave books and papers, very reasonably priced photocopying services, and very comfortable study or seminar rooms.

About three minutes' walk away is the Institute for Commonwealth Studies. Its documents include: seminar papers on the Caribbean, journals printed in the Caribbean, useful tracts on the region (for example, pamphlets commissioned during the 1930s by the Fabian Society), lists of theses on the Caribbean submitted to various British universities, and a fair collection of books on the Caribbean.

The Royal Commonwealth (formerly Royal Colonial) Society is another London-based organization which has been collecting materials from the former British Empire for over a century. The Royal Commonwealth Society Library is particularly strong on pamphlets, and its periodical collection for the nineteenth and early twentieth centuries is especially useful. There is also a good collection of the West Indian *Hansard* in the basement of the building. Delivery of books is usually very prompt, and this library, not very well known among researchers, is never crowded. The Royal Commonwealth Society Building, situated on Northumberland Avenue, is very central.

In the shade of Westminster Abbey, in what is possibly London's most historic sector, are two relatively unknown but essential libraries for the Caribbean scholar. The Foreign and Commonwealth Office Library on Great Smith Street is important for its extensive collection of pamphlets relating to the Caribbean. One must note, however, that pamphlets are not always listed under authors' names or under particular subjects, but under the former colony's name instead. One needs to go through the massive collections entitled *West Indies Pamphlets* to find other valuable documents. This exercise is often time consuming, but it is well worth the effort. In going through *West Indies Pamphlets, Vol. 3, Nos. 44–70,* for example, the author found the following useful items:

J. G. Cruikshank, *"Black Talk" Being Notes on Negro Dialect, in British Guiana with (Inevitably) Chapter on the Vernacular of Barbados.* (Georgetown, Demerara [British Guiana], 1916).
A. A. Cipriani, *The Case for Sugar* (Port of Spain, Trinidad, 1916?)
L. J. Ragatz, *Absentee Landlordism in the British Caribbean* (London, 1928).
Thomas Cameron, "The Early History of the Caribbean Islands," *Scottish Geographical Magazine,* 50 (January 1934).
S. M. Laurence, *Emancipation Centenary in the British West Indies 1834/ 1934* (Bridgetown, Barbados, 1934).

In addition to these pamphlets the Foreign and Commonwealth Office Library possesses extensive runs of the West Indian *Hansard,* historic photographs relating to the region, and government reports (surprisingly up-to-date) from Caribbean states relating to public utilities and judicial and educational questions.

Immediately behind Westminster Abbey on Tufton Street is the little-known library and archives of the United Society for the Propagation of the Gospel. The archives on Tufton Street contain correspondence and reports from the missionaries of the Society for the Propagation of the Gospel, who came to the American and West Indian colonies in the eighteenth century. With the expansion of the British Empire during the nineteenth century, the work spread to other areas in Africa and in the Far East. Equally important is the stock of some twenty-eight thousand volumes in the USPG library. The Caribbean collection is strongest in relation to books, reports, and pamphlets concerning Guyana and Jamaica, and one has the rare opportunity in this library to browse among the shelves and fetch one's documents. The library also lends books for short periods. For the researcher working on East Indians in the Caribbean, the India Office Library, situated at 197 Blackfriars Road, Orbit House, is of immense value. This library specializes in materials relating to the Indian subcontinent, but it holds copies of most of the enquiries into conditions of Indian immigrants in the colonies as well as a good deal of correspondence on this subject. There are particularly good files on the movement for the abolition of East Indian indentureship. Like the collection in the USPG library, that at Orbit House is expertly arranged; the seating arrangement is very comfortable and the service efficient. Orbit House is open between 9:30 A.M. and 6:00 P.M. on weekdays and to 12:30 P.M. on Saturdays.

Outside of London the researcher on the Caribbean can find theses and other material in the libraries at Edinburgh, Cambridge, Manchester, and, increasingly, Sussex universities. However the best single collection outside of London is at Rhodes House, Oxford. Founded by the Rhodes trustees, the library was opened in 1929 and contains some 500,000 books, manuscripts, journals, microfilms, and maps dealing not only with the Caribbean but also with the Indian subcontinent, Africa, and the United States. Of particular interest to scholars of the Caribbean are the Anti-Slavery Society Archives and the personal diaries, papers, and correspondence of some twenty-five hundred former colonial administrators. To the Caribbean scholar the papers of former governors and senior officials like Sir John Chancellor, Howard Nankivell, Sir P. M. Renison, and Sir Gordon Lethem are of particular interest. So too are the papers of the Fabian Colonial Bureau, especially those relating to Sir Arthur Creech Jones and unpublished travelogues relating to the Caribbean as well as Oxford theses on Caribbean topics. The delivery service at Rhodes House is prompt and efficient, the study tables spacious and properly lighted, and there is an inexpensive photocopying service.

All British resource centers require proper identification from prospective users, so the traveler to Britain must provide him or herself with letters of introduction from his or her place of employment. In this connection, the Institute of Historical Research is always willing to provide letters of introduction for bona fide scholars. Security is, more often than not, rather strict, so one must be prepared for thorough searches of one's bags. Most libraries and archives are open between 9:00 A.M. and 5:00 P.M., but the Institute of Historical Research remains open to 9:00 P.M., Mondays through Fridays, and to 5:00 P.M. on Saturdays. The main reading room of the British Library remains open to 9:00 P.M. on Tuesdays, Wednesdays, and Thursdays, and closes at 5:00 P.M. on Mondays, Fridays, and Saturdays. The London University Library remains open to 9:00 P.M. on Monday through Friday during term and to 5:00 P.M. on Saturdays.

83   Archives and Libraries in the United States Containing Materials Dealing with Bermuda, Jamaica, and the Bahamas
Edward W. Chester

Over the years the interest of governmental officials and historical scholars has been focused on such Caribbean islands as Puerto Rico and Cuba, not on such longtime British colonies as Bermuda, Jamaica, and the Bahamas. It is perhaps not surprising, therefore, that research holdings physically located within the continental United States dealing with the British Caribbean are limited. There are bits and pieces of information here and there, but taken collectively these do not begin to rival the large body of materials that one finds in London, the longtime capital of the British Empire.

The diplomatic holdings of the National Archives in Washington, D.C., contain considerable information regarding the intermittent effort between the two world wars to transfer the British West Indies to the United States in full or partial payment of the British war debt. Aside from the diplomatic correspondence itself, one encounters clippings from such island publications as the *Daily Gleaner* (Kingston, Jamaica), the *Mid-Ocean News* (Bermuda), and the *Guardian* (Nassau, Bahamas). Among the topics covered in the Jamaican file are a 1912 visit by William Jennings Bryan, the work of the Rockefeller Foundation, and an assessment of General John J. Pershing. The Bermudian holdings treat such subjects as a ban on American newspapers, the Tercentenary Celebration of the Bermuda House of Assembly, and discriminatory tariff duties. The collection on the Bahamas also deals with the importation of literature from the United States and general commerce with America; of special interest is the correspondence from the years 1920–25, focusing on the illegal liquor traffic from the Bahamas to the United States. There also are occasional annual summaries of each island, written by the American consul there.

United States interest in the Bahamas, Jamaica, and Bermuda has been of a military as well as a diplomatic nature, and much of the available documentation deals with the World War II period, when the United States constructed military bases on a number of Atlantic islands. One important collection is that at the Albert F. Simpson Historical Research Center of the United States Air Force, located at the Air University, Maxwell Air Force Base, Montgomery, Alabama. The major part of the archives here consists of unit histories, which are supplemented by special collections. Although much of the pertinent material appears to be about the non-British bases, there are such important documents pertaining to the British Caribbean as "Survey of Jamaica" and "History of Jamaica Base Command." In contrast, the holdings of the Naval Aviation History office in Arlington, Virginia, only contain a scattering of pertinent material.

The Operational Archives Branch of the Naval History Division at the Navy Yard in Washington, D.C., contains such documents as an overall history of "British Lend-Lease Bases," plus such studies of individual islands as the 1940 "Supplemental Report on Bermuda" and "History of Naval Facilities in Bermuda." The Navy Yard's vast holdings in all fields cover over thirty broad topics and encompass well over 100,000 volumes, plus thousands of rolls of microfilm, hundreds of periodicals, numerous special collections, and a rare book collection. As for the United States Army, there is the Military Research Collection, located at Carlisle Barracks, Pennsylvania. A selected bibliography indicates that one will encounter more about the non-British islands here than about the British ones, but there nevertheless are such items of pertinence as the transcript of an interview of Lieutenant General Betts conducted in March 1971, entitled "Experience as Bermuda District Engineer." There also are well over 100,000 volumes in all fields at Carlisle Barracks, plus original source material including diaries, letters, photographs, personal records, and oral history.

In addition, the British Caribbean offers considerable opportunities for the economic historian. Unfortunately, many business activities postdate World War II, and hence access to documents is often nonexistent. One hardly would anticipate cooperation in obtaining access to the files of the clandestine billionaire recluse Howard Hughes or the fugitive from justice Robert Vesco with respect to their operations in the Bahamas. Nor should one expect Reynolds Jamaica Mines and Kaiser Aluminum and Chemical Corporation, two American bauxite companies active in Jamaica since 1945, to open their records in view of the movement toward nationalization, which has threatened their very existence. Although gambling is now legal in the Bahamas, the casino files do not constitute the type of data traditionally made available to historical researchers. And needless to say, it is difficult to obtain definitive information with respect to flagrantly illegal varieties of enterprise from the past: blockade running from the Bahamas and Bermuda during the American Civil War, rum running from the Bahamas during the era of Prohibition.

There is a substantial collection of monographic material on the West Indies and Bermuda at the American Antiquarian Society Library at Worcester, Massachusetts. Entries in the card catalogue for books, pamphlets, and serials reveal that the Bermudian and Jamaican holdings are four times as extensive as the Bahamian ones. There are many newspapers from all three islands, but the only really substantial runs are for the *Royal Gazette* (1850–82), published at Hamilton, and the *Bermuda Gazette and Weekly Advertiser* (1784–1822), published at St. George's. In contrast, the Williams Ethnological Collection at Boston College, Chestnut Hill, Massachusetts, contains extensive holdings on the racial, natural, and cultural history of the Caribbean, especially Jamaica, from the time of discovery and exploration through the 1940s. Also of interest is the Marine Historical Association of Mystic, Connecticut, whose manuscript catalogue shows several citations under the subject heading "Ports-of-Call" for the Bahamas and Bermuda, with the types of activity noted including trade, yacht and cadet training cruises, whaling, and passenger service.

An unusually comprehensive collection on the non-Hispanic Caribbean is that of the Research Institute for the Study of Man (R.I.S.M.) in New York City. Its library, which focuses almost exclusively on the social sciences, contains published volumes, Caribbean periodicals, dissertations, government documents, and unpublished papers. The most recent list of R.I.S.M. accessions indicates a much heavier emphasis on Jamaica (especially in the area of books and monographs) than on the Bahamas and Bermuda. Lambros Comitas' three-volume-plus-index publication, *The Complete Caribbeana, 1970–1975,* indicates which items in his bibliography may be found at this library.

The Center for Research Libraries of Chicago, Illinois, also has material dealing with Jamaica. This includes runs of the Blue Book from 1892 through 1931, and of the Jamaican *Gazette* from 1960 through 1970. Even more important, there are publications from approximately thirty governmental bodies, especially the Department of Statistics and the Department of Agriculture. A few of these date back into the late nineteenth century, but the bulk of them postdate World War II.

Turning to libraries closer geographically to the Caribbean, the Charlton W. Tebeau Library of Florida History at the Historical Museum of Southern Florida, Miami, possesses selected materials on the history of the Caribbean area, especially the Bahamas and Cuba. Established in 1962, this library houses published material, archives and manuscripts, as well as oral history tapes and transcripts, newspaper clippings, and theses and dissertations. A number of pertinent master's theses were written at the University of Florida at Gainesville between 1929 and 1975. The University of Florida Library, moreover, has a group of special collections, with the West Indies file consisting of 227 manuscript items for the period 1722–1829. Many of the documents referring to Bermuda were written by Governor James Cockburn; there also are letters signed by the different governors of Jamaica or directed to them, including the Earl of Balcarres and Governor Dalling. In addition, one will find there items originating in the Bahamas.

Contributors
Index

Contributors

René V. Achéen *Centre d'Etudes Regionales d'Antilles et Guyane, Fort de France*

Gustavo Anguizola *Department of History, University of Texas at Arlington*

Gustavo A. Antonini *Center for Latin American Studies, University of Florida, Gainesville*

Theresa Armstead-Fairweather *National Archives of Belize*

John P. Bell *Department of History, Indiana University at Fort Wayne*

Ruth Bowe *Public Records Office, Bahamas*

Bridget Brereton *Department of History, University of the West Indies, St. Augustine, Trinidad*

Wallace Brown *Department of History, University of New Brunswick, Fredericton*

Marco Carías Zapata *Department of History, Universidad Nacional Autónoma de Honduras*

Maria de los Angeles Castro *Department of History, University of Puerto Rico, Río Piedras*

Liliane Chauleau *Director, Services d'Archives de la Martinique, Fort de France*

Edward W. Chester *Department of History, University of Texas at Arlington*

Wayne M. Clegern *Department of History, Colorado State University, Fort Collins*

Thomas Fiehrer *Department of History, University of New Orleans*

399

Kenneth V. Finney *Department of History, North Carolina Wesleyan College*

Eileen Goltz *Documents Librarian, Laurentian University, Sudbury, Ontario*

William A. Green *Department of History, Holy Cross College, Worcester, Massachusetts*

Kenneth J. Grieb *Coordinator of International Studies, University of Wisconsin–Oshkosh*

John Hébert *Acting Chief, Hispanic Division, The Library of Congress*

Jean-Paul Hervieu *Archives Departementales de la Guadelupe, Basse-Terre*

B. W. Higman *Department of History, University of the West Indies, Mona, Jamaica*

Harmannus Hoetink *Center for Caribbean Studies, Instituut Voor Culturele Antropologie, Utrecht*

Stanley M. Hordes *State Historian of New Mexico*

Ove Hornby *Institute of Economic History, University of Copenhagen*

John J. Hourihan *Department of Sociology, Howard University, Washington*

Thomas L. Karnes *Department of History, Arizona State University, Tempe*

Derek M. Kerr *Tulane University, New Orleans*

Franklin W. Knight *Department of History, The Johns Hopkins University, Baltimore*

Michael J. Kryzanek *Department of Political Science, Bridgewater State College, Massachusetts*

Tadeusz Lepkowski *Instytut Historii, Polska Akademia Nauk, Warsaw*

Gordon K. Lewis *Institute of Caribbean Studies, University of Puerto Rico, Río Piedras*

Sheldon B. Liss *Department of History, University of Akron*

Italo López Vallecillos *Director, Departamento de Publicaciones, Universidad Centroamericana, José Simeon Cañas, San Salvador*

Christopher Lutz *Co-director, Centro de Investigaciones Regionales de Mesoamerica*

Neill Macaulay *Department of History, University of Florida, Gainesville*

David McCreery *Department of History, Georgia State University, Atlanta*

Paul McDowell *Department of Anthropology, Laurentian University, Sudbury, Ontario*

Murdo J. MacLeod *Department of History, University of Arizona, Tucson*

Woodville K. Marshall *Department of History, University of the West Indies, Cave Hill, Barbados*

Tony Martin *Department of Black Studies, Wellesley College, Massachusetts*

Thomas Mathews *Secretary-General, Asociación de Universidades e Institutos de Investigación del Caribé, San Juan, Puerto Rico*

Mary Noel Menezes *Department of History, University of Guyana, Georgetown*

Hubert J. Miller *Department of History, Pan American University, Edinburg, Texas*

Richard Millett *Department of History, University of Southern Illinois at Edwardsville*

Graeme S. Mount *Department of History, Laurentian University, Sudbury, Ontario*

Joan E. Mount *School of Commerce, Laurentian University, Sudbury, Ontario*

Frank Moya Pons *Fondo para el Avance de las Ciencias Sociales, Santo Domingo, República Dominicana*

David R. Murray *Dean, College of Arts, University of Guelph, Ontario*

Robert A. Naylor *Department of History, Fairleigh Dickinson University, Teaneck, New Jersey*

Thomas Niehaus *Director, Latin American Library, Tulane University, New Orleans*

Louis A. Pérez, Jr. *Department of History, University of South Florida, Tampa*

Hugo Polanco Brito *Archivo de la Arquidiócesis de Santo Domingo*

Marianne D. Ramesar *Institute of Social and Economic Research, University of the West Indies, St. Augustine, Trinidad*

Harold H. Robertson *Department of History, University of the West Indies, St. Augustine, Trinidad*

Dianne K. Rocheleau *International Council for Research in Agroforestry, Nairobi, Kenya*

Mario Rodríguez *Department of History, University of Southern California, Los Angeles*

Richard V. Salisbury *Department of History, Western Kentucky University, Bowling Green*

Brinsley Samaroo *Department of History, University of the West Indies, St. Augustine, Trinidad*

Gail Saunders *Public Records Office, Bahamas*

Thomas Schoonover *Department of History, University of Southwestern Louisiana, Lafayette*

Richard B. Sheridan *Department of Economics, University of Kansas, Lawrence*

William L. Sherman *Department of History, University of Nebraska, Lincoln*

Blanca G. Silvestrini *Department of History, University of Puerto Rico, Río Piedras*

Charles L. Stansifer *Director, Center of Latin American Studies, University of Kansas, Lawrence*

Henock Trouillot *Directeur Générale, Les Archives Nationales, Port-au-Prince, Haiti*

Jaap van Soest *Hogeschool, Willemstad, Curaçao*

Elisabeth Wallace *Department of Political Science, University of Toronto*

Shirley A. Weathers *Department of History, University of Utah, Salt Lake City*

Stephen A. Webre *Department of History, Louisiana Tech University, Ruston*

Howard J. Wiarda *Director of Hemispheric Studies, American Enterprise Institute*

Lee Williams *Curator, Latin American Collection, Yale University Library, New Haven*

Ralph Lee Woodward, Jr. *Department of History, Tulane University, New Orleans*

Miles Wortman *Department of History, State University of New York at Geneseo*

Irene Zimmerman *Latin American Collection, University of Florida Libraries, Gainesville*

Index

COMPOSED BY GRAPHIC COMPOSITION, INC., ATHENS, GEORGIA
MANUFACTURED BY CUSHING MALLOY, INC., ANN ARBOR, MICHIGAN
TEXT AND DISPLAY LINES ARE SET IN TIMES ROMAN

Library of Congress Cataloging in Publication Data
Main entry under title:
Research guide to Central America and the Caribbean.
Includes bibliographical references and index.
1. Caribbean Area—Archival resources. 2. Central
America—Archival resources. 3. Caribbean Area—
Research. 4. Central America—Research
I. Grieb, Kenneth J.
Z1595.R47   1985   [F2161]   972.8′0072   84-40496
ISBN 0-299-10050-2